LEADING THE INCL

Place-based innov
bounded planet

Robin Hambleton

First published in Great Britain in 2015 by

Policy Press
University of Bristol
1-9 Old Park Hill
Bristol BS2 8BB
UK
t: +44 (0)117 954 5940
e: pp-info@bristol.ac.uk
www.policypress.co.uk

North American office:
Policy Press
c/o The University of Chicago Press
1427 East 60th Street
Chicago, IL 60637, USA
t: +1 773 702 7700
f: +1 773-702-9756
e:sales@press.uchicago.edu
www.press.uchicago.edu

British Library Cataloguing in Publication Data
A catalogue record for this book is available from the British Library.

Library of Congress Cataloging-in-Publication Data
A catalog record for this book has been requested.

ISBN 978 1 44730 496 8 paperback
ISBN 978 1 44730 497 5 hardcover

Cover design by Andrew Corbett
Front cover: image kindly supplied by zeber/BigStock
Printed and bound in Great Britain by Hobbs, Southampton
Policy Press uses environmentally responsible print partners

For Isla, Lana and their generation

Contents

List of figures

List of innovation stories

Number in brackets indicates the chapter the Innovation Story appears in

About the author

Robin Hambleton is Professor of City Leadership in the Centre for Sustainable Planning and Environments, Faculty of Environment and Technology at the University of the West of England, Bristol and Director of Urban Answers – a UK based company: www.urbananswers.co.uk

He has worked in local and central government in the UK, held professorial positions in urban planning, city management and public administration at universities in Britain and the USA, and provided consultancy services to public authorities in many countries. He was the founding President of the European Urban Research Association (EURA) and was Dean of the College of Urban Planning and Public Affairs (CUPPA) at the University of Illinois at Chicago.

Preface

Our daughter was born during the night of the first major urban riot in mainland Britain in the 20th century.[1] It was the following morning before we realised that part of the city we had recently made our home had erupted in civil unrest.

The disturbances, which took place in the St Paul's area of Bristol on the night of 3 April 1980, did more than shock the city. The television and newspaper coverage ensured that the riot had a national impact. Films showing large numbers of citizens confronting the police in mass resistance, the sight of angry people burning down their own neighbourhood, the images of conflict and crowd violence on the streets, delivered jarring messages to Prime Minister Thatcher's government, a government that was seen to be increasingly out of touch with the communities it was there to serve.

The civil agitations in Bristol were followed a year later by an English 'summer of discontent'. Urban unrest broke out in a number of inner city areas – including Brixton, Southall, Toxteth, and Moss Side. Lord Scarman was invited by the government to carry out an inquiry into the causes of the riots in Brixton, and his forensic analysis suggested that a cocktail of factors – including insensitive approaches to policing, racial discrimination and social deprivation – had led to a widespread sense of hopelessness.[2]

Sad to say, there have been subsequent episodes of urban disorder in Britain. For example, in 2001 there were major disturbances in several northern English cities – including Bradford and Oldham. As in 1980 and 1981 the areas experiencing unrest were neighbourhoods with sizable ethnic minority populations.[3]

In 2011 my home city of Bristol provided, once again, the prelude to a swathe of urban unrest in cities across England. On 21 April 2011 a campaign against the opening of a Tesco supermarket in Stokes Croft, not far from the location of the 1980 disturbances in St Paul's, turned into a violent street riot when the police sent in 160 officers, in riot gear, to close down a squat in a building close to the Tesco store. Here, unlike the riots of the 1980s, a multi-national corporation was the target of public anger.[4] In August 2011, UK television screens were, once again, filled with disturbing pictures of disorder, looting and violence – this time not just in a string of big cities, but also in smaller towns like Croydon.[5]

Why start a book on leading the inclusive city by highlighting urban disorder?

Because these episodes of social breakdown provide a stark reminder of what can happen if people feel excluded from the mainstream of society. Britain is, of course, not unique. Many countries have experienced social disturbances of one kind or another in relatively recent times. For example, in the summer of 2013 there were riots in the Stockholm suburb of Husby, massive public demonstrations in a string of Brazilian cities initiated by the MovimentoPasseLivre (Free Fare Movement), urban unrest in the Gezi Park area of Instanbul, and riots in the Paris suburb of Trappes.

More recently, in the summer of 2014, there were major outbreaks of urban violence in Ferguson, a suburb of St Louis, Missouri. On 9 August police shot dead Michael Brown, a black teenager. The extent of the civil unrest and public protest provoked by the police action was such that President Obama appealed for calm, and called for a transparent investigation into the death of the unarmed young man. These recurring outbreaks, small skirmishes and demonstrations, as well as the events that make the national and international headlines, should be seen as warning signals for governments and for civil society.

This book focuses on cities partly because most people alive today live in cities and world urbanisation is gathering pace. Cities are not just powerful engines of modern economic growth and expanding service industries, they are also centres of creativity and civilised living offering untold opportunities for their residents. Yet, even in wealthy cities, social and economic divisions are widening. This is troubling not just on moral grounds but because, as continuing outbreaks of civil unrest reveal, unequal cities do not provide secure foundations for economic and social prosperity.

A premise of this book is that the people living in cities, and particularly those who emerge as civic leaders, can play a decisive role in promoting the development of inclusive cities. The book will argue that, in a rapidly globalising world, place matters a great deal – possibly more than ever before. And, more specifically, that place-based leadership can make a significant contribution to the creation of socially cohesive cities – successful, safe and sustainable cities that foster a good quality of life for all.

The book adopts a global approach and will draw on the experience of some of the most innovative cities in the world to provide insights on how to improve the quality of life in cities. While it is important to understand the nature of modern urban problems, it is even more productive to examine what imaginative urban leaders, public servants and activists are doing to create more liveable, child-friendly towns and cities.

Shifts in the global economy have put new fiscal pressures on governments and some countries are now experiencing very severe cutbacks in public spending. These changes require politicians and managers not just to 'do more with less', but also to explore new approaches to public problem solving. In cities across the world efforts are being made to redraw the boundary between the state and civil society in intriguing new ways.

These urban innovations challenge conventional approaches to public service reform. And it can be claimed that strong civic leadership is having a positive and energising effect on the quality of life in many cities. More than that, urban leaders are developing approaches and practices that will be of value to those in public leadership roles in other settings – in rural areas, in regional governance, in national governments and in international organisations.[6]

I hope that the arguments advanced in this book will provide ideas and insights that can aid the development of new thinking about how to advance inclusive approaches to urban governance. The aim here is not to spell out solutions - it is difficult enough to hint at a grammar that the reader can revise and develop in the light of her or his own experience.[7] The book provides carefully chosen examples of bold civic leadership drawn from cities in different countries. Perhaps these various 'Innovation Stories' can inspire fresh efforts to create the inclusive city.

Robin Hambleton, Bristol, UK

A guide to the book

This is an international book about place-based leadership and public service innovation. It aims to offer a contribution to debates about public service reform and to provide prompts and suggestions on how to create inclusive cities.

A book with a stance

Five claims are developed in the narrative:

- Place is important. Public service reform efforts can benefit by starting from an understanding of the experiences of communities living in particular places. This contrasts with approaches that start from abstract ideas about the role, or potential role, of governments, markets and civil society.
- Civic leadership should build inclusive, sustainable cities – not one or the other. In public policy and academic debates about city planning and urban management there is, all too often, a disconnect between social and environmental policy discourses. Social reformers, striving to advance fairness in society, often neglect the natural world on which we all depend. Environmentalists, on the other hand, while they draw attention to climate change and the need for eco-friendly public policy and practice, have tended to be less successful in focussing on who gains and who loses in the urban political process.
- Civic leadership should assert the power of place. This book rejects the view that cities and local communities are helpless victims in a global process of economic exploitation designed to serve the needs of capital. Place-less institutions, meaning organisations that make investment decisions without caring about the consequences for people in the places affected, have gained too much influence in modern society. They have eroded the power of local people to shape the quality of life in the areas where they live. The powers of local governments across the world need strengthening if democracy is to prosper.
- International learning and exchange is vital. Throughout human history cities have provided a supportive setting for all kinds of creative, problem-solving activity. There is great diversity in approaches to city planning and urban governance across the world, but the arrangements for international learning and exchange among cities are under developed. Sharing stories on an international basis about successful efforts to create inclusive cities should be encouraged.
- Academics can make a useful contribution to urban policy-making and public management. This has implications for those who lead the institutions of higher and further education as well as the practice of scholarship. In some countries universities play a major role in urban governance, but more can be done to

support the work of scholars who engage effectively with local stakeholders in the co-creation of new knowledge and understanding.

Engaged scholarship and the aims of the book

The book aims to bridge academe and practice. This is, perhaps, a hazardous enterprise as scholars and practitioners tend to inhabit separate worlds. A consequence is that they often misunderstand one another to the disadvantage of both. Those who aim to enhance dialogue between these realms run the risk of being rejected by both – the messenger may get shot in the back as well as the front! The claim of this book, however, is that those who practice engaged scholarship – meaning academics who execute research and analysis that engages directly with public policy challenges and offers clear recommendations for action in the light of that analysis – can play a useful role, not only in advancing academic understanding but also in contributing grounded advice that can assist governments and communities.

This book sets out, then, to do more than spur new thinking relating to civic leadership and the creation of inclusive cities in a rapidly globalising world. It also seeks to provide direct assistance to busy policy makers, practitioners and community activists who are engaged in public policy making in general, and urban governance in particular.

The four-part structure of the book

The book commences with an opening chapter outlining the whole argument. It introduces the intellectual framework and explains how the book can be 'used' as well as 'read'. Derived from social learning theory, the framework resembles the approach to place-based leadership recommended by the author. Successful leadership starts from an accurate diagnosis, uses appropriate concepts, takes action and constantly learns from that action. This enables all involved to improve knowledge of both outcomes and process, and apply insights to future policy and practice.

The four parts of the book reflect this learning model:

1) Diagnosis: Understanding trends and challenges

The first part of the book centres on diagnosis. It highlights the remarkable urbanisation of the planet, the growth of the multicultural city and the rise of place-less power. It also examines the way approaches to public service reform have changed over the years and notes that, for a variety of reasons, governments are now reconsidering the relationship between the state and civil society. The importance of putting much more emphasis on public service innovation and the co-creation of new solutions to urban challenges emerges from this diagnosis.

2) Concepts: Place, leadership, innovation, and democratic local governance

Part 2 comprises four chapters dealing, in turn, with four key concepts relating to the governance of the city: place, leadership, innovation and democratic renewal. Each chapter draws on the relevant theoretical background to identify a range of helpful concepts that can be used to guide thinking and practice relating to place-based leadership. Examples drawn from innovative cities illuminate the presentation.

3) Experiences: Place-based leadership in action

The three chapters in Part 3 of the book report on the inspirational leadership found in some of the most innovative cities in the world. The concepts introduced in Part 2 are used to identify practical examples of what successful place-based leadership is doing to create inclusive cities in different continents. The experiences are clustered around three interrelated themes that are critical to the quality of life: 1) Developing eco-friendly policies and approaches, 2) Creating people-friendly cities, and 3) Taking advantage of diversity.

4) Lesson drawing: Insights and international learning

Part 4 reflects on the arguments put forward in the book and identifies overall lessons relating to the practice of place-based leadership aiming to create inclusive cities. It examines two major themes: 1) The need to go beyond the notion of the smart city and develop wise cities, and 2) The exciting potential for international exchange and lesson drawing relating to the planning and management of the innovative city.

Innovation Stories

This book contains 17 Innovation Stories drawn from some of the most inventive cities in the world. An innovation story is a new way of documenting examples of successful place-based leadership. Each Story provides a short account of radical change in a particular city and draws out lessons that can inspire bold civic leadership in other places. The aim here is not to identify 'best practice' in urban governance – there is no such thing. Rather a good story enhances understanding and stimulates a creative response. I am most grateful to the civic leaders in all the cities represented for their assistance in co-creating these avenues for social discovery.

Some readers may enjoy reading the chapters in the sequence presented, and this has benefits because later chapters are informed by arguments set out earlier. However, the book is also designed to enable busy policy makers to move directly to specific topics that may be of particular interest – for example, to specific Innovation Stories and experiences. Every chapter provides references to further sources and it is hoped that the endnotes and bibliography provide useful leads for those wishing to pursue particular ideas in more depth.

Location of the Innovation Stories

16. Portland
15. Toronto
3. Chicago
1. New York
9. Curitiba
6. Langrug
17. Ahmedabad
10. Guangzhou
14. Hamamatsu
13. Melbourne
7. Auckland
12. Copenhagen
8. Malmö
5. Enschede
4. Swindon
2. Bristol
11. Freiburg

Overview

CHAPTER 1

Place-based leadership and the inclusive city

Thus the public ruin invades the house of each citizen, and the courtyard doors no longer have the strength to keep it away, as it leaps over the lofty wall. And though a man runs in and tries to hide in chamber or closet, it ferrets him out
Solon, c. 600 BC, on the evils of bad government

Introduction

City leaders, and all those concerned with the governance of urban areas, face unprecedented challenges. This book will identify and discuss many of them. The aim here, however, is not simply to provide an international examination of urban trends and emerging problems. The literature on city planning and urban politics already offers many valuable insights on urban dynamics and public policy making for cities, including numerous texts exploring the ecological as well as the social dangers inherent in current approaches to planning and urban development.[1]

This book is informed by this literature, but it will attempt to go beyond the normal territory of social scientific analysis and critique. By introducing concepts and ideas drawn from different disciplines, and by drawing on the experience of some of the most innovative cities in the world, the book aims to stimulate practical efforts to improve the quality of life in cities. More specifically it sets out to advance the cause of social inclusion in modern societies by highlighting the contribution that place-based leadership can make in tackling social and environmental ills.

This book, then, has a normative stance. It aims to support efforts to change urban policies and practices so that they foster the creation of more inclusive cities. It has an ideological position in line with what Albert Hirschman (1971) calls a 'bias for hope'. It explores the role of place-based leadership in public policy making, and presents practical examples illustrating how civic leadership has promoted more inclusive approaches in specific cities and neighbourhoods. I will explain what I mean by 'place-based leadership' and 'inclusive cities' shortly. At the outset, however, I am suggesting that scholars, and I include here students as well as qualified academics, can play an important role in assisting those charged with making decisions about cities.

Some academics will, I suspect, be troubled by such a suggestion. Traditionally minded scholars argue that researchers should stand aloof from politics and policy-making, and some will warn that direct engagement with the world of practice will compromise intellectual independence. Some will claim, for example, that academics who advise governments will inevitably become 'servants of power'.[2] This is a respectable position to take, but it is not one that I share. On the contrary, I believe that it is vital for academics to think through how their research efforts can have an impact on society. Within the broad field of urban studies, I go further and argue that scholars should be encouraged to put energy and effort into *ensuring* that their evidence-based research has policy influence.[3] This book is, then, aimed at 'doers' as well as 'thinkers'.

My audience is a broad one. As well scholars concerned with cities it includes city mayors, political leaders, elected councillors, city managers, urban planners, public servants, business leaders, trade unionists, voluntary organisations and community activists, as well as policy makers at national and international levels. I also hope that students of city planning, local government and urban sustainability will find the book provides useful insights and pointers.

This opening chapter provides an overview of the main themes that will be explored in the following pages. What is this book about? What are the key concepts that will be used to enhance understanding? What do I mean by 'the inclusive city'? In addressing these questions the underlying philosophy guiding the academic analysis is introduced.

Why focus on the inclusive city?

My starting point is that, during the last thirty years or so, societies across the world have become increasingly divided. Cities are the focus of attention in this book because, as explained more fully in Chapter 2, most people alive today live in cities and, in the thirty years ahead, demographic projections indicate, with some certainty, that we will live in an increasingly urbanised world. Despite the fact that cities are now central to the creation of prosperity, it is the case that, even in very wealthy cities – including the famous, so-called, 'global cities' – social and economic inequalities are on the rise.[4]

For some scholars the rapid increase in urban poverty arising from current approaches to urban development is unproblematic. For example, Edward Glaeser (2011, 70) takes the following view:

> The presence of poverty in cities from Rio to Rotterdam reflects urban strength, not weakness. Megacities are not too big. Limiting their growth would cause significantly more hardship than gain, and urban growth is a great way to reduce poverty.

This is a misguided, neo-liberal view. It is true, of course, to claim that rural poverty can trap people in isolated country areas for generations. It does not however follow that rapid, unplanned urban growth is a sound strategy for development. Nor is it necessary, or wise, to welcome the existence of grinding urban poverty, still less to write off entire communities. As Amartya Sen, the winner of the 1998 Nobel Prize in economics, explains with great clarity, focussing on 'whether the poor too benefit from the established economic order, is an entirely inadequate focus for assessing what has to be assessed' (Sen 2006, 136). He argues that what must be asked is whether the poor can get a better, and fairer, deal, with less disparities of economic, social and political opportunities. Sen suggests that this, in turn, points to a restructuring of international and domestic arrangements.

In contrast to the so-called 'free market' thinking advocated by neo-liberal scholars, this book will argue that it is essential not only to guide and limit the way urban growth takes place, but also to create a just city in which all residents – established and newly arrived – can benefit and develop. Such an approach puts the search for equity, not economic growth, as the central aim of public policy. The book will draw on the works of a growing number of scholars, including economists, who have shown that an obsession with economic development in public discourse and public policy is holding back social progress (Stiglitz 2012). It is encouraging to note that the United Nations has now become much more active in focussing attention on growing inequality. Indeed, urban equity was the central theme of the World Urban Forum (WUF), held in Medellin, Colombia in April 2014. The concept paper prepared for the WUF, *Urban Equity in Development: Cities for Life*, notes that equity is now moving from the fringes of international development policy to take centre stage (UN-Habitat 2014). The Medellin declaration, issued at the end of the seventh WUF, is titled: *Equity as a Foundation of Sustainable Urban Development*. This statement offers no support for neo-liberal models of thinking.

In relation to scholarship on urban inequality, I wish to highlight the valuable analysis provided by Susan Fainstein (2010) in her book, *The Just City*. She presents a devastating critique of modern planning theory arguing that much of it has simply ignored the reality of structural inequalities and hierarchies of power in modern society. By drawing on Rawlsian theories of liberty and justice, as well as detailed examination of the distributional impact of urban planning in Amsterdam, New York and London, she has developed an urban theory of justice that we will refer to later.[5]

This book offers a contribution to these debates about city planning and urban governance by focussing on civic leadership.[6] This is because, as will be explained in more detail in Chapter 5, local leadership matters – it can make a difference to the quality of life in a given city. Put simply, leaders can address or ignore injustice. It is worth stressing that civic leaders are not just those 'at the top' – such as directly elected mayors, political leaders and the chief officers of local government departments. On the contrary, in modern systems of local governance leadership is dispersed and is multi-level. The neighbourhood activist or social entrepreneur can make a significant contribution to place-based leadership alongside the strategic efforts of, say, the city mayor.

A major weakness of planning theory is that it has virtually ignored leadership. This book invites urban scholars, including planning theorists, to pay more attention to the role of leadership in shaping urban environments and local life chances. City leaders are, of course, constrained by wider economic, political and environmental forces that limit their scope for political action – and we will explore the political space available for place-based leadership through numerous Innovation Stories. At the outset, however, we can state that most, if not all, civic leaders – and I define leadership broadly – have at least some scope to bring about improvements in the quality of life for urban residents. Global forces influence but do not determine the urban future. As we shall see, place-less power has grown over the last thirty years but it cannot dictate all that happens in the modern city.

The case for paying more attention to whether or not policies and practices are making cities more inclusive is, at root, a moral one. Dorling (2011), in his imaginative analysis, suggests that the one word that characterises the nature of human society as it is currently arranged worldwide is 'injustice'. Other authors have also drawn attention to the high societal costs of inequality (Lansley 2012; Stiglitz 2012; Wilkinson and Pickett 2010). The case for creating more inclusive societies goes beyond the moral argument, though. As the quotation from Solon at the head of this chapter implies, failure to create good government invites unwelcome forces to 'leap over the lofty wall'. To put it bluntly, if cities become more and more unequal, the quality of life of the well off as well as the poor is threatened. As explained in the *Preface* to this book, even prosperous cities can collapse, at very short notice, into urban violence. It follows that a failure to address the importance of justice in the city is a recipe for political instability. Urban leaders who neglect the importance of social, economic and political inclusion enfeeble the civic foundations of their city.

Recognising the limits of markets

Why are processes that promote social exclusion holding sway? Why is inequality on the rise? To be sure, the growth of global connectivity in recent years has brought spectacular new opportunities to remote regions of the world. By adopting an international perspective we can see that cities, including the rapidly expanding cities and megacities of the global south, are providing billions of people with new economic and social opportunities (Campbell 2012). It follows that it is misguided to focus only on the 'problems' that cities and city regions are now facing. There are many urban success stories, and we will document some of them in this book.

But, and this is the critical point for city leaders and community activists, social inequality is rising at an alarming rate – both within countries and within cities. The reasons for this disturbing trend are complex. Here I want to suggest that a growing obsession with market ideology is largely to blame. In the last thirty years or so many public leaders, local as well as national, came to believe that markets would provide lasting solutions to the problems facing their societies. In the early 1980s, politicians of the right – notably US President Ronald Reagan and UK Prime Minister Margaret Thatcher – argued that 'free markets', not government, provided the right way forward for social and economic progress. Aided by think tanks funded by big business, these neo-liberal politicians were enormously influential – in many countries the ideological landscape slithered to the right.

As Chang (2010) explains with great clarity there is, however, no such thing as a 'free market'. *Every* market has rules and boundaries that restrict freedom of choice. Neo-liberal ideology is, then, built on sand. It is underpinned by an entirely unrealistic, idealised vision of market rule. In practice, as Theodore et al (2011, 16) show, neo-liberalism has 'entailed a dramatic intensification of coercive, disciplinary forms of state intervention in order to *impose* versions of market rule...' (authors' emphasis). With some geographical variation, public policy in many western countries has come to be dominated by an untrammelled belief in the virtues of 'free markets' even though we know there is no such thing.

In recent years various authors have now built a solid critique of this obsession with market-driven approaches to public policy. For example, Costas Lapavitsas (2013) argues that 'financialisation' has transformed the nature of advanced capitalist economies. He shows how the hold of money over society has expanded to the point where private profit has displaced public purpose as the lodestar for many societies. Thomas Piketty (2014), in an extended analysis of the processes shaping the distribution of wealth over the last two centuries, reinforces this argument by demonstrating that modern capitalism is increasing inequality at a formidable rate. Moreover, this accelerating trend is now endangering democratic societies and the values of social justice democratic societies hold dear.

Saskia Sassen adds to the case against neo-liberalism. She argues that soaring income inequality is now caused, not so much by super-rich individuals and massive firms exploiting people, as by the 'predatory formations' in which these vested interests are embedded. In her evaluation of modern capitalism she suggests that the traditional robber barons, so to speak, have been replaced by:

> ... a mix of elites and systemic capacities with finance as a key enabler, that push toward acute concentration... Such systemic capacities are a variable mix of technical, market, and financial innovations plus government enablement (Sassen 2014, 13).

Stated in very simple terms, she argues that, up until the 1980s, the political economy of both capitalist, and communist, countries had a tendency to incorporate people, especially as workers, and that many (although not all) people enjoyed an improvement in living standards. Sassen argues that, in the last thirty years or so, the dynamics of 'incorporation' have been replaced by a relatively new dynamics of 'expulsion'. Because large numbers of people are now no longer needed to facilitate the fabulous concentration of wealth, the predatory processes now work to get rid of people, rather than incorporate them.

For many the international financial crash of 2008/09 has forced a rethink – by individuals, communities and governments (Tett 2009). Michael Sandel (2012) in his acclaimed book, *What Money Can't Buy*, shows why the era of market triumphalism has come to an end. He argues that the financial crisis has done more than cast doubt on the ability of markets to allocate risk efficiently. The global economic convulsions of 2008–2014 have also prompted a deeper sense of unease, a feeling that markets have become detached from morals and a broader sense of public purpose.

Sandel notes that, for many, the solution is to rein in greed, insist on higher standards of probity in the banking industry, and to enact sensible regulations that will prevent irresponsible financial practices in the future. His major insight, however, is to recognise that such an approach is insufficient. Sandel argues that, while excessive greed played a major role in the financial crash, something more troubling was actually happening:

> The most fateful change that unfolded during the past three decades was not an increase in greed. It was the expansion of markets, and of market values, into spheres of life where they don't belong... We need a public debate about what it means to keep markets in their place. To have this debate, we need to think through the moral limits of markets. We need to ask whether there are some things money should not buy (Sandel 2012, 7)

Sandel offers an extended discussion of how, without quite realising it, without debating it, 'we drifted from *having* a market economy to *being* a market society.' (Sandel 2012, 9; author's emphasis). This obsession with market values can crowd out other more important values – for example, sympathy, generosity, thoughtfulness, and solidarity. We will return to Sandel's thesis later. Here we can note that the central argument that I present in this book, that building a more inclusive city is now the most important task for urban leaders in the modern era, is aligned with Sandel's critique of modern society. He argues, rightly in my view, that there are moral limits to markets and that these have gone largely ignored. City leaders, defined broadly, can help to bring moral judgement back into public policy.

None of this is to suggest that markets are a 'bad thing' and that they have no role in the creation of the inclusive city. On the contrary, the successful, inclusive city is one that has a vibrant and diverse economy, and we explore this theme in Chapter 9. The point that needs to be emphasised here, however, is that markets need to serve society, rather than the other way round. The civic leader interested in creating an inclusive city will welcome social and economic enterprises that enhance the quality of life of local residents. They will also stand firm against those powerful economic interests – what I describe as place-less leaders – that are more than ready to exploit local people.[7]

Having outlined some of the main arguments for promoting the creation of inclusive cities I now introduce four substantive themes that will be discussed in more detail later in the book:

- place in public policy
- public leadership

- innovation in public management
- power in modern society.

These can be thought of as intellectual building blocks for thinking about how to create peaceful, multicultural cities in which people live in harmony with nature.

Place in public policy

A central claim in my argument is that 'place' should receive *much* more attention from those who wish to enhance the effectiveness of public policy – particularly those who wish to advance the cause of social inclusion. My intention, here, is not to offend those involved in geography, city and regional planning, architecture, sustainable development and related disciplines who have been striving to advance the cause of place-based analysis and prescription for decades. Rather, my suggestion is that these disciplines are exceptional in having a concern for place.

National governments tend to construct their domestic public policies around sectors – such as the economy, education, health, social care, transport, agriculture, policing, energy and so on. As a result hugely influential central government departments, bolstered by associated policy communities, professions and vested interests, have come to dominate the way public policy is conceived, developed and implemented. This is bad news.[8]

It gets worse. The very way knowledge relating to public policy is constructed limits our understanding. This is because, as Warren Magnusson (2010) reminds us, the social sciences still bear the marks of their origins in the late nineteenth century, when the world was divided up in a new way for the purposes of academic study. The presumption was that this division of labour – between economics, sociology, geography, political science, philosophy and so on – would facilitate scientific study, and it has. This approach, however, has the disadvantage that it works against other forms of analysis and, in particular, it undervalues interdisciplinary studies.[9] Magnusson argues persuasively that urban scholars have been too hesitant in challenging restrictive disciplinary boundaries and that '… this timidity is bound up with an ongoing tendency to see like a state rather than a city' (Magnusson 2010, 41).

He suggests that the traditional disciplines reflect a particular but contestable way of understanding the world, and that the social sciences, in so far as they strive to have policy relevance, tend to 'see like a state' – that is, to produce knowledge that is intelligible to those who seek to govern. His radical argument is that to 'see like a city' holds out many benefits and, in particular, it involves positioning ourselves as inhabitants, not governors.[10] I am sympathetic to this analysis and, in my terms, 'seeing like a city' is consistent with adopting a place-based perspective. I develop this discussion in Chapter 4.

From time to time initiatives emanate from central governments that appear to recognise the potential for developing place-based approaches to public policy. For example, in the UK context, a report by Sir Michael Lyons on local government advocated a place-shaping role for local authorities (Lyons 2007). More recently there have been efforts to develop a Total Place, or whole area, approach to public services (HM Treasury 2010).[11] By examining the totality of public spending in a given area, this place-based analysis of government effort strives to uncover waste and duplication and free up resources so that they can be applied more effectively. More recently Sir Terry Farrell has produced a report on the future of architecture and the built environment in the UK (Farrell 2014). Interestingly the report's title is *Our Future in Place*, and Sir Terry argues, with passion, that we need to develop a much more proactive approach to place-based planning and design.

A central finding of the Total Place pilots was that UK central government departments in Whitehall would have to devolve significant decision-making power relating to 'their' services to the local level for this radical, place-based approach to work. As with previous attempts to develop a Total Approach on a geographical basis Whitehall departments, driven as they are by centralist patterns of thinking, have prevaricated.[12] In 2012, at the invitation of Prime Minister David Cameron, Lord Heseltine, produced a study examining the forces holding back economic growth in the UK.[13] In his radical report he shows how a drift to centralism has weakened local leadership. He recommended transferring £12 billion a year of public spending from Whitehall departments to the local level. This bold proposal represents an attempt to reverse 'a process [of centralisation] that has now continued almost without check for over a century' (Heseltine 2012, 28). A recent paper co-authored by Greg Clark MP, UK Minister for Cities and Constitution, is also full of rhetoric about devolving power and responsibilities to cities (Clark and Clark 2014). In practice, instead of solid proposals for enhancing the fiscal power of elected local authorities, the paper makes unconvincing claims about the importance of small scale, financial 'deals' with specific cities and localities.[14]

The drift of power to Whitehall has taken place over such a long period of time that the UK has, notwithstanding devolution of powers to Scotland and Wales, drifted into an absurdly centralised pattern of decision making. The inevitable flipside is that Britain now has a system of local democracy with inadequate fiscal power. I wish to make an international point here, though. Those adopting a place-based perspective in any country can expect to meet serious resistance from silo-based political and professional power structures, and from higher levels of government that will often tend to think that 'they know best'.

As mentioned earlier, central governments find it formidably difficult to avoid the tendency to 'see like a state' and this weakness is holding back public service reform in many countries. All is not lost, however. As Barber (2013) argues, nation states may find themselves being bypassed by city leaders who are demonstrating – and this is now becoming an international movement – that they can be very effective in using a place-based perspective to solve problems and build city-to-city learning networks (Campbell 2012).

Public leadership: new possibilities?

The nature of leadership in public policy, as distinct from leadership in the private sector is, at last, beginning to receive serious attention from scholars, and this is to be welcomed. It is difficult to see how radical change in public services can be brought about in the absence of bold, forward looking leadership, and yet theories of public leadership appear to be lagging behind the needs of practice. Consider, for example, the shift from local government to local governance.[15] In broad terms local 'governance' refers to the processes and structures of a variety of public, private, and community and voluntary sector bodies at the local level. It acknowledges the diffusion of responsibility for collective provision, and recognises the contribution of different levels and sectors. This is very different from traditional notions of local 'government' in which the operation of the state is the focus of attention.

The implications of the shift from government to governance for local political leadership are significant. Out goes the notion of the 'city boss' determining policies and priorities; in comes the 'facilitative leader' orchestrating the efforts of multiple actors. This is, of course, a caricature of the changes that are taking place in modern city leadership, but it highlights the importance of developing new capabilities relating to 'leadership in partnership working' or 'network leadership'. Yet there are comparatively few texts examining the role of public leadership in settings where the powers and responsibilities of different agencies and actors are dispersed.

Theories of public leadership have, of course, evolved in an effort to remain relevant to changing circumstances (Burns 1978; Grint 1997, 2005; Keohane 2010; Pendleton and Furnham 2012; Scharmer and Kaufer 2013). Contributions linking leadership theories to the urban context, however, have been far and few between. Jim Svara, a highly respected American scholar, provides an exception – he was one of the few urban political scientists to identify the importance of civic leadership back in the 1980s. His pioneering books on local leadership (Svara 1990, 1994) drew attention to the interplay between elected politicians and appointed public servants in urban leadership, and he has worked with colleagues to add to the literature more recently (Svara 2009). In the UK context Prime Minister Tony Blair should be given credit for raising the quality of debate about local leadership (Blair 1998). The Labour Government, elected in 1997, set out to strengthen political leadership in UK local government by, inter alia, introducing legislation creating a more powerful executive role – including the introduction of directly elected mayors in England (Hambleton 1998).

More recently research has examined the role of local leadership in: encouraging public service innovation (Bason 2010); promoting sustainable development (Parkin 2010); stimulating a knowledge-based economy (Gibney et al 2009); sustainable place-shaping (Collinge et al 2011; Sotarauta et al 2014); and promoting local economic development (Swinney et al 2011). While ideas and experiences relating to leadership, including what I call the **New Civic Leadership**, are considered in more depth in Chapters 3 and 5 we can, at this point, highlight three important themes.

First, more attention needs to be given to the role of leadership in bringing about radical change. In a stable world it may not be necessary to innovate that much – doing 'the same as we did last year plus or minus a bit' could well be a satisfactory approach. In such a world the absence of leadership may not be a disaster – managerial models will suffice. In a rapidly changing environment, however, leadership becomes critical because a central role of effective leaders is to change things. Successful leaders help all involved anticipate coming challenges and, inevitably, they disturb the status quo. This applies as much to the leaders of community groups as it does to imaginative city mayors. Indeed, grass-roots activists have much to contribute to the new civic leadership agenda. As Alison Gilchrist and Marilyn Taylor (2011, 123) put it, 'Community development can encourage community leadership that reflects both the population concerned and its own values. In other words, it tries to ensure a style of leadership that is inclusive, collaborative, egalitarian and democratic'.

Second, the shift from government to governance places a premium on facilitative leadership skills. American experience is relevant in this context as governance models have been in use for a longer period of time in the US than in many countries. Various US urban scholars have shown that traditional notions of 'strong' top-down leadership are unsuited to situations in which power is dispersed (Stone 1995; Svara 1994, 2009). Recent research on collaborative leadership in UK local governance supports this argument (Williams 2012). The way leading across boundaries can be supported and developed is a key theme that will be developed in this book.

Third, emotions have been seriously neglected in leadership theory and practice. Again, we can note exceptions. The work by Daniel Goleman and colleagues on emotional intelligence emphasises the importance of using the soft skills of leadership to enhance the quality of relationships (Goleman et al 2002). In relation to urban governance the importance of the emotional dimension of leadership was revealed as a particularly significant feature in a recent Anglo-Dutch study of efforts to tackle social inclusion (Hambleton and Howard 2012).

These three themes will be discussed at some length in subsequent chapters. It may, however, be helpful if I introduce my own definition of leadership at this early stage. In previous work I have defined leadership as: 'Shaping emotions and behaviour to achieve common goals' (Hambleton 2007a, 174). There are other definitions of leadership, and some of these will be considered later. This relatively new definition of leadership will be used to guide the analysis of leadership in this book. Strengths of this definition are that it draws attention to how people feel, and it emphasises the collective, social construction of common purpose.

Innovation in public management

Public service innovation, a relatively neglected topic until a few years ago, is now receiving a high level of attention in public policy circles. Some may feel that the international financial crash of 2008/09 is the main spur to this change in attitude. On this interpretation the present interest in public service innovation represents a response to the significant cutbacks in public expenditure that are now taking place in many countries. Carrying on the same way as before has been removed as an option for many public servants, with the result that innovation has leapt up the managerial 'to do' list. There can be no denying that the onset of austerity following the financial crisis of 2008/09 has spurred interest in public service innovation – at local, national and international levels. The shift in focus nonetheless reflects, in some localities at least, a deeper reconsideration of the changing role and purpose of public service. In some settings this includes a re-examination of the relationship between the state and civil society. In these localities innovation is not seen as a passing managerial response to fiscal pressures.

It is helpful to draw a simple distinction between public service improvement and public service innovation. In the former politicians provide their public servants with clear targets relating to the cost-effectiveness of public services. They require their officials to engage in continuous improvement, to monitor service inputs and outputs, to assess the outcomes arising from public service efforts, and then make adjustments in order to enhance service effectiveness. This is classic performance management – the norms guiding organisational performance are not up for review. Rather, public servants strive to improve by delivering more of the same (or very similar) services to their clients in an ever more cost-effective way. When an organisation engages in innovation it goes beyond the realm of traditional performance management. It undertakes a more radical assessment of its own effectiveness, welcomes unheard of possibilities, and explores entirely new ways of delivering results.

In drawing this distinction between improvement and innovation I am building on concepts first set out by Argyris and Schon (1978) in their influential book on organisational learning. In their vocabulary 'single loop learning' – improvement, in my terms – involves a single feedback loop connecting detected outcomes to organisational strategies. In this model the focus in on improving performance by changing strategies and practices without challenging organisational norms. 'Double loop learning' arises when an organisation realises that it cannot improve performance by doing more of what it already knows how to do. In double loop learning – innovation, in my terms – there is a double feedback loop that connects learning not only to organisational strategies, but also to the very norms that define effective performance.

Both forms of organisational learning have an important part to play in any successful organisation. In stable times strategies emphasising improvement can work well. In times when the organisation's environment is changing rapidly it is almost certainly the case that the emphasis will need to be on innovation. The distinction I am using also aligns rather well with the contrast made by some writers between incremental and disruptive organisational change. Continuous improvement tends to be a fine-grained, incremental process, whereas innovation often involves a degree of disjuncture with past practices (Hartley 2011).

The Whitehall Innovation Hub, established in 2008, has contributed new thinking to public service innovation debates in the UK. Su Maddock, Director of the Hub, recognised from the outset that leadership plays a critical role in nurturing public service innovation – not just in eliminating the disincentives to innovate, but also in creating a public service culture which positively welcomes innovation (Maddock 2009). More recently, a UK charity – known as Nesta – has begun to document innovative practice in public services and explore new ways of working to promote innovation (Gillinson et al 2010; Mulgan and Leadbeater 2013).

For the purposes of this book I define public service innovation as creating a new approach to public service, putting it into practice and finding out if it works. This simple definition makes it clear that innovation involves not just inventing a new idea – it also involves applying it.[16] In addition, it sees innovation as a process of social discovery and learning. We will explore the theme of innovation – particularly place-based innovation – in Chapter 6 and in the many Innovation Stories presented later in the book. At this point I wish to highlight two points. First, in my experience, radical public service innovation usually involves a process of co-creation – a process in which new solutions are generated by working *with* people, not for them. This is an approach that finds favour with other writers on public service innovation – for example, Bason (2010). Second, research carried out for this book suggests that, while managerial models of public service innovation can play a role, truly radical change requires political, not just managerial, leadership.

Power in modern society

There is a vast literature on power and numerous definitions. Here I provide a brief introduction. I focus on the dimensions of power that shape leadership and, in particular, place-based leadership. The Oxford English Dictionary definition of power provides a starting point: 'The ability to do or act'. John Scott (2001, 1) defines *social* power as 'an agent's intentional use of causal powers to affect the conduct of other participants in the social relations that connect them'. The agent might be an individual, a group, an organisation, a political party, a special interest and so on.

Causation is, then, central to the concept of power, and a familiar distinction is often drawn between the exercise of power through inducements or coercion – sometimes described, in colloquial terms, as 'carrot or stick'. Joseph Nye has developed our understanding of international diplomacy by distinguishing between 'hard power' and 'soft power' in modern world politics. He suggests that, while hard power usually rests on inducements (carrots) or threats (sticks) there is another side to power. Soft power co-opts people, it wins them over. In simple terms soft power is:'... the ability to get what you want through attraction rather than coercion or payments' (Nye 2004, x). Giving attention to the use of soft power does not mean abandoning hard power. Rather Nye suggests that power can be viewed as a continuum ranging from softer to harder – or, we might say, from attraction through carrots to sticks. As we shall see, when we examine examples of successful place-based leadership, later in the book, it is often the case that effective civic leaders, while they may not use this language, are making very sophisticated use of soft power in the way they lead.

The concept of power is, however, rather more complicated than a simple continuum between soft and hard approaches. Stephen Lukes (2005), in *Power: a Radical View*, provides a brilliant analysis of power in modern society. In his book, first published in 1974, Lukes draws on a wide literature to argue that there are three dimensions, or 'faces', of power. First, there is the visible exercise of power in public decision-making. This aspect of power absorbs much of the attention of modern, news organisations and dominates public discourse. It focuses on the behaviours of those making decisions about issues where there is an observable conflict of interest. In the American context pluralist scholars, from Robert Dahl (1961) onwards, have argued that examination of actual decisions in cities shows that power in modern society is distributed. Pluralists claim that, in relation to specific decisions, different interests win or lose depending on, for example, the soundness of their arguments, the extent of their political support, their ability to organise and so on. Lukes calls this a one-dimensional view of power.

A second face of power highlights the ability of some interests to prevent issues from ever reaching the public arena in the first place. Pioneered by Bachrach and Baratz (1970), the non-decision-making argument holds that a community may contain groups who are powerful enough to create, consciously or unconsciously, barriers to the public airing of policy conflicts. Lukes argues that this idea of non-decision-making, which he links closely to the notion of a 'mobilisation of bias' (Schattschneider 1960, 71), while it may be hidden from view, is a significant aspect of power as potential demands can be suffocated before they are even voiced.

Lukes goes on to suggest that, while these two dimensions of power have much to offer, they are inadequate because they associate power with actual, observable conflict (or potential conflict in the case of non-decision-making). He points to the existence of a third face of power – the invisible, insidious shaping of desires by the manipulation of group values through misinformation, social engineering and propaganda:

> Indeed, is it not the supreme exercise of power to get another or others to have the desires you want them to have – that is, to secure their compliance by controlling their thoughts and desires? (Lukes 2005, 27).

This third perspective on power offers the possibility of a sociological, rather than a merely personalised, explanation of how political systems prevent political demands from becoming political issues, or even from being made.[17]

During the last forty years or so political scientists and urban scholars have attempted to apply ideas concerning power to the study of urban governance in many cities. Clarence Stone's book, *Regime Politics*, which provides a detailed analysis of the exercise of power in Atlanta from 1946–1988, deserves special mention in this context (Stone 1989). Stone's analysis, which has influenced a generation of urban scholars (see, for example, Davies and Imbroscio 2010), unearths numerous insights on the nature of Atlanta's urban regime, by which he means '… the set of arrangements by which a community is actually governed' (Stone 1989, 6). He points out that: 'The power struggle concerns, not control and resistance, but gaining and fusing a capacity to act – power to, not power over' (Stone 1989, 229).

Earlier I noted, following Fainstein (2010), that modern planning theory has neglected the role of power in modern society. It would be wrong, however, to suggest that all planning theorists have a blind spot in relation to the power structures within which city planning operates. For example, some years ago, Bent Flyvbjerg (1998) provided a detailed analysis of the interplay between rationality and powerful interests in the city planning of Aalborg, Denmark. More recently, Philip Allmendinger (2009) has examined seven schools of planning theory. In this analysis he discusses how various approaches to planning may, or may not, serve different interests in society. These efforts to understand the interplay between political power and planning are important and are to be welcomed. We will return to the theme of power in modern society repeatedly in subsequent chapters.

Dimensions of the inclusive city

Having introduced four themes that need, in my view, to be central to any effective strategy for creating inclusive cities – an understanding of place, a recognition of the importance of leadership, a commitment to innovation and an understanding of power in modern society – I now outline one way of defining an inclusive city. In an international research report on public service innovation Jo Howard and I defined social inclusion as: 'Being able to participate fully in social activities, and/or to engage in political and social life' (Hambleton and Howard 2012, 11). This simple definition worked well enough for the purposes of our Anglo-Dutch comparative analysis of place-based leadership and social inclusion, and the innovators in the three cities we worked with were comfortable with it.

I seek here to broaden this definition of social inclusion and conjure up a vision of a more holistic approach – one that encompasses political, social, economic *and* environmental dimensions. Discussion of definitions is important because, as we shall see, some terms – notably sustainable development – have been so misused over the years that they have become almost devoid of meaning.

I introduce four inter-related themes relating to inclusion, and take the view that they all have a part to play in defining what an inclusive city might look like:

- linking inclusion, inequality and place;
- adopting a 'rights based' perspective;
- enhancing inclusive approaches to democracy;
- including our relationships with the natural environment.

Inclusion, inequality and place

First, we consider the relationship between inequality and inclusion. There is a substantial sociological literature examining the way societies can marginalise and exclude certain groups – on the basis of a person's class, education, gender, race, religion, ethnicity, caste, sexual orientation, age, mental and physical abilities and so on.[18] This is a complex subject, and we must guard against generalising too freely. Wilkinson and Pickett, however, in their influential international study, *The Spirit Level*, conclude that: 'In more unequal societies, more people are oriented towards dominance; in more egalitarian societies, more people are oriented towards inclusiveness and empathy' (Wilkinson and Pickett 2010, 168). These authors suggest that bigger income differences in a society seem to solidify the social structure, and decrease the chances of upward mobility. It follows, then, that activists seeking to advance the idea of inclusion can expect to find common cause with those striving to reduce inequality.

What about the relationship between place and inequality? Does geography matter? The answer is 'yes'. In fact, geography plays a critical role in shaping life chances and this is one of the reasons why, as mentioned earlier, the neglect of place in public policy making is so troubling.[19] The evidence shows – and this is unmistakable – that people are disadvantaged or advantaged by where they live. We can identify three related aspects to the geography of injustice, and I label these as territorial justice, spatial justice and environmental justice.

Davies (1968) coined the term **territorial justice** to describe the idea that public policy should aim to distribute resources to meet the varying social needs of different territorial units. He showed that territorial injustice was widespread, and there is now abundant evidence to show that territorial injustice is rife at a number of geographical levels. At the micro-level there are significant differences in the quality of life between different neighbourhoods in any given city.[20] Uneven geographical opportunity also arises at the urban and regional level. Thus, there are significant differences in the quality of life, and life expectancy, between cities and regions within most countries. In the UK, for example, the existence of a north/south divide in life chances, between those who live in the less well off north and those who live in the relatively prosperous south of the country, is incontrovertible.[21] At the international level De Blij (2009) has shown, in a remarkably incisive analysis, how we are all born into natural and cultural environments that have a profound impact on our individual and collective prospects.

The concept of **spatial justice** overlaps with territorial justice. Soja (2010), in *Seeking Spatial Justice*, provides an extended analysis of the concept arguing not just that social processes have spatial effects, but also that the reverse is true. The concept of spatial justice does not contradict the central argument of territorial justice – that social and political processes create unjust outcomes that can be mapped. It is, however, a more complex concept as it is also concerned with the way spatial dynamics often fuel the creation of this inequality. Soja builds on the work of Harvey (1973), to outline a philosophy of social space. He argues that urban, industrialised capitalism needs space to be arranged in ways that meet its needs. Authors adopting a spatial justice perspective throw light on the socio-spatial conflict between the needs of capital accumulation and social needs.

The concept of **environmental justice** overlaps with both territorial and spatial justice. Environmental justice scholars have shown that poor neighbourhoods receive fewer environmental services, such as street cleaning and open space maintenance, than better off areas that tend to benefit from parks, coasts and forests. Isabelle Anguelovski (2013) describes studies revealing such unfairness as 'traditional' environmental justice – they represent an environmental variation on the idea of territorial justice that I have just described. She notes, however, that environmental justice scholarship is now breaking new ground by examining how marginalised neighbourhoods are attempting to foster holistic forms of environmental action through fresh food and green space initiatives, efforts to foster healthy living, and innovation in relation to the recycling of waste materials. She provides evidence to show how modern environmental justice efforts are closely related to community development, and she highlights the psychological benefits of place-based action:

> Their work encompasses aspects of safety and security that go beyond individual protection against physical, social, or financial damage and harm to include soothing, nurturing, protection, and wellness, that is psychological dimensions of environmental health (Anguelovski 2013, 171).

We will return to the topic of environmental justice shortly.

Critical urban theory has expanded in recent years, and radical intellectuals and activists have contributed fresh insights on the nature of the relationships between spatial patterns of urban restructuring and the needs of capital. For example, Cochrane (2012, 104) shows how territory should 'not be taken as something given, somehow pre-existing and waiting to be filled with politics, but rather as something that is actively formed and shaped through the political process'. Cox (2013) provides a review of recent work on scale and territory – as well as networks theory – and suggests that, because the underlying social structure is often neglected, many of these studies offer insights that are, at best, partial. He is, for example, scathing about the way networks theory ignores the social power structure, saying, 'In network theory mutually supportive individuals working together have replaced the compulsions of capitalism. In some versions, capitalism has been transformed into a blissful cooperation of commodity-owning agents, even while the commodity that the vast majority own is simply their own labour power' (Cox 2013, 59). Critical urban theorists throw light on the processes that give rise to social and spatial inequality (Davies and Imbroscio 2010). The global financial crash of 2008/09 has spurred fresh efforts by scholars to understand modern processes of urban restructuring and the growth of inequality in modern societies (Brenner et al 2012; Harvey 2012). At the heart of critical urban theory lies the claim that cities under capitalism are driven by profit-oriented behaviour rather than by social purpose. For example, Libby Porter and Kate Shaw (2009) show how 'market-obeying' strategies have come to dominate urban regeneration practices in many countries. This results, as often as not, in a process of gentrification that displaces low-income residents.

Critical urban scholars vary considerably in the prescriptions they advocate to tackle the way capitalism commodifies relationships and perpetuates inequality. These proposals range from outright revolution, involving the overthrow of the capitalist system, through to radical social campaigning and action. The recent failures of capitalism have led to widespread public protest. For example, the 'We are the 99 percent' and 'Occupy Wall Street' movements of 2011 inspired the creation of hundreds of nonviolent encampments in cities across the world – in big cities like New York, London, Barcelona, Athens and Cairo, as well as in many smaller cities (Byrne 2012; Graeber 2013).

This discussion of the literature on territorial, spatial and environmental justice suggests that, at the very least, attempts to advance inclusion without considering the dynamics of urban power relations and the role of space and place in these unfolding dynamics will be ineffective.

The right to the city

Our second theme, and it is closely related to the first, considers the value of a 'rights based' approach to inclusion. Marshall (1950), in his classic analysis of *Citizenship and Social Class,* provides a good starting point for understanding this perspective.[22] He argues that there has been, in England at least, an historical progression in the development of citizenship through three main phases as people have claimed more rights: 1) The fight for *civil* rights in the seventeenth and eighteenth centuries created a limited amount of legal equality; 2) The growth of *political* rights in the nineteenth and early twentieth centuries involved conflict with capitalist interests, because these struggles gained citizens' rights to participate in the exercise of political power without limitation by economic status or gender; and 3) The expansion of *social* rights – the right to the prevailing standard of life and the social heritage of the society – stemming (in the UK context) from the growth of the welfare state (for example, free health care, free education, subsidised housing and so on) in the twentieth century.[23]

In other countries the emergence and development of citizen rights will have been different from the UK. Marshall's distinction between three kinds of rights – civil, political and social – is likely to be helpful in any context. It should be noted that Marshall was writing in 1950 and his analysis focuses on the rights of 'citizens'. We know that, because of a rapid rise in migration in the last half century, many residents in any given city may not be recognised as 'citizens' at all (Saunders 2010; Spencer 2011). National laws on the recognition by states of migrant's rights vary enormously. It is the case, however, that in many cities the newly arrived are among the most excluded – and, sometimes, they seem to have no rights whatsoever.

The rights-based approach has gained renewed momentum in recent years as countries have sought to incorporate the notion of the 'right to the city' into their public policy making and, in some cases, into their constitutions. This strategy builds on the 1948 Universal Declaration of Human Rights and was set out in the World Charter on the Right to the City in 2004.[24] Carolyn Whitzman and her colleagues draw on this perspective to offer an insightful collection of essays on the relationship between women's safety and the right to the city. They note that: '... the right to the city is concerned with the right of all individuals living in cities to liberty, freedom and the benefits of city life' (Whitzman et al 2013, 5). This collection stresses how important it is for women and girls to access their rights to the city, and it documents a range of practical strategies – from women's safety audits to gender mainstreaming.[25]

It is important to draw attention to the rights of Lesbian, Gay, Bisexual and Transgender (LGBT) groups in the shaping of the modern city.[26] The laws relating to LGBT people vary greatly by country. In some countries there is no official heterosexist discrimination – for example, Canada, Iceland, the Netherlands, Norway, Sweden, South Africa and Spain. In others same-sex activity or identity is punishable by the death penalty. Again, as we shall see in more detail in Chapter 10, cities and place-based leaders have been, and remain, active in advancing the rights of LGBT groups.[27]

Enhancing the quality of local democracy

A third component of inclusion relates to democracy and, in particular, the degree to which decision-making processes provide for undistorted discourse and recognition of difference. Young (2000), in her wide-ranging analysis of inclusion and democracy, stresses the importance of self-determination and associative activity in promoting social justice. She develops helpful ideas about the norms and conditions of inclusive democratic communication under circumstances of structural inequality and cultural difference, and points to ways in which strong states can promote social justice by creating new bridges between civic associations and state institutions.[28]

In Chapter 3, I discuss alternative approaches to public service reform. Following Hirschman (1970), the argument presented there suggests that two ideal theoretical routes to empowerment now compete for ascendancy in modern societies – exit and voice. Market models provide consumers with the power of exit – dissatisfied customers can take their business elsewhere. Democratic models depend on citizens exercising the power of voice – to express complaints, campaign for changes and offer alternative ideas. There has been much experiment with market and quasi-market approaches in public service management but, as we shall see, the results have been disappointing. In relation to the other route to empowerment we can see that strategies to reform the quality and effectiveness of local democracy have proliferated, and local authorities have become increasingly sophisticated in developing more effective ways of engaging with geographical communities and communities of interest within their jurisdictions (Cornwall 2008; Fung 2004; Oliver and Pitt 2013; Pearce 2010; Smith 2009).

We will explore themes relating to inclusion and democracy – and particularly local democracy – in more detail in Chapter 7. The discussion there embraces ideas designed to enhance the quality of representative local democracy as well as initiatives designed to develop improved approaches to participatory democracy. The rapid movement of peoples across international frontiers means that cities are becoming more and more diverse. These population shifts are discussed in Chapter 2 and the implications for democratic governance in multicultural cities are given explicit attention in Chapter 10. Here we can note that place-based leadership can play a significant role in reshaping local democratic processes to include voices that are often excluded.

Cities across the world are developing a wide variety of approaches to local democracy and there are excellent opportunities for international exchange in this area. It is worth emphasising that research shows that enhancing the quality of local democracy is critical to any effective strategy to reduce urban poverty. For example, a recent analysis of how to reduce urban poverty in the global south shows that two factors are critical: the extent to which the poor are organised and the nature of their relationship with local government (Satterthwaite and Mitlin 2014, 7).

Integrating a concern for the natural environment

Finally, might it be possible to include our relationship with the natural environment in our definition of inclusion? This opens up a big subject and it is one we will return to in Chapter 8. I have already referred to the notion of environmental justice. As adding the environment into my approach to inclusion may seem a little unfamiliar, even controversial, it is important to outline my reasoning in more detail here. Allow me to step back. In the past, there has been an unhelpful divide in thought and action between those concerned with the 'city' and those concerned with 'nature'.[29] Traditionally, environmentalists have focussed on preservation of the wilderness areas of the planet, such as rainforests and tundra. Looking back over the last century or so we can see that many countries established national and/or state parks with the explicit aim of conserving fragile eco-systems. The parks signify a strong commitment to protecting rare animals, plants and fabulous physical natural environments. The city, by contrast, was seen as a human invention and, in many respects, was considered to be separate from the so-called natural world and, in some interpretations, a growing threat to pristine areas.

The separation of living patterns between those residing in the city and those living in rural areas tended to reinforce this unfortunate divide. The scholarly practice of undervaluing interdisciplinary studies compounded the problem. Thus, urban political scientists have long focussed on the social, economic and political dynamics of cities and city regions, whilst paying scant attention to the city as an eco-system.[30] Meanwhile, in the past, ecologists and environmentalists focussed their efforts on advancing understanding of the natural world and did not pay that much regard to the growing impact of human settlements on, for example, climate change and biodiversity, or to the importance of governance in shaping environmental possibilities.

Some will claim that the United Nations Conference on the Human Environment, held in Stockholm in 1972, changed all that. The conference stressed, in line with the 'limits to growth' argument set out by Meadows et al (1972), that any agenda for future development must include the creation of a healthy and productive environment for all human beings. More than a decade later, the World Commission on Environment and Development, chaired by Gro Harlem Brundtland, mapped out a framework for equitable development. Described as sustainable development this approach attempted to balance environmental, social and economic needs (WCED1987).

A problem, however, is that many interested parties have chosen to redefine sustainable development to the point where, in some settings at least, it has become a virtually meaningless expression.[31] Indeed, over twenty years ago evidence was presented showing that economic growth and environmental conservation were uncomfortable bedfellows and fears were expressed that sustainable development was likely to become 'a green cover for "business as usual"' (Jacobs 1991, 59). Others have criticised the way the term has been used: 'Sustainable development remains ambiguous, inexact, ill-defined, unbounded and unmeasurable' (Stewart and Collett 1998, 59). Nigel Taylor (2003) provides a particularly incisive analysis of the meaning of the term 'sustainable development' and shows that fudging together conflicting aspirations is intellectually dishonest.

Erik Swyngedouw builds on and deepens these arguments. He links the current populist discourse relating to climate change and sustainable development to the attempt, pursued by many in power, to adopt a post-political approach to the public sphere. In this post-political world, so the argument goes, words are redefined or diluted in order to emasculate fundamental conflicts. On this analysis it is no accident that sustainable development has become a meaningless term because: 'Post-politics refers to a politics in which ideological struggles are replaced by techno-managerial planning, expert management and administration' (Swyngedouw 2010, 225). In making the link between post-politics and climate change he argues that many involved in green politics have moved from a position of contestation, organised action and radical disagreement, ten or twenty years ago, to one in which they have been co-opted into the service of neo-liberal aims and objectives. He argues that weak definitions of sustainable development, ones that attempt to maximise consensus, stand in the way of clear thinking about what is actually going on.

Mark Whitehead also wonders whether the misuse of the phrase sustainable urban development has led us to the point where we should ditch the term. In the end, he steps back from seeking the burial of sustainable urbanism, as 'Despite its obvious corruption... it is clear that the presence of the principles of sustainable development within urban policy represent a hard-fought victory for those who are eager to see the building of more progressive and just patterns of urbanisation' (Whitehead 2012, 42). The problem of obfuscation nonetheless remains. The word resilience has gained popularity in recent years and, in some circles, seems to be replacing sustainability as the central aspiration for cities. As discussed further in Chapter 8, however, this is also a term that often masks the distributional consequences of city planning and urban management decisions. For example, policies designed to make cities more resilient to the risk of flooding may involve displacing populations and it is poor communities that tend to be disproportionately affected. The post-Katrina reshaping of New Orleans in recent years illustrates the argument – residents of public housing areas have lost out. Edward Goetz (2013, 93) notes that the response to the hurricane has had distributional effects:

> Katrina provided the opportunity for a final push to close down public housing in the city and move toward redevelopment.

Perhaps we need some fresh vocabulary – or modified ways of thinking – that can inject new impetus into the discussion of socio-environmental futures. Here I present a simple framework developed by Richard Rees, a British urban designer, as it helps to bridge the divide between social scientific and ecological perspectives. I will then offer a reminder of the ideas that Gro Harlem Brundtland presented in relation to sustainable development, not least because a key part of her message has been airbrushed out of the discourse. Rees argues that the essential elements of contemporary life – the individual, society and nature – have become separated out, and that they need to be reconnected. Figure 1.1 is derived from his perspective and illustrates a simple way of framing our thinking about sustainable development.[32] Dotted lines are used to signal that the boundaries are porous.

Figure 1.1: The individual, society and nature

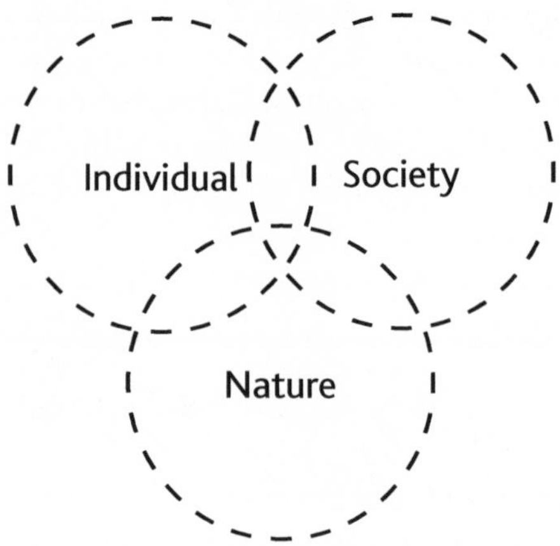

Source: Richard Rees, Urban Designer, UK.[33]

Rees argues, consistent with a growing body of writers on resilient cities and communities, that city leaders, urban planners, architects, designers and others need to embed a fruitful co-existence with nature into urban policy and practice.[34] Our relationship with the natural environment should not be regarded as another policy consideration – it needs to be integral to public policy making. As Timothy Beatley (2011) observes, nature is vital to human experience and he explains how civic leaders can create what he calls 'biophilic cities' – that is, green cities that celebrate the wonder-expanding dimensions of nature itself. Adam Ford (2013), in his book on mindfulness and the art of urban living, extols the virtues of city gardens, allotments and green spaces in keeping us connected to plants and nature and, in passing, he refers approvingly to the guerrilla gardening movement.[35] The philosophical underpinnings for the approach set out in Figure 1.1 – which envisages a move from anthropocentrism to eco-centrism – are well established in green political thought (Eckersley 1992). It is a good sign that some planning theorists are starting to examine the interplay between social and ecological resilience (Wilkinson 2012).

I now return to the Brundtland Commission definition of sustainable development. Please note that it contains two sentences, not one:

> Sustainable development is development that meets the needs of the present without compromising the ability of future generations to meet their own needs. It contains two key concepts: 1) the concept of 'needs', in particular the essential needs of the world's poor, *to which overriding priority should be given*; and 2) the idea of limitations imposed by the state of technology and social organisation on the environment's ability to meet present and future needs. (WCED 1987, 43; my emphasis)

The second sentence, with its strong commitment to addressing the needs of the world's poor, has vanished from view in many academic and policy debates. Some writers on sustainable development not only omit the second sentence, they pay no attention to poverty and unfairness in society at all. Some, however, recognise the challenge here, and they argue that it is essential to move from a traditional environmental perspective, emphasising nature conservation, to a resolute commitment to environmental justice.

As Adebowale (2008) explains, adopting an environmental justice perspective to nature foregrounds the social dimension. It highlights the way society interacts with the environment not just in aggregate terms, but also in relation to the *distributional impact* of planning and urban development policies and practices. As mentioned earlier environmental 'goods' and 'bads' are very unevenly distributed in many societies. It follows that *the distributional effects of urban development should be at the heart of sustainable development.* Unfortunately, much of the time, distributional effects are ignored. Dana Meadows and her colleagues, when they revisited their *Limits to Growth* analysis thirty years on, reinforce this point: 'Current modes of growth perpetuate poverty and increase the gap between the rich and the poor.... In the current system economic growth generally takes place in the already rich countries and flows disproportionately to the richest people within those countries' (Meadows et al 2005, 41–42).[36]

Imagining an inclusive city

The terms referred to in this discussion of the inclusive city – words like 'inclusion', 'inequality', 'rights', 'justice', 'nature', 'sustainability', 'resilience' and so on – are socially constructed. It follows that there can be no fixed and final definitions of what these words mean – they are contested concepts. Moreover, some of these terms will be unfamiliar in some countries – they are likely to have different meanings in different cultures, languages and contexts. Clearly, it serves a useful purpose to try to define terms with precision and, indeed, establishing clarity of meaning is essential for intelligent conversation. Nevertheless, it is critical to be sensitive to cultural variations, and I want to stress here that, in what follows, I am not trying to spell out a fixed definition of the inclusive city. Rather, I hope that the discussion here offers a grammar that the reader can revise and develop in the light of her or his own experience.[37]

For the purposes of this book my definition of the inclusive city is as follows:

> The inclusive city is governed by powerful, place-based democratic institutions. All residents are able to participate fully in the society and the economy, and civic leaders strive for just results while caring for the natural environment on which we all depend.

This is, of course, a utopian vision and I make no apology for that. Utopian thinking is often dismissed as offering idealistic and impractical proposals for social reform and/or radical change. This is to misunderstand the idea, however. I share the view expressed by John Friedmann, who argues that: 'If injustice is to be corrected... we will need the concrete imagery of utopian thinking to propose steps that would bring us a little closer to a more just world' (Friedmann 2002, 104).[38] My approach is consistent with his thinking, with Susan Fainstein's idea of 'realistic utopianism' (Fainstein 2010, 20), and also with the idea of 'visioning' as put forward by Dana Meadows and her colleagues:

> We do not believe vision makes anything happen. Vision without action is useless. But action without vision is directionless and feeble. Vision is absolutely necessary to guide and motivate. More than that, vision, when widely shared and firmly kept in sight, does *bring into being new systems*. (Meadows et al 2005, 272; author's emphasis)

Hanspieter Kriesi and Lars Müller illustrate their excellent analysis of the changing nature of democracy with many stunning photographs and images. They remind us that so-called utopian dreams can come true:

> The photos of Nelson Mandela as president and images of the fall of the Berlin Wall illustrate how once-utopian notions have become a reality (Kriesi and Muller 2013 p9)

In line with the previous discussion the vision of the inclusive city offered here emphasises the importance of five key concepts: place, democratic rights, civic leadership, justice and environmental awareness. The underlying logic here is that: 1) place matters, 2) powerful local self government is critical, 3) all voices in society should have influence, not just the rich and powerful, 4) bold placed-based, civic leadership is fundamental, and 5) the twin aims of policy and practice should be just results and living in balance with nature.[39]

There are different ways of moving towards the creation of inclusive cities. In simple terms we can note that, as mentioned earlier, strategies designed to advance inclusion almost certainly lie on a continuum ranging from modest adjustments designed to diminish injustice, through radical reforms intended to transform social relations and increase equality, through to revolutionary overthrow of the capitalist system of worker exploitation leading to new ways of living. An ongoing and lively debate is taking place, within urban studies and elsewhere, among these different schools of thought. For example, most of the chapters in a collection of essays on *Justice and the American Metropolis*, edited by Hayward and Swanstrom (2011), offer ideas and proposals that are perfectly feasible within the current US political context. Other commentators, for example Marxist urban scholars, argue that injustice is now so embedded in modern society that disruptive change is needed to bring in an era of much greater democratic control of the economy

(Harvey 1973; 2012). Weaver (2014) provides an overview of these alternatives and advocates an emphasis on strengthening social citizenship, a concept I discussed earlier.

In sketching out my utopian vision for an inclusive city I am not suggesting that sustainable development is a concept that should be discarded. I am, however, trying to stimulate fresh thinking in relation to socio-environmental futures. After twenty-five years of misuse the ideals that Gro Harlem Brundtland articulated in relation to sustainable development can benefit from an injection of new vocabulary. In my view, a constructive way forward for city leadership and urban management is to focus more attention on the theme of *inclusion*. If progress towards her objective of giving 'overriding priority' to meeting the needs of the world's poor is to be achieved, it is, frankly, no longer enough to advocate sustainable development.

What about the role of leadership in this context? Some writers on sustainable development have grasped the importance of governance for any future strategy, and this is encouraging. For example, in *Governing Sustainability*, a group of leading sustainable development experts argue that the environmental crisis is, first and foremost, a crisis of governance (Adger and Jordan 2009). In her contribution to this volume Katrina Brown offers a reality check and her analysis makes for grim reading:

> There are many indications that the world is moving further from, rather than closer to, global sustainability, and that the problems of eco-system degradation and entrenched poverty are persistent (Brown 2009, 46).

Surprisingly, even these well-informed writers do not discuss leadership at all, still less, the importance of place-based leadership. This appears to be a serious weakness in the current debate about governing sustainability, and I hope that the ideas set out in this book can make a contribution to filling this gap. Earlier in this chapter I explained, following Sandel (2012), that market-dominated thinking is not delivering satisfactory results for societies. It follows that governments need to intervene, and this is the central reason why public leadership – and particularly public, *place-based* leadership – is so important. In my view, leadership to advance the cause of inclusion should be at the heart of future thinking relating to governing sustainability.

Engaged scholarship and Innovation Stories

In the introduction to this chapter I indicated that this book aims to bridge the worlds of academe and practice. This is not the dominant paradigm in modern scholarship and it is, perhaps, a hazardous enterprise as scholars and practitioners tend to reside in separate worlds. A consequence is that they often fail to communicate very well with each other to the disadvantage of both. In this section

I introduce the idea of engaged scholarship, a phrase that is familiar in American higher education but one that has not yet established itself internationally. It provides an important part of the intellectual underpinning for the analysis of urban dynamics and public leadership that follows. We will examine this topic in more detail in Chapter 11 so that a brief introduction to some key concepts will suffice at this stage.

Ernest Boyer, President of The Carnegie Foundation, had a significant impact on the evolution of conceptions of scholarship in US higher education, and his insights provide a good entry point to a discussion of engaged scholarship. In his influential report, *Scholarship Reconsidered*, he concluded:

> What we are faced with, today, is the need to clarify campus missions and relate the work of the academy more directly to the realities of contemporary life… We proceed with the conviction that if the nation's higher learning institutions are to meet today's urgent academic and social mandates, their missions must be carefully redefined and the meaning of scholarship creatively reconsidered. (Boyer 1990, 13)

In a later article he indicated that:

> … the scholarship of engagement … means creating a special climate in which the academic and the civic cultures communicate more continuously and more creatively with each other (Boyer 1996, 148).

For the purposes of this book I define engaged scholarship as the co-creation of new knowledge by scholars and practitioners working together in a shared process of discovery. This approach, which resembles systemic action research, recognises that there are different ways of knowing (Burns 2007). There is a substantial body of literature on the nature of knowledge, and many typologies have been developed. One helpful distinction is that between 'explicit' knowledge (sometimes described as formal, scientific or professional knowledge) and 'tacit' knowledge (knowledge stemming from personal and social experience that cannot be codified) (McInerney and Day 2007). Engaged scholarship attempts to draw, in an intelligent way, on both categories of knowledge.[40]

Figure 1.2 illustrates how practice and academe are brought together in engaged scholarship. Effective collaboration in the area of overlap between practice and academe requires good relationships to be constructed. In my experience this involves creating spaces in which participants can take risks, raise doubts, always knowing that their views will be respected. Adventurous explorations of this kind can only be productive if co-creators trust each other – this is easy to say, not always easy to do. As with Figure 1.1 I use dotted lines in this figure to emphasise permeability.

Figure 1.2: Engaged scholarship

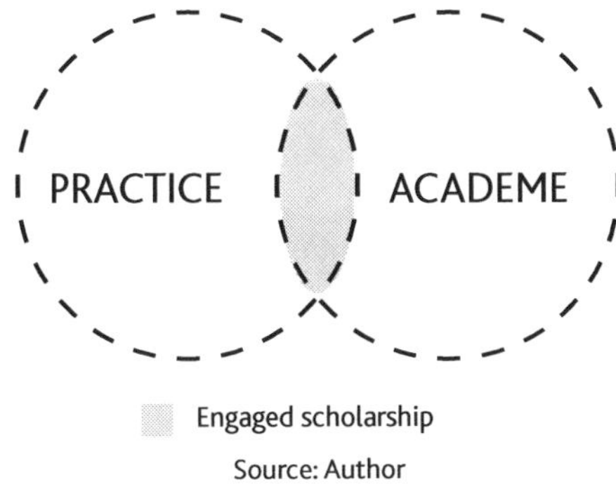

Source: Author

I referred earlier to a study Jo Howard and I carried out examining place-based leadership in three cities – two in the UK and one in The Netherlands (Hambleton and Howard 2012). This research project provides an example of engaged scholarship, and it is also the source of a concept that will be used extensively in this book – the idea of an Innovation Story. The Anglo-Dutch study involved co-creating new knowledge in two senses. First, it bridged the worlds of academe and practice – researchers collaborated actively with practitioners to construct an Innovation Story documenting the leadership of public service innovation in each city. Second, the research develops new understanding by engaging in international dialogue. People from the two countries, with different experiences, shared their ideas and co-created new ways of thinking about civic leadership.

What, then, is an Innovation Story? It is a short, structured narrative describing a particular innovation. It attempts to throw light on how change was brought about and tries to draw out leadership lessons for others. This approach can be applied widely in the public, private and non-profit sectors. It provides a way of exploring the relationships between leadership and innovation – a process that, even now, is not well understood. In this book I am focussing on a particular kind of Innovation Story – that is, stories that advance understanding of the role of place-based leadership in spurring innovations that help to create an inclusive city.[41]

In summary, an Innovation Story employs engaged scholarship and, ideally, it should have the following characteristics:

- **Short.** Busy practitioners and activists may find it difficult to find time to read lengthy case studies. An Innovation Story provides the reader with a concise summary but, by citing sources and providing web-links, it offers the reader a way of investigating further if they wish.
- **Factual and practical.** Much of the literature produced by city authorities – and place-marketing has much to answer for – is designed to promote, or sell, the city. Being economical with the truth, as some city promotion presentations are, is unhelpful. An Innovation Story needs to be based on evidence, and should produce practical knowledge that stands up to scrutiny.

- **Inspirational**. Innovation Stories are not intended to 'prove' that the approach presented is 'the right' way to lead change in the modern city. Rather a good Innovation Story enhances understanding and stimulates a creative response from those hearing the story.

In my experience, and I draw here on my work with cities in a variety of countries, change agents tend to be outward looking in their attitudes, and they are often very interested to learn about creative initiatives tried out in other places. Typical questions are: Why did they do it? What was the impact? Who benefited and in what way? How cost effective was it? These are all good questions, but the one that is most often asked is: *How* did they do it? Practitioners are *action oriented* – they seek ideas on how to bring about positive change. An Innovation Story may not always be able to generate clear answers to this question but it should be suggestive. This is why I believe that the use of the word 'story' is helpful. Storytelling in public policy analysis is a valuable approach to the documenting of experience that can provide inspiration as well as practical insights for public service leaders and activists (Yapp 2005).

There are, however, dangers with the storytelling approach and Daniel Kahneman, in his insightful book *Thinking, Fast and Slow*, discusses two of them: the 'narrative fallacy' and the 'halo effect'.[42] Narrative fallacies arise from our continuing struggle to make sense of the world:

> The explanatory stories that people find compelling are simple; are concrete rather than abstract; assign a larger role to talent… than to luck; and focus on a few striking events that happened rather than on the countless events that failed to happen. (Kahneman 2012, 199)

Kahneman argues that stories don't just simplify, they can also mislead. The halo effect can, unfortunately, boost the power of the narrative fallacy. It refers to a common bias that plays a significant role in shaping our view of people and situations. Psychological researchers have shown how 'first impressions' really do influence our judgements – in both a positive and a negative way – even to the point where we filter out good evidence, received at a later point, that contradicts our first assessment.

Kahneman, by drawing on his understanding of these mental processes, argues that the many business books about so-called successful leaders and companies consistently exaggerate the impact of leadership style and management practices on firm outcomes. To the embarrassment of the authors, who lavish praise on particular business leaders, the admired firms often do not perform that well over time. This is because luck plays a big role in business success but our minds have difficulty in accommodating this fact. The insights that Kahneman provides suggest that we should be very careful in how we interpret the meaning of the Innovation Stories in this book. The focus needs to be on what I call relevant lesson drawing, not a spurious attempt to identify best practice or heroic leadership.

In this book I provide 17 Innovation Stories drawn from cities across the world. No country, no continent, has a monopoly of wisdom on how to lead place-based change to create the inclusive city. In preparing the Innovation Stories I have used the following headings:

- aims and objectives
- outline of the Innovation Story
- leadership lessons
- further sources.

It goes without saying that the approach to social discovery presented in this volume is international. We will examine the theme of international lesson drawing in more detail in Chapter 12.

Conclusions

In this opening chapter I have invited readers to join me in an exploration of the possibilities for strengthening place-based leadership in a rapidly globalising world. Some of my vocabulary may be unfamiliar, but I hope that the argument I am presenting can stimulate fresh thinking about how to promote the creation of inclusive cities – cities in which civic leaders, defined broadly, strive for just results while caring for the natural environment on which we all depend.

My overarching concern is that current economic and social trends are creating increasingly unequal societies, divided societies, unhappy societies, unsustainable societies. In the era of globalisation – the one that we all now live in – place-less leaders, that is, people who are not expected to care about the consequences of their decisions for particular places and communities, have gained extraordinary power and influence. This power needs to be challenged, and people living in particular localities need to regain the authority to decide what happens to the quality of life in their area. To reignite the power of communities in particular places may seem a forlorn hope in an era in which multi-national companies appear to be taking over the reins of international power.

The argument presented in this book is not a pessimistic one, however. The place-less power of modern capital – the power to shift investments internationally, and engage in the ruthless exploitation of peoples in different countries and places – is no longer seen as reasonable conduct by many people. Growing concerns about climate change and the rapid acceleration of unsustainable development are attracting a backlash against the business as usual model of economic development. The need to develop a more responsible form of capitalism now attracts international support, and there is an expanding literature on how to advance prosperity without destroying the planet (Jackson 2009; Hopkins 2011).

Societies, and international organisations like the United Nations, are seeking ideas on how to develop more sustainable futures. I have suggested that Michael Sandel has identified the root cause of many of the troubles that face us today – he shows how, in many countries, we have drifted from having a market economy into being a market society. This obsession with market values is crowding out more important values – notably thoughtfulness, solidarity, caring for others and appreciating the natural environment. It follows that new ways of responding to societal needs, ones that challenge the dominance of market-driven values, are needed.

In many ways place-based leaders – city leaders, voluntary organisations, community activists, public professionals, trade union leaders, local business leaders – are developing an influential role in shaping future possibilities. The chapter has suggested that the following themes are critical in contributing to this agenda: place in public policy; public leadership and community activism; innovation in public management; and power in modern society. Building on these ideas the chapter has articulated a utopian vision of an 'inclusive city' – one in which powerful, place-based democratic institutions enable all to participate, and in which just results and concern for the natural environment guide decision making, not economic growth per se. An effort has been made to refresh the discussion of sustainable development by arguing that *inclusion* should be the new watchword for urban decision-making. Ideas about engaged scholarship and ways of constructing new knowledge have been outlined.

In summary, this book aims to do more than advance thinking relating to civic leadership and public service innovation in a rapidly changing world. It also seeks to provide direct assistance to activists, busy policy makers and practitioners who want to promote the development of inclusive cities.

Part 1
Diagnosis: Understanding trends and challenges

CHAPTER 2

Global trends and our urban future

Even if the Earth's population stabilises toward the end of the century, as many demographers project, urbanisation will continue. The world is on the threshold of change as consequential as any in the history of civilisation
Harm de Blij, *The Power of Place*, 2009

Introduction

The world is becoming increasingly urbanised, and the future wellbeing of both humanity and the planet are inextricably linked with our success or otherwise in dealing intelligently with urban growth and change. In recent years, however, it is globalisation – and not urbanisation – that has become the buzzword in public policy debates.

There is now a massive literature on the impact of globalisation on the future of society. But what does the term mean? Hopkins (2002, 16) defines globalisation as 'a process that transforms economic, political, social and cultural relationships across countries, regions and continents by spreading them more broadly, making them more intense and increasing their velocity'. Hutton and Giddens (2000, vii) adopt a similar perspective in their analysis of globalisation, and suggest that: 'It is the interaction of extraordinary technological innovation combined with the world-wide reach driven by global capitalism that gives today's change its particular complexion' (2000, vii). Moynagh and Worsley (2008, 1) keep it nice and simple and define globalisation as: '... the world becoming more interdependent and integrated'. Underpinning all these definitions is the idea that global economic competition and international cultural exchange, coupled with the remarkable expansion of the Internet and modern communication technologies, are shrinking the planet.

This literature on globalisation is important and it deserves our attention. But our intoxication with all things global may have obscured the fact that another equally important process is also taking place – urbanisation. True, globalisation and urbanisation are inter-related processes, and some writers on globalisation have illuminated this interplay (Birch and Wachter 2011). But, in my view, urbanisation is a distinct process that deserves to be given much more attention. In this chapter I examine the astonishing movement of people to cities and sketch the contours of our global urban future. The urban areas of the world currently have a population of around 3.6 billion. By 2030 the United Nations (UN) expects this urban population to have grown by 1.4 billion. This change signals a spectacular increase in the number and size of cities – a shift that poses many challenges for civic leaders.

This chapter discusses this expansion of cities, considers where this urban growth is expected to take place, and examines the reasons why more and more people are moving to cities. Despite its importance the implications of urban migration for city governance have been sorely neglected. The chapter explores who the urban migrants are, and opens up a discussion of the challenges facing those concerned with the leadership and governance of increasingly multicultural cities.

The explosion of the urban population

The growth of cities is nothing new. But the rapid increase of the urban population in recent decades is unprecedented.[1] While there is variation across the world, many cities are now growing at a formidable speed. A consequence is that more people now live in urban areas than ever before. More than that, ever since 2007, the urban population has outnumbered the rural. There is no doubt that, taking a global perspective, urban growth is set to continue, and that the urban population of the world will continue to climb at a startling pace. This urban expansion represents an extraordinary shift in the geo-politics of the planet that, even now, is not well understood.

First, let's consider the basic figures on population growth. Demographers and geographers argue about the details of this remarkable spatial transformation and there are, in fact, significant definitional challenges. For example, there are notable differences of view regarding how big a settlement has to be before it can be described as an 'urban' area.[2] The UN website does, however, provide us with good data on global urbanisation, and I use this source in the discussion that follows:

> Between 2011 and 2050, the world population is expected to increase by 2.3 billion, passing from 7.0 billion to 9.3 billion. At the same time, the population living in urban areas is projected to gain 2.6 billion, passing from 3.6 billion in 2011 to 6.2 billion in 2050. (UN-DESA 2012, 1)

If we turn our attention to the relatively near future – the period between now and 2030 – the world population is set to rise from just over 7.0 billion in 2011 to around 8.3 billion in 2030 – see Figure 2.1. By then in the region of 5 billion people (or around 60 per cent of the world's population) will live in urban areas. This is a staggering increase in the world urban population in a comparatively short time span. Consider this. The population of Greater London is around eight million. This means that an urban expansion of 1.4 billion (from 3.6 to 5.0) is equivalent to adding over 175 cities the size of London to the global urban landscape in less than twenty years. Except, as we shall see, they won't look that much like London. In marked contrast to spiralling urban growth, the world rural population is projected, as shown in Figure 2.1, to level out and, indeed, to start decreasing in the period from around 2020.

Figure 2.1: World population growth

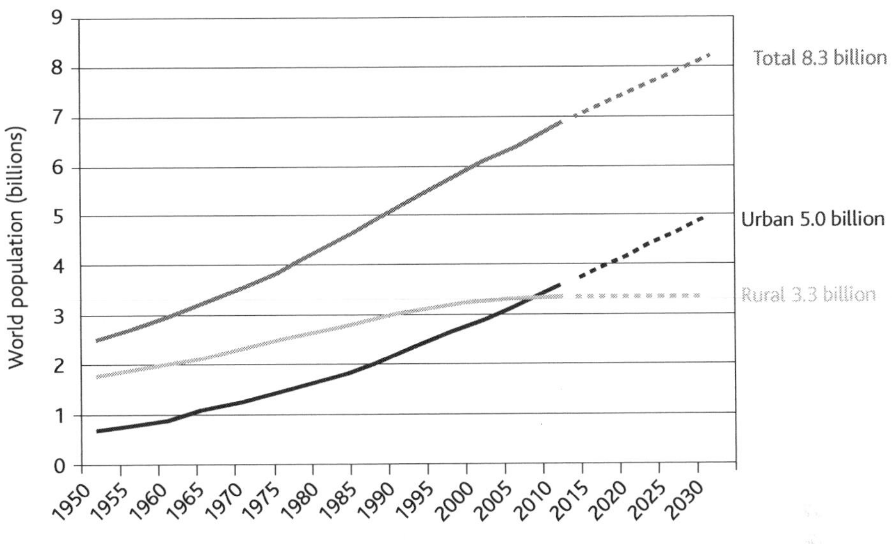

Source: United Nations World Urbanization Prospects, http://esa.un.org/unup

From the point of view of public policy it is important to record that this rapid expansion of cities is mainly happening in areas that have not been dominant in past patterns of urbanisation. Rates of urbanisation vary dramatically between the more and less developed countries. Indeed, in some parts of the world it can be claimed that cities, or at least the central areas of some conurbations, are shrinking. UN demographers are clear that the vast bulk of the projected world population growth will be in the less developed regions of the world (UN-DESA 2012). As Mike Davis points out in *Planet of Slums,* most of the new urban residents are not going to be dwelling in elegant cities made of glass and steel:

> Instead of cities of light soaring toward heaven, much of the twenty-first century urban world squats in squalor, surrounded by pollution, excrement, and decay. (Davis 2006, 19)

Robert Neuwirth, in *Shadow Cities,* estimates that there are about a billion squatters in the world today, and that this number is expected to double by 2030 (Neuwirth 2005, 9).

Birch and Wachter (2011) have assembled a useful collection of papers providing an overview of the various dimensions of global urbanisation, covering population trends, spatial planning, urban governance, finance and other aspects. They point out, politely of course, that the rise of urban populations, with their associated development issues, 'calls into question the tendency of many social scientists to measure and analyse national-level data and to ignore spatial variations' (Birch and Wachter 2011, 4). They are right, of course. In Chapter 1 I explained how 'seeing like a state' distorts understanding and holds back fruitful analysis, and I also suggested that 'seeing like a city' has advantages.

The Stiglitz Commission, set up by President Sarkozy of France, examined global statistical measurements, and concluded that many global metrics – measures like GDP and GDP-per-capita, inflation, and unemployment – are flawed, and made suggestions for improvements (Stiglitz et al 2009). The report makes many helpful suggestions on how to measure prosperity, but even this well respected commission left out 'level of urbanisation'. This is to ignore a critical dimension of societal change. Birch and Wachter lodge this criticism but, in more hopeful vein, they also suggest that world leaders do, at least, now have an increasing capacity to add an urban lens to their assessments. There is evidence that major international organisations – like the United Nations and the World Bank – are redirecting their efforts to take account of urbanisation.[3] And the international organisations representing cities are becoming increasingly effective in pointing to the importance of the 'urban dimension' in international public policy.[4]

Unpacking the dimensions of urban growth

As explained in Chapter 1 place matters a great deal; moreover places are very different. It follows that we must guard against generalising too freely about 'global urbanisation'. However, accepting this caveat, we can identify a number of striking features about international urban trends. The first point to highlight is that urban areas are growing at a faster pace than ever before. This is because, as shown by Figure 2.1, the total world population is rising steeply and because the urban share of the world population is also increasing. Second, today's cities are bigger than ever before. For example, in 1950 the world had two megacities, cities with a population of over ten million – New York and Tokyo. Now it has over twenty. Third, the distribution of the urban population is shifting dramatically. The bulk of urban growth is now taking place in the developing world. I offer a table and a couple of world maps to illustrate aspects of these dynamics.

Table 2.1 lists the twenty largest cities in the world in 1950 and 2025. Figures 2.2 and 2.3 show where these cities are located, and the graphics on the maps give a visual indication of the size of these really big cities. New York City was the largest city in the world in 1950 with a population of 12.3 million, and five other US cities are also listed in the 1950 'top twenty' (Chicago, Los Angeles, Philadelphia, Detroit and Boston). In 1950 Europe had three cities listed (London, Paris, Berlin) and Russia two (Moscow and St Petersburg) – see Figure 2.2. Spring forward to 2025 and, while the US still has two cities listed (New York and Los Angeles), Europe and Russia do not even feature. As Table 2.1 shows almost all of the 'top twenty' megacities in 2025 are in developing countries.

Table 2.1: The largest cities in the world: 1950 and 2025

1950 (Population, millions)			2025 (Population, millions)		
1	New York-Newark, USA	12.3	1	Tokyo, Japan	38.7
2	Tokyo, Japan	11.2	2	Delhi, India	32.9
3	London, UK	8.3	3	Shanghai, China	28.4
4	Paris, France	6.2	4	Mumbai, India	26.6
5	Moscow, Russia	5.4	5	Ciudad de Mexico (Mexico City), Mexico	24.6
6	Buenos Aries, Argentina	5.1	6	New York-Newark, USA	23.6
7	Chicago, USA	5.0	7	Sao Paulo, Brazil	23.2
8	Kolkata (Calcutta), India	4.5	8	Dhaka, Bangladesh	22.9
9	Shanghai, China	4.3	9	Beijing, China	22.6
10	Osaka-Kobe, Japan	4.1	10	Karachi, Pakistan	20.2
11	Los Angeles, USA	4.0	11	Lagos, Nigeria	18.9
12	Berlin, Germany	3.3	12	Kolkata (Calcutta), India	18.7
13	Philadelphia, USA	3.1	13	Manilla, Philippines	16.3
14	Rio de Janeiro, Brazil	2.9	14	Los Angeles, USA	15.7
15	St Petersburg, Russia	2.9	15	Shenzhen, China	15.5
16	Ciudad de Mexico (Mexico City), Mexico	2.9	16	Buenos Aires, Argentina	15.5
17	Mumbai, India	2.9	17	Guangzhou, China	15.5
18	Detroit, USA	2.8	18	Istanbul, Turkey	14.9
19	Boston, USA	2.5	19	Al-Qahirah (Cairo), Egypt	14.7
20	Al-Qahirah (Cairo), Egypt	2.5	20	Kinshasa, Democratic Republic of Congo	14.5

Source: United Nations World Urbanization Prospects: The 2011 Revision, http://esa.un.org/unup/

Figure 2.3 fills out the picture and reveals the spectacular growth of megacities in China, India and neighbouring countries, as well as the emergence of megacities in Africa (Lagos, Al-Qahirah and Kinshasa) and Latin America (Ciudad de Mexico, Sao Paulo, Buenos Aires). The map shows not just that the big cities of the future are mainly in different places than in the past, but that these megacities are set to be truly enormous. These cities have populations that are far bigger than many countries. Indeed, the top ten megacities – those with populations over 20 million in 2025 – will each have a population that exceeds the current total population of whole groups of countries. For example, the combined population of Denmark, Finland, New Zealand and Norway is, at present, less than 20 million. The UN estimates that the number of megacities in the world is expected to grow from 23 in 2011 to 37 in 2025.

Figure 2.2: The 20 largest cities in the world: 1950

Source: United Nations World Urbanization Prospects: The 2011 Revision

Figure 2.3: The top 20 megacities: 2025

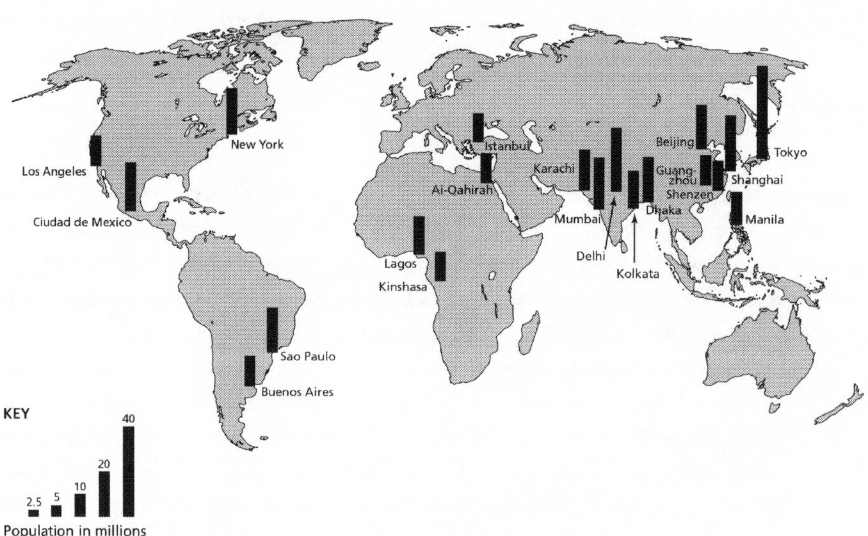

Source: United Nations World Urbanization Prospects: The 2011 Revision

It is, perhaps, not surprising that the megacities tend to attract the headlines and the television documentaries – the world has not seen such massive urban agglomerations before. However, it is a prevailing myth that the megacities contain, or will contain, a large proportion of the world urban population – the reverse is the case. The UN provides data relating to cities in five population bands: less than 500,000 (minor cities); 500,000 to 1 million (small cities); 1 to 5 million (medium-sized cities); 5 to 10 million (large cities); and 10 million or more (megacities).[5] Several striking points emerge. First, taking the distribution of the urban population in 2011 – the 3.6 billion mentioned earlier – we can note:

- most of the world's urban population – slightly more than 1.8 billion (51%) – lived in minor cities (under 500,000);
- around 1.4 billion (39%) lived in small to large cities (500,000 to 10 million);
- around 360 million (10%) of the world's urban population lived in megacities (10 million or more).

Second, the UN predicts that the world urban population will increase by around 1 billion (from 3.6 to 4.6 billion) in the 2011–2025 period. Note that:

- most of this urban expansion – around 620 million (62%) – is expected to take place in cities with a population of *less* than 5 million;
- the number of megacities is expected to grow significantly (from 23 megacities to 37) and these cities are expected to account for 13.6% of the world urban population in 2025.

This discussion highlights the remarkable variation in the scale of the challenges facing city leaders in different localities. At one extreme we can see that developing effective place-based leadership and governance for the growing number of megacities is a pressing priority. But the challenge of improving civic leadership and urban governance is far more widespread. Thousands of cities – large and small – across the world are experiencing rapid urban growth.

City leaders in developing countries face acute challenges arising from urban expansion – relating to, for example, shelter, water, sanitation and public health (Dijk 2006; Sclar et al 2013; Tannerfeldt and Ljung 2006). As Susan Parnell and Edgar Pieterse (2014) explain, Africa is the continent with the fastest rate of urban growth, albeit from a low base level. Before offering some interesting ideas on how to tackle the problems arising from urbanisation in Africa, Pieterse draws attention to the scale of the challenge and to the fact that social unrest is predictable, saying:

> In most African cities and towns, slum life is the norm... It goes almost without saying that this scale of abuse cannot simply reproduce itself indefinitely. (Pieterse 2014, 200–1)

While many cities are expanding rapidly, and I discuss this shortly, some cities are shrinking and need to adapt their city development strategies to changing circumstances.

As discussed in Chapter 1, the quality of life in cities is not at all that it should be. Johnson and Galea (2011) provide an assessment of urban health in low- and middle-income countries. They note that urban poverty has grown with the process of urbanisation:

> In 2002, there were more than 1.1 billion people living on less than US$1 per day, 282 million of whom lived in urban areas. Rising per capita income in low- and middle-income cities is often accompanied by greater income inequality, which places stress on social cohesion and increases the risk of civil conflict. (Johnson and Galea 2011, 352)

We should refer here to the United Nations Millennium Development Goals (MDGs) adopted by world leaders at the UN General Assembly in September 2000. These eight goals frame 21 specific policy targets relating to, for example, eradicating poverty, improving education, reducing child mortality rates and so on. The MDGs have led to a great deal of successful action to tackle poverty, particularly poverty in rural areas. We can note, however, that only one of the targets (7D) refers specifically to the plight of the urban poor. This target calls for a significant improvement in the lives of at least 100 million slum-dwellers by 2020, which is a modest target given that there are probably more than one billion squatters in the world today. In 2012, the UN itself took the view that: '… 863 million people are now estimated to be living in slums compared with 650 million in 1990' (UN Expert Group 2012, 56). It is to be hoped that those working on the goals that will replace the MDGs in 2015 – the Post-2015 Development Agenda – will pay more attention to urban issues and, in particular, the importance of improving urban governance. The Sustainable Development Solutions Network (SDSN) has made a valuable contribution to this debate, and argues rightly for a separate urban goal for the Post-2015 Development Agenda, saying:

> If managed well, urbanisation can create employment and prosperity, and become a central driver for ending extreme poverty and for strengthening social inclusion. If managed poorly, cities will deepen social exclusion and fail to generate enough jobs. (UN-SDSN 2013)

This is not to imply that the UN has disregarded cities and urban areas. On the contrary, starting with an international conference in 1976 in Vancouver, UN-Habitat (the UN Human Settlements Programme) has sought to put the perspective of cities and local communities onto the international global agenda. In the period since 2002 UN-Habitat has stepped up its urban-oriented efforts and has hosted a regular series of World Urban Forum (WUF) conferences at different locations around the world, starting in Nairobi. These events bring together government leaders, city mayors, members of local government associations, non-governmental and community organisations, professionals, academics, grassroots women's organisations, youth and slum dweller groups to share experiences and develop new policies and practices to improve the quality of life in cities.

The studies prepared to support WUF conferences are valuable resources for those wishing to examine urban trends and explore innovative approaches to urban policy and management. The report on the *State of the World's Cities 2012/13* is no exception (UN-Habitat 2012). It shows how policy makers, businesses and activists need to move beyond notions of narrow economic success. The obsession with financial prosperity has led to growing inequalities between the rich and the poor as well as causing serious damage to the environment. The report offers ideas on how to foster a broader sense of urban prosperity, and we will return to explore some of these ideas later in the book. We will, for example, examine innovations taking place in various informal settlements in the Global South. In particular, Innovation Story 6 presents details of an imaginative approach to pro-poor settlement upgrading in Langrug, South Africa.

Urban growth and shrinking cities

Are all cities set to keep on growing, come what may? The answer is no. First, in the long term – at some point in the second half of this century – many demographers expect the world population to cease growing, and some predict that it will decline. De Blij (2009, 24) is cautious, but notes that: 'Predictions of the level at which this [stabilisation of the world population] will take place tend to range from 9 to 10 billion, but we know how risky long-range prognostications are.' Pearce (2010, 293–4), in a racy analysis, is more forthright. He argues that world population could peak as early as 2040 because: '... falling birth fertility means that we will soon reach the point where each succeeding generation of mothers will be smaller than the last'. Danny Dorling (2013) provides an incisive analysis of world population growth projections. He notes that, in 2011, UN global estimates of the world population in 2100 shifted markedly. The projected figure for 2100 jumped from 9.1 billion to 10.1 billion. It is certainly the case that long term population forecasting is a tricky business, but Dorling suggests that the changed projections owe more to politics than to competing technical arguments about how to model demographic trends:

> I think the UN forecasts were increased because it became more politically expedient to increase them, to appear to be warning that the numbers of people might be getting out of control. (Dorling 2013, 33)

Dorling is impatient with the debates about numbers. He argues convincingly that what will matter most is how people behave, not their total numbers.

Second, would a decline in the world population have a significant impact on global urbanisation trends? Here, again, the answer is no. As we shall see, the reasons why people are moving to cities are deep and powerful. These drivers of migration suggest that global urbanisation is here to stay – certainly for many decades. But it is unconvincing to argue, as some do, that inexorable urbanisation is a matter of fact for every place on the planet. The growth rate of some specific cities in the developing world could well falter as they encounter formidable air pollution and congestion problems. For example, as Davis (2006, 2) points out, Mexico City, widely predicted to achieve a population of 25 million in the 1990s, experienced a slowdown in growth such that its population is, twenty years later, not a lot more than 20 million.[6]

Also, not all cities are growing. In contrast to the challenges of a burgeoning urban population many cities in the wealthy west, or at least the central areas of these metropolitan areas, have experienced population decline (Pallagst et al 2014). Most 'shrinking' cities in the last fifty years have been in western industrial countries, especially in the USA, Britain, Germany, and Italy. But there are also some shrinking cities in developing countries, for example, China, and in Eastern Europe, for example, Ukraine.

Older industrial cities like Cleveland and Baltimore in the USA, and Liverpool and Manchester in the UK, have found it a challenge to recover from the period of de-industrialisation, when jobs and population moved to suburban and ex-urban areas. A moving account of urban shrinkage is provided by Gordon Young (2013) in his book on the transformation of Flint, Michigan. While the subtitle is 'Memoir of a vanishing city', the book also contains useful insights on recovery plans. Detroit provides, perhaps, the most vivid example of a shrinking city. According to the US census in the period from 1970–2010 the population of the city declined from 1,511,000 to 714,000 – a startling 53% drop. However, this is a little misleading because these figures relate to the municipality of Detroit – which is the central part of a much larger conurbation. True, the population of the Detroit metropolitan area as a whole has also declined in recent years – from 4.8 million in 2000 to 4.7 million in 2010. But this decline, at minus 2.7% in ten years, is not such a dramatic reduction.

Urban shrinkage is not a new phenomenon. Back in the 1930s scholars involved with the Chicago School of urban sociology documented a process in which urban change can be viewed as a lifecycle that is, in theory, bound to end in decline. But this 'rise and decline' imagery is up for a rethink. Recent scholarship on shrinking cities suggests that 'shrinkage' is a useful term for a multi-dimensional process that has economic, demographic, geographic, social and physical dimensions (Martinez-Fernandez et al 2012). It challenges our understanding of decline as a simple linear downward shift as a city loses its traditional industries. Maybe decline is the wrong word – it implies deterioration when this need not be the case at all.

In this context it seems clear that city leaders and urban planners in cities where the population is descending may be able to develop strategies that break with past practice, ones that are not driven by the obsession with growth and expansion. The experience of cities in former East Germany, that are coping with a post-socialist economic transition, are likely to be of particular interest to those involved in the planning and management of shrinking cities (Wiechmann and Pallagst 2012). The challenges are great – vacated houses, derelict buildings, underused infrastructure – but some cities are breaking new ground in this area. In Detroit, for example, Mayor Mike Duggan is pursuing a *Detroit Future City* initiative, originally developed by former Mayor Dave Bing, which includes a number of innovative initiatives (Detroit City Council 2012).

Urban areas with declining populations often focus on 'bring people back to the city' initiatives. This approach is commonplace in, for example, the US context. Various studies have documented this trend (Gratz and Mintz 1998; Grogan and Proscio 2000), and some city mayors have contributed to this literature (Norquist 1998). This emphasis on revitalising the central areas of cities makes a great deal of sense as cities provide many advantages to their residents – arising from their density, history, infrastructure, networks and cultural capital.

Notwithstanding the existence of shrinking cities, it is fair to say that, from a global perspective, the overall pattern is one of massive urban expansion. Most of the new city dwellers in the coming period will be in developing countries, and here city leadership challenges centre on trying to promote sustainable forms of urban development and supporting the successful integration into city life of the expanding number of new arrivals. Interestingly the growth of cities in Europe and North America has slowed, and the resident population is aging. This produces different problems for city leaders although, as we shall see, most urban leaders – in developing countries as well as in the developed world – share the challenge of responding creatively to the needs of an increasingly diverse population.

Understanding the movement of people to cities

Brugmann (2009) provides a thoughtful analysis of what he calls 'the Great Migration', by which he means the extraordinary movement of hundreds of millions of people to cities in the period since the 18th century.[7] Firstly, he notes that human migration is nothing new. Historians teach us that most cultures, even seemingly sedentary and agricultural ones, have had seasonal migrations since ancient times. In the Middle Ages, for example, many of Europe's peasant families would migrate long distances, on a seasonal basis, to assist with other harvests, brick making, dyke construction and the like. Added to these seasonal flows of migrants it is well established that people with specialised skills were able to ply their trades internationally hundreds of years ago. For example, in the 15th and 16th centuries, skilled stonemasons from northern Italy made a major contribution to the creation of the beautiful Gothic cathedrals of France and England.

However, in the 18th century human migration moved into a new phase. In medieval Europe systems of serfdom tied peasants to the land of feudal landowners. As Brugmann (2009, 38) notes, the decline of the systems of serfdom in the seventeenth century 'enabled the beginnings of the global urban migration process that can still be observed today...' Saskia Sassen has examined the history of migration in Europe and notes that long-distance seasonal-migration '...

eventually developed the elements of chain migration as some migrants stayed at their destinations and started families, thereby building linkages for more migrations from their communities of origin' (Sassen 1999, 10). Seasonal migrants started to take up permanent residence in cities as a way of improving the quality of life for themselves and their families.

Sassen's notion of 'chain migrations' remains a helpful way of understanding the modern urban migration process – a family member establishes a foothold in a city, learns how to prosper, builds local relationships and then encourages others to follow. The advantages of the pioneers are made available to later migrations of family or community members. Those with desirable skills are often invited to become citizens: 'German records for the eighteenth century show, for instance, that about half of the burghers in trading towns were migrants' (Sassen 1999, 8).

The steady emancipation of European peasants from their indentures to landowners coincided with major crop failures, and with the efforts of cities to rebuild their populations and labour forces after plagues and various epidemics and setbacks. With the rise of the merchant classes, the spiralling of global trade and the emergence of new industrial technologies the scene was set for an extraordinary European migration to cities in the 18th and 19th centuries. Europe became the first predominantly urbanised continent, with its powerful city-states shaping societal progress ahead of the creation of modern nations. Brugmann believes that this history does much to explain the efficiency and vibrancy of many European cities, and the richness and resilience of Europe's urban culture.

In 1900 the world population stood at 1.65 billion and it is estimated that 220 million (or 13%) lived in cities. As shown in Figure 2.1 the world population now stands at around 7 billion and approximately 3.6 billion (or 51%) live in urban areas. Even allowing for the fact that a proportion of urban population growth stems from the birth rate of those living in cities, these figures suggest that there was an astonishing movement of people from rural areas to cities in the 20th century. No population movements in world history have come close to matching the scale or global reach of this urban migration and, as Figure 2.1 indicates, it is set to continue.

It is important to note that urban growth has taken place in different ways in different economic regions of the world, and that, as discussed further below, the future scenarios for urban expansion have different time lines in different world regions. Nevertheless, it is helpful, following Brugmann (2009, 41–2), to identify three general stages in urban migration:

- **Regional urban migration**. Pioneer individuals and families make the decision to break with their rural tradition and head for a regional town. A process of chain migration and investment transforms the town into a fully-fledged city. The nature of the city's politics, economics and culture shifts, and the traditional symbiotic relationship with the rural hinterland is disrupted. This 'first stage' urban migration continues apace in smaller cities all over the world, and it is this migration, as mentioned earlier, that will account for a large part of world urban growth in the coming period. The UN estimates that cities with a population of fewer than 500,000 will grow by 117 million between 2011 and 2025.

- **National urban migration**. Having established themselves in regional towns, migrant families may embark on a second stage of migration to a large city, in some cases a megacity, in their home country. By taking advantage of ethnic and family contacts, migrants create new networks that support their specialisation in established or newly emerging industries, and underpin the development of new political and social movements. The UN estimates that 393 cities with a population in the range 500,000 to ten million will be added to the world urban system in the 2011 to 2025 period. This will increase their combined population by 623 million, equivalent to slightly less than the combined populations of the USA, Brazil and Japan.
- **International urban migration**. In a third stage migrant families emigrate from their home country and seek a better quality of life in a foreign city. The immigrant settlement of North America provides a vivid example of international urban migration. Between 1846 and 1940 it is estimated that 55 million people migrated across the Atlantic to start a new life in North America. Unsung in the American and Canadian legends of pioneer nation-building, most of these emigrants headed for the expanding cities, not the rural regions. In more recent times international migration has increased markedly, and it is estimated that, in 2010, 214 million people moved to a foreign country, almost always to a foreign city. Some receiving cities are now experiencing 'dynamic diversity' – meaning the rapid arrival of large numbers of immigrants from a range of countries into a given city (Hambleton and Gross 2007). We will explore the challenges arising from dynamic diversity later in this chapter and, also, in Chapter 10.

Castles and Miller, in their wide-ranging examination of international population movements, characterise the modern era as 'the age of migration'. They note that: 'International mobility of people seems certain to grow, leading to greater ethnic diversity in receiving countries, and new forms of transnational connectivity' (Castles and Miller 2009, 18).

Who are the urban migrants?

Brugmann is keen to demonstrate that those who move to cities should not be viewed as pathetic victims of wider economic and social forces:

> The end of ancient seasonal migrations, which connected the economics and social life of towns and their agricultural hinterlands, was often provoked by large-scale events like revolutions, wars, colonisation, plagues and famines. But the patterns of migration and settlement of those who fled the countryside to rebuild their broken

> livelihoods in cities shows that theirs was not a passive, impulsive victimised response. Throughout the centuries and even today, urban migrants have generally responded to the pushes and pulls of major events as active agents, not as passive victims. (Brugmann 2009, 38–9)

To support this claim Brugmann (2009, 42–54) reports on recent research carried out in Madurai, a city of over one million located in an agricultural region in southern India. Based on interviews with migrants to the city, and with villagers who have stayed away, the research established a clear pattern. The psychological profiles of rural households who tended to stay in the countryside tended to be more 'accepting'. Those who moved to the city were more likely to be restive, more wishful. A high proportion of urban migrants are, in other words, a self-selected breed. This is an important insight that flies in the face of the conventional media-produced image of urban migrants.

> Many planners and political leaders fail to note the migrant's tenacity and methodical ways, and many critics of globalisation conceive the migrant as a victim, constrained by corporate capital and established institutions. But the city is by economic nature a centre of empowerment, where new strategies are hatched between established pushes and pulls. (Brugmann 2009, 52)

The three-step categorisation of types of migration outlined above is helpful, but it simplifies a much more complex reality. First, it should be stressed that migrants do not necessarily flow through the three stages in a sequence. A crisis in a particular country – for example, the outbreak of a war – may spur migrant families to move a large distance, even to emigrate, without any intermediate steps. Second, the reasons why people migrate are varied and we discuss this further below. Migrants may be 'economic migrants' seeking better employment prospects and some may have travelled abroad to study. Others may have been forced to move as a result of factors beyond their control – for example, religious persecution, political oppression, wars, famines and so on. Third, we also need to ask questions about the definition of migration: 'When is a migrant a migrant?' Some migrants may see themselves as visitors, or temporary residents, rather than permanent migrants. In the European Union, for example, there is now free movement of peoples among 29 countries. This leads to an ebb and flow in modern patterns of international migration that make accurate predictions difficult.

Before going further we should recognise the significance of regional variations. We have already established that in some parts of the world – for example, in China, India and parts of Africa and Latin America – cities are growing at a truly breathtaking speed. In these cities civic leaders need to focus not just on how to cope with helter-skelter growth, but how to shape the process of urbanisation to achieve public purpose. In other world regions, some cities are losing population and civic leaders face the rather different challenge of how to reinvent their cities – to hold onto their residents and/or attract new migrants.

In Chapter 10 we will explore in more detail the dynamics of urban migration and consider who the new cosmopolitans are. Here we can note that, in simple terms, there are two kinds of migrants – those who have to (or think that they have to) migrate, and those who choose to migrate of their own volition. We should turn for a moment to consider the highly qualified migrants who can, to a great extent, exercise choice regarding where they wish to live. There is a growing recognition among city leaders that key players in the modern knowledge economy – sometimes referred to as the creative class (Florida 2002) – are vital to any serious hopes of urban prosperity. These talented and creative people – scientists, engineers, professors, artists, designers, architects, writers, think tank researchers, editors, inventors and the like – as well as people in allied professions – like high tech industries, financial services, business management and so on – have strong views about where they want to live.

While it is unwise to generalise too freely, people in the creative class appear to be attracted to areas that can offer, according to Florida (2002; 2005), a certain kind of lifestyle, including good cultural facilities, lively nightlife, rich social interactions, a diversity of people, including gay and transsexual people, strong spatial identity, and a high quality environment. This research is based on American cities and the details may not be transferable to other countries and contexts. However, the idea of focussing on how to attract talented people provides useful insights for civic leaders. It seems clear that successful cities will need to give much more attention to creating the right 'people climate' rather than believing that sorting out the 'business climate' is the key to economic health.

Dynamic diversity in the modern city

The argument we are unfolding here is that the interplay between globalisation and urbanisation is producing cities that are now much more multicultural than they have been previously. More specifically migration – the remarkable growth in the number of people moving across international frontiers – is altering the nature of urban life in many cities. These changes present new challenges for place-based leaders. Earlier in this chapter I referred to the problems that arise with national-level datasets and the way that they reflect an absence of efforts to 'see like a city' (Magnusson 2010). Unsurprisingly we encounter this problem once again when we seek to understand urban migration. Thus, organisations like the United Nations estimate the foreign-born by country and do not compile data at the urban/metropolitan scale. It has been left to urban scholars to create the beginnings of a global database on urban migration. By working with colleagues in numerous countries Marie Price and Lisa Benton-Short have built up a picture of urban immigrant destinations, and I draw on their work in the following discussion (Price and Benton-Short 2007; 2008).

The term gateway city refers to a metropolitan area where large numbers of immigrants have settled. Such cities have become increasingly important because urban economies are becoming more and more reliant upon new, and increasingly large, flows of foreign workers to undertake specific jobs – often in relatively low paid positions in the service sector. Price and Benton-Short (2007, 104) suggest that: '... the discourse about inclusion/exclusion of newcomers has intensified as growing numbers of foreign-born peoples in urban areas challenge basic assumptions about citizenship, identity and belonging'. A consequence is that immigrant gateway cities are often characterised in polarising terms. On the one hand they are seen as vibrant centres of cosmopolitan culture underpinned by transnational capital and world trade. On the other hand they are also portrayed as tense localities with heightened polarisation along racial and class lines.

In a book on governing cities in a global era Jill Gross and I suggested that some gateway cities exhibit dynamic diversity. In employing this phrase we sought to draw attention to the speed of change taking place in some gateway cities. We used it to mean the rapid arrival of large numbers of immigrants from a range of countries into a given city (Hambleton and Gross 2007, 218–220).[8] Cities experiencing dynamic diversity face, what Gross (2007) describes as, a set of 'diversity-democracy' challenges – meaning challenges for democratic governance arising from dynamic diversity. She examines the way gateway cities – for example, Toronto and Paris – are adapting their systems of democratic engagement to cope with the changing needs of their populations and, in more recent work, she discusses the multi-level governance of migrant residents in capital cities in North America and Europe (Gross 2012).

What is the scale of the dynamic diversity challenge? Earlier in this chapter I noted that, in 2010, the UN estimates that 214 million people moved to another country – a vast number. But where are these people going? Price and Benton-Short (2007) attempt to provide the answer. Three caveats should be made before we consider their findings. First, this analysis uses census-derived data on foreign-born residents. The authors note that this source has limitations. Census dates and frequency vary by country and it is clear that censuses represent a minimum documented figure for the foreign-born. Irregular or 'illegal' migrants are highly unlikely to submit returns. There are also different definitions of foreign-born. Most states define the foreign-born as individuals born outside the territorial state. However, in some countries, for example, the Netherlands, the definition of foreign-born considers the children of immigrants to be foreign-born even though they were born in the host country. Second, the authors do not analyse the impact of immigrants *in* the cities they have moved to. That requires detailed empirical work in individual gateway cities. Third, the data reflect a range of reporting years, mostly from 2000 to 2005. In some metropolitan areas there are now considerably more foreign-born individuals than the data suggests. These caveats aside, what the analysis does provide is a helpful picture of the global flows of immigrants *to* cities around the world.

The research presents information on the foreign-born for 145 cities in 52 countries. The focus here is on metropolitan areas with a population of more than one million people. The following are some of the main highlights to emerge from this analysis:

- Nineteen metropolitan areas have more than one million foreign-born residents. New York (with 5.1 million) has the most, and the other seven conurbations with over 1.5 million foreign-born residents are: Los Angeles (4.4 million); Hong Kong (3); Toronto (2.1); Miami (1.9); London (1.9); Chicago (1.6); and Moscow (1.6).[9]
- Roughly 100 metropolitan areas have more than 100,000 foreign-born residents, and cities in this category are to be found all over the world. North American and European cities stand out as key immigrant destinations but all world regions feature.
- A growing number of metropolitan areas have a relatively high proportion of foreign-born residents. Some immigrant cities in the Middle East, for example, have very high proportions. These oil-rich states have established various temporary worker programmes that have resulted in thousands of labourers – often enjoying very few rights – migrating to these regions. Dubai tops the list of cities for a high percentage foreign-born (with 83%) and Muscat (44%), Jiddah (37%) and Riyadh (31%) are not that far behind.
- Other metropolitan areas with a very high proportion of foreign-born residents are Toronto (45%), Hong Kong (43%) and Vancouver (39%). Toronto is exceptional, and we will discuss this city further in Chapter 10. We can note here that some 70,000 immigrants arrive in the city annually from approximately 170 different countries, and there are now over 2 million foreign-born residents in the metropolitan area.

Diversity can bring great vibrancy to urban society, so long as new groups are integrated – socially, politically and economically. Indeed, the global city can be defined by the intermixing of cultures and ideas. Developing and adopting policies that head off conflict between insiders and outsiders is a challenge. A theme that we will revisit later is that imaginative place-based leadership in particular cities, and in specific neighbourhoods within cities, can break new ground in building multicultural understanding and intercultural collaboration. The cities that are already experiencing dynamic diversity have valuable insights to share with urban areas that are less familiar with the challenges of leading and managing the multicultural city.

Conclusions

In this chapter I have discussed various themes relating to global urbanisation. My purpose here is partly to set the scene for subsequent chapters, and partly to argue that urbanisation has been – and is being – overshadowed by a preoccupation with globalisation in public and academic discourse. This is troubling and reflects, perhaps, a tendency of nation states, and the media in those states, to 'see like a state'. Fortunately there are some strong counter currents – largely unsung – and we shall consider them in more detail in subsequent chapters. These counter-currents speak to the importance of local identity, the meaning of community and the power of place in a rapidly globalising world.

In this context we should recognise the valuable contributions of the United Nations. In this chapter I have drawn extensively on the work of UN population experts who continue to provide excellent information on world urbanisation prospects (UN-DESA 2012). Alongside these efforts UN-Habitat has provided world leadership in relation to policy analysis for cities, and continues to generate fresh ways of thinking about the future of cities (UN-Habitat 2012). The various organisations that represent cities nationally and internationally are also making an increasingly important contribution – some of this work in fruitful collaboration with the UN. This locally driven research and analysis is helping not just to create new ideas about the future possibilities for cities, but also to sketch out practical strategies to tackle urban problems. In particular, I would highlight the work of UCLG (United Cities and Local Governments) – the global network of cities, local and regional governments. This international network of local authorities is making an important contribution to our understanding of cities and city futures. For example, the reports from the UCLG Global Observatory on Local Democracy – the 'GOLD' reports – provide an invaluable analysis of the role of local governments in addressing current and future urban challenges (UCLG 2008; 2011; 2014).

Urbanisation is not a new process but, in this chapter, I have suggested that the pace and scale of urbanisation take us into unfamiliar territory. The addition of 1.4 billion to the world urban population in the period between 2011 and 2030 is extraordinary – and difficult to imagine. Strong place-based leadership will be essential if we are to guide this spectacular urban growth in a way that creates inclusive cities in the sense outlined in Chapter 1. There are profound implications here, not just for the effective leadership and governance of the growing number of megacities, but also for the hundreds of cities set to absorb vast numbers of new arrivals.

Alongside this turbo-charged urban growth, an urban expansion that is taking place mainly in developing countries, the chapter has drawn attention to the fact that some cities are shrinking. This downsizing is no less challenging as it involves cities redefining their roles, and breaking new ground in relation to urban planning and management. The chapter has drawn attention to urban migration – it is now the case that millions of people are moving across international frontiers every month, and most of them are moving to foreign cities. This growth in urban migration has major implications for city leadership, local democracy and urban governance – implications that are little understood. The cities that have experience of dynamic diversity can provide valuable lessons for those that have not yet encountered a rapid shift towards a multicultural future.

In closing this chapter I wish to offer a different take on global trends and our urban prospects – the perspective of an artist. Sebastian Salgado, the internationally renowned photographer, has produced a wonderful collection of stunning images of the world-altering phenomenon of mass migration (Salgado 2000). With photographs taken over a seven-year period in 35 countries Salgado offers many moving insights into humanity on the move. He writes:

> I also came to understand, as never before, how everything that happens on earth is connected. We are all affected by the widening gap between the rich and poor, by the availability of information on population growth in the Third World, by the mechanisation of agriculture, by rampant urbanisation, by destruction of the environment, by nationalistic, ethnic, and religious bigotry. The people wrenched from their homes are simply the most visible victims of a global convulsion entirely of our own making. (Salgado 2000, 8)

Salgado asks us to pause and reflect on the human condition. He suggests that the human race seems bent on self-destruction and he offers his powerful photographs as a way of understanding the point we have now reached.

CHAPTER 3

The changing nature of public service reform

All private effort, all individual philanthropy, sinks into insignificance compared with the organised power of a great representative assembly like this
Joseph Chamberlain, Mayor of Birmingham, speaking to Birmingham City Council, 10 November 1875[1]

Introduction

In the 1860s Birmingham, like all the other industrial cities of England, was a bleak and forbidding place with insanitary streets, dilapidated housing and grinding poverty. The historian Tristram Hunt provides a particularly vivid account of the miserable living conditions, and suggests that, at the time, it was 'a disgusting city' (Hunt 2004, 324). Joseph Chamberlain, who arrived in the West Midlands in 1854 and became a successful businessman, was inspired by the Revd George Dawson and other civic activists to stand for election to the city council in 1869. In 1873, at the age of 37, he was to become Mayor of Birmingham and, as we shall soon see, in a short space of time he led a successful effort to transform the quality of life for the residents of the city. He pursued an entirely new approach to the philosophy and functions of municipal government.

As the above quote from his speech on the importance of the City Council implies, he imagined the city as an organic whole whose purpose was to improve the quality of life for all its citizens. Hunt (2004) describes this approach as a 'municipal gospel', encompassing a firm belief that elected local authorities could be much more effective in helping communities solve problems than distant politicians in Westminster. Chamberlain's strategy, involving well-managed civic investment to reverse the process of urban decay, provides a remarkable early example of public service reform in action. We will return to the achievements of Chamberlain, Dawson and their colleagues in Birmingham shortly.

Here, however, I want to note how Joseph Chamberlain's civic leadership efforts highlight two themes that we will revisit during this and subsequent chapters. First, important public service reforms often stem from place-based initiatives of various kinds. For example, if we track back to the origins of modern social, health, education and housing services we usually find inspirational activists who were moved to take action at the local level. Found in the voluntary sector, in religious institutions, in trade unions, in local businesses, in local government, in local political parties and elsewhere, these change agents were often driven by a passionate belief in their ability to change society for the better, and they acted on their beliefs.[2]

Second, cities are clearly very important players in the public service innovation process. In the previous chapter I explained how cities have expanded rapidly in the last 150 years. Europe led the way in this process of urbanisation and it is, perhaps, not surprising that we see many examples of bold local government leadership developing in the big cities of Europe in the 19th Century. In the period before 1830 local government was not, on the whole, a particularly important public institution. In those days, in England at least, the tasks of local government were primarily administrative and judicial. The problems of urban squalor thrown up by urbanisation and the Industrial Revolution changed all that. These major new challenges were too much for this traditional system of local government to cope with. Many societies responded by creating powerful, elected local authorities to guide societal change.

This chapter, after noting the role of place-based civic leaders in developing public services in the 19th Century, will turn to consider the public service reform efforts of the last thirty years or so. Three competing approaches to reform will be considered. These reflect the use of two different empowerment mechanisms – the exercise of choice and the expression of voice – plus a third approach that depends on self-improvement by public service providers. It will be suggested that these routes to reform embody very different ways of conceiving the desired relationship between the state and the people it is there to serve. Reforms pursued in many countries in the name of **New Public Management** (NPM) will be criticised as they are built on a flawed understanding of this relationship. An alternative approach, which I describe as **New Civic Leadership** (NCL), will be outlined. This involves strong place-based leadership acting to co-create new solutions to public problems by drawing on the complementary strengths of civil society, the market and the state. This leadership strategy emphasises the importance of moving beyond public service improvement to focus on politically driven public service innovation.

Public services – place-based origins

Public services are closely linked with human rights. Traditionally they have been provided by the state for the people. However, in some countries – for example, the UK and the USA – the state does not provide all the services itself. It allows private sector companies to provide some of the services (for example, electricity, gas and water in the UK) and then attempts to regulate the performance of these providers. The history of public services varies by country, but we can note that, in most developed countries, widespread public service provision emerged in the mid to late 19th Century.

Often, as in the case of Birmingham, it was local governments that pioneered the introduction of new services – for example, public gas and water services, as well as public health, town planning, education and housing provision. In developing countries public services are not, on the whole, as extensive. For example, in some countries water services may only be available to the relatively wealthy. Here I outline the emergence of local government leadership in the UK and the influence it had on public service development. A similar narrative can be developed to explain the emergence and growth of public services in other developed countries. My aim here is not to provide a comprehensive history – rather I wish to highlight the role of place-based leadership in advancing public service innovation.

As noted in the introduction to this chapter, it was the growth of cities in the 19th Century and, more specifically, the emergence of dreadful living conditions in the pitiful urban slums, which provoked a governmental response. The Municipal Corporations Act 1835 introduced the idea of multi-purpose elected local authorities into England and Wales to replace self-electing, and frequently corrupt, medieval corporations. Hunt (2004), in his thought-provoking overview of the Victorian city, provides an excellent analysis of the growth of local government power, and he catalogues many remarkable examples of urban leadership and civic action in a string of vibrant provincial cities – including Birmingham, Bristol, Glasgow, Leeds, Liverpool and Manchester.

Here I refer again to Joseph Chamberlain's extraordinary achievements in Birmingham in order to illustrate a wider trend. In his in depth study Peter Marsh shows how Chamberlain, 'won widespread, amazed respect for his achievement in civic affairs. That achievement… established a new composite of policies for urban government known as municipal or gas-and-water socialism that inspired emulation throughout the industrialised world' (Marsh 1994, 77). Chamberlain was Mayor of Birmingham from 1873–1876 and, in this period, he obtained powers from Parliament to take over the failing, privately owned gas and water companies. This was, in effect, reverse privatisation. Using new revenue streams he made spectacular improvements to the city – creating public spaces in the town centre, improving housing and streets, creating parks, libraries and a fabulous City Museum. This transformation of the central area was one of the first radical efforts at urban regeneration in an industrial city – and Birmingham was soon dubbed 'the metropolis of the Midlands'. As Marsh notes, Chamberlain introduced important innovations in public finance:

> The slum clearance would justify civic expenditure on the commercial heart of the town, while the revenue from the commercial improvement would help pay for the renovation of the slums. (Marsh 1994, 93)

The key lesson I wish to draw from Joseph Chamberlain's bold, place-based leadership is that he was able to redefine and expand the nature of public service. As Marsh (1994, xiii) writes, 'In order to enhance the wellbeing of urban, industrial England, Chamberlain insisted upon widening the accepted social and economic parameters of political action' (Marsh 1994, xiii). In the context of 21st Century urban politics Chamberlain can be criticised for adopting a paternalistic style of leadership. In his model, working people were intended to benefit from, but not be partners in, his various municipal enterprises. But this is to miss the point. In the 1870s, from a strong political base in an English provincial city, he pioneered an outgoing and extremely effective approach to public service reform – one that created an astonishing level of civic pride in the city. Understanding the need to redraw the boundaries of public action and, as part of this, to erode the power of capital to exploit people, remain central challenges for urban political leaders today.

Public service reform – three alternative strategies

We now leap forward a century or so to consider recent efforts to reform public services. First we should record the steady expansion of public services, particularly in the period since World War II, and celebrate the enormous public benefits welfare states now deliver to citizens in many countries. In the UK, for example, the state expanded a wide range of public services that are free at the point of delivery – education, health care, libraries, social work support, art galleries, museums, public open spaces, roads and cycle paths, homelessness support, clean streets, fire and rescue services, police services, refuse collection/recycling services, consumer protection, social security and so on. In addition, a range of valuable public services are provided by the state that require some payment by service users – for example, social housing, swimming pools, leisure centres and public transportation. Many welfare states in the developed world provide similar, or more, services, and the quality of life for millions of people is much the better for it.

However, in the 1970s, in the UK at least, a process of questioning whether the welfare state was continuing to deliver high quality public outcomes emerged. Was the welfare state model we had developed as cost effective as it could be? Was reform necessary? I now take the UK as an example to illustrate a wider discussion about the drivers of public service reform efforts in recent years. In an earlier analysis Danny Burns, Paul Hoggett and I examined the build-up of large, highly professionalised departments designed to mass-produce public services (Burns et al 1994). We noted that the dominant organisational form was bureaucratic. For each service there emerged: a defined department or division; an administrative hierarchy of control; a set of procedures designed to ensure uniformity of treatment; and groups of professionals or specialists to perform the tasks. While, at their best, such departments provided an impartial and fair service 'for' the population, service users began to complain that they were often inflexible, and that they frequently displayed a 'we know best' attitude in their dealings with the public.

Discontent with this model of public service grew and, in 1994, we identified three main options for tackling bureaucratic paternalism. These are illustrated in Figure 3.1.[3] Starting at the bottom of the diagram, in the 1970s, we find large public service organisations staffed by professionals. Imbued with a strong commitment to public service these professionals worked hard to provide services 'for' people – and they tended to describe the people they served as 'clients'. The critique that emerged was that these organisations, while they were well meaning in intent, often failed to connect adequately with the lived experience of service users. The professionals, or at least some of them, exhibited a paternalistic style.

The diagram identifies three routes to reform. These three options continue to compete for attention in public policy circles today, and it is a safe bet that they will remain a central feature in public service reform debates in the future. The different strategies are often collapsed together in academic and public policy debates and this is a big mistake. For example, politicians sometimes use generic terms like 'modernisation' without any clear explanation of what values underpin reform proposals. So, what are these three distinct pathways for reform?

The first broad alternative, shown on the left of Figure 3.1, rejects the very idea of collective and non-market provision for public need (Walsh 1995). Centring on the notion of privatisation it seeks to replace public provision with private – it strives to extend market models, particularly the idea of competition, into the realm of public services. The strategy involves not just selling off public assets, but also emphasises the commodification of services, and favours the introduction of so-called 'quasi-markets' (Le Grand 2007). Defenders of this strategy claim that, by enabling consumers to exercise choice between competing providers, these organisations will become more responsive.

The second alternative, shown on the right of Figure 3.1, aims to preserve the notion of public provision, but seeks a radical reform of the manner in which this provision is undertaken. It seeks to extend, not reduce, democracy. It strives to replace the old, bureaucratic paternalistic model with a much more democratic approach, often involving radical decentralisation to the neighbourhood level and new approaches to citizen involvement. We explored this reform strategy in some detail in our book, *The Politics of Decentralisation* (Burns et al 1994). In more recent years numerous writers have contributed valuable insights on how to democratise public service provision, and we will draw on this literature in Chapter 7 (Cornwall 2008; Oliver and Pitt 2013; Taylor 2011; Wainwright 2003; Warburton 2009). This citizen-oriented approach to reform is leading to a radical reshaping of the role of the third sector in many societies.

The third sector – variously described as the voluntary sector, the non-profit sector, the social economy or civil society – is becoming increasingly important in many societies. In some countries, the third sector has played an important role in welfare services since World War II – for example, in Germany and the Netherlands. In others, for example the UK, it was not until the 1990s that the government decided to outsource a range of public services, including social housing, to third sector providers. A consequence of the growth of the third sector in recent years is that the boundaries between the state and civil society are now blurred by the emergence of a class of organisational hybrids. By this I mean, following Evers and Laville (2004), third sector organisations that have some characteristics that resemble the state (for example, formal rules and regulations) and other characteristics that we associate with market organisations (for example, use of contracts). Brandsen and Pestoff (2006) have developed a useful conceptual framework for understanding these developments. It distinguishes co-production, co-management and co-governance and we will return to these ideas shortly.

Note that the market approach treats people as *consumers* of services, and the democratic approach treats people as *citizens* with a right to be heard. This, as we shall see shortly, is a crucial distinction. Advocates of market models often mask their intent by continuing to describe service users within 'quasi-market' systems as 'citizens'. This is to mislead as the model depends, entirely, on individual consumer power, not the collective power exercised by citizens.

The third broad strategy for public service reform, shown running up the centre of Figure 3.1, has become increasingly influential in recent years. It attempts to distinguish a *managerial* as opposed to a *political* response to the problems confronting public service bureaucracies. This strategy borrows from the two competing political models in a way that simulates radical methods, but in a form that preserves existing power relations between the producers and users of services. In this model citizens are redefined as *customers*. There is now a substantial literature, drawn mainly from private sector experience, on the customer orientation, customer driven service delivery and the like (Osborne and Plastrik 1997, 157–202; Bernard et al 2011).[4]

Figure 3.1: Public service reform strategies

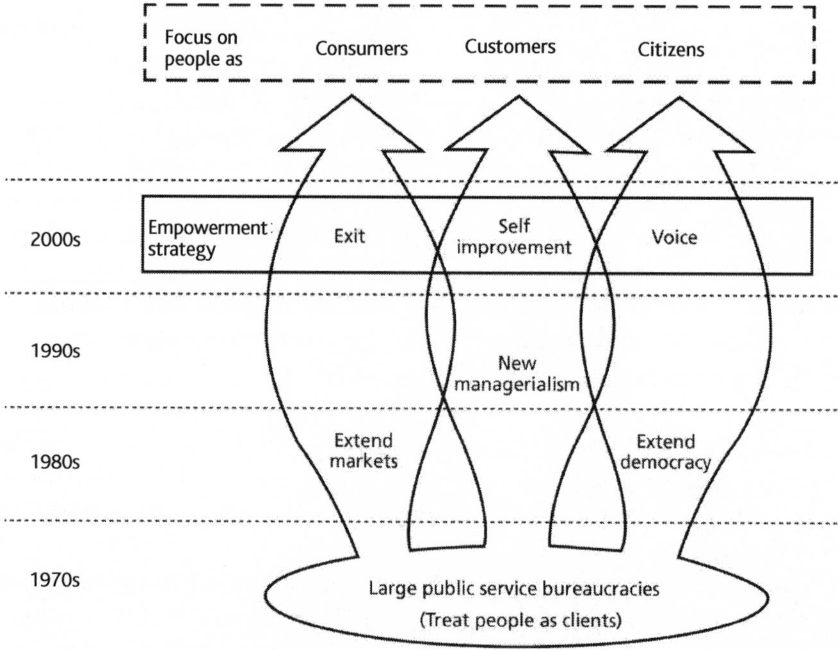

Source: Adapted from Burns et al (1994) Figure 1.1, p 22

Understanding the drivers of public service reform

The rhetoric surrounding public service reform efforts often fails to distinguish the philosophical underpinnings of the strategies that are advocated. This failure leads to confusion and poor decision making, hence my suggestion that the distinctions – between clients, consumers, customers and citizens – shown in Figure 3.1 are absolutely critical. The analysis presented here draws on the distinction Albert Hirschman articulated between two ideal theoretical notions of empowerment – exit and voice (Hirschman 1970). He argues that members of an organisation, a nation or any other form of human grouping, have essentially two ways of responding to unsatisfactory performance: they can *exit* (withdraw from the relationship); or express their *voice* (in an effort to complain or set out proposals for change). He also has interesting things to say about a third concept – loyalty – and we will come back to that shortly.

As Figure 3.1 implies, the power of exit is associated with the workings of markets – hence my use of the word 'consumer' to describe the focus of this approach. Voice, on the other hand, is by nature political and, not surprisingly, ties in with the idea of the free citizen exercising the right to vote, protest, demonstrate and so on. Hirschman notes that, while both exit and voice can be used to assess organisational performance, voice is by nature more informative in that it provides reasons why people are unhappy.

The third strategy for reform identified in Figure 3.1 – new managerialism – is not derived from Hirschman's work. This is because it is *not*, in fact, an empowerment mechanism at all. Rather, it comprises a managerial response to changing public pressures. In place of the unsettling signals of exit and voice, this approach reaches for private sector management techniques – market research, user satisfaction surveys, complaints procedures, customer care programmes, mystery 'shopping' visits, interactive websites, focus groups and the like. This panoply of techniques is intended to provide more gentle and manageable feedback. The key point about feedback as opposed to pressure is that it doesn't force the organisation to change – rather it is about establishing a relationship with customers or, in management-speak, customer intimacy.

If we now step back we can distinguish 'four Cs' that can help us understand the competing values that lie at the heart of many current public service reform debates. These words draw attention to the nature of the relationship between the state and the people it is there to serve (Burns et al 1994, 51). The four Cs are:

- **Client** – This implies a dominance of the client by the professional and is the word often used in traditional public administration.
- **Consumer** – This implies a free agent in the market place interested solely in the product or service provided. In Hirschman's terms it is the consumer who has the economic power of exit.

- **Customer** – This implies giving attention to the experience of the person using the service of the organisation and, ideally, building a relationship with this person
- **Citizen** – This is someone who has a right to influence public decisions affecting the quality of life, and responsibilities in relation to other citizens. In Hirschman's terms it is the citizen who has the political power of voice.

These distinctions may seem unimportant, and it is true that translation of these words into other languages can be problematic. However, it is clear that they speak volumes about the ethos underpinning given public service reform efforts, and we ignore these distinctions at our peril.

In Chapter 1 I introduced Michael Sandel's argument that many societies have shifted, without realising it, without debating it, from *having* a market economy to *being* a market society (Sandel 2012, 9; author's emphasis). The misguided take-up of market and quasi-market approaches in public service reform efforts – often described by academics as **New Public Management** – illustrates Sandel's argument rather well.[5] A substantial number of criticisms of the competitive model in public services – of the idea of treating public service users as consumers in a market place – can be identified. While these limitations have been set out in some detail (Whitfield 1992 and 2012; Dowding and John 2009), they have not received sufficient attention in public policy debates. Here I list six concerns.

First, in many public service situations there is nowhere else to exit to. For example the poor cannot move home easily, or possibly at all, so suggesting that dissatisfied consumers can relocate to a different area that provides better services is nonsense. Second, many public services are collectively produced and collectively enjoyed – for example, clean air, public parks, streets, footpaths, libraries, museums and so on. The public benefit cannot be sliced into individual purchases. Third, the quasi-market approach can create 'two tier' systems of service – with reasonably high-quality services for the wealthy and articulate, able to operate successfully in the curious quasi-market systems, mirrored by declining services for the less well off.

Fourth, from a management point of view, the need to specify requirements in detail in advance of letting a contract leads to a highly centralised form of control that works against innovation and local learning. Fifth, the market mechanism can be viewed as an attack on the local polity in that, by fostering a self-interested and individualistic approach to decision-making, it works against debate and deliberation of collective concerns and needs. A sixth argument, developed at some length by Hirschman in his discussion of the value of loyalty, is that the ready and widespread use of exit can lead to the unnecessary demise of otherwise salvageable enterprises. These are all powerful arguments.

In addition, we can note the core philosophical argument articulated so well by Sandel. He shows how emphasising self-interested behaviour erodes the quality of life:

> At a time of rising inequality, the marketization of everything means that people of affluence and people of modest means lead increasingly separate lives. We live and work and shop and play in different places. Our children go to different schools. You might call it the skyboxification of American life. It's not good for democracy, nor is it a satisfying way to live. (Sandel 2012, 203)

However, Sandel makes an even more important point in relation to public service reform. He asks us to consider, on a case-by-case basis, whether commercialising a practice could, in and of itself, degrade it. His suggestion here is not just that markets thrive on selfish behaviour, they diminish and corrupt other norms:

> Economists often assume that markets do not touch or taint the goods they regulate. But this is untrue. Markets leave their mark on social norms. Often, market incentives erode or crowd out nonmarket incentives. (Sandel 2012, 64)

Put simply, markets crowd out morals. The notion that markets don't taint the goods they exchange is implausible. It is clear, then, that extending markets, or so-called quasi-markets, into public services does great damage to the public service ethos. They trample over the idea that caring for others and the pursuit of public purpose lie at the heart of a civilised society.

This discussion suggests that civic leaders would be wise to examine carefully what the implications are of treating people as consumers or customers – the key words used by those advocating **New Public Management** approaches. Managerial models built around these concepts should not be dismissed out of hand. There is much to be said for enhancing the quality of the service encounter in public service systems and the private sector can offer valuable experience and insights in relation to, for example, customer care. But it is a serious mistake to believe that the private sector offers a superior level of responsiveness to service users than public sector organisations. As we shall see in Chapter 6 sophisticated local authorities are well ahead of the very best private companies when it comes to public service responsiveness, and Innovation Story 3 provides a concrete illustration. The evidence suggests, then, that, while reform efforts that treat people as consumers or customers – see Figure 3.1 – can play a role in improving the quality of public services, it is more productive for the state to focus on strategies that respect and value people as free and responsible citizens.

The dangers of 'nudge' in public policy

Before moving to consider afresh the potential for place-based civic leadership to engage with citizens and advance the cause of public service reform, we should make a short detour to sound a warning note about the disturbing advance of 'nudge' thinking in some public policy circles. I refer here to the idea of covertly nudging people to behave in ways the state or, more accurately some individuals working for the state, thinks are good for us (Thaler and Sunstein 2008). Parts of UK central government claim that it is acceptable, even essential, to try to change our behaviour without us realising that our behaviour is being changed.

This is an extraordinary state of affairs and the paper from the UK Cabinet Office, which sets out how to go about implementing nudge policies, is no cause for comfort (Dolan et al 2010). It is hardly surprising that every page in this document is stamped with the statement 'Discussion document – not a statement of government policy'. It is almost as if the authors realise that this material is not just sensitive, but probably unacceptable to citizens concerned to defend their civil liberties. Knowing this provides little comfort to UK citizens as, in 2010, the Prime Minister set up a Behavioural Insights Team, known as the Nudge Unit, in the Cabinet Office, with the explicit purpose of manipulating the behaviour of British citizens.

Edward Bernays, in his path-breaking book, *Propaganda,* examines mass manipulation in modern societies, and his early guide to public relations provides the lodestar for the new paternalists. His opening sentence is, perhaps surprisingly, devoid of spin: 'The conscious and intelligent manipulation of the organised habits and opinions of the masses is an important element in democratic society' (Bernays 1928, 1). But you will not find his book cited by Thaler and Sunstein or the Behavioural Insights Team. Still less will you find reference to the insightful critique of these practices provided by Vance Packard in his excellent analysis, *The Hidden Persuaders* (Packard 1957). We have known for decades, then, that ruthless private sector companies, unprincipled politicians and their servants, take the view that people must be controlled by manipulating their instincts and emotions rather than by appealing to their reasoning.

In a democratic society governments have a portfolio of legitimate policy instruments that they can use to influence the behaviour of the population. Over and above managing services in a sensible way (by, for example, using intelligence when designing government application forms, training public servants to be creative and so on), there are four legitimate policy levers available to governments. Governments can, after due debate:

- pass legislation to ban undesirable behaviour (for example, require those travelling in vehicles to wear seat belts)
- regulate behaviour that may damage the wellbeing of others (for example, impose no smoking restrictions in indoor public spaces, apply penalties on those who pollute the environment)
- tax actions (in various ways) to discourage certain kinds of behaviour (for example, impose high taxes on units of alcohol purchased in bars or shops); and
- take active steps to educate free citizens about the merits and demerits of life style choices and options for the future (for example, co-design imaginative campaigns with communities to promote healthy living, safe sex, physical exercise, a balanced diet and so on).

The latter strategy blends into the co-creation of new knowledge to solve societal problems, and we discuss the way the state and civil society can work together shortly.

Nudge is, by comparison with these well-established methods, rather sinister. While practice varies we can note that steps taken in the name of nudge are usually surreptitious. Hidden from view, the paternalistic bureaucrats we criticised earlier in the chapter are attempting to make a comeback. To be fair, the American advocates of nudge approaches do acknowledge that it is a paternalistic model of government:

> ... the approach we recommend does count as paternalistic, because private and public choice architects are not merely trying to track or to implement people's anticipated choices. Rather, they are self-consciously attempting to move people in directions that will make their lives better. (Thaler and Sunstein 2008, 6)

Note that there are no worries here about who knows what is 'better'. It is the appointed officials. The use of the phrase 'choice architects' to describe these bureaucrats is, in itself, a nice example of the obfuscating language nudge enthusiasts like to use. The sixteen-member British Behavioural Insights team was privatised in 2014. This, in itself, is troubling. The unit has left the Cabinet Office and is now owned by three parties: one-third by the government, one-third by a charity called Nesta, and one-third by the staff. The UK taxpayer has, then, paid the officials in the Nudge Unit good salaries to develop ideas and public service innovations for a period of four years. Now these officials have been allowed to part-privatise the intellectual assets the public purse paid for. It would seem that they are about to make vast sums of money selling their services back to the government. This is because these individuals will no longer be bound by civil service pay grades and, it seems, will be able to earn massive bonuses.[6] As Edward Bernays (1928) explained, almost a century ago, there is money to be made from manipulation.

There are three reasons why nudge initiatives in public policy should be viewed with concern. First, the idea that public servants, or arms length policy advisers, should be using psychological tricks to manipulate the behaviour of the population is offensive in and of itself (whether or not such dupery is announced beforehand). Second, it is deeply worrying that concepts and ideas, imported from behavioural psychology, are being allowed to taint the honesty and integrity of government. As Elaine Glaser explains:

> This modish wonkery is all about eroding vital distinctions between government, psychology and marketing... We are no longer appealed to as citizens. We are simply flawed units to be prompted into spending more and costing the state less. The propaganda lies not only in the political–corporate manipulation of the public but also – most

> insidiously – in the way it is cloaked in the language of ideology-free empiricism and the semblance of autonomy. (Glaser 2013)

Any government that claims to care about transparency in public decision-making would have difficulty defending these manipulative techniques. Third, and this illustrates the breathtaking insensitivity of those involved, at this point in time politicians and governments are experiencing very high levels of public distrust. In this context, to even begin to think that introducing a strategy designed to change behaviour without changing minds is an intelligent move, smacks of both incompetence and arrogance. The UK House of Lords Science and Technology Select Committee has become concerned about the work of the Nudge Unit. In July 2014, Lord Selborne, the chair of the committee, wrote to Oliver Letwin, the Cabinet Office minister responsible for the Unit, questioning positive claims made about the performance of the unit. He notes that the Unit has not published an annual report since its 2011–12 update, and that the absence of data means that independent evaluation of the work of the Unit is being frustrated.[7] In the British context, and perhaps elsewhere, it looks as if the arguments used to see off the bureaucratic paternalism of the 1970s will need to be reinvigorated to tackle the new bureaucratic paternalists of the 2010s.

The New Civic Leadership

We now begin to explore the notion of civic, or place-based, leadership in a little more detail. First let's glance back to the origins of public services. At the beginning of this chapter I suggested that place-based leaders played a major role in creating the modern welfare state by, amongst other things, promoting the development of effective, multi-purpose local governments in the 19th Century. They invented a wide range of new public services and generated the political will to implement them. Central governments, to their credit, picked up these ideas and nationalised them. The achievements of the place-based leaders – the local activists, the elected politicians, the many public-spirited campaigners – were breathtaking. In the discussion that follows my aim is not to advocate a return, in some sort of mechanistic way, to a golden era of municipal leadership. Rather, I am suggesting that modern urban leaders can draw inspiration from the political drive and enthusiasm of the civic leaders that have gone before them. Imaginative approaches to place-based leadership offer a promising way forward for public service reform in the coming period, not least because they provide opportunities for creative collaborations linking the state and civil society.

There are four steps to this argument. First, we consider the movement from government to governance. As mentioned in Chapter 1 this is a shift that is taking place in many societies. Second, we note that this shift invites a reconsideration of the relationships between civil society, markets and the state. Third, we refer to the emergence of new ideas relating to nonmarket values in public service reform – particularly, loyalty and civic identity. Finally, we examine the importance of moving beyond the notion of public service improvement to engage in the co-creation of public services. We now consider each of these steps in turn. The overall argument here, and it will be developed in the rest of this book, is that a focus on what I call **New Civic Leadership** (NCL) can provide a significant advance on the outdated notion of **New Public Management** (NPM) – a notion that has held public service innovation back for far too long.

From government to governance

Numerous writers have suggested that we are moving from an era of government to one of governance (Pierre and Peters 2000; Denters and Rose 2005; Mossberger et al 2012; Pierre 2011).[8] Government refers to the formal institutions of the state. Government makes decisions within specific administrative and legal frameworks and uses public resources in a financially accountable way. Most importantly, government decisions are backed by the legitimate hierarchical power of the state. Governance, on the other hand, involves government *plus* the looser processes of influencing and negotiating with a range of public and private agencies to achieve desired outcomes.

A governance perspective encourages collaboration between the public, private and non-profit sectors to achieve mutual goals. While the hierarchical power of the state does not vanish, the emphasis in governance is on influencing and coordinating the actions of others. There is recognition here that government cannot go it alone. As Jon Pierre (2011, 20) puts it, 'Governance could be defined as processes through which public and private resources are coordinated in the pursuit of collective interests. Thus, as a concept, governance is more encompassing and broad than government'.[9] A word of caution is needed. This movement from government to governance is unfolding, if it is happening at all, in different ways in different countries. For example, McCarney and Stren (2003), in a valuable collection of essays, explain how urban governance in developing countries has had a different trajectory than in developed countries. The long-established existence of the informal city, operating outside any regulatory framework and led by non-state actors, in many developing countries means that it is unwise to imply that the transition from government to governance is an appropriate way to characterise changes in approaches to urban government in all countries. With this important qualification made we can move to our second step, and consider the debate about the changing relationships between civil society, markets and the state.

Civil society, markets and the state

We have already discussed the role of markets and the state in relation to public service reform. What about the role of civil society? Marilyn Taylor (2011) provides a useful overview of the long and distinguished history of the concept, and she also provides a helpful introduction to related terms – for example, community, communitarianism, social capital and mutuality. She explains how in Europe, with the collapse of feudal society, the idea of civil society emerged out of the separation of the realm of the state from the realm of the private. She suggests that civil society provides a foundation for reciprocity, mutuality and co-operation beyond the calculus of pure exchange. Walzer (1992, 7) defines it as 'the sphere of uncoerced human association and also the set of relational networks – formed for the sake of family, faith, interest and ideology – that fill this space'. Antonio Gramsci adds a more radical interpretation – he argues that civil society is the arena in which the fight for cultural and ideological hegemony takes place. He fears that the institutions of civil society may become servants of the ruling class and it follows that: 'The superstructures of civil society are like the trench-systems of modern warfare' (Gramsci 1971, 235).

Edwards (2009) explains that the idea of civil society embodies an ethical understanding of social life, one that prescribes social norms and values mutuality. Oliver and Pitt emphasise the practical implications of this understanding:

> ... the norms and values of a civil society are embodied in voluntary associations where skills of co-operation are developed. In political terms, a return to civil society calls for a return to a manageable scale of social life emphasising voluntary associations, churches and communities. (Oliver and Pitt 2013, 56)

Reciprocity, co-operation, association, connection, solidarity, community – these are the words that recur in discussions of the nature of civil society.[10]

Jacob Norvig Larsen (2012) notes that the familiar division between civil society (community, third sector), markets (economy, business), and the state (public sector, politics, government) is often illustrated by means of a triangular diagram. He explains how the reality is more complex, and that new configurations of social action are now emerging in the space 'inside' the triangle. He illustrates his argument with examples drawn from urban regeneration initiatives in Denmark. His analysis is in line with the argument presented by Lucas Meijs (2012), who suggests that the reinvention of Dutch civil society involves three models: 1) The service delivery organisation, 2) The campaigning organisation, and 3) The mutual support organisation. These authors remind us that there is a danger that civil society, like its close cousin community, could become idealised in ways that are unsustainable, even unethical. There are divisions within civil society that civic leaders need to understand and respond to.

Hodgson (2004) also notes that the state can have difficulty in dealing with this complexity, and may be tempted to manufacture a civil society to suit its needs. She argues that such a move might actually undermine civil society and she concludes, 'There needs to be recognition that authentic civil society is a complex, diverse, organically developing entity that cannot be manufactured to suit the needs of government.' (Hodgson 2004, 160).

Taking account of these complexities, Figure 3.2 suggests that it is helpful to present the relationships between civil society, markets and the state not as a rigid triangle, but as three overlapping spheres of influence.[11] The diagram uses dotted lines to signal the way ideas flow between these sectors. The borders between these concepts are clearly porous and, indeed, some actors may find themselves operating in more than one sector at one and the same time. Earlier in the chapter I suggested that it is helpful to distinguish co-governance, co-management and co-production (Brandsen and Pestoff 2006). Stated simply:

- **Co-governance** refers to an arrangement in which the third sector participates in the planning and delivery of public services
- **Co-management** refers to an arrangement in which third sector organisations produce services in collaboration with the state
- **Co-production** refers to an arrangement where citizens produce their own services at least in part

This classification suggests that co-governance involves developing more strategic relationships between the state and the third sector than the other two – it involves third sector participation in policy formulation. Co-management refers to interactions between organisations. Co-production refers to voluntary efforts by individual citizens.

Figure 3.2: Civil society, markets and the state

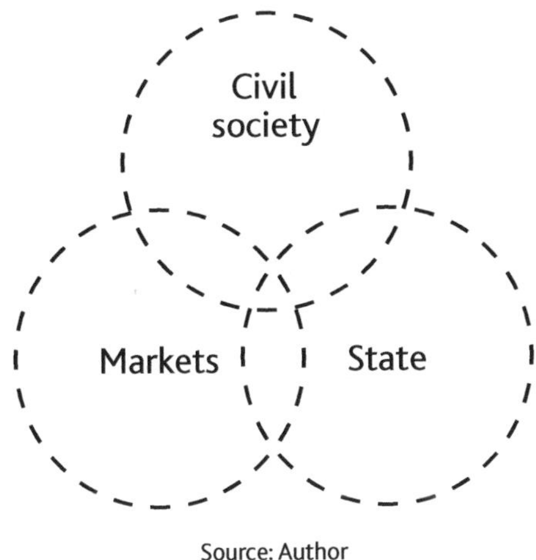

Source: Author

Figure 3.2 provides a fresh way of examining the argument presented earlier in this chapter relating to the core values underpinning public service reform efforts. The discussion of the drivers of change, summarised in Figure 3.1, suggests that civic leaders would be unwise to focus their efforts on viewing people as consumers and/or customers. The promotion of individualistic self-serving behaviour is, relatively speaking, a blind alley for those seeking a significant advance in public service effectiveness. As many of the Innovation Stories in this book will illustrate, civic leaders within the state are making important strides forward by engaging creatively with civil society. In terms of Figure 3.2 the most promising possibilities for public service reform are not to be found in the promotion of quasi-markets (the overlap between markets and the state). The zones that are fertile with possibilities are in the other two areas of overlap – between civil society and the state (for example, innovative approaches to community care, social housing, public health) and between civil society and markets (for example, through the creation of social enterprises, co-operatives, credit unions). But why might the engagement of civil society work? In order to answer this question it is useful to return to Albert Hirschman's incisive analysis of empowerment.

Loyalty and civic identity

As well as distinguishing, with great elegance, the strengths and weaknesses of exit and voice, Albert Hirschman also presents a theory of loyalty (Hirschman 1970, 76–105). Hirschman notes that, as a rule, loyalty holds exit at bay and activates voice: 'When loyalty is present exit abruptly changes character: the applauded rational behaviour of the alert consumer shifting to a better buy becomes disgraceful defection, desertion, and treason' (Hirschman 1970, 98). Loyalty is a precious asset – civil society contains it in abundance; successful place-based leaders understand this, connect to it and strengthen it.

In Chapter 1 I presented a vision of an inclusive city – a city governed by powerful, place-based democratic institutions. In such a city all residents are able to participate fully in society, and civic leaders strive for just results while caring for the natural environment. In subsequent chapters we will explore how civic leaders in cities across the world are working hard to create inclusive cities that try to match up to these demanding criteria. Here I want to highlight the importance of loyalty – a concept that overlaps with civic or community pride.

In discussing loyalty it would be easy to slip into a process of making vague claims about community and shared purpose in modern society. In the UK context this was a feature of Prime Minister Cameron's flimsy rhetoric about the idea of creating a 'Big Society'.[12] Enthusiasts for 'public value' also veer in this direction by making ill-defined claims about what the concept actually means. In particular, the theory fails to address issues of power in modern society. As I explained in Chapter 1 understanding and addressing power relations is central to any effective strategy to create the inclusive city. The literature on public value offers no practical suggestions on how to prevent powerful interests determining what constitutes public value. A consequence is that this concept has lost any purchase that it might once have had – it becomes 'all things to all people' (Rhodes and Wanna 2007, 408).[13]

Anyone with even modest experience of urban politics knows that communities are conflicted and that loyalties are in tension (Hoggett 1997; 2009).[14] Competing feelings – to the past, to the familiar, to the future, to sectional interests, to new arrivals, to new possibilities and so on – are part and parcel of modern urban life. Moreover, all individuals have *multiple loyalties or identities* – to their home area, to their class, to their place of origin, to their age group, to their ethnic group, to their political party, to their social network, to their sports club, to their work and so on. Some will have loyalties to a religion or way of viewing the world.

In subsequent chapters we will explore these themes in more detail. For example, in Chapter 7 we will discuss approaches to democratic participation, and in Chapter 10 we will give particular attention to the theme of diversity in the modern city. Here I want to suggest that policy makers cannot expect to succeed in exercising legitimate political leadership unless they develop a sophisticated understanding of the *publics* they are there to serve – of the *differences* between communities and individuals – as well as identifying what unites them. This includes understanding the experiences of people whose views may be marginalised for a variety of reasons – for example, new migrants (Thorp 2009) or disabled people (Roulstone and Prideaux 2012).

Civic leadership, at its core, needs to understand these various conflicts and tensions, and rise above them to deliver actions that speak to the common good. This is easier said than done. But the idea of appealing to the loyalty that residents feel towards their locality, their city, the place where they live, is full of potential. In my view, the significance of place-based identity, including the attachment newcomers feel to their new city, has been neglected in urban political science and urban studies. We will explore the meaning of place in more detail in Chapter 4 and the opportunities for place-based leadership in Chapter 5. Here I want to suggest that emotional attachment and shared commitment to a locality are undervalued in the prevailing public policy discourse.

Bell and de-Shalit (2011), in *The Spirit of Cities*, attempt to provide a corrective. They argue that, contrary to the claims of those wedded to neo-liberal ideology, social units at the local level do have the political and economic wherewithal to oppose the place-less logic of globalisation. In a subtle analysis Bell and de-Shalit argue that each city has an *ethos* – a set of values and outlooks that are generally acknowledged by people living in the city. They assemble case studies of nine cities from various parts of the world to develop a narrative suggesting that cities reflect, as well as shape, their inhabitants' values and outlooks. They argue that:

> … many people do want to experience particularity, to maintain and nurture their own cultures, values, and customs that they believe are constitutive of their identities, and without which their communal way of life would be substantially diminished. Hence, we want to suggest that cities have been increasingly the mechanism by which people oppose globalisation and its tendency to flatten cultures into sameness. (Bell and de-Shalit 2011, 5)

These authors suggest a new word – civicism – to express the sentiment of urban pride, to parallel the way patriotism is used to convey national pride. This new word may do damage to the English language, and it may even be unnecessary, but this is not to undermine the value of their perceptive analysis of the way people feel about the place where they live.

Place-based loyalty and commitment can provide a particularly important contribution to the achievement of the environmental objectives of local governance. In Chapter 1 I stressed the importance of integrating a concern for the natural environment into urban strategy and practice. Efforts to create sustainable communities have mushroomed in recent years, and many localities are now able to point to active collaborations between the state and civil society designed to release new energies to tackle climate change, encourage recycling and promote community-based problem solving. In the UK, for example, we can identify many notable initiatives. Some of these have stemmed from state leadership and the government has provided good guidance on the development of skills to create sustainable communities (Egan 2004). Other important initiatives have been driven by grassroots civic action – such as the Transition Movement, which seeks to enhance the resilience of communities in the face of climate change (Hopkins 2011). Rob Hopkins, founder of the Transition Movement, has provided a highly accessible guide for civic activists in *The Power of Just Doing Stuff* (Hopkins 2013). A key feature of these initiatives is that they draw strength from a strong sense of place and from the belief that local community action can make a difference.

Leading the co-creation of public services

In Chapter 1 I suggested that it is helpful to distinguish between public service improvement and public service innovation, and I introduced theories relating to organisational learning to illustrate my argument (Argyris and Schon 1978). I provide a brief recap. In efforts to improve services public servants strive to provide more for less; organisational norms are not up for reconsideration. Rather, the aim is to deliver more of the same (or very similar) services to the population in an ever more cost-effective way. When an organisation engages in innovation it goes *beyond* the realm of traditional performance management. In public service innovation – which I defined earlier as creating a new approach to public service, putting it into practice and finding out if it works – public servants question established norms and explore entirely new ways of delivering results. This is exciting and talented public servants love doing this. As often as not, successful innovations span across the divide between the state and civil society.

We examine the leadership of public service innovation in more detail in Chapters 5 and 6. Here I want to draw attention to the critical role that place-based leadership can play in co-creating fresh ways of defining challenges and generating novel solutions. The idea of working *with* communities of interest and place, rather than *for* them is long established in the field of community development.[15] Earlier in this chapter I explained how many public servants in the period up to the 1970s, in Britain at least, saw themselves as providing professional, high quality services 'for' their clients. The motives were not bad, but the methods used often left a lot to be desired.

I have suggested that, over the years, the language relating to public service reform has changed. More important, the underlying philosophy of how to govern effectively has leapt forward. Community pressures of various kinds have brought about these moves towards a more citizen-friendly approach. Social movements, many and varied, should be praised for bringing about this shift. But it is also appropriate to recognise the invaluable contribution of those working in countless, local community development projects in cities and localities across the world. These workers have supported grassroots activists and their efforts should be praised not only for their practical achievements but also for the way they have reshaped our understanding of the relationships between the state and civil society (Oliver and Pitt 2013; Taylor 2011).

Their political efforts to promote civic activism, coupled with the energetic leadership of municipal governments, have transformed the way public authorities work with citizens to solve societal problems. As various Innovation Stories in this book will show, place-based leaders are pioneering new forms of citizen involvement. We should mention here, the potential for information and communication technologies (ICT) to play a role in community-based public service innovation. It is still early days, but evidence is starting to accumulate which suggests that ICT can play a valuable role alongside face-to-face innovations in citizen involvement (Smith 2009).

A feature of successful innovation in modern public services is a willingness to work across the boundaries of civil society, markets and the state. Figure 3.2 can, then, provide a starting point for fresh thinking. How can people in these three realms share ideas and experiences and co-create new solutions? Burns (2007) identified the value of adopting a systemic approach to achieving holistic change in complex social and organisational settings – sometimes described as whole system change. Bason (2010) reviews alternative approaches to the co-creation of public services and, in line with the ideas advocated by Burns, suggests attention should be given to the innovation ecosystem. Mulgan and Leadbeater (2013) extend this argument and suggest that systemic innovation is an important way forward for public service reform.

The co-creation of public services – a process that embraces co-governance, co-management and co-production – has important implications for place-based leadership. Leadbeater hints at the leadership agenda that is now opening up:

> In more open, emergent systems, with many players operating in more fluid environments, and where the task is to create solutions rather than repeat tasks, then successful leadership will be more like leading a community of volunteers, who cannot be instructed. Leadership is likely to be far more interactive and distributed rather than concentrated and instructional. (Leadbeater 2013, 50)

This idea of interactive leadership fits well with the idea of facilitative leadership that I introduced in Chapter 1. We will explore this idea, which I describe as **New Civic Leadership**, in more detail in Chapter 5 when we examine the changing nature of place-based leadership. The Innovation Stories documented in this book provide concrete evidence to support the argument not just that place matters, but that place-based leadership can make a difference – sometimes a big difference.

Conclusions

We started this chapter with a reminder of the origins of the modern welfare state. Back in the 19th Century, in developed countries, political activists working at the local level in the industrial cities, drove forward the idea of providing *entirely new* public services to meet collective needs. It was recognised that capitalist interests were focussed entirely on exploiting people, and a range of progressive social movements and left leaning politicians pressured governments to intervene. I have suggested that central governments are, frankly, not that good at inventing solutions. But they play an important role in learning from pioneering localities that are breaking new ground, and spreading ideas relating to public service innovations. This process of local invention coupled with national take up does much to explain why, in Britain at least, we now have public libraries, public schools, city museums, public parks, public transport, public health services and all the other welfare services we now enjoy. In developing countries the trajectory of the advance of public services is more complex but, again, there is strong evidence to support the view that the discovery of new ways of meeting the needs of society have stemmed from local pressures.

The chapter has examined the public service reform efforts of the last thirty years or so and it has been suggested that three competing drivers of reform have emerged – economic competition, political voice and self-improvement by public service professionals. The latter is important – public servants motivated to provide high quality services are to be found all over the world, and their caring commitment to public service should be celebrated. The analysis presented in this chapter suggests, however, that at root there are only two competing ways forward for radical public service reform.

On the one hand there is **New Public Management** (NPM). The underlying idea here is to import private sector management techniques into the public sector. Construct quasi-markets in the public sector and give consumers choice, get closer to the public service customer, latch onto the self-interested behaviour of individuals and households – these market-driven values are the guiding lights of NPM. The evidence suggests that this obsession with markets is not delivering the hoped-for results. Indeed, it is my suggestion that they are damaging the public service ethos in many countries and that this narrow, uninspiring agenda should be rejected.

Many citizens, politicians and public servants are aware of the limitations of the misguided NPM model. More than that, they are profoundly uncomfortable with the 'two-tier' services and divided societies such policies are creating. They reject this neo-liberal analysis of the way modern society should work. Rather than collapsing into being a market society – a competitive dog-eat-dog society of self-interested consumers acting with little or no consideration for others – many cities and countries are committed to advancing the public good and protecting the values that uphold the welfare state. This alternative strategy, one that captures a public-spirited sense of commitment, I describe as the **New Civic Leadership** (NCL).

Following Sandel (2012), this approach understands that self-interested behaviour crowds out more important values – solidarity, thoughtfulness, caring for others, and a commitment to community. More than that, it recognises that the pursuit of self-interest threatens the civic foundations of modern life – if societies continue to become more and more unequal it is inevitable that urban unrest will follow. The chapter has suggested that, notwithstanding the challenges, there is good reason to be optimistic. It has outlined the ideas that can underpin a new approach to progressive, place-based civic leadership – ideas that are drawn from some of the most innovative cities in the world. Key elements in **New Civic Leadership** are an understanding that government cannot go it alone, that local political leaders need to reach out to other stakeholders in civil society, that loyalty and a local sense of identity are invaluable resources, and that co-creation of public services can generate radical, new solutions. These themes will be explored and illustrated in the following chapters.

Part 2
Concepts: Place, leadership, innovation and democratic governance

CHAPTER 4

Understanding place and public policy

We shape cities, and they shape us
Jan Gehl, *Cities for People*, 2010

Introduction

A crucial argument of this book is that place should play a much more prominent role in public policy making. Place is, as I explained in Chapter 1, a neglected dimension in public policy – particularly at the national and state levels. This is because higher levels of government are disabled by departmentalism. They construct their public policies around functional domains – for example, the economy, education, health, social care, transport, agriculture, policing, energy and so on. Because departmental thinking is so deeply embedded in both the design of these government institutions and in the thought processes of the public servants they employ, political leaders are often not well served when it comes to comprehending the overall impact of public policy on particular places.

This is one of the reasons why local government is so important in modern societies. Locally elected leaders and their officials tend, on the whole, to have a more holistic understanding of the challenges particular communities are facing. For example, the socio-geographical intricacies of a city, or a neighbourhood, are more readily grasped than those of a vast territory. Also, in an important sense, local government politicians and their public servants are literally closer to the people they are there to serve. They possess tacit knowledge of what it is like to live in the place they govern.

True, city and county halls can also be victims of 'silo thinking' and have many imperfections. But, in my view, and I draw here on my experience of working in policy-making roles in both local and central governments, departmentalism tends to be more entrenched in the *modus operandi* of higher levels of government. This is partly because the realities of life at the street level are more distant. But it is also because the departmental culture generates particular 'ways of seeing' the world (Berger 1972). Questions and challenges tend to be framed in a departmental way and the gathering of evidence usually reflects departmental priorities and preferences.

A consequence is that the effectiveness of central government decision-making is impaired. As I noted in Chapter 1, Warren Magnusson discusses this phenomenon and suggests that national governments tend to 'see like a state', rather than 'see like a city'. His claim that policy makers should attempt to see like a city – an approach that involves '... positioning ourselves as inhabitants, not governors...'

(Magnusson 2010, 53) – is consistent with my argument that place-based policy-making should be strengthened.

But what do we mean by 'place'? And what, exactly, are the benefits that can flow from bolstering the power of place-based leaders in modern societies? In this chapter I will address these questions in a four-step fashion. First, I consider the question: What do we mean by place? Second, I outline the main arguments why it is useful for policy makers to pay more attention to place. Third, I examine some of the roles that place can play in public policy making. And, fourth, I sound a warning note about the privatisation of public space in the city.

It is helpful to illuminate the argument about the significance of place in public policy making by offering a concrete example. Later in the chapter I therefore present an Innovation Story, the first of many in the book, to illustrate the effectiveness of place-based leadership. This relates to the High Line, a now famous public space, located on a disused, elevated railway line on the west side of Manhattan in New York City. This success story demonstrates the extraordinary power and wisdom that a local sense of place and place-based activism can bring to public policy making.

What do we mean by place?

Human geographers, environmental psychologists, architects and planning theorists have advanced our understanding of place a good deal in the last forty years. Yi-Fu Tuan, in his influential book, *Space and Place*, provides a thoughtful examination of the ways in which people feel and think about space (Tuan 1977). He notes that space and place are basic components of the lived world; yet we tend to just take them for granted. These words are, for example, often used interchangeably without too much thought. His great insight is to show how, while the meaning of space can merge with place, they have rather different emotional roots. For him place is associated with security (consider, for example, the saying: 'There is no place like home'), while space has connotations of freedom (for example, the recognition that: 'We all need space to develop').[1]

Tuan argues not just that we are attached to the one and long for the other, but that the ideas of space and place require each other for definition:

> What begins as undifferentiated space becomes place as we get to know it better and endow it with value… From the security and stability of place we are aware of the openness, freedom and threat of space, and vice versa. (Tuan 1977, 6)

Tuan also shows how place exists at different scales:

> At one extreme a favourite armchair is a place, at the other extreme the whole earth. Homeland is an important type of place at the medium

> scale. It is a region (city or countryside) large enough to support a people's livelihood. (Tuan 1977, 161)

Tuan's presentation of how to understand place is highly respected. But, in the years since he wrote his classic text, place has become a rather contested concept in the broad field of spatial studies. Scholarly contributions – in geography, sociology, city planning, architecture, urban design, ecology and environmental psychology – continue to debate the meaning of place. Indeed, there is a vast literature, some of it highly theoretical, on the perception of place, the psychology of place, the sense of place and the design of place (Canter 1977; Gehl 2010; Massey 2005; Relph 1976).

In an early, influential contribution, one that questioned traditional conceptions of place, Manuel Castells outlined the contours of 'the informational city'. He claimed that we were witnessing 'the historical emergence of the space of flows, superseding the meaning of the space of places' (Castells 1989, 348). His analysis was prescient, particularly when one recognises that he was writing before the invention of the World Wide Web. In modern life the widespread use of the Internet means that information does, indeed, flow very rapidly through networks and across vast distances. It enables people to act across space in a way that was virtually unimaginable thirty years ago. But, in my view, Castells goes much too far when he claims that: 'The fundamental fact is that social meaning evaporates from places, and therefore from society…' (Castells 1989, 349).

Great power is, undoubtedly, exercised by those who control information flows in the modern world, but it is misguided to suggest that the growth of this 'network society' erases the meaning of place. On the contrary, it is my contention that, in a turbulent world of swirling information flows and concealed power relations, place-based social meaning, far from evaporating, becomes *more* significant and more sought after – and, in an ontological sense, more important. Social action to bring about progressive change can, of course, be creatively deployed across space. The Arab Spring, starting in 2010, is just one example of a current political struggle providing evidence to support the argument that citizens can use the Internet to assist people who may be very far away. And the Occupy Wall Street movement of 2011 provides another good example (Byrne 2012). But daily life – taking the kids to school, working on an allotment, attending a place of worship, getting to the local surgery and/or day centre and so on – is place-bound and, it should be said, place-strong. In other words, notwithstanding all the wonders of mobile phone technology and the like, much of life remains, *and will always remain*, stubbornly place-dependent. Thus, we can surmise that place, if nurtured, valued and connected to the power of other places, can become a source of resistance to the place-less 'space of flows'.

In making this argument I am not attempting to appeal to a romantic notion of a stable time when we all lived in peaceful places fixed in space – and where everyone felt 'at home'. This static conception of 'community' is a myth. There is no doubt that cities have always been places in flux – any given neighbourhood or locality is a social construct that is evolving (Cresswell 2004; Massey 2005). The old idea of a fixed conceptualisation of a place is long past its sell-by date. But it is, in my view, misguided to then suggest that place no longer matters as a source of identity and social commitment. The evidence presented in this book – and particularly the various Innovation Stories – suggests that place still matters a great deal to people and, more than that, it can provide a sound building block for social action.

Urban scholars and writers on planning and urban design recognise this well enough. Indeed, as we shall see, urbanists, planning theorists and urban designers have contributed many valuable insights on how to shape urban places so that they foster inclusiveness and conviviality (Healey 2010; Jacobs 1961; Shaftoe 2008). The Danish architect and urban designer, Jan Gehl, deserves special mention in this context. His perceptive understanding of the interplay between place and civil society is remarkable, and his work as a professional urban designer, some of it with his colleague Lars Gemzøe, has had a significant impact on many cities – including, cities as far apart as Copenhagen, Melbourne and San Francisco (Gehl 2010; Gehl and Gemzøe 2000). We will refer again to Gehl's work in Chapter 9.

A word of caution is needed. We should avoid over simplifying the argument about what place means. Place is a genuinely difficult concept to define, and Lineu Castello, a Brazilian urbanist, illustrates this point rather well in his extended analysis of the meaning of place (Castello 2010). I wish to draw two insights from his book. First, he makes it clear that it is not easy to define place: '… place is one of those concepts, like "passion", whose definition is damaged when put into words' (Castello 2010, xiv). It follows that we should be alert to the subtleties of how the word can be imbued with complex meaning. Second, and it is a closely related point, people lie at the heart of any sound conceptualisation of place: 'It is, after all, people who *make* places, frequent them and use them. It is they who make a space into a *place*' (Castello 2010, 231; author's emphasis).

This people-centred approach recognises that citizens often care a great deal about their surroundings and the enjoyment they get from them. It is hardly surprising, therefore, that lively public debates usually accompany proposals for urban redevelopment projects and/or major modern buildings in cities. The impact of these buildings on a given place – whether for good or ill – can stir great controversy, and often attract a high level of media and public interest. In this context it can be claimed that urban design is becoming more newsworthy and this should be welcomed. For example, Sir Richard Rogers, architect of the Pompidou Centre in Paris and the Lloyd's of London building, is now a famous public figure able to attract significant media attention when he contributes a public lecture on aspects of urban design (Rogers, Stirk and Harbours 2012).

For the purposes of this book I define place as: Somewhere somebody cares about. Following Tuan and Castello, I am suggesting that people imbue places with meaning, and places may often be associated with important feelings of identity. My definition is a broad one and it may be that it does not go very far in serving the needs of, for example, social geographers and environmental psychologists. But this loose definition has attractions that are consistent with the analysis presented by Tuan. It allows us, firstly, to conceive of places existing at many geographical levels; secondly, to encompass people's fleeting engagement with places as well as deep feelings of attachment and geographical rootedness; and thirdly, it recognises that people have multiple loyalties to many places. Most important, for the purposes of this book, it enables us to divide decision makers into two distinct categories: place-based leaders, who care about the place they are making decisions about, and place-less leaders who don't.

In Chapter 1 I explained how the growth of multi-national companies and the centralisation of power in very big, remote institutions means that some of the most influential figures in the modern world are, what I call, *place-less leaders*. Place-less leaders are unconcerned with the impact of their decisions on particular places. In contrast to place-based leaders these decision-makers care little or, possibly, not at all, about whether particular places prosper or collapse.

Why bother about place?

In the discussion below I offer five sets of reasons why place should be given more attention in public policy. These arguments are intertwined but it is useful to separate them out for the purposes of exposition.

- place-based identity
- environment, local loyalty and the quality of life
- enhancing governmental effectiveness
- places as building blocks for democracy
- the need to combat place-less power

These themes will be extended and developed in subsequent chapters. And the various Innovation Stories in this, and later, chapters provide solid evidence to fill out the picture.

Place-based identity

In their analysis of nine modern cities in four continents Bell and de-Shalit (2011) argue that each one has a distinctive ethos. The aim of their book, *The Spirit of Cities*, is to counter the claim that, in an age of globalisation, local social units no longer have any meaning – and that there is no local political will to oppose economic globalisation. They set out in rich detail why the identity of a city matters in a global age, suggest that urban pride is a seriously neglected topic, and put forward a word to help fill a gap in our vocabulary. Noting that patriotism, referring to national pride, serves nations states well enough, they advocate 'civicism' as a new word to convey how we feel about being a member of a city or a smaller community.

In the past city politicians and their professional staff have often failed to appreciate the importance of both the feelings people have for their home area and the social significance of neighbourhood life. Hence many cities experienced misguided approaches to urban planning and rebuilding in the second half of the 20th Century. For example, in Britain and the USA whole neighbourhoods were swept away in the name of urban renewal. Mindy Thompson Fullilove (2004), in *Root Shock*, provides a detailed account of the impact of urban renewal on African American communities. She shows how, when neighbourhoods are destroyed, residents suffer a traumatic shock to their sense of wellbeing. In many, but not all, cities awareness of the social significance of places has increased – in progressive cities approaches to urban regeneration are more sensitive and sophisticated than they were in the past. Those teaching degrees in city planning, architecture, and community development can claim to have influenced professional practice for the better.

Successful city leaders recognise that our attachment to neighbourhoods is created by personal experience, including events that happen there – from local community celebrations to major street festivals. Nicola Bacon notes correctly that effective urban policy works with the grain of these feelings of community identity:

> People's sense of belonging, resilience and connectedness to others affects their wellbeing and quality of life, their capacity to act individually and collectively, and a community's level of crime, health and educational achievement. (Bacon 2013)

The Innovation Stories presented later in this book provide many examples of city and community leaders generating collaborative advantage by working with local people, rather than for them. Many start from the premise that place-based identity matters. I will say a little more about local loyalty and quality of life in a moment.

Here, however, the general point I wish to draw out is that, in line with other studies, like the ones by Tuan (1977) and Castello (2010) mentioned earlier, places have significant meanings for people. Many people have a sense of attachment to their city and/or their 'home area', in some cases a strong sense of attachment, and it often forms part of their identity. A sense of attachment is often given cultural expression through sports clubs, social activities, community events, and it can underpin commitment to civic engagement – of which more in a moment. The mental maps of such imagined places will vary considerably between individuals, and it should also be recognised that these perceived localities are not fixed and bounded entities.

Economic, social and political changes mean that urban neighbourhoods are constantly being reshaped as the urban economy shifts and develops. People move in, people move out, and areas take on new meanings for different social groups. It is also important to emphasise that, as mentioned earlier, feelings of identity and attachment are not all geographically rooted. Social networks often cut across space and, in modern multicultural cities, many households have very strong economic and emotional links to friends and family in other countries and continents. Michel Laguerre (1999, 18), for example, explains how immigrants can, by maintaining ongoing relations with their homeland, create a transnational space:

> The politics of location does not define exclusively the politics of identity. Some minorities are now experiencing the social spaces of two nations simultaneously: they live here but maintain their active participation in homeland affairs.

The expansion of Internet-based social networking in recent years gives this argument added force because it can strengthen feelings of attachment and identity that transcend place. To argue that place has significant meaning for many people is, then, not to argue that other forms of attachment are unimportant.

In this discussion we should also note that place-based identity is not an untrammelled good – it can have a downside. As the geographer Harm de Blij (2009) argues, the confines of place can impose limits on human thought and action, and can lock communities into an unequal position. Even in wealthy metropolitan cities we can find neighbourhoods that, for a variety of reasons, have been largely excluded from the general rise in prosperity. These communities may come to feel culturally or economically trapped in a locality. Barry Quirk, in commenting on this trend, notes that the economic restructuring of a city or city region may foster an undesirable, sense of identity in some communities – one that looks inwards and backwards. He notes that in the West this narrowing of vision, often coupled with a fear of others '... can be found in poor white communities as much as in poor ethnic minority communities' (Quirk 2011, 108). This discussion will be familiar to those who work in community development. While the notion of 'community' has many plus points, it also has a dark side in that communities can be oppressive and exclusive (Taylor 2011).

In this context we should refer to 'gated communities'. In essence, these are residential areas designed in a way that permits their residents to exclude other people. By their very nature they work against the idea of creating an inclusive city. We will return, later in this chapter, to examine the growth of urban gating, and to consider the way public space is being privatised in too many cities.

Environment, local loyalty and the quality of life

A second set of arguments for giving more attention to place in public policy is that places have a direct impact on the quality of our lives. For example, as I explained in Chapter 1, we are all advantaged or disadvantaged by where we live. Place has impacts on the quality of life at many different levels – from the neighbourhood to the global scale (Smith et al 2007; De Blij 2009). It is an inescapable fact that people live in specific places and experience their home area 'in the round'. It follows that the quality of the local environment matters a great deal. In practice the quality of this environment, including access to services, often varies remarkably between neighbourhoods in any given city. For example, access to shops, markets, fresh food, libraries, schools, open space, surgeries, banks and other local services can vary considerably. This accessibility is significant for all households, but it is even more important for people who are, for one reason or another, not that mobile – for example, families with young children, people who are infirm or disabled, or poor families.

We need to add in, here, the neglected ecological dimension. In Chapter 1 I suggested that the individual, society and nature are inextricably linked – see Figure 1.1 – and that our relationship with the natural environment should be embedded in public policy making. In Chapter 3 I extended this discussion and noted that new kinds of relationship are developing between the state and civil society – for example, services are now provided via co-governance, co-management and co-production. The areas of overlap between civil society and the state are replete with possibilities for creative collaborations. Following Hirschman (1970), I suggested that loyalty is a precious asset that is not always appreciated by urban decision-makers. I refer to these arguments at this point because it is at the local level – in the neighbourhood or home area – that many of these collaborations occur. In other words, they are place-based. There is little doubt that the quality of life in an area can be enhanced if the loyalty, feelings and energies of local people can be conjoined with the activities of public agencies.

Rob Hopkins, founder of the Transition Movement, grasps the significance of this argument when it comes to tackling climate change. In *The Power of Just Doing Stuff*, (2013, 41) he notes correctly that 'most of us care deeply – not just about our families, but also about our community, the place we live, and the future our children will inherit. What we need are tools that help us to find a creative, active and empowering response'.

His book provides numerous examples of people taking local action to transform the places where they live and work. It is important to note that some of the most successful initiatives – for example, the *Totnes and District Local Economic Blueprint* – do not involve community activists 'going it alone'. Rather, they involve creative collaboration between the elected local authorities and enthusiastic community leaders bringing new energies to the table of local policy making and practice. In other words they flourish in the area of overlap between the state and civil society.

The Transition Movement builds on previous traditions of local, place-based action. For example, urban designers and city planners have attempted, over the years, to develop policies and practices that create sustainable communities, and these all depend on place-based analysis and action. In the UK context, Sir John Egan has provided useful national guidance on the skills needed to create sustainable communities – but his ideas will resonate in cities across the world (Egan 2004).

More broadly we can note that planning, architecture and urban design are, in their nature, place-based. These professions have advanced both knowledge and practice relating to the planning and design of urban neighbourhoods as well as cities as a whole. As a consequence, there is now a good deal of helpful advice on how to design not just for a post-carbon world, but also to promote healthy living by encouraging walking and cycling, and by providing ready access to open spaces, recreation facilities and parkland (Barton, Grant and Guise 2010; Boone and Modarres 2006; Condon 2010; Gehl 2010). In this context Mark Tewdwr-Jones (2011) is surely right to urge planners to pay much more attention to the meaning of place. In a far-sighted analysis of the future of architecture and the built environment in the UK, Sir Terry Farrell calls for a more united approach from the built environment professions (Farrell 2014). He argues that these professions should be guided by a common pursuit of place quality, and that 'place reviews' should be built into the ongoing public leadership of every locality.

Enhancing governmental effectiveness

The aims of bringing political power closer to the people, by strengthening local government, and of adjusting public policy more carefully to meet the needs of particular geographical areas within the local authority have had a longstanding appeal. In the introduction to this chapter I referred to the fact that higher levels of government are often plagued with problems of departmentalism. The tendency for national politicians to 'see like a state', rather than 'see like a city', creates serious obstacles to the process of designing and delivering effective public policy (Magnusson 2010).

Occasionally central governments appear to recognise that this is an unsatisfactory state of affairs, and then embark on place-based initiatives of various kinds. The history of government-driven 'area initiatives' is a long one. In the USA, for example, the Model Cities Programme, launched in 1966, was an important American initiative targeted on needy areas (Marris and Rein 1972). The idea was to develop new antipoverty programmes by involving citizens and municipalities in place-based action in various selected cities. Many US area-based experiments were to follow, including President Clinton's Empowerment Zones (launched in 1994), and President Obama's Health and Human Services (HSS) efforts to assist rural hospitals, clinics and clinicians (launched in 2012).

Meanwhile, UK central government has tried out a plethora of area initiatives over the years, from the Total Approach of 1972 through to more recent efforts, such as Total Place (launched in 2010) and Community Budgets (launched in 2011). Andrew Tallon (2013) provides a useful overview of UK Area Based Initiatives (ABIs). As discussed in Chapter 1, these efforts are, on the whole, sound in intent. This is because place-based analysis of government policies and spending patterns can uncover duplication of effort and, if handled in an imaginative way, a 'whole area' approach to public services has great promise (HM Treasury 2010). Resources can be redirected, new connections with civic partners can be made, and experiments can be tried out. However, area-based initiatives of this kind will only have a lasting impact if they succeed in making the transition from being seen as pioneering programmes – that is, as special arrangements of one kind or another – to being embedded in mainstream policy and practice. This means, in the UK context, shifting power and authority away from Whitehall to elected local authorities so that effective, holistic engagement with service users, families and communities can be advanced.

This takes us back to the important role that local government can play in modern societies. As discussed further in Chapter 7, elected local authorities are in a good position to develop effective place-based approaches to public policy and management. In Chapter 3 we saw how, in the UK, the creation of powerful, elected local authorities in the 19th Century enabled major advances to be made in tackling the social and economic challenges of the time. These place-based efforts not only resulted in major improvements in health and life chances for residents, they also fostered a high level of civic pride. In more recent times local authorities have continued to act as drivers of urban innovation. For example, in the 1970s, English local councils took the lead in developing place-based approaches to public involvement and problem solving.[2] In a recent contribution to the debate about education policy, Kathryn Riley (2013) looks at the role of place in schools and in the lives of young people today. She provides vivid accounts of how schools in the USA, UK and South Africa are using place-based approaches to help young people establish 'their place in the world', giving particular attention to the challenges facing rapidly changing inner city schools.

In the last thirty years or so local authorities have, as mentioned in Chapter 2, established themselves as world leaders in relation to tackling urban problems – see, for example, the reports from United Cities and Local Governments (UCLG 2008; 2010; 2011; 2014). This discussion of local government leadership leads us to our fourth argument for paying more attention to place in public policy.

Place as a building block for democracy

Places provide spatial units for the exercise of local democracy. Indeed, it can be argued that healthy national democracies depend, for their existence, on the political underpinning provided by vibrant local democracies. The longstanding and fundamental arguments for local government are highly relevant in this context. John Gyford offers an insightful discussion, focussed on the UK experience, of the relationships between place and local democracy and I draw on his ideas here (Gyford 1991). Developed in similar ways in many different countries, over a period of more than 150 years, local governments provide democratic building blocks for nation states and, ultimately, for international democratic institutions.

Gerhard Banner (1996), an experienced German city manager, summarises three of the main arguments for local government rather well when he suggests that the purpose of local government is to organise the common good at the local level with regard to three critical matters: democracy, community and services. First, as already mentioned, local government underpins democracy – it supports political pluralism and contributes to political education, as it acts as a school in which democratic habits are acquired and practised. Second, it can facilitate the growth of self-organising capacity in local communities. Local government can support and encourage a variety of forms of civic engagement, and experiments in co-governance are now on the rise. Third, it can improve the responsiveness of service providers to the diverse needs and requirements of different communities, an argument that gathers additional weight in complex multicultural cities.

A fourth important argument for local government is that it promotes social innovation. Having a diversity of geographical power centres in a country adds to the innovative capacity of that country's governance. This is because different areas have the political legitimacy to try out different approaches and learn from experience.

The notion of place is embedded in all these arguments for local government. Place injects meaning into both representative democracy and participatory democracy. Take representative democracy first. It usually involves the election of politicians on a geographical basis. While electoral systems vary across countries, from 'first-past-the-post' systems to various systems of proportional representation, the idea that elected figures are held to account by citizens living in particular territories is widely accepted as a sensible way of organising representative democracy. This electoral accountability might be to the city as a whole as with, for example, a directly elected city mayor. Or it might involve accountability to a relative small area in the city. For example, in many countries local politicians are elected on a ward, or district, basis.

Second, place also provides a basis for numerous kinds of participatory democracy. Local authorities across the world have been inventive in developing new approaches to citizen involvement, and many of these efforts are, not surprisingly, place-based (Cornwall 2008; Fung 2004; Oliver and Pitt 2013; Smith 2009). We will examine these ventures further when we discuss democratic urban governance in Chapter 7.

The need to combat place-less power

Earlier I suggested that place-less decision makers have gained too much power in modern society. Here I provide a short account of what has happened to a chocolate factory in Keynsham, a small town near where I live in Bristol, to illustrate my argument. In 1824 John Cadbury, a Quaker, began selling drinking chocolate in Birmingham, England. Cadbury developed the chocolate business with his brother Benjamin and it was very successful. His son, George, is famous for building a model village, Bournville, near Birmingham, in the 1890s to provide factory workers with good housing and living conditions.

In the 20th Century Cadbury's Dairy Milk Bar was particularly popular, and Cadbury became the most famous chocolate brand in the UK. The company expanded rapidly and merged with J.S. Fry and Sons, a Bristol based chocolate manufacturer famous for making the world's first chocolate bar in 1847. To improve production a state of the art chocolate factory, called Somerdale, was built on the edge of Keynsham, in the 1930s. In its heyday, the factory workforce was over 5,000. Consistent with Quaker values the factory included good social facilities and extensive sports grounds.

In September 2009 Kraft Foods, a major American company, made a £10.2 billion takeover bid for Cadbury which was rejected. However, Kraft Foods were not to be deflected. Importantly, in their continuing negotiations to buy Cadbury, Kraft Foods stated clearly that they would retain the Somerdale Factory. In 2007 Cadbury had indicated that it planned to close the factory and move production to Poland and a campaign to stop this happening was in full swing. Workers at the factory, and the residents of Keynsham, welcomed the pledge from Kraft Foods. In February 2010 Kraft Foods purchased Cadbury for £11.5 billion.

The Chairman of Cadbury, Roger Carr, and the Chief Executive, Todd Stitzer, having arranged for truly enormous personal financial gains (£12 million in the case of Mr Stitzer), via share sales arising from the sell-off to Kraft Foods, resigned. Within days of acquiring Cadbury, Kraft Foods announced, on 9 February 2010, that they intended, after all, to close the Somerdale Factory, with the loss of 400 jobs. Amoree Radford, who campaigned to keep Somerdale open, said to the BBC (14 January 2011) that she had no reason to believe Kraft Foods would go back on its commitment: 'I believed them and the employees believed them. The plant is very productive. It is very profitable. Kraft said they wanted to expand it and wanted to be environmentally friendly. So, of course, we believed them – who wouldn't?'

Here then is a classic example of the exercise of place-less power. Irene Rosenfeld, Chairman of Kraft, and her senior executives in Kraft Foods, renamed in 2012 as Mondelez International, work in offices in Northfield, a suburb to the north of Chicago. From their vantage point in Illinois they decided to close a productive factory and do untold damage to a small town in another country 5,000 miles away. They did this, not because the factory was failing, but because the lower labour costs in Poland would enable them, they believed, to make even more money than they were already making. Unite, the union representing the factory workers, were able to show that, during this period, the profit margins of Cadburys UK were over 12%. From a place-based perspective, from the point of view of the people depending on the factory for a living, this decision makes no sense at all.

But it is worse than that. Subsequent increases in raw material costs, disproportionate growth in the pay of Polish workers, plus rapidly increasing fuel costs – 16 to 18 LGV (Large Goods Vehicle) lorry loads of chocolate per day are now shipped back to the UK from Poland – mean that the move of production to Poland was not only ecologically thoughtless but, also, of doubtful wisdom, even in a narrow economic sense. Sad to say, the experience of the workers in the Somerdale Factory is not that unusual. The capitalist economy, with its ceaseless pursuit of maximum profits, regardless of other values, is bound to lead to what David Ranney calls, in his perspicacious analysis of industrial closures in Chicago, 'global decisions' resulting in 'local collisions' (Ranney 2003).

The critique of place-less power I am offering here is consistent with the argument put forward by Sandel (2012). He suggests that the obsession with market driven models of decision-making crowds out other important values. Place-less decision makers in, for example, multi-national companies, decide whether or not to invest in particular places, and/or to withdraw investment from particular places, on the basis of narrow calculations of potential profit and loss. Such an approach pays no attention to local history, identity, solidarity, or the feelings of local communities. Even more startling, distant decision makers often fail to make sound economic decisions as measured by their own narrow metrics.[3] This is because their knowledge and understanding of the local economy is often poor or non-existent.

Having summarised the main reasons why place matters we now turn to consider the ways in which place is being incorporated into public policy.

Place in public policy

It would be wrong to imply that place has not featured in public policy making in the past. Indeed, a key theme of this book is to highlight the remarkable success of place-based approaches in a variety of countries, and to draw attention to the important *leadership lessons* that can be drawn from these positive experiences. There are, perhaps, three main ways in which place arises in current public policy discourse: place making, place marketing and place shaping. These phrases may seem unfamiliar to some readers – they certainly have more currency in some countries than in others. My purpose here is not to create a typology of different approaches to place-based leadership, still less claim the existence of watertight categories. Rather my aim is to offer a short introduction to three main themes relating to place in modern public policy. Two of them display wisdom; one is questionable.

Place making

First, the art of place making is clearly well established. Indeed, it has been central to the practice of city planning and urban design for centuries, and it is possible to argue that the art of place making is as old as cities themselves (Duany et al 2003; Hall 1988; Girouard 1985; Sepe 2013). Place making refers, then, to the planning, design and construction of places – it lies at the heart of most professional courses in city planning, architecture and urban design. We have already referred to the ongoing, and lively, debates within urban theory relating to what constitutes a sense of place, and we have touched upon the theme of urban quality. There are several strands to place making and four influential approaches should be mentioned.

Our starting point is the classical view of urban place making which emphasises physicality – the design of public space, gateways, vistas, landmarks, squares, elevations and so on (Cullen 1961). The focus here is on the three dimensional design of the urban form. A second approach, pioneered by Lynch (1960, 1981), emphasises the 'imageability', or legibility, of the city. Lynch and others highlight the importance of city planning in helping to create mental maps, which people can use to guide their movements around the city.

Third, Jane Jacobs, in her classic book *The Death and Life of Great American Cities*, stressed that urban places depend for their success on public activity (Jacobs 1961). Jacobs, and the many urban designers she has inspired, emphasises street life, a rich juxtaposition of land uses, permeability of the urban form, a mixture of building types and intense use of public space. An important off shoot of this approach is urban time planning and the encouragement of the evening, or 24 hour, economy (Montgomery 2007). A fourth approach, one that draws on all the others, can be described as sustainable urban design. I use this phrase here as a banner for all those, qualified professionals or not, who pay attention to the role of nature in the urban setting, to the implications of climate change for place making and who are committed to the creation of child-friendly, healthy urban places (Academy of Urbanism 2011; Barton et al 2010; Girardet 2008; Gehl and Gemzøe 2000; Sepe 2013; Shaftoe 2008; Williams et al 2000).

In Chapters 8 and 9 we will return to discuss the role of planning and urban design in modern place making, and we will provide examples of place-based leadership that have led to high quality urban places – in, for example, Freiburg, Germany and Copenhagen, Denmark.

Place marketing

We now turn to a second strand in the debate about place and public policy – place marketing. This approach emerged in a significant way in the late 19th Century, in parallel with the emergence of product marketing in the expanding industrial economies. The idea of selling a place was very much an American invention. The early development of Los Angeles provides a classic example of place marketing – one that generated massive profits for the owners of real estate in what was to become a city. In his forensic analysis of 'real estate capitalism' Davis (1990) shows how the 'place' of Los Angeles was invented, marketed and sold to pioneers. Hollywood and California remain as world leaders in the business of selling dreams.

Stated simply, place marketing involves generating an image or proposition – sometimes described by those involved in city branding as a 'Unique Selling Point' (USP) – about a place, and then striving to project this image through the media, promotional campaigns and a variety of publicity materials, as in the marketing of a product or business. In Chapter 2 I discussed the global pressures that are spurring cities to compete with each other. A consequence is that urban investment in place marketing has spiralled in recent years. Indeed, there is now a major international industry devoted to place marketing, or city branding, as some prefer to call it (Anholt 2010; Dinnie 2011; Zavattaro 2013).[4] Shortly I will explore whether we may be able to make a distinction between place 'marketing' and place 'branding'. For a moment, however, let's treat them as a single perspective on urban politics and city leadership. Place marketing, or branding, stems from the world of commerce, often draws on techniques developed in the tourism industry, and is used not just to market the attractions of particular cities, but also to promote particular quarters or areas within a given city.

A problem with place marketing, as with product marketing, is that the advertising can become misleading. The urge to sell can result in a distortion of the truth. For example, Allan Cochrane (Cochrane, 2007, 112) notes that, 'The emphasis of place marketing is increasingly on redefining – or reimagining – each individual city in ways that fit with dominant perceptions of success'.

The key phrase here is 'dominant perceptions'. What are these dominant perceptions? Where do they come from? Whose interests are served by allowing them to influence public spending? And who is paying for all this? Claire Colomb, in a thoughtful analysis of the politics of place marketing in Berlin, shows how the city branding firms, in the period since 1994, have created a series of discourses that legitimise pro-business, political and economic choices (Colomb 2012). Like place marketing in many other cities, the search for competitive economic advantage by Berlin's city leaders has involved numerous attempts to appropriate local cultures. This, not surprisingly, has met resistance as local communities, artists and activists reject the imposition of simplistic messages – like Berlin's 'Poor, but sexy' slogan – on the places where they live and work. Opposition parties in Berlin have noted that, in the context of a city with a significant debt, these efforts at image making are an unnecessary waste of money. And, of course, radicals have subverted the various messages. Nevertheless the commodification of the city continues and this is troubling.

In Chapter 1, following Sandel (2012), I argued that the current obsession with market values is crowding out more important values. The city branding industry provides abundant evidence to support Sandel's argument that, without a serious debate about the role and reach of markets, we are drifting from having a market economy to being a market society. Cochrane (2007), for example, shows that place branding is not limited to selling the city to outsiders. The infatuation with selling now means that city branding messages are often played back to the residents of the cities themselves. These superficial efforts to promote city pride usually involve a dumbing down of place-based meanings and community identities.

The growth of this idea that places can be 'sold' is, in my view, disturbing and I wish to raise a few doubts about it. Civic leaders who strive to create an inclusive city would be wise to consider four critical questions relating to place marketing. A first question: Is this a good use of our limited resources? Any expenditure on promoting the city represents expenditure that could be spent on other objectives. It follows that city leaders need to ask the question: Why, *exactly*, are we doing this? The marketers need to present a convincing intellectual case setting out, with precision, why treating the city as a commodity is a great idea for all those who live in the city and, as part of this, they need to specify who, within the city, they expect to benefit. Annual monitoring of whether said benefits actually accrue to those identified beneficiaries would add rigour.

Second, and I recognise this is a more subjective dimension, I want to ask: Does it feel right to market the place we live in as if it were a commodity? This speaks to the argument, developed at length by Sandel (2012), who suggests that some goods in life are corrupted or degraded if turned into commodities. It follows that asking: 'Do we really want to sell or market our place?' is a legitimate question that needs to be answered. The literature on place marketing and city branding is largely silent on this fundamental philosophical point. Two American sociologists provide an interesting chapter on 'Places as commodities' and note that 'Places have a certain *preciousness* for their users that is not part of the conventional concept of a commodity' (Logan and Molotch 1987, 17, authors' emphasis). This sentiment cannot and should not be bought and sold.

Third, the propagation of a favourable image necessitates, in many instances at least, a process that, in itself, drives social exclusion. This is because the audiences for place marketing are, on the whole, relatively wealthy. For example, attracting the international tourist is usually seen as requiring spending on city centre amenities, not neighbourhoods in need. But it is even more troubling than that. The city branding firms are busy trying to appropriate and sanitise social histories. A colourful past can, it seems, be marketed to visitors in a way that disregards alternative interpretations of urban history. Not surprisingly, this can cause offence to the communities portrayed in sanitised, tourism-oriented social histories.

Fourth, and I draw here on a conversation with the mayor of a global city who does not want to be identified. In an interview about place marketing the mayor in question, who was clearly not in favour of city branding at all, asked me: 'Do you buy a book because it has been marketed well, or do you buy a book because it is good literature?' This mayor believes that word-of-mouth stories about what the city is really like are what matters. He is very proud of his city, indeed his passion for the city is boundless, but he wants understanding about it to be communicated through direct experience and authentic stories – not by marketing or branding. Nonetheless, even this powerful mayor felt it was difficult to opt out of place marketing altogether.

Here, then, are some challenges for those involved in place marketing and city branding. Some cities are well aware of these issues and are developing approaches that attempt go 'beyond branding'. For example, the City of Tacoma, Washington is working with residents to articulate a vision for the city that is rooted in the history and assets of the city. On the upside it is just possible that that innovative approaches to city branding, those that give visibility to the multiple strands of place-based identity, could have a constructive role in creating the inclusive city. However, against the grain of conventional wisdom, I am suggesting that current approaches to place marketing and city branding need to be questioned.

Place shaping and city development strategies

Having sounded some warning notes about place marketing I now turn to an important topic for civic leaders: place shaping and city development strategies.

In contrast to place marketing this is an area where investing effort really pays off, and several of the Innovation Stories presented later in the book provide compelling evidence to support this claim – from Copenhagen, Denmark to Curitiba, Brazil. There is, perhaps, a degree of confusion over what place shaping means and what city development strategies involve. I now seek to clarify these terms, while recognising that usage in different countries and contexts varies.

The idea of place-shaping, a concept that is much broader than place making, gained currency in the UK context when Sir Michael Lyons, at the request of the Labour Government, prepared a far reaching report on the future role, function and funding of local government (Lyons Inquiry 2007). In his report, which was titled *Place-shaping: A Shared Ambition for the Future of Local Government*, Sir Michael suggested place-shaping should be seen as the key role for elected local authorities. 'Throughout my work, I have promoted a wider, strategic role for local government, which I have termed 'place shaping' – the creative use of powers and influence to promote the general well-being of a community and its citizens' (Lyons Inquiry 2007, 3).

In practice Sir Michael was trying to combat the extreme centralisation of the British state that I referred to in Chapter 1. He was striving to enlarge the political role of UK local authorities and, in particular, to shift power from the central state to the localities across the country. Despite the soundness of his analysis the then-Labour Government was deaf to his arguments. His recommended shift in power did not take place. But, on the plus side, the report did stimulate fresh thinking about the wider purposes of elected local government. In this book I am using place shaping in the way Sir Michael intended. My definition of place shaping is: Elected local authorities adopting a strategic role to shape the places they govern in order to promote the well-being of all the people who live there. Hopefully this notion resonates internationally.

I highlight two points about this definition of place shaping. First, it is very different from traditional definitions of local government. The traditional view of local authorities is that they are seen as organisations that can play an important role in the 'administration' of a range of local public services. Place shaping envisages a far more outgoing and proactive role for local government. Local civic leaders do not 'administer' public services, they set agendas and strive to improve the local quality of life. Second, place shaping is concerned with much more than the planning and design of the built form and its relationships with nature. As the discussion of place making set out above makes clear, these are vital components of successful civic leadership. But place shaping is more strategic and broader than place making. It includes many activities that do not impact the physical environment at all, and it is concerned with the overall efforts of place-based leaders to shape the quality of life in their locality.

How do city development strategies fit into this discussion? Well-prepared strategies for urban development are invaluable in assisting local political leaders enhance their place shaping performance. At this point, it may be helpful to step back and say a few words about the changing nature of city and regional planning.

This is a big subject, and it is also clear that experience varies internationally. However, we can, perhaps, make a helpful generalisation. City and regional planning, or urban planning if you prefer, is a political and a technical process concerned with the use of land and the creation of sustainable cities. But it has changed its stripes.[5]

Over a period of thirty to forty years, urban planning has shifted from a focus on 'land use planning' to a concern for 'spatial planning'. Non-specialists can be forgiven for thinking that these phrases mean one and the same thing. But, in the world of planning practice, they signal rather different concepts. In simple terms the ethos of planning, in many countries at least, has shifted from the preparation of plans designed to control the pattern of urban development, to a more proactive process in which planners seek to bring about particular kinds of development (Morphet 2010).

Traditional land use planning centres on the preparation of a visual, or diagrammatic, presentation of future developments. Sometimes described as master plans, at others development plans, the intention is to map the location of future infrastructure and, as often as not, to designate zones for particular kinds of activity. Attention centres on the regulation of urban development. Who might propose and implement the developments is neglected in this approach. Rather the role of planning is seen as *controlling* what developers do, whether they are private or public, to achieve public purpose.

Spatial planning is rather different. It focuses on the process of *coordinating and integrating* the actions of different agencies and actors in a locality in order to achieve political objectives. As Yvonne Rydin argues: 'Spatial planning not only emphasises stakeholder engagement but also is based on the idea of integrating policies across different tiers of government and different policy sectors through such engagement' (Rydin 2011, 25). There are, of course, many ways of approaching spatial planning. Some focus sharply on the promotion of economic growth, while others seek prosperity without economic growth (Jackson 2009; Rydin 2013). Yet others focus on advancing the cause of equity in the modern city (Krumholz and Forester 1990).

City development strategies involve application of the spatial planning approach I have just described. Viewed internationally we can see that cities are becoming increasingly active in preparing robust city development strategies. The international network of cities and local governments (UCLG) has promoted a creative process of city-to-city learning in relation to urban strategic planning that has been very productive. In a policy paper, that presents a helpful analysis of 21st Century city development strategies, UCLG provides a global overview of experience:

> City Development Strategies (CDS) have evolved in the last decade as a tool to address new challenges and to provide a space for innovative policies which actively involve all stakeholders. Besides socio-economic

> and spatial development, it is increasingly relevant to address poverty reduction and climate change. (UCLG 2010, 10)

This UCLG study provides a useful definition of urban strategic planning, identifies the challenges facing urban leaders, offers an analysis of the strengths and weaknesses of alternative approaches to urban strategic planning, and identifies a number of sensible recommendations. The study includes extensive analysis of practice in different continents, and it is a valuable resource for all those wishing to strengthen the role of planning in supporting place-based, civic leadership.

The power of place-based action

In this book I present a selection of inspiring Innovation Stories designed to illustrate the effectiveness of place-based leadership in action. I have chosen the High Line, New York City – a public park 'in the sky' – as the first Innovation Story because it helps to set the political tone for the arguments about place-based leadership that will follow. First, the High Line is a remarkable story of fine civic leadership that advances our understanding of how to create an inclusive city – of how to expand public space in the city, even against the odds. Second, and this may be surprising, it is not a story about top civic leaders, powerful figures with all the right connections, setting the agenda and making things happen in a city. On the contrary the most senior politician in New York City – then Mayor, Rudy Giuliani – thought the idea was a loser and rejected it. This, then, is a story about *grassroots civic leadership*, about two young men who, with no background in city planning or urban design, saw the exciting potential of a disused, elevated railway line – a structure that the powerful in the city wanted to see demolished.

In Chapter 1 I explained what an Innovation Story is. Here, I offer a brief recap. An Innovation Story, as I define it, is a short, factual account of an example of bold, place-based leadership. All the Innovation Stories in this book follow a structured format:

- aims and objectives
- outline of the Innovation Story
- leadership lessons
- further sources

A key feature is that each story attempts to identify leadership lessons. I invite you to read Innovation Story 1 as it provides an inspiring example of what place-based leadership can achieve. It shows that local activists possessed not only superior place-based knowledge, but also passionate feelings about what the future should be for 'their' place in the city. As we shall see powerful figures in City Hall were able to learn from the activists and, to their credit, change their approach.

Formal city leaders became active partners in a remarkable success story. So this first Innovation Story, as well as demonstrating the power of grassroots initiative, provides an excellent example of politicians and professionals learning how to see things a different way.

INNOVATION STORY 1

Grassroots leadership: the creation of New York City's High Line Park

Aims

On the west side of New York City an abandoned stretch of elevated railway line has been transformed into the High Line, an extraordinary public park running above the streets. Arguably one of the most innovative city parks in the world, the High Line provides an unexpected oasis of green, car-free space in the heart of Manhattan. Dubbed a 'park in the sky' it is now enjoyed by local residents, workers in the city and large numbers of visitors. The story of the High Line is one of community-based vision and tireless political advocacy to find a creative public use for an obsolete piece of industrial infrastructure.

Friends of the High Line (FHL), founded in 1999 by two local residents, Joshua David and Robert Hammond, is the reason why the park exists today. Against the odds, and in the face of a strong property lobby that had persuaded the city government to demolish the elevated track, FHL and its supporters have succeeded in creating a 1¾ mile linear public park.

This Innovation Story provides a short account of how FHL went about achieving their goal of transforming the rail track into a public space capable of accommodating large numbers of visitors and a variety of public and commercial activities, whilst embodying its industrial past and wildness following more than twenty years of abandonment. It is an account of tenacious community leadership resulting in the creation of much needed public space in one of the world's busiest cities.

Innovation Story outline

Between 1934 and 1960 the High Line operated as a railway for freight trains carrying meat, agricultural goods and post to the warehouses and factories of New York City's west side. The elevated track was built to remove dangerous freight traffic from the street level. In the 1950's however, the rise of the interstate highway network heralded the demise of the transportation of goods by rail. Declining use combined with an urban renewal project led, in 1963, to the demolition of the lower section of the line, and finally, in 1980, the last freight train rolled along the remainder of the elevated track.

Following its closure, the future of the High Line was disputed. An early local advocate for the line's preservation was the West Side Rail Line Development Foundation. In 1984 the community group succeeded in purchasing the High Line for a mere $10, a decision that was overturned three years later, following the efforts of a group of property owners with interests in the land beneath the High Line. The latter became the influential Chelsea Property Owners (CPO) alliance. Their goal was to demolish the remainder of the elevated track. They argued vigorously that the disused High Line was an eyesore hindering neighbourhood revitalisation, attracting anti-social activities and was a safety hazard to underlying property and the public.

The property owners received strong support from the city authorities. Mayor Rudy Giuliani agreed with their view that the dilapidated High Line was standing in the way of local economic development, and he signed a demolition order in December 2001 shortly before leaving office. This decision is critical to understanding this Innovation Story. City Hall was against a creative redesign of the High Line. It was community leaders – place-based activists not employed by the state – that provided the vision and energy to drive the initiative forward. In this instance the vigour and commitment came from members of the gay community. As David and Hammond explain:

> Josh and I are gay, and a lot of our friends are gay, so a disproportionate number of our early supporters were gay men. Not just because of Josh and me, but also because the High Line runs through two famously gay neighbourhoods, Chelsea and West Village.[1]

In 1999 the owners of the elevated rail line – CSX Transportation – commissioned a study on future options for the track. This recommended light rail use and a greenway. In the same year, at a public meeting to consider these recommendations, locals David and Hammond met, and in the absence of any other preservation lobby, co-founded FHL as a not-for-profit organisation with a mission to preserve the High Line and to reuse it as a public open space.

In the face of the powerful demolition lobby the idea of reinventing the tracks as a new kind of public space seemed a hopeless fantasy. Yet the work of FHL gained momentum as local residents, art and fashion celebrities, architects and designers, civic organisations, and some businesses began to share David and Hammond's belief that reuse of the line as a park was possible. Evocative photographs, taken during 2000/01 by respected photographer Joel Sternfeld, brought the High Line debate to national attention. His inspiring images highlighted in *The New Yorker* and later to become an art gallery exhibit and book *Walking the High Line*, revealed a mysterious, almost magical, wild space in the heart of the city. In 2001 Adam Gopnik wrote that: 'The most peaceful high place in New York right now is a stretch of viaduct called the High Line.'[2]

The two co-founders and their fellow activists worked tirelessly to secure support from a number of influential politicians and agencies. In time, FHL gained support from: Christine Quinn, the local councillor and, later, Speaker of New York City Council; State representatives; City Planning officials, such as City Planning Commissioner Amanda

Burden; and, most decisively, the new mayor of New York – Mayor Bloomberg. On 11 September 2001 the terrorist attacks on the World Trade Centre in New York City had a profound impact not just on US foreign policy but also on the feelings of all New Yorkers. Some wondered if it was safe to continue to live in the city. David and Hammond were shaken by the events and took a while to work out how to react, but they developed a persuasive argument:

> We said we were committed to the future of New York City, this was a future-oriented project, and this was not the time to be tearing things down... The demolition of the High Line was going to be very destructive... People were not up for anything that disruptive[3]

An early, and critical, step was taken by Mayor Bloomberg when he reversed the previous mayor's demolition order, and from 2002 onwards, the City of New York made High Line preservation and reuse city policy.

The High Line story is one of legal complexity involving rail track owners, the owners of adjoining property, the State and City of New York and not for profit organisations. Rezoning to allow for residential use and provisions to enable underlying property owners to transfer their development rights to neighbouring landowners – involving density transfers – proved critical to securing public funding for the park's development.

In 2005, CSX Transportation donated the majority of the High Line to the City of New York, and CSX, the City and the State entered into an agreement that secured the preservation of the High Line as a trail – an official designation forming part of the national 'Rails to Trails' initiative. This, in turn, made possible the reinvention of the High Line as a public park. Work on the park began in 2006 and the first, southernmost, section (below 20th Street) opened in 2009, followed two years later by the second section (from 20th to 30th Street). The park is wheelchair accessible and has elevators at a number of its access points. Title to the third and final section (30th to 34th Street) of the elevated track was handed over by CSX to the City of New York in 2012 and is due to open sometime in 2014.

Whilst the City of New York funded much of the capital costs of the first two sections of the park, FHL is funding the majority of the final section through a major capital campaign. Philanthropic and private donations have been significant. The City of New York entered into an agreement with FHL making FHL responsible for day-to-day park maintenance and operations, and FHL is responsible for funding more than 90% of these on-going costs.

Community involvement has been a central feature of FHL's activities. Throughout the design process, FHL, in conjunction with the design team of James Corner Field Operations, Diller Scofidio + Renfro, and landscape designer Piet Oudolf, held a series of Community Input sessions to present, review and refine the design plans. The result is a very high standard of urban design. FHL makes much use of new social media to keep the community involved in the project, and continues to engage with its longstanding group of donors and volunteers with special programs like the High Line Council and volunteer activities.

Visitor numbers to the park are significant. In 2012 over 4 million people visited, many engaging in the park's programme of free and low-costs events, educational initiatives, and members-only events geared specifically towards New Yorkers. Roughly half the visitors are locals. Whilst the High Line's achievements are celebrated and the knock on benefits for surrounding businesses welcomed, some local residents are expressing concerns that the park's success, combined with rezoning to allow new residential development, is leading to gentrification of adjoining neighbourhoods. Mindful of these concerns, FHL is working to fulfil its original aims of achieving a park that is a special place for all New Yorkers.

Leadership lessons

- Local residents can take on enormously powerful vested interests and win. The community-based organising of Friends of the High Line (FHL) provides an inspiring and successful example of passionate place-based leadership by community activists
- The co-founders of FHL recognised the importance of securing a broad coalition of interests spanning, community, business, political, cultural and technical actors to advance the goal of creating a new kind of city public open space
- Initially the city authorities failed to recognise the potential of the High Line and decided to demolish it. However, and to their lasting credit, they changed their position. Mayor Bloomberg demonstrated wise leadership in this context – he decided that the city authorities should drop their opposition to a redesign of the High Line and City Hall became enthusiastic backers of the project
- FHL demonstrated great imagination in sharing and promoting the vision of a 'park in the sky'. Artists, designers, landscape architects, botanists, photographers, film makers and many others have played an active part in galvanising support
- Professional planners, lawyers and real estate experts played a critical leadership role in coming up with solutions to significant technical obstacles relating to development rights and public responsibilities
- Leaders of radical change need to have emotional resilience in order to hold onto their vision. As Joshua David and Robert Hammond, Co-Founders of FHL, make clear: 'The key to starting anything is being comfortable with lots of rejection'[4]

Sources

David, J, 2002 *Reclaiming the High Line*, New York: Design Trust for Public Space

David, J, Hammond R, 2011, *High Line: The inside story of New York's city in the sky*, New York: Farrar Straus Giroux

Gopnik, A, 2001, A walk on the High Line, *New York Journal* 21 May, 44

Sternfeld, J, 2009, *Walking the High Line*, 3rd edn, Gottingen, Germany: Steidl

Friends of the High Line: www.thehighline.org/
City of New York Parks and Recreation: www.nycgovparks.org/

Endnotes

[1] David and Hammond 2011, 35
[2] Gopnik 2001
[3] David and Hammond 2011, 39
[4] David and Hammond 2011, 21

Gated communities and the city of fear

The High Line provides a good example of a successful effort to expand public space in the city. Unfortunately, for those who are striving to build inclusive cities, there are some strong counter currents. Powerful economic forces are working to reduce public space in the city. One of the most troubling trends in modern urban development is the growth of gated communities. The literature on the 'gating' of the modern city is expanding rapidly (Atkinson and Blandy 2006; Davis 1990; Glasze et al 2006; Low 2003). Ed Blakely (2007, 475), who has studied gated communities for more than twenty years, provides a discerning definition, and we will use this as our starting point. In his view gated communities are 'residential areas with restricted access, such that spaces normally considered public have been privatised. Physical barriers – walled or fenced perimeters – and gated or guarded entrances control access'.

Note the key elements – privatisation of public space, restrictions on who can enter, and physical barriers to prevent unauthorised access. It follows that gated communities are, *by definition*, exclusionary. They are designed to exclude unwanted people. As we shall see, in the discussion of privatising the city that follows, these three building blocks of the gating of the city – privatisation, new controls on people and physical design to enforce exclusion – arise in commercial as well residential urban development. First we consider residential areas.

Gated housing areas

Mike Davis was one of the first writers to recognise the threat that gated communities pose for the inclusive city. His prize-winning book on Los Angeles, *City of Quartz*, includes a chapter on 'Fortress LA' in which he records the insidious growth of walled off communities. Never short of a vivid turn of phrase, he describes a 'frenzied... residential arms race as ordinary suburbanites demand the kind of social insulation once enjoyed only by the rich' (Davis 1990, 246). In his prescient analysis he draws attention not just to the privatisation of public space in and around the city, but also to the growth of private security firms and state-of-the-art electronic surveillance. Evan McKenzie (1994) was also ahead of his time in highlighting the growth of 'private government'.[6]

As predicted by Davis, more recent years have seen the emergence of, what Stephen Graham (2010) describes as, the new military urbanism. From this militaristic perspective 'mixed up' cities, bringing together a rich diversity of people, are seen as bad news. They are perceived as:

> ... problematic spaces, beyond the rural or exurban heartlands of authentic national communities... The construction of sectarian enclaves modelled on Israeli practice by US forces in Baghdad from 2003, for example, was widely described by US security personnel as the development of US-style "gated communities" in the country (Graham 2011, 124).

Military urban designers strive, therefore, to construct enclaves, or colonised zones, that can be defended against external threat. This approach may well be required in a war torn country. The problem, as Graham explains, is that insidious militarism is permeating the fabric of cities and urban life across the world, including in cities where it makes no sense at all. Thus, the number of gated communities in cities worldwide is growing at a formidable rate (Glasze et al 2006; Bagaeen and Uduku 2010). Designers of gated communities may assert that they are aiming to create place-based identity for their residents, but this flimsy claim attempts to mask the fact that they are actively destroying the inclusive city.

The reasons why people choose to live in fortified enclaves of this kind are complex, but a recent, international comparative study suggests that the main driver is a perceived need for security (Bagaeen and Uduku 2010). Many residents of gated communities appear to believe that, by living behind a barrier that separates them from 'others', they will make their lives safer. Fear is not the only motive. For example, some people purchase, or rent, houses in gated communities out of a desire for social exclusivity. Joining a wealthy club, accessed only by the affluent, is seen as a status symbol, rather like owning a very expensive watch. But the accumulating international evidence suggests that it is fear that has resulted in the rapid growth of gated communities in the period since the 1980s.

Let's examine this argument. The idea of people banding together and creating a fort in order to defend themselves in a hostile world has a tradition going back thousands of years. Historic fortress settlements, relics of a lawless era when the state could not provide security for citizens, can be found in societies across the world. In the past, creating walled towns and villages made a great deal of sense. Building a high wall around a community, and constructing a restricted number of strong gates in the wall, provided a defence against external aggression. At a basic level this urban form could protect residents from large wild animals as well as from armed enemies.

How relevant is this argument today? Fortunately, in most countries, residents are no longer threatened by attacks from wild animals. Moreover, the expansion of civilisation, democracy and the rule of law have, in large parts of the world, made fortress living as redundant as the need for cannons on the battlements. However, in a strange and unsettling way, the obsession with security lives on, even in cities with low crime rates. Bauman (2006) analyses this dysfunctional feature of modern life and takes the view that we have created a fantastical 'derivative fear.' This can be thought of as a way of thinking that generates a feeling of insecurity, which comes to guide behaviour whether or not a menace is actually present. Those that stand to gain from exploiting these groundless fears – the designers, financiers and builders of gated communities, security firms and the like – have not been slow to fan anxieties about crime because an increase in fear will generate more profits for their fear-dependent companies.

A helpful parallel can, perhaps, be drawn with the gun control lobby in the USA. The National Rifle Association (NRA) continues to defend the right of all Americans to bear arms. In earlier, lawless times the idea of individuals carrying guns for personal defence had legitimacy. Now it is clear that, when comparisons are made with other countries, high levels of gun ownership can be shown, and this is incontrovertible, to *diminish* public safety on American streets and, worse than that, in American schools. The growth of gated communities is contributing to widening social segregation in the city, and this trend, like the growth in gun ownership, is actually *decreasing public safety*.[7]

Setha Low (2003), in her detailed study of life 'behind the gates', adds to our understanding. She presents evidence to show that gated communities in the USA are no safer than other suburbs. Indeed, in a further twist to the argument, she notes that residents of these enclaves may actually be paying out to be less safe, in that, 'Gates, in fact, may contribute to placing residents at increased risk by marking the community as a wealthy enclave where burglary is lucrative and by creating a social environment characterised by lack of social integration' (Low 2003, 131).

Local authorities in some countries, for example, in the UK and the USA, are able to require developers to provide a specified number of social housing units for less well off tenants. Conditions of this kind are intended to promote a social mix in housing developments and to provide low paid workers with housing opportunities. However, developers of upmarket housing projects in central London and New York City are designing schemes, and getting them built, that introduce *explicit* social segregation. In these projects poorer residents are forced to use separate entrances, dubbed 'poor doors', and even bicycle storage spaces, rubbish disposal facilities and postal deliveries are being segregated (Osborne 2014). It is troubling to note, then, that in some cities we now find that gated housing projects are deliberately designing in separate gates for the rich and the poor. It is a practice that resembles the British Victorian upstairs/downstairs distinction, with a grand entrance for the rich and a servant door round the back of the house.

The theft of public space

So much for gated residential areas. What about the privatisation of public space more generally? In many countries business interests have come to play a dominant role in urban place making and, in a growing number of cases, this has resulted in a massive erosion of the public realm. This shift in power relating to the spaces we live in, a shift from public to private control, first became visible in the USA with the upsurge in the building of suburban shopping malls in the 1950s and 1960s. The shopping mall, the privatised alternative to the marketplace or town square, has become an extremely popular model for retail development in the last fifty years, and not just in the USA.

Margaret Kohn provides an incisive analysis of American experience with this growth in private government, and she shows how the privatisation of public space undermines the opportunities for free speech. She opens her book with the story of the arrest, in 2003, of a lawyer in the Crossgate Mall in Guilderland, New York, for wearing a T-shirt with the slogan 'Give Peace a Chance' (Kohn 2004). The lawyer believed, wrongly as it happened, that his right to political expression in a shopping mall was protected by the First Amendment to the US Constitution. His mistake was in not realising that this right is not protected in a *privately owned* place. The security guards, and the police officers that handcuffed him and removed him from the mall, were on solid legal ground.[8]

The business takeover of public space is not just an American phenomenon. In a telling analysis of the erosion of the public realm in modern Britain, Anna Minton shows how models of urban development designed to suit private sector interests are transforming UK cities:

> As the twenty-first-century corporate estates take over large parts of the city, the last decade has seen a huge shift in landownership, away from streets, public places and buildings in public ownership and towards the creation of new private estates, primarily given over to shopping and office complexes... At the same time, control of the streets is being handed back to the estates, reversing the democratic achievements of the Victorians... Today, there has been no public debate about the selling of the streets... (Minton 2009, 20–1)

Minton's study is meticulous and thought provoking. In particular, her work contributes to our understanding of fear in the city. She notes that the private sector controlled developments, which are now emerging in many cities across the world, aim to create environments which make a profit and which feel safe. However, these developments, while they may make vast profits for private interests, are *not* enhancing safety in the city.

On the contrary, they are making the city a far more fearful place. This is because the process involves us handing over our collective and personal responsibility for our safety to private companies. A consequence is that we are drifting towards a more authoritarian and less democratic city. In more recent research, co-authored with Jody Aked, Minton extends this argument by showing that well-intentioned efforts, such as the UK government-backed *Secured by Design* policy, is creating high security environments that appear threatening. This study examines the militarisation of poor neighbourhoods and the roll-out of CCTV in schools and reaches a worrying conclusion: 'Our research suggests that the physical environment we are creating is contributing to declining levels of trust and growing levels of fear' (Minton and Aked 2012, 17).

In addition Minton is rightly scathing about the quality of the environments the market is creating:

> These places are everywhere but feel like they're nowhere in particular, devoid of local culture and history and the distinctiveness that brings. Instead they try very hard to import their own culture and vitality, but it doesn't work, creating fake, themed environments where everything is controlled and far from unplanned and spontaneous. (Minton 2009, 186)

While these changes in urban development are alarming, my message for the future is not a gloomy one. This is because many city leaders *reject* this notion of the privatised city – they have developed urban strategies to *expand* the public realm. Indeed, as various Innovation Stories presented later in the book will show, some of the most successful cities in the world are demonstrating that it is perfectly possible to resist efforts to privatise the public realm and create an increasingly permeable urban fabric. Innovation Stories 12 and 13, on Copenhagen and Melbourne, illustrate not just how to challenge narrow, market-dominated thinking but also how to expand public space. Interestingly, many of the private interests in these cities have realised that extending the public realm is actually good news for businesses. These progressive cities are also enhancing public safety. This is because they recognise that the safest places are well populated. In well-designed cities residents, workers, users and casual passers-by all provide 'eyes on the street' to informally police the public realm (Jacobs 1961; Shaftoe 2008). Place-based leadership, described in more detail in the next chapter, is the key reason why some cities are *not* becoming 'could be anywhere' sites for the commercial exploitation of people.

Conclusions

Over fifty years ago, Jane Jacobs, a radical thinker and reformer, wrote an incisive critique of top-down, modernist planning and urban government in the USA. Her analysis is still highly relevant for those concerned with urban leadership and city management in cities across the world today. She argued that politicians, planners, urban administrators and the like were far too ready to impose idealised, ready-made, one-size-fits-all forms of development on the city. In her view this whole approach was misguided because it disregarded the inherent complexity and singularity of urban life. For her the daily experiences of living in particular streets and neighbourhoods, with all their idiosyncratic qualities, is what mattered – the particular places in the city and the way they functioned needed to be understood. Her book is full of sound advice, nowhere more so than in relation to local place shaping:

> Planning for vitality must promote continuous networks of local street neighbourhoods, whose users and informal proprietors can count to the utmost in keeping the public spaces of the city safe, in handling strangers so that they are an asset rather than a menace, in keeping tabs on children in places that are public. (Jacobs 1961, 421)

In this chapter I have provided an introduction to the meaning of place and set out the main reasons why place should be given much more attention in public policy. The discussion has considered three main ways in which place features in urban policy-making – place making, place marketing, and place shaping. In an effort to clarify thinking I have defined these various terms. By drawing insights from the practice of a number of innovative cities, and on my own experience of working with policy-makers in a number of cities across the world, I have suggested that place making can and should play a vital role in urban leadership. In contrast to this view, I have questioned the relevance and usefulness of current approaches to place marketing. Finally, I have discussed place shaping and the role of city development strategies. I concluded that these are key elements, indeed essential components, of effective place-based leadership.

A vital question that runs through this chapter is: Whose place are we talking about? I have suggested that defending and expanding the public realm should be the focus of attention for *all* civic leaders today. I have noted that holding onto public space and, indeed, holding onto public purpose, is now increasingly difficult because of the unhealthy growth in place-less power. The public, or civic, realm is under attack from economic forces that see the city as a profit-making machine. Particularly troubling is the fact that these forces are also helping to create unsafe, fearful cities, and that an increasing number of people seem to think they will be safer if they live in fortified compounds. This is not a good sign.

Fortunately, there are plenty of examples of place-based leaders in cities who are actively mapping out a different future for cities – one that *expands*, rather than diminishes, the public realm. In this chapter I have presented the first Innovation Story of the book – the story of the High Line in New York City. It shows how community-based activists can, if they have imagination, energy and tenacity, make a significant impact on the quality of life in a city. Here local activism has created a beautiful 'park in the sky' that is open to all. In the next chapter we will turn to examine the nature of place-based leadership in more detail, and more inspirational Innovation Stories will follow.

CHAPTER 5

Place-based leadership

Make no little plans. They have no magic to stir men's blood and probably will not, themselves, be realised. Make big plans, aim high in hope and work...
Daniel H. Burnham, Chicago, 1909. Quoted in Carl Smith, *The Plan of Chicago*, 2006

Introduction

Civic leadership is place-based, meaning that those exercising decision-making power have a concern for the communities living in a particular place. But what does place-based leadership involve? How can it be conceptualised? Can we have too much place-based leadership? In this chapter I address these questions.

Wise civic leadership cultivates a public sense of place. Civic leaders, by standing up for local communities against place-less power, can energise collective action at the local level that would not otherwise happen. However, a word of caution is needed. It is possible to take the argument for strengthening place-based power too far. As explained in the previous chapter, gated communities – areas within cities that have been privatised – are on the rise. Some may feel that these zones are clear examples of place-based leadership in action. This is *not* what I am advocating. No doubt the residents of these enclaves identify with the place where they live, but these are private spaces. They are designed to exclude people and, as such, they destroy the public realm. Place-based leadership, in the sense I am using it, *expands the public space* in the city – in both the physical and the political sense.

The discussion in this chapter moves through four main stages. First, we discuss the changing context for place-based leadership. Powerful forces, some of them global in reach, impact localities. These drivers of change can be strong, but they do not neuter civic leadership. It is helpful to think of them as shaping the context within which place-based leadership is exercised. Successful civic leaders pay attention to these forces, in a way that resembles how a successful sports coach assesses the strengths and weaknesses of opposing teams. Second, I provide a graphic visualisation of the way these external forces 'frame', or place constraints on, local leadership. This approach is intended to advance understanding of the flows of influence and power that shape the prospects for particular places.

Third, we step away from the world of local governance to examine debates about the changing nature of leadership in modern societies. What insights can the literature on leadership offer? In the fourth step, I explain in more detail what place-based leadership comprises. I suggest that, in any given locality, there are likely to be five realms of civic leadership. Civic leaders are to be found both inside and outside the state – many different kinds of people can be successful civic leaders, and the Innovation Stories in this book illustrate how imaginative leadership can emerge from diverse sources. The areas of overlap between these realms are fertile grounds for public service innovation. I outline a process model of civic leadership to give a sense of how local leaders can make a difference, not just by enabling constructive action to take place in their localities, but also by reshaping the context within which they operate. The discussion also touches on purpose-driven leadership and considers how civic leaders can transcend parochial thinking.

Towards the end of the chapter I introduce our second Innovation Story. This one is about the introduction of the directly elected mayor model of governance to Bristol, UK in 2012. It explores how the institutional design of the governance arrangements of a place can be modified to spur innovation in city leadership.

Contextualising place-based power

Civic leaders in particular cities do not operate in a vacuum. The power of urban governance is shaped by a variety of political, economic, social and environmental forces. Here I outline these pressures. A key theme in this discussion is that the political space available to local leaders is *not fixed* – the frame can be expanded.[1] In Chapter 3 I explained how, in the 19th Century, place-based leaders in the provincial cities of England – and I used Mayor Joseph Chamberlain of Birmingham as a classic example – were able to *enlarge the power of place* dramatically. As the Innovation Stories in this book show, it remains the case that confident, talented leaders can use local power to improve the quality of life in their localities. They can take on place-less forces and advance the right to the city. But it would be foolish to believe that place-based power in the modern world is unconstrained.

The first point to stress is that national context matters. Some countries attribute a very high societal value to independently elected local authorities and grant them substantial autonomy – for example, Sweden. In others the central state has weakened local government to the point where the locally elected politicians cannot even decide on the level of local tax they wish to impose on their citizens – for example, the UK.[2] Scholars writing in English have dominated the literature on urban development and urban governance. Often these writers have focussed their research efforts on experience in North America and/or Europe. These studies have generated many valuable insights on the exercise of local power (Ranney 2003; Denters and Rose 2005; Skelcher et al 2013). Transatlantic research has, for example, advanced our understanding of urban regimes, and this work has, in turn, influenced thinking relating to urban governance and civic capacity (Stone 1989; Mossberger 2009; Pierre 2011). A focus on developed countries can, however, provide only a partial picture of the ways cities are governed in the modern world. It is encouraging to see that scholarship on urban governance in less developed countries is now being given more attention in the international discourse (van Dijk 2006; McCarney and Stren 2003; Parnell and Pieterse 2014).[3]

These various studies of urban governance draw attention to the importance of the institutional relationships between local government and higher levels of government. For example, there are some fairly obvious differences between federal and unitary systems of government. In the former it is usually the intermediate tier (state, province or similar) that has constitutional responsibility for local government, while in the latter the central state has a direct relationship with local government. In many countries, whether or not they have unitary systems of government, local government enjoys constitutional protection. This safeguards the local polity from unwanted interference emanating from higher tiers of government. In other countries, local authorities exist at the whim of the central state, and local leaders may even see themselves as local administrators working for national government.

Alongside constitutional and cultural differences, Denters and Rose (2005, 243) draw attention to the growing importance of multi-level governance 'involving complicated patterns of vertical and horizontal relationships between municipalities which cross borders and produce new economic and political spaces'. These patterns, sometimes described as network governance, are shaped by socio-political history and the changing dynamics of local/central relations in any given country. Skelcher et al (2013, 43) remind us that 'cities have deeply embedded institutional legacies'. These legacies may establish norms, or expectations, that constrain the political space, or agency, for local actors in both fairly direct and in more subtle ways.

While recognising the importance of these influences we should be careful not to overstate the significance of the institutional legacy. Spurred on by local social movements and public pressures, civic leaders can invent new practices that add to, or even replace, the existing normative framework. In certain circumstances they may, as demonstrated by Joseph Chamberlain in Birmingham in the 1870s, be able to throw aside past norms relating to local government. Anselm Strauss (1978) suggests that social order is 'negotiated order' and that the products of negotiation (understandings, agreements, rules and so on) all have temporal limits. Viewed in this light we can surmise that the local/central relationship, or the institutional legacy, in any given country always has the potential to be modified – possibly quite radically.

Contrasting perspectives on the power of place

Urban political science reveals two main logics relating to the power of place in modern societies: an economic logic and a political logic. We will add a third lens, but let's take the two well-established perspectives first. Hank Savitch and Paul Kantor (2002) provide a helpful overview of these drivers of urban development, and I draw on their analysis here. The economic logic claims that cities are required to tussle in a competitive marketplace and must strive to promote economic growth at all costs. Tiebout (1956) made this claim over fifty years ago, when he suggested that people and industry choose their locations based upon a simple cost–benefit ratio of goods and services available. Building on this 'public choice' perspective, Peterson (1981) suggests that, owing to local resource deficits and the need to maintain their competitive position, cities have become dependent on higher levels of government and private investment for survival. On this analysis urban dependency increases as the world becomes more global. Labour and capital are mobile, people follow jobs, and industry opts to move to more distant locations where the cost of land and labour is lower. A central claim of this economic logic is that cities must conceive of themselves as business corporations – as efficiency-maximising organisations, which must strive to enhance economic productivity as determined by the needs of capital.

A contrasting way of explaining the behaviour of cities is provided by the political logic. This suggests that cities, far from being business corporations, are political entities with, in democracies, elected civic leaders who are accountable to their citizens. Cities have particular socio-cultural values, histories, traditions and identities. It follows that civic leaders should be expected to pursue policies and practices relating to the needs and values of their residents, not the requirements of place-less capital. Opinions differ on the most appropriate political strategy to adopt. For example, David Harvey (2012, xv–xvi) offers a Marxist analysis and suggests that 'The traditional city has been killed by rampant capitalist development, a victim of the never-ending need to dispose of over-accumulating capital driving towards endless and sprawling urban growth no matter what the social, environmental, or political consequences'.

He argues that the whole capitalist system of perpetual accumulation has to be overthrown and replaced. Susan Fainstein, while agreeing with much of Harvey's diagnosis of the problem, argues for a strategy of 'non-reformist reforms'. She argues that:

> … transformational movements aimed at a more egalitarian society must find a rationale based in human motivation rather than historical inevitability and, if not committed to or expecting revolution, must seek to achieve their aims through politics. (Fainstein 2010, 19)

Political parties from across the political spectrum present alternative visions of how to create a fairer, more prosperous society – with some being more convincing than others.

A third logic shaping the space available for place-based leadership is ecological. As I explained in Chapter 1 – see Figure 1.1 – it is essential for civic leaders to build a concern for the natural environment into the heart of their approach to urban governance. The rapid increase in greenhouse gas concentrations, and the potentially disastrous climatic consequences, suggest that city leaders, public managers and others need to pay much more attention to the ecological footprint of current policies and practices. Boone and Modarres outline seven pathways to sustainable development (2006, 185–89). They advocate a precautionary approach rather than adopting a blind faith that all will be better. Their suggestions tie in with the advice of others seeking a more sustainable approach to urban policy making and practice (Girardet 2008; Condon 2010; Parkin 2010; Pearson et al 2014). These authors, and the many who share their values, recognise that the dominance of market thinking is not contributing to human progress. Tim Jackson puts it this way:

> There is a sense … in which individual prosperity is curtailed in the presence of social calamity. That things are going well for me personally is of little consolation if my family, my friends and my community are all in dire straits. My prosperity and the prosperity of those around me are intertwined. (Jackson 2009, 1)

His book is focussed on finding a credible vision of what it means for human society to flourish in the context of ecological limits.

This environmental dimension has been serious neglected in urban political science and public administration, and this limitation needs to be rectified. Some may argue that ecological imperatives do not amount to a distinct perspective – they may feel that the political and/or economic drivers will, for good or ill, carry (or not carry) the environmental arguments. This is to misunderstand the nature of the sustainability crisis now facing modern societies. Nature needs a distinct seat at the urban governance table if cities are to be ecologically resilient.

Framing the power of place

The above discussion suggests that place-based leaders are not free agents able to do exactly as they choose. On the contrary, various powerful forces shape the context within which civic leaders operate. These forces do not disable local leadership. Rather they place limits on what urban leaders may be able to accomplish in particular places and at particular moments in time.[4] Figure 5.1 provides a simplified picture of the forces that shape the world of place-based governance in any given locality. To the three forces just discussed, I add – at the top of the figure – the constraints imposed on localities by laws, regulations and government policies.

Let's run through this figure. At the bottom of the diagram, are the non-negotiable environmental limits. Ignoring the fact that cities are part of the natural ecosystem is irresponsible, and failure to pay attention to environmental limits will store up unmanageable problems for future generations. This side of the square is drawn with a solid line because, unlike the other sides of the square, these environmental limits are non-negotiable. On the left hand side of the diagram are socio-cultural forces – these comprise a mix of people (as actors) and cultural values (that people may hold). Here we find the rich variety of voices found in any city – including the claims of activists, businesses, artists, entrepreneurs, trade unionists, religious organisations, community-based groups, citizens who vote, citizens who don't vote, children, newly arrived immigrants, anarchists and so on.

The people of the city will have different views about the kind of city they wish to live in, and they will have differential capacity to make these views known. Some, maybe many, will claim a right to the city. We can assume that, in democratic societies at least, elected leaders who pay little or no attention to these political pressures should not expect to stay in office for too long. Expression of citizen voice, to use Hirschman's term (1970), will see them dismissed at the ballot box. On the right hand side of the diagram are the horizontal economic forces that arise from the need for localities to compete, to some degree at least, in the wider marketplace – for inward investment and to attract talented people. Various studies have shown that, contrary to neo-liberal dogma, it is possible for civic leaders to bargain with business (Savitch and Kantor 2002). Recognising the power of economic forces, including the growth in global competition between localities, does not require civic leaders to become mere servants of private capital. For example, a detailed study of the governance of London, New York, Paris and Tokyo concluded that 'Global forces are not making the politics of place less important. Globalism and local governance are not mutually exclusive but are deeply entwined… important differences remain in the ways particular world city-regions are mediating international forces' (Kantor et al 2012, 241).

Figure 5.1: Framing the political space for place-based governance

Governmental framing
Socio-cultural framing
Place-based governance
Economic framing
Environmental limits

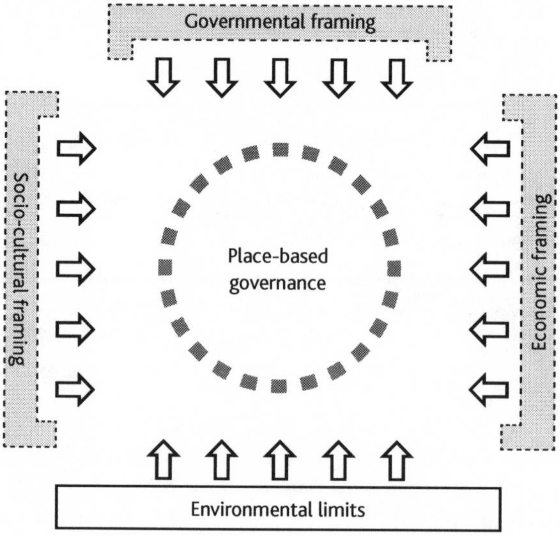

Source: Author

On the top of Figure 5.1, as mentioned, we find the legal and policy framework imposed by higher levels of government. In some countries this governmental framing will include legal obligations decreed by supra-national organisations. For example, local authorities in countries that are members of the European Union (EU) are required to comply with EU laws and regulations, and to take note of EU policy guidance. Individual nation states determine the legal status, fiscal power and functions of local authorities within their boundaries. As mentioned earlier, these relationships are subject to negotiation and renegotiation over time.

It is clear that Figure 5.1 simplifies a much more complex reality. This is what conceptual frameworks do. In reality the four sets of forces framing local action do not necessarily carry equal weight, and the situation in any given city is, to some extent, fluid and changing. The space available for local agency shifts over time, and a key task of local leaders is to be alert to the opportunities for advancing the power of their place within the context of the framing forces prevailing on their area at the time.

The figure indicates that place-based governance, shown at the centre, is porous. Successful civic leaders are constantly learning from the environment in which they find themselves in order to discover new insights, co-create new solutions and advance their political objectives. Note that the four forces are not joined up at the corners to create a rigid prison within which civic leadership has to be exercised. On the contrary the boundaries of the overall arena are, themselves, malleable. Depending on the culture and context, imaginative civic leaders may be able to disrupt the pre-existing governmental frame and bring about an expansion in place-based power. We will return to the theme of place-based leadership shortly, but now we step back and consider the nature of leadership in general.

Leadership – an orientation

There is a large literature on leadership – and it is expanding.[5] Here I consider four overlapping perspectives before recapping on my own definition of leadership:

- personal qualities of leaders
- leadership and institutional design
- the nature of the leadership task
- the context for leadership

The aim here is not to provide a comprehensive review of leadership theories. Our purpose is more focussed. First, we seek to identify insights that can enhance our understanding of **public leadership** – that is, leadership that serves a public rather than a private purpose.[6] Second, we are hoping to unearth ideas from the literature on leadership that can contribute to a normative theory of place-based leadership. By this I mean generate practical ideas that can assist those involved in civic leadership to do better. Writings relating to leadership and local politics are, therefore, of particular interest to us, particularly those that speak to the relationship between leadership and place.

The personal qualities of leaders

Our first theme considers the personal qualities of leaders and is, perhaps, the most familiar aspect of leadership to the non-specialist. For example, the modern mass media tends to focus on the personal qualities of senior public figures. There is a widespread belief that these qualities matter and there can be no doubt that charismatic leaders can make a significant impact on society. Inspiring individuals – like Nelson Mandela, of South Africa, and Aung San Suu Kyi, of Burma – can have a major impact on the direction of travel for a whole of society. Personal qualities such as vision, strength, resilience, persistence, energy, inventiveness, passion, humility and judgement are associated with successful leadership in both the public and the private sectors.

A focus on the role of influential individuals dominated early thinking relating to leadership. Thus, the 'Great Man' (sic) theory of leadership, developed in the 19th century, placed the emphasis on the characteristics of the individual leader – 'heroic' figures, with the 'right' personality traits and skills were the focus of attention. This emphasis on developing the capacity of individuals to be effective leaders still dominates management studies. Airport bookstores heave with self-help manuals claiming to provide practical advice that attentive readers can use to improve their capacity to lead.[7]

In more academic vein we can note, as Jones (1989) observes, that the biographical, or case study, approach to the study of leadership can, by examining the personal conduct and behaviour of known leaders, provide valuable insights on the exercise of leadership. This approach has, over the years, developed into a significant body of literature focussed on drawing insights from inspirational leaders (Adair 2002). This biographical approach has tended to dominate discussion of urban leadership within political science (Stone 1995; Flanagan 2004). Academic studies of famous US city leaders include books on Robert Moses of New York City (Caro 1975), Mayor Harold Washington of Chicago (Rivlin 1992) and Mayor Richard J. Daley, also of Chicago (Cohen and Taylor 2000). David Siegel (2014) has made a useful addition to this literature with his book on the leadership qualities of successful Canadian city managers. Interestingly, his study is not focussed on political leaders. Instead, by examining the leadership traits, skills and behaviours of five exceptional chief administrative officers, he draws attention to the important leadership role of municipal managers.

The role of individuals in urban leadership has received attention in Europe with, for example, studies of Joseph Chamberlain, mayor of Birmingham (Marsh 1994), and Herbert Morrison, Leader of the London County Council (Donaghue and Jones 1973). The literature now also includes a growing number of biographies of respected city leaders – the autobiography by Ken Livingston, the first mayor of London, provides a recent example (Livingstone 2011). Added to this are the many personal profiles of public leaders written by journalists, and some of these take the form of an extended analysis. For example, Bissinger (1997) provides a highly readable 'fly on the wall' study of personal emotion and energy in action in his book about the way Mayor Ed Rendell lead Philadelphia in the period from 1992 to 1997.

The focus on personal qualities raises a question: What are the qualities that *really* matter? There is no simple answer to this question, but Nannerl Keohane (2010, 88), in her perspicacious analysis of leadership, argues that the most valuable attribute a leader can possess in any context is good judgement:

> Making judgements often involves reasoning; but there is an inner core of judgement that has more to do with a person's innate reactions than with intellectual dexterity or anything that could be conveyed through teaching.

Having identified this quality Keohane does not, then, go on to argue that leaders are born and not made. On the contrary she discusses how the faculty of judgement can be refined, honed, and improved by experience and reflection. Her book contains many insights on how to develop personal leadership skills. In particular, by drawing on Hannah Arendt's work on Kant's political philosophy, she suggests that, at root, leadership involves the use of imagination and 'enlarged thought'. This idea of 'enlarged mentality', which entails broadening your perspective to take into account the views of others affected by your judgements, goes to the heart of what I call, in this book, the **New Civic Leadership**.

Leadership and institutional design

Our second theme stems from organisation theory. It highlights the fact that there is a critical relationship between leadership and institutional design. The argument here is two-way. First, the design of an organisation, or institution, can help or hinder the exercise of effective leadership. Second, organisational leaders have a crucial role in shaping both the structure and the culture of their organisation. The origins of an organisational perspective on leadership can be traced to the introduction of 'scientific management' in private sector companies in the early 20th century (Taylor 1911). This approach – exemplified by the Taylorism and Fordism of production line management in large factories – stressed the important role of leaders in designing procedures and practices in order to establish control over the workforce. According to Taylor workers were incapable of understanding what they were doing and that was why managers/leaders had to enforce compliance. The machine became the model for business leadership and management, and this was, of course, the heyday of hierarchical 'command and control' forms of leadership and management.

Peter Drucker (1954), in his classic *The Practice of Management*, challenged this view. He and other writers, notably McGregor (1960) in *The Human Side of Enterprise*, argued for forms of leadership that provided clear objectives, but created scope for self-direction and innovation in the achievement of those objectives. In more recent times management bestsellers, like *In Search of Excellence* (Peters and Waterman 1982), have urged managers to stop managing and start leading their organisations. Allied to these efforts to liberate talent within organisations there has been an upsurge in efforts to engage in strategic management (Stacey 1993; Joyce 2012). A key theme here, and we will return to it in Chapter 6 when we discuss the role of leadership in public service innovation, is that modern organisational leadership needs to be strategic. According to Stephen Bungay, a respected management consultant, this involves deciding what really matters, communicating this message and then giving people space and support to deliver – it involves a move from 'mission command' to 'directed opportunism.' (Bungay 2011, 83)

In many ways shifts in thinking and practice within the world of public administration have paralleled changes in the private sector. As explained in Chapter 3, in the early 20th century many western countries, in a drive to advance fairness and justice in society, developed large public bureaucracies to deliver welfare – health, education, social care, housing, planning and so on. In the early days these services were 'administered' rather than 'managed'. The idea of redesigning institutions, including local government, to strengthen leadership and management emerged much later – in the UK it was in the 1960s and 1970s. The relatively new ideas about leadership drew not just on private sector concepts, but also on international exchange between public service professionals and policy makers. We will examine the influence of international exchange in relation to place-based leadership in more detail in Chapter 12.

Here we can note that, in many countries, efforts have been made to strengthen the leadership of local government by redesigning both the officer and the elected member structures of local authorities. If we take Britain as an example, we can note that in the 1970s local corporate planning gained credibility and many ideas were imported from the private sector, such as goal setting and Management by Objectives (MbO) (Stewart 1971). The new post of Chief Executive was created to lead and manage the officers and advise the politicians. Previously the most senior officer in UK local government was usually known as the Town Clerk – whose main role was to co-ordinate the administration of essentially separate local government services.

In the last decade or so debates about the institutional design of local governments, in Europe at least, have focussed on strengthening the capacity of elected politicians to exercise executive leadership (Berg and Rao 2005; Leach 2006; Swianiewicz 2007). Several European countries – for example, Germany and Italy – have introduced directly elected mayors right across their systems of local governance in the belief that this can strengthen local leadership (Hambleton 2013). In this context it should be noted that Australia is actively considering widening the use of the directly elected mayor form of governance (Sansom 2012). Clarence Stone, a leading American urban political scientist, suggests, however, that we should not place all our eggs in the institutional design basket. In a perceptive essay on the mayoral leadership of four US cities – Atlanta, Boston, Hampton, and New Haven – he argues that institutional design matters, but resources decide:

'The experience of mayors in the United States shows that leadership rests on informal arrangements, not simply on the formal powers of those who hold local executive offices' (Stone 2005, 180).

The English experience is illuminating. As mentioned in Chapter 1, shortly after the Labour Government was elected in 1997, Prime Minister Tony Blair, in a remarkable intervention, wrote a pamphlet urging local authorities to develop a highly visible, outgoing approach to community leadership (Blair 1998). The underlying theory was that institutional redesign could bolster improved approaches to local leadership. The Labour Government was quick to pass legislation creating not just a new, directly elected mayor and strategic authority for London, but also opportunities for all English councils to develop new leadership models (Hambleton 1998; Hambleton and Sweeting 2004).

The London reforms strengthened the political leadership of the capital (Sweeting 2002; Travers 2004). The Local Government Act 2000, while it required most English councils to strengthen their political executives, did not insist on the introduction of directly elected mayors (Copus 2006). In practice most councils chose to create a cabinet of senior councillors to lead the locality, which was not the intention of the Prime Minister. However, the English directly elected mayor debate has reappeared in recent years. The UK Coalition Government, elected in 2010, introduced legislation – the Localism Act 2011 – enabling the larger cities in England to opt for a directly elected mayor model of governance if they wished. We examine the role of directly elected mayors in local leadership in Chapter 7 when we discuss leadership in democratic local governance. And Innovation Story 2 discusses the impact of the mayoral form of governance introduced into Bristol in 2012. Here we can note that in many countries, not just the UK, governments are reviewing the design of their local government arrangements with a view to introducing institutional changes that reformers believe will strengthen local leadership.

The nature of the leadership task

This discussion of the impact of institutional design on public leadership paves the way for our third perspective and a deeper question: What is the nature of the leadership task? Burns (1978) draws a very helpful distinction between transactional and transformational approaches to leadership. Stated simply the traditional paradigm defined leadership as a 'transaction' between a leader – often described as the 'boss' – and a follower, or 'subordinate'. A typical exchange is pay for doing a job, but other exchanges can take place – such as the favours and feelings psychologists suggest are traded in social exchange theory. Transformational leadership is different in nature from transactional leadership. Burns argues that the former is both more complex and more potent – the transforming leader tunes into the feelings and emotions of followers, and seeks to stimulate enthusiasm and commitment through a process that is more like bonding than bartering. Sashkin and Sashkin (2003) build on the work of Burns and suggest that transformational leaders couple self-confidence with an orientation towards the empowerment of others, and recognise the importance of building a values driven organisational culture.

This leads to a key point about the leadership task that I wish to emphasise: emotions matter. In a far-reaching analysis, Hoggett (2009) notes that politics, as taught and researched in universities, has relatively little to say about identity in politics, and even less to say about the role of emotion. Similarly, leadership theories, and particularly theories relating to public leadership, have neglected the emotional dimension of leadership. In recent times there has, thankfully, been an expansion of interest in emotional intelligence (Goleman et al 2002) and some scholars have started to examine the role of feelings in organisational dynamics (Iszatt-White 2013). For example, Heifetz and Linsky (2002) argue that successful leaders promote adaptive change, and that this necessarily stimulates resistance because it challenges people's habits, beliefs and values. Along with other writers, they suggest that leaders need to cultivate emotional resilience in order to stay open even when they experience personal attack (Haslam et al 2011). A recognition of the importance of emotions suggests that leaders need to speak from the heart:

> Speaking from the heart requires being in touch with your own values, beliefs, and emotions. Yet in your professional life, this may conflict with pressures to be rational – that is, to "be in your head". But when you are leading people through adaptive change, it is their hearts (not their heads) that hold them back. (Heifetz et al 2009, 270)

In this context, some writers believe that women leaders tend to exhibit a higher level of emotional intelligence than male leaders – and there are plenty of examples to support this argument. Sara Parkin, an influential UK activist in relation to sustainability, provides a good example – she has written eloquently on the need for a more passionate approach to public leadership (Parkin 2010). Nannerl Keohane devotes an insightful chapter of her book on leadership to the question 'Does gender make a difference?' She concludes that there is some evidence to suggest that women often do lead differently – they tend to be more collaborative, have a greater concern for colleagues and subordinates, and tend to be less fussed about status. She stresses, however, that it is important *not* to label some styles of leadership as 'feminine' and others 'typically male' as this: '... itself imposes stereotypes on complex behaviour and helps perpetuate biases that have provided obstacles for women leaders throughout history' (Keohane 2010, 152–3). She hopes that more women will provide leadership in future and that they will be regarded as 'leaders', not 'women leaders'.

Barry Quirk, a highly respected local government chief executive in the UK, suggests that a core task of leadership involves valuing the contributions of team members and others. He notes correctly that public service leaders have a significant advantage when it comes to motivation:

> Valuing contribution may be crucial, but contribution to what? Most managers will say, 'contribution to organisational purpose'. But they would be wrong. People want to contribute to far wider goals than the narrow objectives of any organisation. And this is where public service organisations have a massive motivational edge on their private sector counterparts. In local government this is easier still. The common cause that conjoins those who work in local public service is the welfare of the local community. (Quirk 2011, 138)

Another highly respected local government chief executive in the UK also emphasises the importance of values-based leadership. Mark Rogers, President of the UK Society of Local Authority Chief Executives for 2013/14, encourages council chiefs to tell their own personal stories about why they care about what they are doing:

> ... we should talk more about our own personal background, because our leadership is very personal. The chief executive's role is fundamentally characterised by the ability to make good judgement calls. And by their nature they are subjective. No two people would lead a council in the same way. (quoted in Wiggins 2013, 11)

These two chief executives highlight the importance of socially aware, public leadership. In this context it is encouraging to note that recent theoretical work on leadership is starting to pay attention to the interplay between public leadership and civic capacity. Peter Sun and Marc Anderson (2012, 317) define civic drive as: '... the desire and motivation to be involved with social issues and to see new social opportunities'. They explore the relationship between transformational leadership and civic capacity, and argue that understanding this dynamic is critical for public leaders. However, they go further and suggest that, because societal norms are changing, business leaders also need to show that their companies are able to function as responsible, corporate citizens within their communities.

This discussion of facilitative leadership suggests that modern local government leadership is concerned with fusing the capacity to act. The absence of formal authority puts more emphasis on personal style. It requires leaders to understand the feelings of others and to develop their collaborative leadership skills (Marshall et al 2011; Forester 2013). As Sue Goss and Paul Tarplett (2010, 276) observe:

> Some of the skills needed are close to good coaching skills; i.e. an ability to listen carefully and really hear what is being said, understand the language in its context and to ask good questions that throw light on a problem.

Successful boundary spanners strive to build strong interpersonal relationships and establish trust and reciprocal relationships (Williams 2012). Three important insights stem from this consideration of the relatively new, collaborative style of leadership. First, this approach recognises that leadership resides in groups and communities, not just in individuals. Second, depending on the requirements, different people need to take on the leadership role – leadership is dispersed and is multi-level. Third, the role of formal leaders shifts to focus on facilitating, encouraging and supporting others and it implies making an emotional connection – articulating the values that leaders are committed to. It involves speaking with emotion about shared purpose.

The context for leadership

So far so good – leaders matter, institutional design matters and the nature of the task matters. What about the context for leadership? There is widespread agreement in the literature that an effective approach to leadership in one setting might not be appropriate in another. Again Nannerl Keohane offers helpful insights. She stresses that leaders need to tune their efforts to the context both within and outside their organisation:

> The size and culture of an organisation, the expectations of followers, the purposes the organisation is intended to pursue, and its history and traditions are all relevant in considering what kind of leadership is most likely to succeed. Behaviour by a leader that seems perfectly appropriate in some contexts may appear quite out of place in another. (Keohane 2010, 10)

On this analysis the accomplishments of leaders depend to a large extent on how well they respond to, and influence, the organisational environment in which they find themselves. This context varies greatly. For example, to make a very simple point in relation to managerial leadership, the context for a first-level supervisor in an organisation is very different from the context experienced by the chief executive. This implies the need for different styles of leadership suited to the context. Sometimes called situational leadership, at other times contingent leadership, this approach has become popular within the field of management studies. For example, Hersey (1984) suggests that leadership style should be adapted to the 'readiness level' of subordinates. And Baghai and Quigley (2011) sketch out eight archetypes of 'leader and followers' relationships.

In an influential analysis of American mayoral leadership, Yates (1977) outlines a typology of leadership styles based on the dimensions of political activism and the amount of political and financial resources they possess. In his model the strongest type of mayor – which he describes as the Entrepreneur – has sufficient resources to act decisively on substantive policy issues. By contrast the weakest category in his typology – the Broker – lacks financial and political clout and this limits their vision to mediating conflicts between various interest groups. Studies of this kind suggest, then, that a well-positioned city, one that is being flooded with inward investment, provides a rather different context for the exercise of local political leadership than, say, one that is in a declining region that appears to be unattractive to outside investors. In turn, this context has implications for leadership style. Figure 5.1, presented earlier, sets out a way of considering the forces that shape the context for place-based leaders in modern societies.

Successful local leaders, partly because they are place-based and possess extensive tacit as well as policy knowledge, are able to read the geo-political and socio-economic context of their place better than most. In Chapter 1 I drew attention to the importance of tacit knowledge. The term refers to knowledge that stems from personal and social experience that cannot be codified. Because it is difficult to pin down it tends to be neglected by political scientists and urban scholars in general. Yet, this knowledge about the 'feel' of a place is critical. In Chapter 3 I suggested that loyalty and civic identity are crucial to successful civic leadership – these emotions vary by locality but they can provide a powerful resource for civic leaders.

For example, in the city where I live – Bristol, England – there is a fairly well established feeling that we, the citizens of Bristol, are a bit quirky, a bit challenging, some would say a bit bolshie. This is partly explained by the proud and lengthy history of rebellious public protest in the city, partly by the diversity of the city, partly by the existence of strong artistic communities who give expression to the local culture – up to and including the famous street art of Banksy and others. As we shall see, in Innovation Story 2, Mayor Ferguson, who became the first directly elected mayor of Bristol in 2012, is very responsive to what we might call the soft cultural landscape of social feelings and beliefs. The context for local leadership has, then, an important emotional dimension. There is not much literature on this notion, although Bell and de-Shalit (2011) offer a helpful analysis of the way the spirit of a city can be cultivated and nourished.

Research on mayoral leadership in the US has documented a move towards facilitative leadership (Svara 1990; 1994; 2003). This shift represents a response to the changing environment in which elected mayors find themselves. In Chapters 1 and 3 I have discussed the movement from urban government to urban governance (Denters and Rose 2005; Hambleton and Gross 2007). While this is not a pattern of change that is present in all cities, the idea of urban leaders working proactively to influence other stakeholders in their city to achieve shared goals is now high on the list of most elected mayors and city council leaders. The growth in partnership working in public policy puts a premium on knowing how to lead when you are not in charge. In his study of official leadership in the city Svara (1990, 87) argues that the facilitative mayor '...accomplishes objectives through enhancing the efforts of others. This distinction makes a great difference in the orientation of the mayor. Rather than seeking power as the way to accomplish tasks, the facilitative mayor seeks to empower others'.

We may conclude, then, that the city 'boss', going it alone, has long been an anachronism. This idea, stemming from the old-fashioned command and control model of management referred to earlier, envisages the local authority political leader determining policy for city council services and then imposing it on the bureaucracy.[8] The changing context for civic leadership requires facilitative leaders able to reach out to other stakeholders in efforts to influence the decisions of public and private agencies to improve the local quality of life.[9]

This review of four perspectives on leadership represents a canter across a rapidly expanding and complex field. Moreover, we have not had space here to review the ideas about leadership that prevail in non-western cultures. For example, ideas about leadership in China are very different from those found in the west. In particular, as Wang and Chee (2011, 106–111) note in their excellent book on Chinese leadership, China has a 'high-context' culture. This means that communication is invested with a great deal of subtext – a consequence is that leaders need to become highly skilled at understanding what is meant rather than what is actually said. Readers operating in different cultural settings will need to consider how relevant the four themes outlined above are to their own cultural context.

Defining leadership

How then do we define leadership? In Chapter 1 I gave my own definition of leadership and I provide a recap here. My definition draws on both the leadership literature and on my personal experience of leadership in communities, in government and in higher education in Britain and the USA: 'Leadership involves shaping emotions and behaviour to achieve common goals' (Hambleton 2007a, 174).[10] This definition puts emotions front of stage and also emphasises the importance of leaders adopting an inclusive approach to the identification of the aims and purposes of collective endeavour.

This definition implies a wide range of activities aimed at generating both new insights and new ways of working together. It prizes respect for the feelings and attitudes of others as well as a strong commitment to collaboration. It is imaginative, involves risk-taking and involves 'being able to put yourself in the situation of someone else' (Keohane 2010, 89). My approach to the study of place-based leadership is informed by this perspective, and I wish to emphasise, again, that the feelings people have for 'their' place have been seriously neglected in both the leadership literature and the public service innovation literature. Following Hoggett (2009, 175) I take the view that approaches to leadership need to develop a form of 'passionate reason'. How we feel is not a distraction from reason – on the contrary: 'Not only are our feelings essential to our capacity for thought but they are themselves a route to reason' (Hoggett 2009, 177). This idea of emotional engagement is central to what I call the **New Civic Leadership**.

Understanding place-based leadership

Civic leaders are found in the public, private, and community/voluntary sectors and they operate at many geographical levels – from the street block to an entire sub region and beyond. It is helpful to distinguish five realms of place-based leadership reflecting different sources of legitimacy:

- **Political leadership** – referring to the work of those people elected to leadership positions by the citizenry. These are, by definition, political leaders. Thus, directly elected mayors, all elected local councillors and Members of Parliament are political leaders. Having said that we should acknowledge that different politicians carry different roles and responsibilities and will view their political roles in different ways.
- **Public managerial/professional leadership** – referring to the work of public servants appointed by local authorities, state and central governments, and third sector organisations to plan and manage public services, and promote community wellbeing. These public managers bring professional and managerial expertise to the tasks of local governance.
- **Community leadership** – referring to the many civic-minded people who give their time and energy to local leadership activities in a wide variety of ways. These may be community activists, voluntary sector leaders, religious leaders, higher education leaders and so on. The potential contribution to civic leadership of an independent and engaged voluntary and community sector is important here.
- **Business leadership** – referring to the contribution made by local business leaders and social entrepreneurs, who have a clear stake in the long-term prosperity of the locality.
- **Trade union leadership** – referring to the efforts of trade union leaders striving to improve the pay and working conditions of employees in public, private and voluntary sector organisations. Elected by their members these leaders enjoy democratic legitimacy within their organisations.[11]

These roles are all important in cultivating and encouraging public service innovation and, crucially, they overlap. I describe the areas of overlap between these different realms of leadership as **innovation zones** – areas providing many opportunities for inventive behaviour – see Figure 5.2. This is because different perspectives are brought together within these zones and this can enable active questioning of established approaches. Heterogeneity is the key to fostering innovation. Civic leadership has a critical role in creating the conditions for different people to come together – people who might not normally meet – to have a creative dialogue, and then to follow through on their ideas. I present the circles in Figure 5.2 as dotted lines to emphasise the connectivity, or potential connectivity, across the realms of civic leadership.

It can be claimed that the areas of overlap in Figure 5.2 are conflict zones, not innovation zones. It is certainly the case that these spaces often provide settings for power struggles between competing interests and values. And it is important to acknowledge that, within these settings, power is unequally distributed.

It is possible that formalised partnership settings – administrative arrangements designed to link local stakeholders together in order to further collaboration – can operate as innovation zones. But in my experience this is often not the case. Recent research on public service innovation suggests that it is the more informal, open-ended, personal interactions that matter in a creative process (Hambleton and Howard 2012; 2013). This creativity can be cultivated if leaders step out of their own 'realm' of authority and engage with the perspectives and realities of others. This means going into what one public service leader in our Anglo-Dutch research project described as one's 'ZOUD' – or Zone of Uncomfortable Debate. Here, different approaches, values and priorities collide.[12]

Figure 5.2: The five realms of place-based leadership

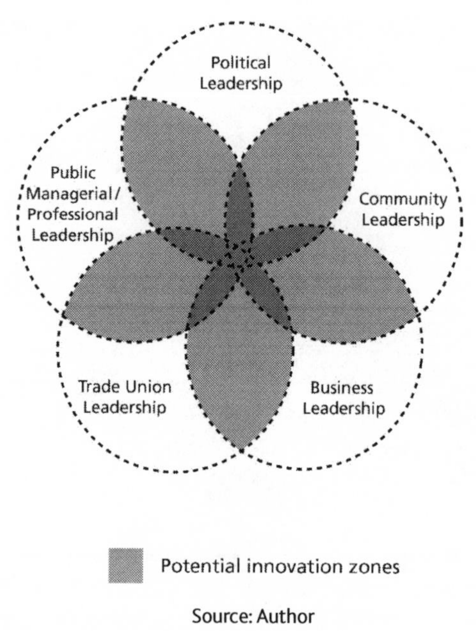

Source: Author

A limitation of Figure 5.2 is that, while it shows clearly enough that the realms of civic leadership overlap, it gives the appearance of essentially separate fields of action. In practice the process of place-based leadership is much more dynamic than the figure implies – effective public leaders in a city are cutting across the realms of civic leadership on a day-to-day basis. Figure 5.3 is a reworking of the same figure. The shape of each realm is now shown, not as a contained circle, but as a petal that is inextricably linked to the other four realms. The line outlining the realms of civic leadership is a single line. This is designed to signal *the importance of unifying the separate realms of civic leadership in a single purposive process.* This idea of unified action resonates with the notion of 'as one' behaviour advocated by other writers on leadership (Baghai and Quigley 2011).

Wise civic leadership is critical in ensuring that the innovation zones – sometimes referred to as the 'soft spaces' of planning (Illsley et al 2010) or 'space for dialogue' (Oliver and Pitt 2013, 198–99) – are orchestrated in a way that promotes a culture of listening that can, in turn, lead to innovation (Kahane 2004). New ideas emerging in the field of urban planning resonate with the argument I am putting forward. For example, Balducci and Mantysalo (2013) suggest that successful urban planning involves the creation of 'trading zones', meaning arenas within which different stakeholders exchange ideas for action without necessarily developing shared agreement on core values and motives. This notion of trading zones is close to the idea of innovation zones set out in this book.

Figure 5.3: Unifying the realms of place-based leadership

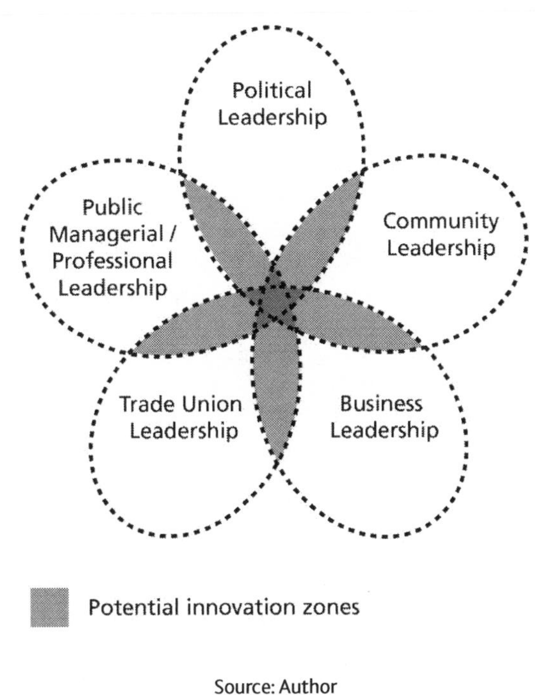

Source: Author

The point I wish to highlight from this discussion of innovation zones, or trading zones, is that place-based leadership can shape the quality of the exchanges that take place in these spaces. It is true that these arenas are often experienced as conflict zones – there are many clashes of values in the modern city. The role of leadership is to orchestrate a process of social discovery within these zones that is constructive and forward looking. Adam Kahane (2004, 129) puts it this way:

> We have to bring together the people who are co-creating the current reality to co-create new realities. We have to shift from downloading

> and debating to reflective and generative dialogue. We have to choose an open way over a closed way.

In sum, leadership capacity in modern society is dispersed. Our systems of local governance need to respect and reflect that diversity if decisions taken in the public interest are going to enjoy legitimacy. Further, more decentralised approaches – both across localities and within each realm of civic leadership – can empower informal leaders to be part of the dialogue (Howard and Lever 2011). Figure 5.3 simplifies a more complex reality. It is not intended to show how the dynamics of local power struggles actually unfold. The relative power of the five realms varies by locality. Moreover, the realms shift in influence over time. The interactions across the realms are also complex and, of course, there are many different interests operating within each realm. Nevertheless I believe that the notion of five different realms – with leadership stemming from different sources of legitimacy within each realm – provides a helpful way of framing discussion about civic leadership.

Earlier in this chapter I explained how various forces shape the context within which place-based leadership is exercised and I set this out in diagrammatic form in Figure 5.1. Having now explained the five realms of place-based leadership it is possible to advance the presentation by locating the five realms within this broader context – see Figure 5.4.

Figure 5.4: Place-based leadership in context

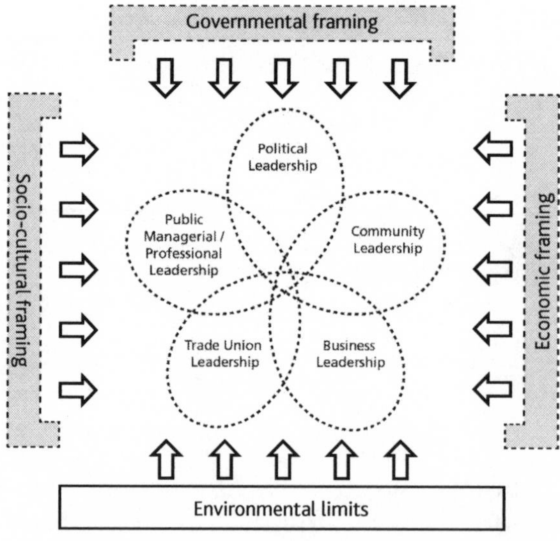

Source: Author

Skelcher et al (2013, 24) provide an interesting framework, a kind of flow chart, for the analysis of governance transitions. In their model they identify two forces shaping the agency exercised by local actors: ideational context and the institutional legacy. They argue that, aside from the imaginative agency of individuals and groups, governance change is driven by two factors – the big ideas that take hold within a community of actors (the ideational context) and the normative logics inherent in the institutions of government (the institutional legacy). An attractive feature of their model is that they show how emergent practices can, in turn, reshape the big ideas and the institutional legacy.

My own model is aligned with their approach – see Figure 5.5. The main differences are that I suggest that four forces, not two, shape the space for local action. My analysis suggests that environmental limits are critical, and I also try to bring out the tensions between the political and the economic drivers of local change, rather than collapsing them into one ideational driver. Figure 5.5 has the benefit of highlighting the dynamic possibilities for place-based leadership. Before we leave this discussion of place-based leadership it is important to draw attention to two important matters – the purpose of place-based leadership and the need for local leadership to transcend parochialism. We touch on these two themes briefly here but we will revisit them in subsequent chapters.

Figure 5.5: A process model of civic leadership

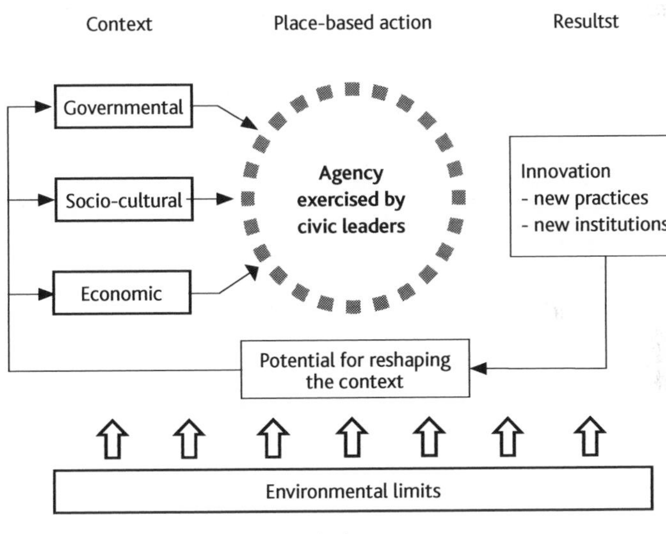

Source: Author

Purpose-driven local leadership

Leadership is inextricably linked with purpose. Stone (1995) examines modern urban politics and observes that aimless interaction requires no leadership. In contrast, in cases where a compelling vision emerges from an inclusive process and is then articulated by a leader or leaders, the results can be inspiring. A clear statement of purpose (or mission) can provide a formative experience, shaping the identity of group members, and articulating shared values and aspirations. In the mid-1990s Sir Steve Bullock, who is now the directly elected mayor of the London borough of Lewisham, and I were commissioned by UK local government to develop national guidance on local political leadership (Hambleton and Bullock 1996). In carrying out this research we asked leading figures in UK local government what they thought constituted successful local political leadership, and the indicators of good leadership that emerged are summarised in Figure 5.6.

There is no suggestion here that the indicators listed in Figure 5.6 are comprehensive or appropriate in all settings. Rather they are offered as a possible set of aspirations for local political leadership and to stimulate fresh thinking. In Chapter 1 I introduced the notion of the **inclusive city**. The statement set out there of what this would mean could be used as a starting point for the discussion of the purpose of civic leadership in any given city – not as a prescription but as a prompt.

Figure 5.6: Indicators of good local political leadership

- *Articulating a clear vision for the area*

  Setting out an agenda of what the future of the area should be and developing strategic policy direction. Listening to local people and leading initiatives.

- *Promoting the qualities of the area*

  Building civic pride, promoting the benefits of the locality and attracting inward investment.

- *Winning resources*

  Winning power and funding from higher levels of government and maximising income from a variety of sources.

- *Developing partnerships*

  Successful leadership is characterised by the existence of a range of partnerships, both internal and external, working to a shared view of the needs of the local community.

- *Addressing complex social issues*

  The increasingly fragmented nature of local government and the growing number of service providers active in a given locality means that complex issues that cross boundaries, or are seen to fall between areas of interest, need to be taken up by leaderships that have an overview and can bring together the right mix of agencies to tackle a particular problem.

- *Maintaining support and cohesion*

  Managing disparate interests and keeping people on board are essential if the leadership is to maintain authority.

Source: Adapted from Hambleton, R. and Bullock, S. (1996) *Revitalising Local Democracy – The Leadership Options*. London: Local Government Management Board.

Transcending parochialism

Back in 1975 US Senator Mark Hatfield (Republican – Oregon) advocated the introduction of neighbourhood government legislation in the USA – the Neighbourhood Government Act 1975. His aim was to bring about a massive transfer of tax monies from higher levels of government to the neighbourhood level. The legislation went nowhere, but it provides us with a warning note. This Act was intended to make rich neighbourhoods formidably wealthy at the expense of less well off areas. In advocating a much stronger role for place-based leadership in urban governance I am not seeking to promote this kind of selfish, parochial behaviour. Rather, following George Frederickson (2005), I am suggesting that place-based leaders should be guided by 'instincts of appropriateness' and what is understood to be right and fair. Place-based leadership calls for the ability to hold onto the ethical purpose of governance while also containing the uncertainties and complexities inherent in the leadership role.

Frederickson, as well as grasping the importance of facilitative leadership in the modern city, also makes a strong case for leaders to transcend the geographical limitations of municipal boundaries:

> Although they are working from the vantage point of particular jurisdictions, leaders practicing ... governance see the big social, economic, and political context in which they are embedded... To serve a city well, its leaders must transcend the city. (Frederickson 2005, 6)

It follows that civic leaders must be able to build strong grassroots relationships alongside their horizontal and vertical relationships. Local leaders need to be able to see the bigger picture, but at the same time remain connected with people across the city, in ways that empower them to take action.

In this context it is useful to refer to the experience of those working in communities that have a history of conflict, even violent conflict. Kahane (2004) provides many valuable insights on how to develop an open way of becoming more human, not just increasingly clever – even in high-conflict situations. Unfortunately, there are many high-conflict situations around the world. Here I refer to the efforts to bring about peace in the island of Ireland. The International Fund for Ireland (IFI) has made a major contribution to the peace process. Paddy Harte, who was an advisor to the IFI for over twenty years, highlights the importance of supporting community leaders who can transcend the language of conflict:

> In my experience, people with a passion for their community will always be the spark that ignites community spirit and they form a very precious part of economic and social regeneration. It is vitally important that these very valuable people are supported... I have worked with some remarkable community leaders and without them no real change would have been possible. (Harte 2013, 17)

Harte shows how the building of community leadership has played a critical role in moving power away from paramilitary organisations, and fostering local place-based action to bring communities together. In the island of Ireland, and particularly in the areas just to the north and south of the border, we find a growing number of inspirational community leaders who demonstrate how it is possible to transcend narrow self-interest in their approach to public affairs.

Can a Directly Elected Mayor make a difference?

There are different ways of organising the political leadership of a city, and we will consider the main institutional forms of urban governance in Chapter 7. Here I want to introduce the second Innovation Story of the book to illustrate how redesign of governmental arrangements can have a significant impact on the nature of urban leadership. Directly Elected Mayors (DEMs), while commonplace in many countries, are still a relatively new phenomenon in British politics. Legislation enabling local authorities to adopt the DEM form of governance was only introduced in England in 2000 and, by 2012, only 16 local authorities – not much more than 3% of those entitled to do so – had decided to introduce a DEM model of governance.

The UK Coalition Government, elected in May 2010, embarked on an effort to encourage the large cities in England to introduce DEMs, believing this would strengthen urban leadership. We will return to consider the arguments for and against directly elected mayors in Chapter 7. At this point it is sufficient to say that the Localism Act 2011 required the twelve largest cities in England, outside London, which already had a directly elected mayor, to hold referendums on whether or not to adopt elected mayors. Two of the listed cities – Liverpool and Salford – decided to introduce mayors under existing legislation. This meant that citizens in ten cities participated in citywide referendums in May 2012.

Nine English cities said 'no'. Bristol was the only city to vote 'yes'. In fact, the year 2012 witnessed two startling developments relating to civic leadership in Bristol. First, in the referendum, held in May, the citizens of Bristol bucked the national trend and voted in favour of a DEM to lead the city. Second, following a lively contest between fifteen candidates, George Ferguson, an Independent, was elected as mayor of Bristol in November 2012. Again Bristol bucked the national trend. Party politics is deeply ingrained in English local government and the fact that an Independent candidate, that is, a politician not attached to any political party, was able to win the citywide contest attracted national news.

Mayor Ferguson indicated from the outset that he would like the City of Bristol to be seen as a place that is willing to experiment with new ideas. Innovation Story 2 provides an account of the introduction of the directly elected mayor form of governance into Bristol, and reflects on the style of leadership Mayor Ferguson has adopted during his first year in office.

Independent city leadership: Mayoral governance in Bristol

Aims

In May 2012 the citizens of Bristol decided in a referendum that they would like to introduce a Directly Elected Mayor (DEM) form of governance into the city. The election of the new mayor took place in November and, to the surprise of many observers, the winning candidate was an Independent, that is, a candidate who ran for office without the backing of any political party or political organisation. George Ferguson, an architect and urbanist with a track record of carrying out successful regeneration projects in the city, was sworn into office at a ceremony held in an unusual setting – Brunel's Old Station, a historic building close to the city's main railway station – on 19 November 2012.

This Innovation Story discusses the introduction of a radically new model of urban governance into an English city, and reports on some of the early changes that have taken place during Mayor Ferguson's first year of office. Advocates of the mayoral model of governance claim that cities with directly elected mayors benefit because mayoral leadership can combine strong, outgoing leadership with clear accountability. The citizens of Bristol, admittedly on a low turnout in the referendum (24%), agreed that change in the institutional form of urban governance was needed, and they ushered in a new era of local political leadership. Mayor Ferguson will now hold office until the next mayoral election in May 2016. He has indicated, from the outset, that he wants to see Bristol become 'a test bed for urban innovation'.

Innovation Story outline

Research carried out before the mayoral election reveals significant differences of view among stakeholders in the city about whether having a DEM form of governance would make much difference.[1] In this research we obtained the views of councillors, professionals working in public agencies (including the local authority) and civic leaders (in the community and business sectors). When asked 'How much do you agree or disagree with the view that a directly elected mayor will improve leadership of the city?' the councillors were pessimistic – only 28% agreed with this view. In contrast over 70% of both the public professionals and the community/business leaders agreed with this view. This survey evidence provides a useful benchmark of attitudes, and it also gives an indication of what respondents felt should be the priorities for the new administration.

A nasty budget crunch was the first major challenge for the new city leader. Mayor Ferguson took up office only weeks before the city budget for 2013/14 had to be finalised. The front-page story of the *Bristol Post*, on the weekend before the swearing-in ceremony, had the headline: 'Baptism of fire. New mayor will have to find £25 million of cuts in 6 weeks' (17 November 2012). In practice, the situation was considerably worse than that. Once Mayor Ferguson had clarified the financial details he discovered that central government was requiring him to make £35 million in spending reductions. This amounted to cutting more than 10% out of the city revenue budget in one year.

These drastic cuts were imposed by the UK central government as part of a national programme of spending reductions; they were not of the mayor's doing. In a speech on 22 November 2013 Mayor Ferguson said: 'I like a challenge, but I would have preferred a smaller budget challenge!' The mayor created small, cross-party groups to examine budget options. In a matter of a few weeks this approach led to the development of a number of creative ideas on how to respond to the budget crisis. The reductions were painful, but Mayor Ferguson adopted a facilitative style and drew on the knowledge and skills of many experienced councillors to make the savings.

It is still, of course, early days for the new mayor and certainly too early to judge whether the mayoral model can be viewed as a success or not. But Mayor Ferguson has already taken a number of steps designed to set a new tone in relation to urban governance in the city. For example, the municipal offices in Bristol have been called the 'Council House' since they were built. On his first day in office Mayor Ferguson changed the name of the building to City Hall. His intention here is to signal that the council building should be seen as a public place, a resource for the city – not the 'house for the Council'. There can be no disputing the fact that the city is now seen as having much more visible leadership. In 2012, before the direct election of a mayor, 24% of citizens thought that Bristol had visible leadership. A year or so after the election this figure leapt to an astonishing 69%.[2]

Mayor Ferguson sees the role of mayor as being very different from the role of a Council Leader (the most senior politician in the pre-mayoral era). He believes as mayor he is leader of the place, not leader of the local authority: 'My leadership is not about what the Council does, it's about how Bristol changes, about how the city feels. The mood change is really important'.[3]

He has radical ideas about the use of public space in the city. For example, he moved ahead swiftly with a *Make Sundays Special* scheme for the summer of 2013. By drawing on the successful experience of cities in other countries – for example, Bordeaux – he decided to 'liberate the streets' in the centre of the city for five Sundays in the June-October period. On these days traffic was excluded from the central area, and community groups, activity leaders, artists and street performers took over the public space. The initiative has proved popular with residents and children and there are plans to build on this experiment in future years.

In June 2013, in recognition of the progress made towards becoming a low carbon city, and the plans for major investment in public transport and energy conservation, the city won the award of European Green Capital 2015. Mayor Ferguson is the first to praise his predecessors for their good work on environmental issues over a number of years, but it is also true that he is personally very active in creating a people-friendly eco-city.

Mayor Ferguson has chosen to take his salary in Bristol Pounds, the local currency designed to run alongside sterling. Launched in the city region in September 2012, the Bristol Pound encourages shorter supply chains that are less dependent on fossil fuels, and aims to build better connections between communities and local businesses so that local wealth is recycled. Hundreds of independent Bristol-based traders now accept the currency.

When asked about his leadership style he said: 'It's leadership by encouragement and inspiration. I think if you take an optimistic attitude to things people will buy into it. Some people won't. But when you look at the people who are giving me a hard time, its odds-on that there's some sort of political side to it'. In relation to what difference direct election makes he is forthright: 'Being elected by the whole electorate creates a huge difference to my authority to do things. It also gives me the courage to make changes that, otherwise, would be very difficult to make'.

Leadership lessons

- Central governments can introduce legislation to enable individual cities to choose their own form of urban governance. This flexibility can act as a spur to experimentation with different ways of doing things which can, in turn, be shared with other localities
- The Directly Elected Mayor (DEM) form of governance provides a high level of visibility to the leadership role. There is no doubt at all that Mayor Ferguson is a much more visible public figure than previous leaders of the City of Bristol. This prominence stems partly from the process of direct election (involving more than 20 public debates and a good level of media coverage), and partly from the open approach to leadership taken by the Mayor. For example, he makes extensive use of Twitter to communicate with the public and is frequently seen walking about the city. Despite his heavy workload, Mayor Ferguson tries to prioritise responding to the media and is very well known in the city.
- The DEM model of governance enhances the legitimacy of the political leader of the city. This legitimacy arises from the nature of the election process (citizens chose this particular person to be city leader), and also from the sheer numbers involved. We can note that, even though the voter turnout was, at 28%, relatively low, Mayor Ferguson received more personal votes than most Members of Parliament. For example, Mayor Ferguson's tally of 37,353 votes is more, in actual numbers, than the number of votes Prime Minister David Cameron received in the safe Tory seat of Witney
- The DEM model of governance appears to strengthen place-based leadership in that the person elected is granted authority directly by the citizens of the city, rather than by some kind of indirect process. Mayor Ferguson's slogan, in his text book electoral campaign of 2012, was 'Bristol 1st' and he constantly makes the point that he is answerable to the population of the whole city, not a particular group of councillors in City Hall
- It is possible for a DEM to have a strong commitment to the development of the role of councillors in the governance of the city and, as part of this, to strengthen the neighbourhood governance of a city. Mayor Ferguson is keen to expand the role of

Neighbourhood Partnerships in the city, not least because he believes that more people should be directly involved in local governance.

Sources

Hambleton, R, Howard, J, 2013, Place-based leadership and public service innovation, *Local Government Studies* 39, 1, 47–70

Hambleton, R, Howard, J, Marsh, A, Sweeting, D, 2013, *The prospects for mayoral governance in Bristol*, The Bristol Civic Leadership Project. March. University of the West of England, Bristol: Bristol, http://bristolcivicleadership.net

Hambleton, R, Sweeting, D, 2014, Innovation in urban political leadership: Reflections on the introduction of a directly elected mayor in Bristol, UK, *Public Money and Management* 34, September, 315–322

For City Council activities: http://www.bristol.gov.uk

For the Bristol Pound: http://www.bristolpound.org

For Bristol Civic Leadership Project: http://bristolcivicleadership.net

Endnotes

[1] On behalf of two universities (University of the West of England, Bristol and the University of Bristol) the author is co-leading a research project – the Bristol Civic Leadership Project – designed to examine the impact of the mayoral model of the governance on the city and to provide advice to civic leaders. The first report from this study documents how various respondents felt about the prospects for mayoral governance in the city (Hambleton et al 2013). The survey work was carried out before the mayoral elections in November 2012 so that the study has built up a good picture of attitudes 'before' the model of urban governance was changed. Further research is in hand to discover whether people's hopes and fears about the model were, or were not, justified. In an earlier study we examined the performance of civic leadership in Bristol before there was any suggestion of having an elected mayor (Hambleton and Howard 2013).

[2] These figures are derived from stratified public opinion surveys of Bristol citizens carried out, as part of the Bristol Civic Leadership Project, in September 2012 (658 respondents) and January 2014 (648 respondents).

[3] This and subsequent quotes attributed to Mayor Ferguson are from a personal interview carried out by the author on 23 April 2013.

Conclusions

Daniel Burnham, the influential American architect and city planner, is probably best known for his work, with Edward Bennett, on the visionary *Plan of Chicago* published in 1909. The plan, a startling document by any standards, had a major impact on the development of Chicago. Burnham's imaginative approach to planning and civic leadership has influenced generations of urban planners, and not just in the USA. The quote at the beginning of this chapter, attributed to

Burnham by Charles Moore, his friend and biographer, sums up his ambitious approach to place-based leadership: 'Make no little plans'. Burnham was certainly far sighted, but it would be quite wrong to picture him as the 'go it alone' heroic leader taking command of the city region. As Smith (2006, 71) shows in impressive detail: '... creating the *Plan* was an immensely complex undertaking that included the efforts of many people'.

In this chapter I have suggested that powerful forces shape the context within which place-based leadership is exercised. Influential place-less leaders – in globalised corporations and central governments – may care little about the quality of life of particular communities living in particular localities. A key challenge for place-based leaders is to understand how to use their local power to negotiate with place-less organisations to bring about desirable outcomes and enhance the power of local democracy. The analysis presented here suggests that place-based leadership can, depending on the context, work to expand the amount of political space available to local communities.

The chapter has provided an introduction to theories of leadership and, by drawing on this literature and on the practice of innovative cities in different parts of the world, has outlined a way of conceptualising place-based leadership. This posits the existence in any given locality of five overlapping realms of leadership: political, managerial/professional, business, community and trade union. The areas of overlap between these realms can be construed as innovation zones – areas providing opportunities for learning and exchange between people with different backgrounds, experiences and knowledge. Cities are riven with conflicts and, in many settings, there is dispute and friction between diverse interests. It follows that potential innovation zones can easily become conflict zones. Successful civic leaders set the tone for local conversations and orchestrate a shared process of social discovery. They can turn conflict zones into innovation zones.

In Chapter 3 I noted the shift from government to governance and offered a critique of **New Public Management** (NPM). I suggested that NPM should be discarded in favour of a different idea – **New Civic Leadership** (NCL). This approach to leadership involves reshaping the boundaries between the state and civil society, and invites us to reconceptualise the nature of public leadership. Innovation Story 2 on mayoral governance in Bristol provides an example of what I have in mind. In a globalising world, in which place-less leaders have been granted too much power, reformers need to advance the collective power of local communities to shape public policy outcomes. In this chapter I have attempted to sketch out the main components of this **New Civic Leadership** – a place-based approach to public policy making and community empowerment.

CHAPTER 6

Leading public service innovation

What we need to add to our list of managerial skills is improvisation – the art of adjusting, flexibly adapting, learning through trial-and-error initiatives, inventing ad hoc responses, and discovering as you go
Frank J. Barrett, *Yes to the Mess*, 2012

Introduction

Frank Barrett is an accomplished jazz musician. He is also a professor of management and public policy and, in his recent book, he constructs an intriguing conversation between the worlds of jazz improvisation and organisational innovation. His way of thinking provides many valuable insights, and we will draw on his analysis in this chapter. Early on he sets the tone:

> Human beings are at their best when they are open to the world, able to notice what's needed, and equipped with the skills to respond meaningfully in the moment. Improvisation grows out of a receptivity to what the situation offers and thus the first move is a "yes to the mess". (Barrett 2012, xii)

Whilst we did not know it at the time, Barrett's analysis aligns closely with findings emerging from research Jo Howard and I were carrying out on the leadership of public service innovation in the UK and The Netherlands (Hambleton and Howard 2012). Our action/research collaboration with three innovative cities indicates that a key role for civic leaders is to create a culture in which risk taking and experimentation are valued and encouraged. This is consistent with Barrett's view that leaders need to embolden people to try something new, knowing that the results will, in all likelihood, be unexpected and 'unexpectable', including errors. This is not the dominant culture in public service organisations in most countries. On the contrary, too much of the time, the people who get promoted in public bureaucracies are those who can offer a 'safe pair of hands'. There is a tendency for those who never take risks to get rewarded; the fact that conservative behaviour constantly misses opportunities is rarely penalised.

In stable times playing it safe, always taking the cautious route, might be acceptable. An adjustment here, a tweak there, a bit less of this, a sliver more of that, might enable organisations to survive and, in some circumstances, do tolerably well. But, as Donald Schon (1971) explained in his sagacious book, *Beyond the Stable State,* we do not live in stable times. He argued, and many books have followed to reinforce his thesis, that we are experiencing an unprecedented and accelerating rate of change. His central conclusion is that, 'Our need is to develop institutional structures, ways of knowing, and an ethic, for the process of change itself' (Schon 1971, 11). We will return to Donald Schon's ideas shortly.

The opening section of this chapter provides an orientation to the expanding field of public service innovation, and highlights the importance of place-based innovation. Writers on innovation often seem to neglect the politics of place as a key driver of social innovation. This is, perhaps, because the dominant discourse relating to public service innovation tends, even now, to be dominated by managerial and/or technological ways of seeing. Too many think tanks, and their followers in the media anxious for newsworthy claims and counter claims, see innovation as a technological fix. This chapter will attempt to provide a corrective by suggesting that, while scientists and technical experts have a vital contribution to make to social progress, radical public service innovation is more likely to be driven by groups of people working together in specific places solving particular problems. In the words of one very effective green activist – bold innovation is likely to stem from local groups 'just doing stuff' (Hopkins 2013).

This chapter contains four Innovation Stories showing how local leaders are bringing about place-based innovation to advance the cause of social inclusion. Thousands of similar stories could be told. The ones identified here can, perhaps, best be seen as harbingers of different ways of moving towards the creation of the inclusive cities I outlined in Chapter 1. Innovation Story 3 explains how Mayor Daley of Chicago introduced a three-digit phone number – 311 being the number used in the USA – to provide instant access to public services within seconds. This story shows how professional, well-educated employees, when assisted by sophisticated information technology, can bring about a massive boost in citizen accessibility to public services.

The next two Innovation Stories outline the experiences of two local authorities that have broken entirely new ground in relation to helping families suffering extreme social and economic difficulties. The Swindon Family LIFE Programme in England is an imaginative initiative designed to co-create a new approach to working with families facing multiple difficulties. Innovation Story 4 describes the way a range of public service providers are working with the families themselves to break new ground by focusing, not on the needs of families, the traditional centre of attention in public service provision, but on ways of reframing thinking and practice relating to helping families in chronic crisis.[1] Innovation Story 5 describes the Social GP Programme that has been developed in the Dutch city of Enschede. This story outlines the development of a new approach to tackling deprivation on an area basis. It records an interesting mix of shared governance at the strategic level, and bold innovation on the front line of service delivery.

In Chapter 2 I noted that many of the most challenging problems facing those concerned to create inclusive cities are to be found in the rapidly expanding cities in the developing countries of the world. Innovation Story 6 outlines the creative initiative taken in Langrug, an informal settlement not far from Capetown, South

Africa. The efforts to improve the quality of life in Langrug have attracted local, national and international attention – not least because they employ inventive approaches to co-production and social inclusion.

These Innovation Stories pave the way for a discussion of themes and challenges relating to the leadership of effective, place-based social innovation to create more inclusive cities. The emerging argument, revealed in glimpses in the Innovation Stories, is that leading effective public service innovation involves the development of new ways of leading and new ways of being a leader.

Public service innovation – an orientation

As mentioned in Chapter 1 public service innovation is now a hot topic in public policy circles. The onset of austerity in many countries, following the financial crash of 2008, has forced politicians and managers to focus on new ways of doing things. Carrying on the same way, plus or minus a little bit, is not going to cut it. Across the world we find cities reconsidering the way they relate to the citizens they are there to serve. There can be little doubt that acute financial pressures on the public purse are forcing many cities to reconsider the way they can best serve their citizens. But something much more interesting than conventional 'cutback management' is taking place in many cities. As Charles Leadbeater argues, the changing resource outlook is fostering a wave of place-based innovation with committed people '... solving real-world problems that matter to them, where they live and work' (Leadbeater 2014, xi). Here I highlight three related themes relating to public service innovation that emerge from the argument presented in earlier chapters.

From public service improvement to public service innovation

In Chapter 1 I drew a distinction between public service improvement and public service innovation. While this change may not be front-of-stage in every country, it is an important one for all those interested to enhance the quality and effectiveness of public services. Let's recap on this argument. Improvement lies within the realm of traditional performance management. In public service organisations adopting an improvement strategy, politicians will, typically, set performance targets, require their public servants to monitor inputs and outputs, assess outcomes and progress towards the targets, and then make adjustments to enhance service effectiveness. The focus of organisational effort is, as a rule, on delivering more of the same (or very similar) services to clients in an ever more cost effective way. This was exactly the model we used when I worked in corporate planning in English local government in the 1970s (Hambleton 1978). And this approach – often described as performance planning – remains very popular in public management practice today (Joyce 2012, 196–207).

When an organisation engages in innovation it steps *beyond* conventional performance management. It undertakes a more radical assessment of its own effectiveness. It explores new ways of delivering results and leaders cultivate a willingness in their staff to try out new ideas. As I explained in Chapter 5, a shift towards a public innovation ethos requires a strategic change in organisational leadership. It involves a move 'from mission command to directed opportunism' (Bungay 2011, 83). In Chapter 1 I drew on organisational learning theory, as developed by Chris Argyris and Donald Schon (1978), to clarify this shift. These authors distinguish between 'single loop learning' – improvement in my terms – and 'double loop learning' – innovation in my terms. In the former valuable learning takes place and adjustments are made that can be very beneficial – but the underlying organisational norms are not challenged. There is a single feedback loop. The central question asked is: How can we get closer to achieving our targets?

When leaders strive for public service innovation they recognise that the organisation cannot deliver a significant increase in effectiveness by doing more of what it already knows how to do. In double loop learning the very norms that define effective performance are up for review. In contrast to single loop learning members of the organisation are not just thinking about how to achieve specified targets. They are actively asking: Are these sensible targets in the first place? In practice, and I readily acknowledge this, there is often an area of overlap between what we might describe as radical improvement and innovation, and I am not, here, trying to establish watertight categories. Rather I am attempting to highlight an important difference in organisational culture – in particular, a difference in attitude to risk taking. Signalling whether risk taking is welcome or unacceptable is a key task for civic leaders. The vocabulary is important here – sensible leaders advocate the benefits of an experimental approach. Advocating being risky feeds the media and the population at large the wrong message. Explaining why new ideas are being trialled, on a 'let's try this and see' basis, has proved to be far more persuasive with the citizenry.

Renegotiating the relationships between the citizen and the state

Our second theme concerns the changing relationships between the governed and those governing. In Chapter 3 I distinguished three broad approaches to public service reform and these are shown in Figure 3.1. I offered a critique of traditional bureaucratic management, outlined the weaknesses of market and quasi-market models in public services, and pointed to the importance of public service organisations treating people as citizens – not as clients, consumers or customers. That chapter reviews the changing relationships between civil society, markets and the state. In Figure 3.2, and the associated discussion, I highlighted the potential for new kinds of collaboration in the areas of overlap between civil society and the state, and between civil society and market. A new vocabulary is emerging to help us imagine and understand new forms of collaborative endeavour, and I sketched out the distinctions that can be made between co-governance, co-management and co-production (Brandsen and Pestoff 2006). Chapter 5 developed this argument and suggested that the areas of overlap between the different realms of place-based leadership provide innovation zones, areas where significant opportunities for public service innovation can arise – see Figure 5.3.

Christian Bason notes, correctly, that the central idea behind co-creation is that new solutions are designed *with* people, not *for* them. He observes that co-creation is strongly connected to notions of 'participatory design' and 'co-design' and he writes: 'Involving people inside and outside the organisation throughout the process of creation is the key…' (Bason 2010, 8). While the idea of co-creation may be relatively new to private sector companies and central governments, it is important to note that co-production of public services, an approach involving elements of co-creation, has been well-established practice in the field of community development for decades. Marilyn Taylor notes, for example, that 'community management has long been part of development policy in the global South, where the absence of state provision places a premium on local knowledge and resources in the delivery of services and the management of water and other amenities' (Taylor 2011, 33).

There is, in fact, a significant body of evidence from citizen involvement initiatives in developing countries to show that local ownership of projects and active participation in development processes represents a creative approach to community problem-solving (Leavy and Howard 2013). Innovation Story 6, on pro-poor settlement upgrading in South Africa, provides but one example of how the Global North may be able to learn from the Global South.

Systemic innovation – making new connections

In Chapter 5 I discussed the changing nature of the public leadership task. I suggested that the changing context for civic leadership, notably the shift from government to governance, requires facilitative leaders able to reach out to, and build successful relationships with, other stakeholders. Individual public agencies 'going it alone' are not going to be effective in the modern world. However, action-oriented advice on how to exercise leadership in partnership settings remains thin on the ground. Useful books on collaborative public management are available, but these do not say a great deal about the changing nature of leadership in collaborative settings (Agranoff 2012; Agranoff and McGuire 2003). In the UK context Paul Williams does, however, provide a step forward in his helpful discussion of 'leaders as boundary spanners' (Williams 2012, 100–113). And Richard Margerum, in his analysis of collaboration in relation to natural resource management and environmental planning in the USA and Australia, offers useful insights on the role of political leadership in shaping collaborative activities (Margerum 2011, 247–56).

Why are these comments about the challenges facing collaborative leadership relevant to this discussion of public service innovation? Because public leaders and managers are discovering, little by little, that it makes a great deal of sense to adopt a whole systems approach to tackling many community problems. This is because the most intractable challenges facing modern societies are fiendishly complex, and solutions lie beyond the competence of any individual organisation or agency.[2] Take the challenges facing families in chronic crisis. As Innovation Stories 4 and 5 illustrate in vivid detail, such families, attract the attention of multiple agencies – from health, education, housing and social care through to the police and probation services. In the absence of systemic understanding individual agencies could well take action in relation to such families that, unintentionally, perpetuates the problems the interventions are designed to address.

Mulgan and Leadbeater (2013) offer useful insights on the challenges facing those who wish to engage in systemic – or 'joined up' – innovation. The analysis they present draws on current private sector thinking, which suggests that successful companies of today 'widen the lens' to consider the way their products and services fit within a wider system of innovation (Adner 2012).[3] These ideas are useful. However, a weakness with this approach is that, possibly because it stems from private sector experience, it tends to neglect the potential role of political power to reshape the system. The Innovation Stories in this book provide substantial evidence to show that facilitative, political leadership can play a decisive role in reconfiguring the way services are organised and delivered – place-based political leadership can actively promote and drive systemic innovation.

Defining public service innovation

We will develop these themes relating to public service innovation later in the chapter. At this point it is helpful to recap on the definition of innovation I presented in Chapter 1. My definition of public service innovation is: Creating a new approach to public service, putting it into practice and finding out if it works. Innovation is, in my view, much more than having a bright idea. Coming up with something new is the easy bit – it's putting the idea into practice and discovering how well it works that's the tough part. Influenced by Donald Schon's ideas on public learning, my definition of innovation not only embraces application of the new idea in the world of practice. It also suggests that innovation should be seen as a process of local social discovery and that it is, therefore, incumbent on those involved to attempt to identify lessons from experience with the innovation. Public service innovation is, then, closely aligned with the notion of lesson drawing in public policy (Rose 1993; 2005). The Innovation Stories in this book resonate with this approach. In each case an attempt is made to draw lessons, or potential lessons, from the story for the practice of public leadership.

New technology as servant: the Chicago 311 service

When it comes to service responsiveness via the telephone the public sector puts the private sector to shame. In an emergency, in the UK, you can dial 999 anywhere in the country – a competent person answers the phone straight away and you receive immediate help.[4] This responsiveness outperforms the very best in the private sector on four counts.

First, this is a three-digit number. You can remember it and dial without having to waste time looking up the number on the Internet or elsewhere. Second, there are no choices to make. Forget about an automated voice saying 'Please choose from the following options'. Third, someone answers the phone. Forget about 'You are now in a queue and your call will be answered shortly' or, worse than that, 'All our customer service lines are busy, please try later'. Fourth, a professionally trained phone operator helps you immediately. Forget about 'Please hold while I check whether we can deal with this'.

Some will say: 'Fair enough. You are right to say that the private sector is way off the pace when compared with our 999 telephone service, but this is our national emergency number. Local authorities cannot possibly deliver this astonishing quality of service.' Wrong answer.

In the USA the national emergency number is 911 (covering ambulance, fire and police, as does 999 in the UK). In many cities, and here I will highlight Chicago's experience as I lived there and used this service for five years, there is a 311 non-emergency number operating alongside 911. In Chicago, if you want information about public services, or you need to request a non-emergency service, all you do is dial 311 – any time, night or day. You will speak straight away to someone who can help you. That's it.

Innovation Story 3 explains how, behind this breathtaking simplicity, is a prize winning combination of well-trained people and up to date technology. The 311 rapid response service is not limited to Chicago. Baltimore Police Department deserve recognition for setting up the first 311 help line in the early 1990s. When President Bill Clinton endorsed the approach in a campaign speech in 1996 a number of elected mayors picked up on the model, and 311 is now in operation in a large number of US cities – from New York to Los Angeles and from Detroit to Houston. Some other countries have emulated this American innovation. For example, the Beijing Services and Information Centre provides a similar level of responsiveness, except here the number is 12345, and cities like Toronto in Canada also offer a 311 service.

In the Chicago example, Mayor Daley wanted to change the relationship between those providing services and those requesting them. His civic leadership introduced a seismic shift making city services much more accessible to everyone. Mayor Rahm Emanuel, who was elected Mayor of Chicago in 2011 after Mayor Daley retired, is now enhancing the 311 service by making use of new technology – he launched a new online 'Open311' service in 2012.

INNOVATION STORY 3

Seeing like a citizen: the Chicago 311 service

Aims

The purpose of the 311 system in Chicago it to provide a 'one-stop' service for those wishing to access city services. The idea is to provide a highly responsive level of public service over the telephone and, more recently, via the internet.

Chicago residents can telephone 311 – 24 hours a day, 7 days a week – to report service needs, check the status of previous requests, obtain information regarding city programmes or events and file police reports. In addition, the 311 service provides a back-up facility for the 911 emergency communications service.

Innovation Story outline

Mayor Richard M. Daley became frustrated with departmentalism in Chicago City Hall in the mid 1990s. He found it difficult to establish how well different departments were responding to requests made by citizens for information and/or service action. In January 1999, in a bold reform, he introduced the 311 system into city government. In taking this step he was aiming not just for improvements in public service efficiency: 'We decided to consolidate all the separate complaints procedures run by different departments into one system in order to improve accountability and transparency – as well as strengthen responsiveness. We certainly wanted service improvements. But, more than that, we wanted citizens to feel that public servants were working for them.'[1]

Over 2,000 city employees were trained in how to use the new system and, in 2000, Mayor Daley created 311 City Services as a separate unit of government. In the years since then the service has continued to improve and develop. Mayor Daley again: 'In the beginning the focus was on complaints but it soon expanded into cultural events. We tried to make the service as inclusive as possible – ranging from responding to complaints to providing information about events in the city.'

The service request and delivery process of the 311 service is as follows:

- A service request is created and routed automatically to the proper department
- The caller receives a service request number to simplify follow up
- A checklist of steps to resolve the problem is generated
- The checklist is translated into work orders or other appropriate action
- City staff respond to the request
- The response is monitored and any additional activities are assigned as needed

Behind this elegant simplicity is a prize winning combination of well-trained people and up to date technology. First, there is a team of 69 highly trained operations personnel who strive to ensure that every caller gets a prompt, courteous and helpful response. Currently headed by Audrey Mathis, a director with extensive previous project management experience in city government, the team works in a spacious call centre. The office is well designed and phone operators are enthusiastic and committed.

Second, the 311 staff are supported by a sophisticated computer system that routes requests electronically to the appropriate department to take the necessary action. More than that, this system enables supervisors to monitor the progress of any given job and deal quickly with any problems that might be causing delay.

The City of Chicago has a population of 2.7 million and, in 2012, the 311 centre, dealt with 3.8 million calls. About half of these – around 1.9 million – were requests for information and were dealt with then and there.

'When does the Taste of Chicago event begin?', 'How can my child apply for a summer job?', 'What's this I hear about Lake Shore Drive being closed to vehicles so that cyclists can "Bike the drive"?', 'Where is the nearest location for community tax assistance centres?'. These are the kinds of questions that will be answered within seconds by 311 staff as the information is only a keystroke away.

What about the other calls – the 1.9 million service requests? For example, 'Can you fix the broken street light at the corner of my block?', 'Do you know about the offensive graffiti scribbled on the underpass?'. Also, what about those citizens who don't call the 311 number, but instead call a local authority department directly? Will this duplicate action and create confusion? No. Whoever answers the phone in any department simply enters the request into the system, and it is handled in the same way as requests made direct to the 311 number. Citizens can also, of course, make service requests via the Internet or through mobile phones and these are also integrated into the system.

Don't speak English? Don't worry. The 311 operators have access to a language bank and can request the services of a qualified translator in over 100 languages.

Mayor Rahm Emanuel, elected as mayor of Chicago in 2011, after Mayor Daley retired from office, is keen to enhance the quality of 311 by making use of new technology. In 2012, he launched a new online 'Open311' service request system to go alongside the well-established 311 service. This enables citizens to track service requests via the internet – from the time they are submitted to the end point when citizens receive an email indicating the issue is resolved. Unlike the one-to-one communication of existing 311 call centres, Open311 technologies use the internet to provide many-to-many communication – citizens can use the system to exchange information around a single topic or concern. In launching the new system, which includes the 'Service Tracker' capacity, Mayor Emanuel stated: 'The new system brings an unprecedented level of transparency and accountability to City government... and it also provides an open government information platform upon which to build new applications'.[2]

Leadership lessons

- Powerful elected local authorities decide whether or not they want to have a 311 service, not state or national governments. Local leaders in the US have the authority to innovate, and this is not the case in all countries
- Directly elected mayors in the US and Canada are leading the way in using new technology to make city hall bureaucracies more open, transparent and responsive. They have the political legitimacy to initiate bold changes of this kind
- 311 services can assist neighbourhood-based politicians (called aldermen in Chicago) and community-based organisations by providing detailed information on public service performance on a neighbourhood basis
- Professional, well-educated employees, appointed by local authorities to bring about public service innovation, can have a major impact on the quality of public service delivery and responsiveness
- 311 starts from the point of view of the citizen – it draws on local knowledge, experiences and priorities. This idea of 'seeing like a citizen' can help public bureaucracies move away from 'seeing like a state.'

Sources

The City of Chicago provides more information at: www.cityofchicago.org/311
Many US and Canadian cities have 311 websites. For example:
Houston – http://hfdapp.houstontx.gov/311/index.php
New York – http://www.nyc.gov/apps/311/
Toronto – http://www.toronto.ca/311/
For more on Open311 visit: http://open311.org/

End notes

[1] The quotations from Mayor Daley stem from a personal interview carried out by the author on 23 April 2012

[2] Mayor Emanuel, public announcement, 20 September 2012

Working with families in crisis: the Swindon Family LIFE programme

The Chicago Innovation Story shows how bold civic leadership can enhance the quality of public services for all citizens and service users in the city. Our next Innovation Story examines a radical initiative designed to focus support on a small minority of the population – families in chronic crisis. The Family LIFE initiative in Swindon, England, is an imaginative effort designed to co-create a new approach to working with families facing intense difficulties. The acronym LIFE stands for 'Lives for Individuals and Families to Enjoy' and this, in itself, points to the radical nature of the reform process that Swindon's public service agencies have embarked on. Instead of focussing on the needs of the families –

the traditional centre of attention in public service provision – the programme sets out to reframe thinking and practice.

As described in Innovation Story 4, the heart of the initiative is the belief that new sets of relationships need to be developed between public services and families in chronic crisis, and that the main focus should be to develop the capabilities of families, not 'meet needs'. This innovative approach, which is based on a methodology developed by *Participle*, a social enterprise providing public service consultancy advice, involves a dedicated team working very closely with a small number of families to develop the capabilities of the families to meet their aspirations.

The Swindon Family LIFE approach, which is led by Swindon Borough Council working in partnership with a range of public service providers (including the health service, police service and voluntary organisations) and the families themselves, has attracted national attention. In 2010 Swindon was selected by central government to be one of sixteen Community Budget pilots designed to develop new approaches to working with 'families with complex needs'. A striking feature of the approach is the way that political and managerial leaders have set a tone which positively welcomes innovation. The Family LIFE team has not disappointed. By adopting a systemic approach they have assisted many troubled families improve their situation and have also saved the taxpayer money.

INNOVATION STORY 4

Breaking new ground in working with troubled families: the Family LIFE programme in Swindon

Aims

The origins of the Family LIFE programme can be traced back to 2007/08. Public service professionals in Swindon – from the Borough Council, the Primary Care Trust, Wiltshire Constabulary, Probation and the South West Strategic Health Authority – were becoming increasingly concerned about the relative ineffectiveness of public services to improve the lives of families with multiple problems, despite the high level of spending on each family – identified in some studies as being in the region of £250,000 per family per year. The families tended to have a long history of difficulties – for example, domestic violence, anti social behaviour, adults with mental illness, children taken into care, threats of eviction, unemployment and children not in education.

In simple terms the aim of the Family LIFE initiative is to improve outcomes for troubled families by working with them in a different way. The acronym stands for 'Lives for Individuals and Families to Enjoy'. As well as raising family self esteem and capabilities the approach strives to obtain much better value for money from public spending.

Innovation Story outline

A key turning point was when, following various informal conversations with agency leaders, the Strategic Health Authority and the Swindon Borough Council agreed to commission *Participle*, a social enterprise, to develop a different way of working with families experiencing multiple difficulties.[1] The LIFE programme and methodology was co-developed by *Participle* and Swindon public agencies working with families, schools and staff during 2008 and 2009.

Sue Wald, Head of Commissioning for Children and Adults, recalls the discussion: 'That really was the start as we had identified that there was a problem with the existing model. *Participle* said: "Give us twelve of your most difficult families and we'll spend time with them…"' [2] *Participle* sent three staff to live in accommodation near the families and, after three months, the team prepared a presentation for elected members and senior executives. The findings showed that not only did the families feel isolated, but that professional staff also felt relatively powerless in being able to create positive change. Servers and served were utterly frustrated.

Sue Wald remembers that: 'The presentation had an electrifying effect.'[3] The research found that professionals were spending 74% of their time on administration, 12% on indirect work and only 14% on face-to-face contact with the families. This evidence created a platform for new thinking in public service delivery.

The next step in the innovation process was provided by a series of workshops with staff from right across the organisations involved, including the voluntary sector. Around 150 members of staff attended five different workshops. These provided an opportunity not just to feed back what the families said about the services they were receiving, but also enabled professionals to offer their own views on how they were working with the families.

These and other discussions facilitated by *Participle*, led to the suggestion that the Swindon Family LIFE programme should develop a new set of principles:

- 80/20 working (meaning professionals aiming to spend 80% of their time on face-to-face working and 20% on other)
- Meeting people 'where they are at'
- No agenda
- Honesty and compassion
- Opening up opportunities for change[4]

A multi-professional Family LIFE Programme team was created to develop the model by working with the families. The local authority was successful in attracting a 'Think Family' grant from the Whitehall Department of Children and Families, and this provided invaluable core funding for the two year period April 2009 – March 2011. Partner agencies agreed to second staff into the team of eleven (from health, housing, police, social services etc).

The approach involves three key features:

- A team of people working in new ways – building purposeful relationships between families, workers and the community
- Building capabilities for families and workers – to release new resources
- Building local community capacity – social networks, skills and training opportunities, enterprise opportunities, peer to peer learning

This is a very demanding model for all the members of the Family LIFE Programme team because preconceived notions of how to operate needed to be set aside. The radical nature of the model is illustrated by the fact that: the families select the workers to work with them (not the other way round); the workers are given no information about the families; the workers receive training in 'stripping off the system' (ie preconceived patterns of working); and the workers are expected to share some of themselves in their relationship building with the families.

In April 2011 Swindon was selected by central government to be one of sixteen national Community Budget pilots which later changed into the Troubled Families Initiative. Swindon responded by using the lessons from the Family LIFE Programme, as well as integrated working and Family Nurse Partnership experience, to expand to a model for working with 370 Troubled Families. The LIFE Team has been strengthened and now includes education psychologists as well as social workers and staff seconded from the police and housing.

Ofsted, the national Office for Standards in Education, Children's Services and Skills, provides independent inspection reports to the UK Parliament. Their analysis indicates that the Family LIFE Programme has had positive impacts for families and is good value for money.[5]

Leadership lessons

- The top leadership of the council – the political leader (Councillor Roderick Bluh), senior councillors and the chief executive – have set a tone for the council that expects innovation to take place. For example, Gavin Jones, the chief executive, stresses that leaders and managers need to be 'comfortable about being uncomfortable'.
- The culture of the organisation places a high value on critical self-reflection and shows an interest in personal as well as professional development.
- Leaders in Swindon have welcomed inputs from knowledgeable outsiders. Staff working for *Participle*, the social enterprise that has worked with Swindon to co-create the Family LIFE approach, have brought skill and energy to the innovation process.

- At various points in the story different leaders have been entrepreneurial in seeking external funds to underpin the public service innovation agenda.
- The institution of Swindon Borough Council has been redesigned to make it more effective. For example, staff from the National Health Service have been integrated with local authority staff to deliver integrated services for children, families and adults, whilst commissioning across adults, children and health has also been integrated.
- The LIFE Team has created a distinctive culture and narrative for all those working with it. This is built on coaching and empowering families whilst also challenging families to think of new possibilities for themselves. The leadership of the team, and continued reflective working and supervision, supports this culture.

Sources

Participle website: http://participle.net

Bunting, M, 2011, Tough love for troubled families, *The Guardian*, 9 February

Cottam, H, 2013, *The Life Programme: An interim report*, July, London: Participle

Hambleton, R, Howard, J, 2012, *Public sector innovation and local leadership in the UK and the Netherlands*, June, York: Joseph Rowntree Foundation

Ofsted, 2012, *Good practice resource – Working with families through the 'LIFE' programme: Swindon Borough Council*, November. www.ofsted.gov.uk/resources/good-practice-resource-working-families-through-%E2%80%98life%E2%80%99-programme-swindon-borough-council

Endnotes

[1] *Participle* is an innovative social enterprise that aims to build a new settlement between individuals, communities and government. In recent years it has established a good track record for developing bottom up processes of learning, often involving communities 'at the bottom of the heap'. More: http://participle.net.

[2] Interview with Sue Wald on 29 March 2011.

[3] Bunting 2011.

[4] From *Participle* Swindon Family LIFE Project presentation. *Participle* has developed a four stage methodology for its work and this has been deployed in Swindon: 0) Invitation, 1) Aspirations, 2) Capabilities, and 3) Opportunities.

[5] Ofsted 2012.

Tackling social disadvantage in Enschede, the Netherlands

The City of Enschede and three local housing associations have initiated a Neighbourhood Coach Project that is developing a new way of tackling problems of multiple deprivation.[5] This project, which is also known as the Social General Practitioner (GP) approach, represents, in the Dutch context at least, a new model. In many countries the medical GP is often the first point of contact for a patient requiring advice and assistance relating to their health. In simple terms the GP draws on a wide general knowledge, and a variety of health service providers, to meet the needs of the patient. While the parallel is not exact, the general idea behind the Social GP model is the same. Social GPs act as individual counsellors to people who face multiple or complex problems. The Social GPs are 'empowered to empower'.

Innovation Story 5 describes the background to the development of the Social GP approach, examines how the model works and offers some reflections on the leadership of this bold approach to public service innovation. Like their colleagues in Swindon, civic leaders in Enschede recognise that social exclusion is a multifaceted phenomenon. Social and economic deprivations are, in many cases, associated with issues in other domains of life – for example, disadvantage in education or poor health. Policies aimed at improving the life chances of households experiencing multiple problems face three major challenges:

- many of these households are served (or feel 'raided') by a small army of social professionals employed by numerous social and medical care organisations – an integrated approach is lacking;
- a minority of these households slip through the net and do not receive support at a point when emerging problems are at their early stages, and preventive action can avert future crisis;
- the care provided by professionals can be paternalistic and may make clients dependent on professional support rather than empowering them to take decisions about their lives into their own hands.

The Social GP approach aims to address these three related sets of challenges. In the City of Enschede some 25 institutional providers of specialised services agreed to grant the Social GPs informal decision-making power across various spheres of life – health, housing, education, safety, welfare and/or employment – while decision-making authority formally remains vested in the organisations.

INNOVATION STORY 5

Tackling urban deprivation: the Social GP programme in Enschede

Aims[1]

The Velve-Lindenhof neighbourhood is part of the City of Enschede, a town of approximately 160,000 inhabitants in the East of the Netherlands. In 2007 the Dutch central government identified this area as one of the 40 most deprived neighbourhoods in the country. Like the other 39 neighbourhoods, Velve-Lindenhof suffers from the combined effects of social, economic and physical disadvantage, which harms its socioeconomic climate and has a negative impact on the individual life chances of the people living there. Launched in 2008, the Dutch *Neighbourhood Policy Initiative* aims to improve the life chances of residents in these deprived areas.

In the Enschede case, local leaders decided to try the Social GP model in the Velve-Lindenhof neighbourhood. The aim is to improve the life-chances of over 600 residents. The Social GPs (also described as Neighbourhood Coaches) pursue an outreach approach; through house calls they make contact with residents who might be experiencing multiple or complex problems. This strategy is designed not just to provide a more integrated approach to multi-problem households, but also to promote appropriate preventive action.

Innovation Story outline

In the Velve-Lindenhof neighbourhood the Social GP model is summarised in the slogan: 'One family, one plan, one coordinator'. For each household (one family), one Social GP replaces a range of specialised frontline workers, unless specialist expertise is called for. The Social GPs act as individual counsellors to residents of the neighbourhood. Based on the ambitions and competences of the residents the Social GPs agree ways in which the families can address their problems, and start building a better future (one plan of action).

Like medical GPs, the Social GPs try to meet the needs of individuals directly themselves, unless the complexity of the situation calls for the expertise of a specialist. In case of referral to 'the second line', the Social GP continues to govern the implementation of the plan of action. Their central position in both the governance of the network of professionals, and in the actual service delivery, is designed to enable the Social GPs to work across professional boundaries in an integrated manner (one coordinator). Moreover, the approach takes the ambitions and competencies of individual residents as the starting point and aims at empowering, rather than caring for, these individuals.

The Social GP model builds on previous initiatives in the neighbourhood but is more radical. At the strategic level it is based on shared governance: a coalition of 25 community and governmental organisations has agreed voluntarily to introduce this integrated approach to the social emancipation of residents and multi-problem households. In order to implement this strategy, at the operational level, four Social GPs were empowered to act decisively in pursuit of an integrated plan of action that had been worked out with the individual families.

In a formal sense, the model was based on an agreement of 25 organisations. However, in an informal sense, Hans Weggemans, the Director of Enschede's Social Support and Welfare Department, and Fons Cateau, Director of a local housing company, took a lead. Their leadership was influential in encouraging the various organisations to try out a new approach. The initiative was taken in a context in which the Dutch national government, in its new *Neighbourhood Policy Initiative*, had invited the municipality of Enschede and its local partners, including housing associations, to develop a Neighbourhood Action Plan for the Velve-Lindenhof. The Social GP initiative was supported by the three housing associations with property in the neighbourhood. A think tank, comprised of innovation-minded officials from a variety of municipal departments and community organisations and a number of independent experts, was established. The ideas developed in this group were then discussed and agreed upon in a meeting of the managers of the 25 organisations. Based on this agreement a plan of action was developed and the programme started in 2008. For the professional social welfare officials the fact that the costs of the new project would be funded by a special subsidy provided by the three local housing associations, was crucial for the acceptance of this plan.

A research team at the University of Twente has carried out an evaluation of the programme.[2] This research has shown that the GP's had sufficient expertise and competences to fulfill their central role and they were able to cooperate with professionals from partner organisations. They were also successful in realising the ambitious objectives regarding their work process. Moreover they produced outputs that were largely in line with the objectives of the model. They achieved improvements in the social competences of the residents, particularly for those who really needed it. Moreover, it was shown that longer support resulted in larger improvements. Finally the Social GPs succeeded in realising many improvements in the social situation of the residents, although more results and stronger indications for effectiveness were found in some fields than in others.

The researchers asked professionals and managers from all participating organisations to assess the plans of action developed and implemented by the Social GPs according to a list of eight criteria. These included measures like responsiveness, flexibility, effectiveness, tailor-made and so on. On the whole the plans of action received high scores (mainly over 3 on a scale of 1 to 4) from both the participating organisations and the Social GPs themselves. The research team also asked the respondents to compare the plans of action that the Social GPs have worked out with conventional plans of action developed and implemented elsewhere in Enschede. The findings reveal that the experimental approach is considered to produce better results in terms of all of the criteria. The respondents are particularly positive about the flexibility and efficiency of the plans of action, and their capacity to provide for integrated and tailor-made service provision.

Leadership lessons

- An informal alliance of managerial and community leaders at the strategic level set the stage for this innovative project. The fact that the initiative was shared with an influential and widely respected community organisation – The Velve-Lindenhof Community Council – was important in establishing the legitimacy of the programme.
- The innovative project was initiated in the context of a collaborative network involving 25 organisations. The involvement of middle managers, front line workers and external experts from various organisations at an early stage contributed to the successful adoption of this innovation.
- The programme combines strategic leadership with a distinctive model of frontline, or street-level, leadership at the operational level. The four Social GPs are 'empowered to empower' and they have the legitimacy and authority to span organisational boundaries.

- At the operational level, the legitimacy of the new model was strengthened by the careful selection of the Social GPs (experienced people with different but complementary backgrounds). The tactful operation of the Social GPs in relation to the partnering organisations (collaborative rather than confrontational) has also contributed to the success of the experiment so far.
- The experiences with the 'one family, one plan, one coordinator' approach implemented by the team of neighbourhood coaches have been widely shared with other municipalities and have been brought to the attention of central government. This contributed to the legitimacy of the innovative concept, inspiring other Dutch cities to start social innovations of their own along the lines of the Social GP Programme.
- There are challenges of transition from a neighbourhood focus to a citywide approach. To run a highly visible pilot project, endorsed by national government, in one neighbourhood is one thing. To extend such a programme to the city level, in a context where additional funding is no longer available, presents a new set of challenges.

Sources

Denters, B, Klok, PJ, Oude Vrielink, M, 2012, 'The Social GP Programme in Enschede' in R Hambleton, Howard J, *Public Sector Innovation and Local Leadership in the UK and the Netherlands*, June, 19–25 York: Joseph Rowntree Foundation.

Oude Vrielink, M, Klok, PJ, Denters B, 2012, *Handling tensions in cross-boundary working: The case of the Enschede neighbourhood coaches.* Paper presented at the NIG conference Leuven 29–30 November.

Klok, PJ, Denters,B, Oude Vrielink, M, 2013, *Effectiveness of the social general practitioner: The case of the Enschede neighbourhood coaches*, Paper presented at the EURA conference, Enschede 3–6 July.

Endnotes

[1] This Innovation Story draws directly on the analysis of the Social GP programme provided by Bas Denters, Pieter-Jan Klok and Mirjan Oude Vrielink. This initial assessment appears as Chapter 4 in *Public Sector Innovation and Local Leadership in the UK and the Netherlands* (Hambleton and Howard 2012). I am most grateful to them for giving me permission to draw on this material in this chapter.

[2] Bas Denters, Pieter-Jan Klok and Mirjan Oude Vrielink have written several publications outlining the findings of this research – see sources above.

Pro-poor settlement upgrading in South Africa

As discussed in Chapter 2, city leaders in developing countries face formidable challenges. The evidence presented there suggests there are probably more than one billion squatters in the world today – yes, that's equivalent to more than 1,300 cities the size of London. Truly enormous numbers of people have moved to cities in the hope that the city will provide them, and their families, with opportunities for a better life. However, as Tanja Winkler has argued in the South African context, the residents of informal settlements 'live without security of tenure and they also live with very little, if any, access to urban infrastructure, including access to taps and functioning toilets' (Winkler 2013a, 12). She argues, and it is a compelling analysis, that public policy in South Africa, until not that long ago, aspired to the misguided aim of eradicating informal settlements by 2014. Now, thankfully, progressive policy makers realise that erasing slums is a non-starter. Rather, the challenge is to transform the way state institutions work with the residents of informal settlements.

Shack/Slum Dwellers International (SDI) is a network of community-based organisations of the urban poor in 33 countries in Africa, Asia and Latin America.[6] Launched in 1996, SDI aims to promote community-to-community learning and exchange relating to pro-poor strategies, and strives to influence governments and international organisations. SDI believes that the only way to manage urban growth, and to create inclusive cities, is for the urban poor to be at the centre of urban development strategies. The ethos of SDI is very much in line with the idea of co-creating solutions that I mentioned earlier in the chapter. Consistent with well-established community development practice, SDI argues that, when communities own the process of settlement upgrading they are able to ensure that it is sustainable and continues to prosper over time.

Evidence suggesting co-creation of solutions is an effective strategy finds support in a recent study of 84 participatory research projects involving people living in extreme poverty and marginalisation in 107 countries (Leavy and Howard 2013). These authors provide a useful chapter explaining why development that is sustainable requires meaningful participation of the people affected. Some 70% of the studies they examined highlighted that *how* people experience interventions in their lives is as important to them as *what* the intervention can offer them. Moreover, successful strategies bring local assets such as knowledge, culture and networks to the development process.

Innovation Story 6 provides an outline of the pro-poor settlement upgrading taking place in Langrug, South Africa. It is a good illustration of the kind of strong community engagement found in SDI projects across the Global South. In 2012 Langrug, an informal settlement of less than 5,000 people in the Stellenbosch Municipality, won the South African Planning Institute's (SAPI) award for good 'community/outreach' planning. This award is granted to a community that has embarked on an exemplary participatory and/or outstanding community development project that has improved the quality of community life and/or overcome difficult local circumstances.

INNOVATION STORY 6

Pro-poor settlement upgrading, Langrug, South Africa

Aims

Langrug, an informal settlement of around 1,900 shacks in Stellenbosch, Western Cape, is home to about 4,100 people. The settlement was established in 1992 to accommodate seasonal labourers working on the surrounding wine farms. A large dam construction project increased the number of residents significantly in recent years. The residents still find seasonal work on the nearby farms, from September to March, and also work in shops, restaurants and other businesses in nearby Franschhoek. The settlement was, however, constantly struggling with basic service delivery like water, sanitation, electricity and waste management.

The Stellenbosch Municipality is faced with a growing housing waiting list. By 2009 the Municipality already had more than 20,000 families living in informal settlements. The local authority decided to undertake a radical rethink of its approach to housing and created a new Informal Settlements Management Department. This Department approached the South African SDI alliance (Slum/Shack Dwellers International) to develop an innovative approach to settlement upgrading. The alliance comprising of two key social movements, Federation of Urban and Rural Poor (FEDUP) and Informal Settlement Network (ISN), supported by NGO Community Organisation Resource Centre (CORC), is a bottom-up agglomeration supporting the urban poor around service delivery and housing issues. Through advocacy and lobbying from the grassroots, the organisation has had a significant impact since 1994 via the People's Housing Process, and other related policies, to influence the manner in which cities are planned and developed. The aim is to promote a people-driven, pro-poor approach to housing and urban development.

Innovation Story outline

The number of households living in informal settlements in and around the City of Cape Town is increasing. Tanja Winkler estimates that, in 2010, there were approximately 181,000 such households, and that this number is set to rise to 260,000 by 2019, a 43% increase.[1] She argues that conventional house building programmes cannot possibly meet the challenges facing people living in informal settlements. Apart from anything else, the country simply cannot afford to build the number of housing units required.

The South African government has begun to encourage alternative approaches. The 2009 National Housing Code includes a programme for in-situ, informal settlement upgrading. Winkler argues that, while focussing attention on in-situ upgrading is a step in the right direction, the requirements of the Upgrading of Informal Settlements Programme (UISP) are extremely cumbersome. Nevertheless, the settlement upgrading has introduced a number of service delivery innovations and social organisation changes leading to a longer-term development linked to UISP.

In October 2010 senior officials from Stellenbosch Municipality and FEDUP/ISN and CORC visited the SDI Ugandan Federation to see people-centred planning in action.[2] This helped all those involved imagine new ways of working. Following the learning exchange, a strong mobilisation strategy was laid out to develop leadership capacities and a leadership structure for Langrug. This mobilisation strategy was strongly linked to community based data collection; mapping and community led implementation became the key planning concepts underpinning a Municipal-wide formal agreement between the Municipality and the alliance. Subsequently, in 2011, a Memorandum of Understanding (MoU) was signed between Stellenbosch Municipality and the alliance to create an Urban Poor platform and finance mechanism to fund community prioritised projects. This finance mechanism provided resources to survey, map, enumerate and profile the settlements across the municipality with a view to bringing about comprehensive upgrading.

By early 2012, the community leadership had established block committees in every part of the settlement to manage projects and deepen accountability. For example, the installation of additional flush toilets, creating play parks around communal toilets, and developing grey water management systems were noteworthy projects. University support for these efforts was important. Staff and students at Worcester Polytechnic (WPI) worked with the community over a period of two years to develop an effective water, sanitation and hygiene programme. WPI along with the residents, Municipality and alliance helped develop the Langrug WASH Facility, that brings together new ways of thinking about communal facilities.

This community facility caters for a range of activities including using hot water showers, solar water geysers, post office, women's hair salon etc all managed by the residents. The new WASH Facility was co-designed and co-created by all partners. A municipal field worker from Stellenbosch supported the local team as they designed and built the facility. The WASH Facility may be a modest step, but it has improved the quality of life for residents enormously. It brings together a very wide range of services in a concerted effort. Johru Robyn, the lead officer on the upgrading efforts for Stellenbosch Municipality, raises a good question: 'Who would have imagined a toilet block could become the focal point for such a wide range of interaction and collaboration?'[3]

In 2012, the partnership invited academic staff and masters degree students from City and Regional Planning and Landscape Architecture, University of Cape Town (UCT) to develop a long term plan for the development of the settlement. The work of the students and academic staff critically questioned the role of UISP policy and stressed the importance of developing a community vision for Langrug. This involves developing both short-term and long-term proposals.

In the longer term the planning work by the UCT students outlined ideas for providing better transport connections between the informal settlements, including Langrug, and nearby towns – for example, Franschhoek, Paarl and Stellenbosch. The long-term plan, in line with UISP guidance, also envisages securing a right for residents to remain on the land. The Stellenbosch Municipality has embraced new strategies to deal with informal settlements and this is a key feature of this Innovation Story.

In 2012 Langrug won the South African Planning Institute's (SAPI) award for good 'community/outreach' planning. This award recognises that the Langrug settlement upgrading effort of recent years is an outstanding community development project. It has improved the quality of life and pioneered an imaginative approach to community-based problem solving in difficult circumstances.

Leadership lessons

- Co-creation of practical solutions, with a strong emphasis on community engagement, can be very effective in generating new ways of thinking and acting. Here, with only the most slender of resources and with formidable challenges, a partnership based approach has demonstrated a strong impact.
- Imaginative municipal leaders can discard past ways of doing things and engage in radical rethinking and risk taking .
- All communities contain able community leaders and people with rudimentary skills who, with the right kind of support and encouragement, can bring fresh thinking and ideas to the process of community development. Resident leaders in Langrug have demonstrated a willingness to take on leadership roles.
- Financial agility has allowed leaders to deliver small-scale improvements at a rapid pace. This attention to small victories has strengthened the leaders role in the community.
- International learning and exchange can provide practical insights and inspiration. In the Langrug case a visit to see people-centred planning in Uganda was an important step to develop the capacities of the urban poor.
- Universities can play an important role in supporting local community action, and learn from grassroots planning. The learning benefits for students participating in such initiatives are invaluable. Moreover, with the right guidance from faculty, student projects can contribute energy, ideas and practical suggestions for community improvement.
- Cross-sectoral collaboration involving local government, NGOs and academics working with communities can be very effective in coming up with new ideas and practical solutions.

Sources

Partners in the project, 2013, *'This is my slum': The upgrading of Langrug*, http://sasdialliance.org.za

Winkler, T, 2013, The challenges facing our South African cities, *Quarterly Roundtable*, No 27, July. Cape Town: The Helen Suzman Foundation Series

For information on informal settlement upgrading: http://sasdialliance.org.za

Endnotes

[1] I draw here on a public lecture presented by Tanja Winkler on *The Future of Our Cities* organised by The Helen Suzman Foundation, Johannesburg, 30 July 2013. Winkler, a senior lecturer in the School of Architecture, Planning and Geomatics, at the University of Cape Town, presented statistics based on the City of Cape Town's 2010 GIS data.

[2] The main source for the narrative that follows is a report *'This is my slum'. The upgrading of Langrug*. Jointly prepared by partners in the project the report is available at: http://sasdialliance.org.za

[3] Personal communication, 14 February 2014

Leading public service innovation

The four Innovation Stories presented in this chapter illustrate very different ways of moving policy and practice towards the creation of the inclusive city. This is deliberate. There is no single route map for political activists and reformers, and this fact should be celebrated. Effective action designed to advance the cause of social and environmental justice in the city can, and does, travel along multiple pathways. In this context it is worth emphasising that, as I noted in Chapter 5, successful place-based leadership needs to be tuned to the context within which leadership is exercised. Places are different. What works in Swindon might not be right for Chicago. Intelligent action in Langrug might not be right for Enschede. This is why the discovery process must be locally rooted in specific places and particular communities. Effective public leadership needs to be energised by local priorities and culture, the political dynamics of the locality, and the strengths of the governing arrangements in place as well as the assets of the local community. At the same time, wise civic leadership is mindful of the need to test the constraints placed on local political action by place-less power. In Chapter 12 I explain in more detail why there is no such thing as 'best practice' in urban governance. What the Innovation Stories in this book provide are insights into relevant practice, not best practice.

Given the importance of local context we are, perhaps, faced with a challenge. If places are so different we have to ask: Is it possible to generate insights relating to the leadership of public service innovation that might have general applicability? The extreme localists will say 'no'. They will claim that local culture, political power structures and history – local distinctiveness if you will – mean that nothing can be learned from elsewhere. In my work with city and county politicians in different countries I have often encountered this view. It is a position that needs to be challenged. Whilst best practice does not exist, it is possible to draw useful insights from other places. I am suggesting that we should develop a grammar around the theme of inspirational place-based leadership. I introduced the idea of a grammar, or series of grammars, in Chapter 1. In line with this idea we can identify useful themes relating to place-based leadership, insights that can enhance the possibilities for developing progressive, public leadership. This is *not* a script for good local leadership – rather it is a set of ideas that the reader can revise and develop in the light of her or his own experience.

The following discussion draws directly on the Anglo-Dutch study of innovation in place-based leadership that I mentioned earlier (Hambleton and Howard 2012).[7] This research suggested that effective public leadership is multi-level and that the key task of senior figures is, in effect, to orchestrate a process of social discovery. In Figure 6.1 I provide a sketch map of this orchestration process. This figure simplifies a complex and highly interactive process. The diagram is offered to enhance understanding – to provide a framework for thinking about the leadership of public service innovation. I am certainly not suggesting that there are five separate components in this process. On the contrary, Figure 6.1 is intended to emphasise the flows of ideas and influences that characterise effective processes of social discovery.

Figure 6.1: The orchestration of social discovery

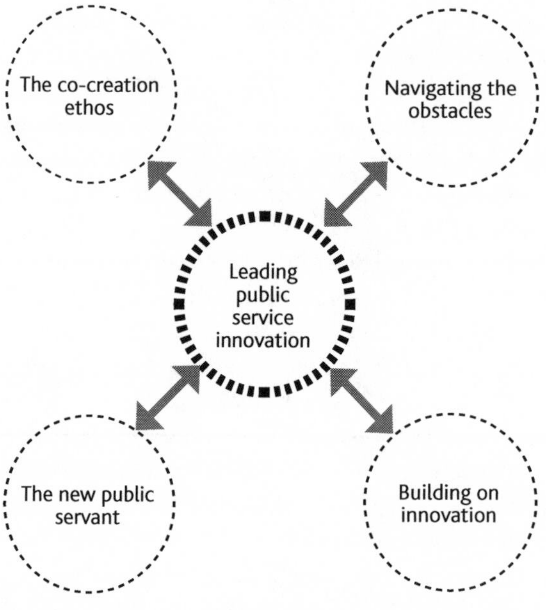

The co-creation ethos

Navigating the obstacles

Leading public service innovation

The new public servant

Building on innovation

Source: Adapted from Hambleton and Howard (2012, p 33)

At the centre of Figure 6.1 is the core task of leading public service innovation. In the absence of strong leadership shaping emotions and behaviour to create inclusive places, it is difficult to see how progress can be made in tackling social exclusion. I unpack the elements of this leadership task in the text below. However, Figure 6.1 suggests that four other factors interact with this leadership task. These relate to: the importance of developing a co-creation ethos; the need to redefine the nature of what it means to be a public servant; understanding ways of navigating the obstacles to innovation; and the challenges associated with building on innovation. I now discuss each of these five themes relating to place-based leadership and social inclusion in the following order:

- the co-creation ethos
- the new public servant
- leading public service innovation
- navigating the obstacles to innovation
- building on innovation – from prototype to wider influence.

These themes are richly inter-related, but it is helpful to separate them out so that leaders, reformers and activists can use them to reflect on their own experience.

The co-creation ethos

The first key theme to emerge from the Anglo-Dutch research project, and related research, is that effective innovation in public services needs to be firmly based in an ethos of collaboration. Going beyond mainstream ideas about co-production, which brings non-state partners together with the state to inform and deliver services, co-creation implies a process in which various stakeholders in and outside the state come together to invent something new. To make a real difference this commitment to co-creation needs to imbue the whole innovation process – from the earliest stages of conceptualising and planning a service, through to delivery, and forward to thinking about how to adapt and improve an innovation, and share it with others.

An important feature of co-creation is that it implies an assets-based approach. Such an approach identifies and builds on capabilities and interests, and seeks to create opportunities for change. Yes, it is concerned to address social needs, but it breaks away from a conventional 'needs based' approach to service planning and delivery. Thus, for example, the Swindon and Enschede initiatives focus explicitly on identifying and strengthening the capabilities of families, and the families shape plans and activities directly.

The Anglo-Dutch research identifies three insights into how governments might respond to this challenge. First, we found that *asset-based, co-creative approaches are built on values and principles of engagement.* The initiatives we studied were underpinned by important values, in particular: trust, authenticity (genuine commitment, personal motivation, passion, respect), and, what we describe as, an asset-oriented ethos (seeing people as a resource not a problem). For example, the approach developed in Swindon requires workers to put themselves into their work, their personal as well as their professional self. The premise is that in order to build genuine relationships of trust, you need to give something of yourself. This suggests that local authorities interested in radical innovation need to think about how to support and communicate a values base in their work.

A second factor that has emerged as significant for effective co-creation is *timeliness*. Timeliness is important in two ways. One is to be aware of the stage reached in the process of co-creation – when to nurture, when to step back, when to intervene, when to bring in other players. The second way relates to the need to manage the tension between the slow pace required for working in ways that build trust and meaningful relationships, and the speed at which innovators want things to change.

A third factor is the need for leaders to *recognise the assets within their own organisation* – to spot talented people and help them to do what they do well. The notion of co-creation implies quite a deep change in mind-set for those leading, managing and delivering public services. In line with long established approaches to community development it requires those serving the public to develop sophisticated listening skills and, more than that, it requires a much sharper focus on assets than tends to be the case in most public service settings. A focus on assets also means working with a holistic and inclusive understanding of 'place', rather than a sectoral or departmentalised one. Clearly senior leaders can play a crucial role, in terms of creating space for people to come together across sectors and departments, identifying innovative people and supporting them.

The new public servant

The co-creation approach calls for new ways of working. In the Anglo–Dutch project we have called this theme the 'new public servant' in an effort to stretch thinking about what modern public service might look like. The managers of the initiatives in our case study cities stressed the importance of working differently. The new ways of working that are being tried out in the cities we studied could be perceived as rather risky. Part of the risk involved is that of engaging with service users as co-creators, reframing the relationship between professionals and residents from one of us/them, professional/problem, to one of collaboration and mutual respect.

Sharing information and decision-making with less powerful partners means sharing power in real and meaningful ways. In Swindon, families choose which Family LIFE team member they want to work with. This stands usual practice on its head. In traditional models, the client has no choice, and all the power is with the public servant. The Social GPs in Enschede have been given informal decision-making powers to work across service areas to work in a holistic way with individual residents, and to empower them to take actions for themselves. Along with radical innovations taking place in other localities, these Innovation Stories are in the process of redefining what it means to be a public servant.

Managers at senior and middle levels have a key role in helping front-line staff to develop new ways of working – building truly collaborative relationships with residents is easy to say but can be very challenging in practice. In order to work in a boundary-spanning way, co-creative/collaborative leaders, managers and front line workers need to give new emphasis to a particular set of skills and capabilities. These include personal resilience, emotional literacy, and the ability to take risks and to hold the risk on behalf of others. Training for leading innovation may need to be re-examined, as many leadership training programmes tend to perpetuate the traditional model.

Leading public service innovation

We now turn to the core task lying at the heart of Figure 6.1. What should leaders do in order to lead in a way that cultivates radical innovation and social inclusion at one and the same time? Our Innovation Stories suggest that place-based political leadership is critical in setting a tone that welcomes public service innovation. Local political leaders, and this issue is neglected in the literature, can play an enormously influential role in shaping the emotions and behaviour of public servants and the wider community in ways which can foster social inclusion.

However, it is not just politicians who are important place-based leaders. As explained in Chapter 5, there are five important realms of civic leadership in any given locality. The way these five realms of local leadership – political, public managerial/professional, community, business, and trade union – inter-connect and overlap is illustrated in Figure 5.3. The Innovation Stories presented in this book show that leaders from all five realms of civic leadership can play a vital role in stimulating public service innovation. More than that, the stories also show that leaders from all five realms have demonstrated a willingness to take bold steps to bring about greater social inclusion in their cities.

In this section we identify and discuss the key elements of an effective approach to the leadership of public service innovation as created by scholars and practitioners working together in the Anglo-Dutch research project. The model is summarised in Figure 6.2.

Figure 6.2: Leading public service innovation

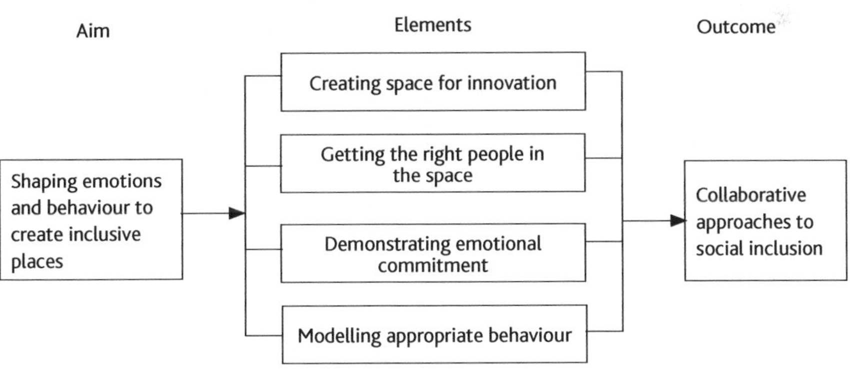

Source: Hambleton and Howard (2012, p 36)

This simple model envisages three steps. The practice of leadership is, of course, far more turbulent and challenging than this neat sequential model implies. In reality there are many feedback loops, cross-connections, setbacks, and surprising twists and turns, both good and bad. Our model does not attempt to map this complexity. The model starts with a clear aim. By building on the definition of leadership set out earlier, we defined the aim of civic leadership designed to advance social inclusion in a very simple way: Shaping emotions and behaviour to create inclusive places. This is an overall aim – each locality in the Anglo-Dutch study has many more specific objectives relating to social inclusion. But these complexities need not detain us here. As shown in Figure 6.2 the desired outcome is: Collaborative approaches to social inclusion. This, again, is only one measure of progress, and each city evaluates its own performance against many more specific criteria. But this broad desired outcome will suffice for the purposes of our discussion of leadership.

Four core elements of leadership emerge from our research. We stress that these four elements are connected and that effective leaders blend them together. But understanding can be increased if we separate them out. Two relate to 'what' leaders do, and two relate to 'how' they do it:

What do leaders do to promote innovation?

- Leaders create new spaces, or settings, for people from different backgrounds to come together and learn from each other.
- Leaders get the right people into the spaces they have created.

How do leaders promote innovation?

- They model ways of working that encourage openness and courageous behaviour, and they help others to overcome their fear of change or failure.
- They show their own personal commitment and are aware of others' emotions.

In Figure 6.2 these four elements are set out as separate strands. In practice a leader may take action that, in any one moment, is delivering on several of these elements at once. The Anglo-Dutch study discusses each of these elements in some detail (Hambleton and Howard 2012, 35–39). Here we just touch briefly on each one.

First, it is crucial to create space for connectivity and exchange. Bringing different kinds of people together to talk in a structured, purposeful way may be as important as investing in building the capacities of individuals to bring about change. This insight is consistent with the argument, presented in Chapter 5, that the creation of innovation zones, where people with different perspectives can be brought together, can enable creative questioning of established approaches. Cities across the world are experimenting with this idea of creating spaces for innovation.

It is one thing to create a space for innovative thinking and practice, and another to get the right people involved. Getting the right people into the space requires strategic leadership from the top. For radical innovation to prosper it is often the case that senior political and managerial leaders will need, not just to protect the creative spaces against the demands of short-term financial imperatives and political pressures, but also to identify suitable people to work on innovation initiatives. Senior leaders are, then, involved in 'innovation talent spotting'. They need to develop a flair for identifying latent talent and they need to empower emerging leaders who they recognise as having strong collaborative skills, to take initiative, and to give them permission to explore and experiment. These people, who are to be found in all five realms of place-based leadership, are the *boundary spanners*, or bridges between organisations and groups. Typically, they are comfortable working between levels of an organisation, between organisations and across the interface between civil society and the state.

The third element concerns emotional commitment. Innovation in public services often requires working against the grain – swimming hard against the prevailing current or culture. This can be very demanding and a consequence is that the effective leadership of public service innovation requires strong emotional commitment to the innovation. Leaders must *believe* that change is necessary, and manage other people's fear of change or of failure. The Anglo-Dutch research project found that leadership of public service innovation is more likely to be successful – particularly when it comes to fundamental rethinking of roles and relationships – when leaders adopt a transformational, rather than a transactional approach. This means exhibiting a kind of behaviour that engages with people's emotions, their passions and enthusiasms, and their fears, rather than leading through the logic of incentives and bartering.

In Chapter 5 I discussed the distinction between transformational and transactional approaches to leadership, and noted that a transformational approach involves speaking with emotion about shared purpose. Frank Barrett reinforces this argument when he discusses affirmative competence:

> Problem solving by itself will not generate novel solutions. What's needed is affirmative belief that a solution exists and that something positive will emerge... Leaders need to do what jazz musicians do – anticipate that when people are encouraged to try something new, the results will be unexpected... Innovative cultures maximise learning by nurturing a mind-set of enlightened trial and error that allows managers to take advantage of errors to offer new insights. (Barrett 2012, xi–xii)

The fourth element, sometimes described in business management books as walking the talk (Taylor 2005), involves leaders signalling through their behaviour what they want for their organisation. For an organisation to embrace innovation, leaders will set the tone by taking some risks themselves. This is true at all levels of the organisation. In particular, they will be role-modelling the leadership skills of boundary crossing, building bridges between different groups of people with something to contribute to a shared place. For senior leaders, building bridges entails getting out of their office, organisation and comfort zone. Leaders who are concerned with the future of their locality – at whatever scale – need to be connected with others, know what actors in other realms are thinking and doing, and bring different interests together. This means working through, ideally on a regular basis, the Zone of Uncomfortable Debate (ZOUD).[8] The ZOUD refers to an unspoken process that prevents people from questioning current practices too closely. Civic leaders need to be adept not just at recognising the zones of uncomfortable debate, but also at encouraging staff and colleagues to move into and out of this zone.

Navigating the obstacles to innovation

The Anglo-Dutch research suggests that the major obstacle to innovation is fear – different forms of fear, arising from perceptions of risk. These fears include:

- fear of failure – what happens if things go 'wrong'?
- fear of departing from the norm – the notion of 'best practice' can blunt fresh thinking;
- fear of freedom – professionals becoming too dependent on rules and procedures and losing confidence in their own judgement;
- fear of the new – will I be able to cope well in this new situation?
- fear of friction with colleagues – is everyone else up for this?
- fear of the other – people are often used to working with colleagues who are like themselves (for example, other professionals within the local authority) and may resist working with people who are dissimilar.

The research confirmed that those charged with leading public service innovation are highly likely to encounter fears of this kind. We were also able to identify a number of strategies that leaders can use to manage or navigate these fears, and two are highlighted here.

One strategy for navigating people's fear of risk, is to try out an innovative idea below the radar. New initiatives are often heralded as breaking new ground and, as a result, they tend to be under the spotlight from a very early stage. They may attract the attention of the media or, more likely, the attention of vested interests that find the innovation unsettling. Local politicians and public sector managers need to find ways to be more agile, and this may mean getting on with and testing out a new idea quietly without waiting for permission.

A different leadership strategy is to identify the risks, and hold the risk on behalf of others. This means empowering, training and supporting your staff to make decisions and take risks. Public service leaders need to insulate the innovators from potential attack – from vested interests, the media and so on – in order to give an innovation time to develop and take root, or fail and start afresh. Leadership is therefore about giving people the encouragement to experiment, and permission to fail. This is what I mean by holding the risk for others.[9] George Ferguson,

Mayor of Bristol, understands the importance of taking risks, and Innovation Story 2 provides insights on his approach to city leadership. In his first State of the City address, given on the anniversary of his election, he stressed the importance of innovation: 'We should never set out to fail but we should never allow fear of failure to prevent us from succeeding. It's about being bold...' (Ferguson 2013).

Building on innovation – from prototype to wider influence

What about the fifth component in Figure 6.1 – the idea of building on innovation? The Anglo-Dutch research project suggests that the language currently being used in debates about spreading public service innovation is seriously flawed. It is commonplace to hear politicians and policy makers, even think tanks, talking about 'scaling up' or 'rolling out' an innovation. Or, worse still, of 'replicating' a break through. All these ideas are misconceived as they fail to recognise that public service innovation is, at its heart, a process of local social discovery. Stated bluntly, you can't cut and paste successful innovation. How then, can learning about innovation be shared? How can inspiring innovations ignite processes of local social discovery in other places? Three suggestions emerge from the Anglo-Dutch project (Hambleton and Howard 2012, 40–43). Here we have space only to mention them: connectivity across 'place'; the capacity to learn from failure; and the role of leaders in inspiring wider change in and between organisations, including the use of storytelling.

One way to build on innovation is to establish stronger connections between local (or neighbourhood) leaders and citywide/strategic leaders. The role of the boundary spanner, who can make wise links between the strategic vision and local community-based assets, becomes critical. This idea of developing more porous organisations suggests that the Innovation Zones, the areas of overlap between the five realms of civic leadership shown in Figure 5.3, should be expanded. It is essential for political leaders and the managerial/professional staff they employ to open up spaces of dialogue with civic leaders from the other realms of place-based leadership.

Earlier in this section, in the discussion relating to the obstacles to innovation, I indicated that fear of failure is a major factor discouraging experiment and the exploration of new ways of doing things. This research, consistent with the analysis presented by Barrett (2012, 41–65), suggests that attitudes to failure need to change. Public service leaders need to embrace errors as a source of knowledge – and be able to learn from failure. In this context it may be helpful to draw a distinction between 'prototypes' and 'pilots'. A prototype is expected to be flawed and to be reinvented: it exists in order to put ideas into practice and to enable adjustments to be made when notion and reality do not conjoin.[10] On the other hand a pilot implies the existence of an idea that is to be tested out before being applied at a larger scale. If this distinction is accepted, the implication is that policy makers should focus more on prototype initiatives, on exploring by doing, than piloting projects. It is, of course, difficult for politicians to advocate risky behaviour and to admit that some of their initiatives have failed. However, I suggest that the language of experiment, prototyping and learning through doing could all feature more boldly in political discourse about public service innovation.

If my criticisms of the lazy language of 'best practice', 'rolling out' pilots, or 'scaling up' initiatives are correct, what can leaders do to take forward a public service innovation from its incubation stage? A good way to build on innovation is to share experiences, not as recipe for action in other places, but as a way of encouraging others to experiment, to collaborate, and to identify and build on their own assets. Earlier we identified emotional commitment as a key aspect of leadership for innovation, and this is equally important if innovative practices are to have an impact more widely. People need to feel an emotional connection if they are to take risks of their own, and move away from the practices they have become very used to, and which they have invested in.

This is where the idea of an Innovation Story came from. As I explained in Chapter 1, an Innovation Story is different from a conventional case study. It involves the co-creation of a narrative about an innovation coupled with an explicit effort to identify lessons for leadership. A clear and concise Innovation Story, one that examines a bold and successful innovation, can be inspirational. Attempting to highlight lessons involves cajoling plausible insights from the narrative. Different readers can consider whether the lessons are robust and can, of course, identify other lessons that are more appropriate to their needs. The use of stories, or metaphors, can create non-literal linkages that can inspire fresh thinking. I agree with Yapp (2005) when he suggests that there is room to expand the notion of storytelling in relation to public policy.[11]

Conclusions

In stable times there is not that much need for innovation in public policy. Doing pretty much what we did last year, plus or minus a bit, might not be very inspiring but, in stable times, the chances are the outcomes would not be disastrous. In this chapter I have argued, in line with the analysis presented by Donald Schon (1971) that we do not live in stable times. On the contrary the world is changing rapidly, so rapidly that conventional performance management approaches to public services are found to be wanting. This changing environment means that public policy makers, and civic leaders from all walks of life, now need to focus much more sharply on how to bring about constructive public service innovation. Subsequent chapters will extend and develop this argument. For example, Chapter 8 will highlight how the problems arising from global warming require a step change in environmental awareness and action – and the Innovation Stories provided there will show how place-based leaders are responding.

This chapter has suggested that much of the literature on public service innovation has neglected the importance of place-based innovation. For too much of the time discussion of public service innovation is dominated by a technical and/or managerial discourse – a discourse that is disconnected from politics in general, and from the innovative power of community-based action in particular. Technological breakthroughs can, of course, make a difference to the quality of public services. Innovation Story 3, on the remarkable 311 service in Chicago, illustrates how new technology, when used to support service users and staff, can contribute to enhanced public service responsiveness. The other Innovation Stories in this chapter – which discuss inventive practice in Swindon, Enschede and Langrug – record extraordinary examples of bold innovation designed to tackle social and economic exclusion. An important theme in all the Innovation Stories is that it is people, not technology, that are the driver of radical public service innovation. Langrug, for example, shows how significant change to tackle social exclusion can be undertaken on a shoestring.

The chapter has suggested: that many public service organisations are moving from an 'improvement agenda' to an 'innovation agenda'; that radical innovation involves a reconsideration of the relationships between citizens and the state; and that a whole systems approach to public innovation is desirable. By drawing on an Anglo-Dutch study of public sector innovation in three cities, the chapter has mapped out some ideas and suggestions on how to go about leading public service innovation in a locality. It has been suggested that it is helpful to view the central leadership task in public service innovation as the orchestration of social discovery. This has profound implications for the nature of civic leadership in the coming period. The various Innovation Stories show what this might mean in practice.

In closing this chapter I would like to highlight the importance for public service innovation of improvisation and the idea of breaking rules. I have suggested that the world is changing rapidly and that, as a result, public organisations are unlikely to increase their effectiveness by doing more of what they already know how to do. It follows that the old Manchester saying is still relevant today: 'Never forget, only a dead fish always swims with the current'.[12]

CHAPTER 7

Democratic urban governance

Sicinius Velutus: 'What is the city but the people?'
Citizens: 'True. The people are the city'
William Shakespeare, *Coriolanus*, Act III, Scene I (circa 1608)

Introduction

A central argument of this book is that the reach of place-less power is expanding and that this is bad news for local communities. The behaviour of place-less, unaccountable decision makers is creating divided societies across the world. Why is this the case? Because these decision makers neglect the social calculus. They do not believe it is important to consider the consequences for particular communities of the decisions they make.

This is an extraordinary state of affairs – one that has been highlighted with painful clarity by the global financial crash of 2008/09. The distant decision makers in the big financial institutions and multi-national companies have been shown to be completely out of touch with social reality. They need, and this is a massive challenge for them, to rethink their values and raison d'etre so that they can become organisations that understand the importance of local communities. Societal progress requires them to shift from exploiting people to serving them. This may seem to be an ambitious task, but there are many voices arguing for a push towards more responsible forms of capitalism, ones that recognise the resourcefulness of all communities and ones that generate local wealth and prosperity.[1] It is my argument that successful efforts to change societies from a culture of exploitation to a culture of service will require a significant expansion of place-based power.

Local governments can be expected to be key players in bringing about this new social order. Indeed, they are already doing this. This chapter explains why strong local democracy has a vital role to play in rebuilding the power of place in modern societies. First, I recap on the problems associated with the exercise of place-less power. Second, I ask: What is local government for? This is a big subject but it is important to go back to fundamentals. Third, I discuss the various dimensions of democracy and consider the possibilities for combining representative and participatory democracy. Fourth, and now the argument becomes more specific, I examine options for the institutional design of local governance. It will be suggested that how we organise our systems of local government can make a significant difference to the quality of local democracy in a locality. Innovation Story 7 shows how the New Zealand government redesigned the governing arrangements of the metropolitan area of Auckland in order to create a platform for more effective and more inclusive civic leadership.

In a fifth section I examine citizen involvement and I present a simple conceptual framework – a ladder of citizen empowerment. There has been a significant, pretty much worldwide, expansion in various forms of participatory democracy in recent decades, and this proliferation of efforts to reinvent democracy offers much encouragement and many valuable insights. Innovation Story 8 outlines the remarkable reshaping of urban governance in Malmö. When compared with other countries Swedish local authorities are enormously powerful, and Sweden's national policies for local government will be of interest to all those interested to strengthen local democracy. Within this context Malmö provides an inspiring example of decentralised management and community involvement.

Place-less power – the central challenge

In Chapter 1 I introduced the concept of power in modern society. I outlined various ways of conceptualising power drawing, for example, a distinction between hard and soft forms of power. In simple terms, while hard power relies on inducements or threats, soft power attracts support by winning people over (Nye 2004). I also referred to the three 'faces' of power identified by Stephen Lukes (2005): 1) the visible use of power in public decision-making, 2) the subtle exercise of power by interests who manage to keep certain conflicts off the public policy agenda (referred to as non-decision-making), and 3) the insidious shaping of desires by the manipulation of group values through misinformation and propaganda. Here I want to advance the discussion of power by highlighting the distinction between place-less power and place-based power.

It is incontestable that place-less power has grown significantly in the last thirty years or so. By place-less power I mean the exercise of power by decision-makers who are unconcerned about the impact of their decisions on communities living in particular places. In Chapter 4 I suggested that distant decision-makers often miss opportunities because they lack local knowledge, and I stressed that the modern requirements of global capital accumulation are distorting intelligent decision-making in modern societies. We have arrived at a situation where private sector managers are not just driven by the importance of making a profit. The dominant model of capitalism operating today requires managers to maximise profits to the exclusion of all other values.

Defenders of private sector management claim that 'triple bottom line' leadership and management can be introduced to mitigate this fundamental drawback. For example, some years ago, John Elkington argued that forward-looking businesses should measure their performance against three criteria – economic prosperity, environmental quality and social justice – not just the economic (Elkington 1997). This is a good idea, but his arguments have fallen on deaf ears. Where is the solid evidence that large numbers of big companies are now actually using 'triple bottom line' planning and budgeting? And in those big companies that are, how many are giving equal weight to these three performance criteria?

Sadly, the evidence points in the opposite direction. Judged as a whole the major companies in the private sector have become even more obsessed with narrow profit making than ever before. Leave aside, for a moment, the fact that the 2008/09 global financial crisis stemmed from the self-interested behaviour of those leading the banking industry and consider, for a moment, the example I provided in Chapter 4.

Here I explained how an American multi-national company (then Kraft Foods, now Mondelez International), took over the Cadbury chocolate company in 2010. Despite promising to retain the successful Somerdale chocolate factory in Keynsham, near Bristol, the new owners reneged on their public promise within days of taking over the British company. Senior decision makers in Kraft Foods were not interested in the 'triple bottom line'. Rather, they acted with unseemly haste in closing the economically successful Somerdale site and moving the chocolate factory operation to Poland. The decision to shut the factory made 400 workers redundant and did untold economic damage to a small English town. This is a vivid, and well-documented, example of the crass misuse of place-less power.

But the important point I wish to stress here is that the closure of the Somerdale chocolate factory is not an isolated incident. Multi-national companies are missing opportunities to foster locally rooted wealth creation all the time. This is because place-less decision makers rarely concern themselves with local economic development, still less with thoughtful consideration of the impact of their decisions on the quality of life of particular communities in particular places. Otto Scharmer and Katrin Kaufer (2013, 111–12), in their book on modern business, are surely right to argue that business leaders tend to operate in an overly selfish way – with 'an organisational ego-system awareness' when our economic reality is now shaped by 'globally interdependent eco-systems'. They note, correctly, that many business leaders view the concerns of others as 'externalities'. These authors show how forward thinking companies realise that, in our inter-connected world, this is not just foolish, it is out of date business thinking.

One way to combat place-less power, and to redress the growing inequalities that stem from the exercise of this form of irresponsible capitalism, is to enhance place-based power. This is a central reason why all societies need strong, healthy local democratic institutions led by people who care about the local communities living in 'their' place. The inclusive city has, then, to be a democratic city. The rest of this chapter discusses local democracy, and explores the way political voice is being developed and strengthened in cities across the world.

What is local government for?

The form and functions of local government in any given country will reflect national traditions, history and culture. There are hundreds of thousands of local governments in the world today. It follows that it is unwise to generalise too freely when attempting to answer the question: What is local government for? However, we can identify some important themes and principles that are relevant to any discussion of local democracy.

First, local government is a political institution. The origins of modern local government lie in political activism – people have created local governments to serve public purpose. The nature of this activism, the context within which it has taken place and the timing of when it occurred, will vary by nation. In most countries, however, the invention and emergence of elected local democracy was (and is) intertwined with broader social movements designed to advance the cause of democracy in general. Stated simply, efforts by oppressed peoples seeking emancipation explain the existence of modern local government.

For example, in the UK, the appalling living conditions of those struggling to survive in the expanding industrial cities of the 19th Century spurred widespread political protest and demonstrations. In Chapter 3 I referred to the remarkable achievements of Joseph Chamberlain, the Mayor of Birmingham, and his colleagues, in transforming the conditions of those living in urban squalor during the 1870s. However, the lasting accomplishments of Chamberlain, and the other highly effective Victorian leaders of British cities, would not have been possible without the political action, and sacrifice, of the radical activists who went before them.

Chartism deserves special mention in this context. The Chartists, who drew strength from earlier political movements, like the Tolpuddle Martyrs, were an influential political and moral force in the UK in the 1830s and 1840s. They, and other radical activists, paved the way for the kinds of local government reforms that were to come later in the 1870s and 1880s. The Chartists sought a more democratic system of governance – votes, a secret ballot, no property qualification for Members of Parliament (MPs), payment for MPs (so that poor citizens could serve) and so on. Their leaders were thrown in prison for sedition. As I explained in Chapter 1, citizens have, over the years, banded together to claim civil, political and social rights (Marshall 1950). These efforts to advance a rights-based approach to social justice, including the struggles to establish a 'right to the city', have gained momentum over the decades. The campaigning techniques used by the Chartists are, then, well understood by community activists today.[2] Without political activism of this kind there would be no local governments. And, as argued persuasively by Ines Newman (2014), without continued political activism local democracy will wither.

Apart from the fact that local government is driven by the political project of enhancing democracy, what are the other characteristics that distinguish local government? Five features stand out. First, local governments are elected. Local people choose who they want to represent them. A variety of local government electoral systems are in use around the world – for example, some countries use 'first-past-the-post' voting systems, while others employ various systems of proportional representation. Second, local government is multi-purpose. Local authorities, in the sense I am using, carry out more than one function, and the range of functions varies by country. This enables the elected politicians to exercise choice in relation to policy priorities among these functions. Third, local government has responsibility for the exercise of governmental functions in defined territories – local authorities are place-based.

Fourth, to deserve the name, local governments are able to set local taxes and raise their own revenue without interference from higher levels of government. Local/central relations vary cross-nationally. In many countries local governments enjoy constitutional protection, but this is not the case in some countries. For example, as I noted in Chapter 1, successive central governments in the UK have taken powers away from elected local governments to the point where local citizens can no longer decide how much they can tax themselves. Fifth, local governments are corporate bodies. On the whole, the powers of local authorities are vested corporately in the council as a whole. They are not vested in the majority party, nor individual politicians, nor in the officers elected politicians decide to appoint.

This description of the powers and functions of local government is, it has to be admitted, rather dry. The larger point that I wish to emphasise is the vital role that local governments have in exercising place-based leadership. In my view the purpose of local government is to provide place-based leadership for the common good.[3] The four underpinning purposes are:

- to defend our political liberties against a potentially autocratic central state and other external forces;
- to support a community-based approach to public service innovation tapping local energies and resources;
- to provide outstanding public services to meet the needs of all residents and enhance the quality of life;
- to create eco-friendly prosperous communities able to adapt to changing circumstances.

In Chapter 3, following Hirschman (1970), I drew a distinction between two ideal theoretical notions of empowerment – exit and voice. Consumers in a well-regulated and fair market can use their power of exit to take their business elsewhere if they feel the organisation serving them is not performing well. This power of exit (the market mechanism) works well in relation to the consumption of products – for example, a pint of beer, a chocolate bar, or a meal in a restaurant. I suggested that this power is, however, and for a variety of reasons, of very limited usefulness in the public realm. This is because public policy is concerned with collective goods – it provides numerous services and benefits that cannot be individualised. It follows that the power of voice – citizens signalling their priorities via the ballot box and other means – offers much more promise than market mechanisms as a way of improving the performance and creativity of public policy. Local government rests, then, on the power of voice. And, as we shall see, local authorities have become increasingly effective in not just listening more effectively to the views of citizens, but also in co-creating new solutions to public challenges by building voice into the heart of public service innovation.

Dimensions of democracy

A remarkable speech by US President Abraham Lincoln, delivered in November 1863, provides a useful starting point for our discussion of the dimensions of democracy. In the Gettysburg Address, one of the most influential speeches in American history, Lincoln argued passionately for a 'new birth of freedom… for government of the people, by the people for the people'. His speech has been an inspiration for all those who believe in democracy ever since. But, as David Held (1987) observes, there are many 'models of democracy'. How to achieve 'government of the people, by the people for the people' remains a work in progress.

It is worth emphasising, as Amartya Sen (2006) explains, the idea of democracy is not a 'Western' invention. For example, in early 7th Century Japan, the Buddhist prince Shotoku, insisted in 'the constitution of seventeen articles,' promulgated in A. D. 604: 'Decisions on important matters should not be made by one person alone. They should be discussed with many' (Sen 2006, 53). Sen notes that this is six hundred years before the Magna Carta was signed in England in the 13th Century.[4]

For the purposes of this discussion of democratic urban governance a helpful distinction can be made between representative theories of democracy and participatory theories. In the former, often called the classical theory, it is the competition for leadership that lies at the heart of democracy. Candidates compete for office in free and fair elections and, once elected, the chosen representatives are expected to get on with the job of making decisions in the public interest. In the latter, the role of citizens involves much more than casting a vote in an election and waiting to see what happens. In participatory democracy citizens are much more actively involved in the decisions that affect their lives. Advocates of participatory democracy argue that it has intrinsic educative benefits as well as instrumental benefits. Sometimes it is argued that we have to choose which system we prefer. This is a false choice. As the Innovation Stories presented in this book attest, some of the most successful cities in the world have been very successful in combining representative and participatory approaches.

A brief comment on the evolution of democratic theory may be helpful at this point. Joseph Schumpeter, in his influential book *Capitalism, Socialism and Democracy,* emphasised that it is competition by potential decision makers for the people's vote that is the key feature of democracy (Schumpeter 1943). In Schumpeter's theory the only means of participation open to the citizen are voting for leaders and discussion. Campaigning, direct involvement in decision-making, through arrangements like participatory budgeting, and community control do not feature. Carol Pateman points out that Schumpeter offers a curiously narrow interpretation of democratic theory, one that obscures the fact that not all classical theorists shared his view of participation. She sets out a number of arguments to underpin the development of a participatory theory of democracy (Pateman 1970, 22–44). In practice, the representative model came under intense challenge from social movements in the 1960s, and a plethora of different forms of participatory democracy emerged.

Given this background, what are the important dimensions of democracy today? Smith (2009, 12–26) provides us with a useful presentation of various 'democratic goods'. I draw on his analysis here, and include an additional dimension – civic leadership. This approach generates five dimensions of democracy as follows:

- inclusiveness
- popular control
- considered judgement
- transparency and efficiency
- civic leadership.

Our touch on each of these dimensions here will be fleeting, but we will revisit these themes in subsequent discussions. First, uneven participation remains a persistent concern in systems of urban governance. Fair systems of local democracy are inclusive – they include all voices. This is easy to say, less easy to do. A number of issues arise in relation to the inclusiveness dimension of democracy. First, who counts as a citizen? As explored more fully in Chapter 10, many of us live in cities that are increasingly diverse and many residents are, for one reason or another, excluded from the political process. Also, what about the voices of children? And who is representing the voices of children yet to be born? Second, in relation to the representative system, how are individuals selected to stand for election? Self-selection may replicate existing inequalities. For example, feminists note that women are under-represented in just about every electoral assembly you can think of.[5] Third, and most important, to what extent do the institutions of urban governance provide equality of voice? Are resources provided to ensure that those with less experience and confidence are able to affect the outputs of the institution?

A second dimension concerns popular control. Who sets the public policy agenda? Is participation limited to safe topics in order to suppress conflict? To what extent does local authority decision making respond to the views expressed by citizens? A common criticism of participation 'exercises' is that they have little or no effect on decisions. Too often those in power ignore the citizen inputs, or use the views expressed as a gloss to endorse decisions made elsewhere. We will return to these questions later in the chapter when we discuss the ladder of citizen empowerment.

A third important dimension concerns considered judgement. Effective citizen involvement needs to go beyond discovering the self-interested preferences of various stakeholders. High quality decision-making processes need to provide adequate opportunities for public deliberation. This requires the creation of spaces in which participants can not only learn at least something about the 'facts', but also comprehend the views of other citizens with quite different backgrounds and experiences. As Smith (2009, 25, author's emphasis) notes, it is doubtful whether democratic institutions can be designed 'to *ensure* citizens achieve… considered judgement'. However, as I suggested in Chapter 5, civic leaders can encourage the development of considered judgement. They can create innovation zones in which different stakeholders can exchange views and learn from each other – see Figure 5.3 and associated discussion.

Fourth, transparency is fundamental not only in building trust and confidence in the political process, but also in ensuring efficiency. Having open processes of decision-making has several virtues. First, transparency diminishes the opportunities for improper, or corrupt, behaviour by politicians and/or their officials. Second, transparency enables community activists, the media and the public at large to scrutinise the activities of elected representatives and hold them to account. Third, transparency enhances efficiency because it strengthens the quality of decision-making without requiring everyone to participate in every decision. Many people are not that interested in politics and many have very limited time to contribute to local political processes. Openness can, then, help to deliver accountability without incurring the high costs of running large-scale, continuous direct participation. Fourth, information and communication technologies are creating an expanding range of possibilities for enhancing the efficiency benefits of transparency, particularly if local authorities make the data they hold readily available. For example, in 2011 San Francisco passed open-data legislation to enable citizens and government to work together on the creation of a number of apps designed to use technology to address pressing needs (Townsend 2013, 227–30). We will return to the role of information technology in urban governance when we discuss new ideas relating to the smart city in Chapter 11.

The fifth dimension of democracy is civic leadership. As discussed at length in this book effective local democracy depends on the existence of effective place-based leadership. Indeed, I have defined local government as place-based leadership for the common good. In Chapter 5 I set out a model that distinguishes five realms of civic, or place-based, leadership: political, public managerial/professional, community, business and trade union. These realms of leadership overlap and influential civic leaders can emerge from any of the realms.

Here I would like to highlight the critical role of elected local government politicians in exercising civic leadership. Electoral arrangements vary by country. But in many we find politicians who have been elected 'at large' (that is, by all those entitled to vote in a city – for example, directly elected mayors), and politicians, called councillors in the UK, who have been elected to represent geographical units within the city. In some countries there is more than one level of elected local government – for example, there is a two-tier system of counties and districts in parts of England. And in many countries there are elected neighbourhood councils (sometimes called parish councils, town councils, community councils, local boards or similar) providing locally accountable government for small areas within a locality. These variations in democratic structure can make a significant difference to the political vitality of an area, and need to be understood by would-be reformers.

The important point I wish to stress here, however, is not just that local politicians matter – it is that the roles they choose to exercise are changing. Traditional representative work can be expected to continue – it is essential. But it is increasingly the case that many local politicians are expanding their political repertoire. For example, many councillors in the UK are giving much more attention to community problem-solving activities, and some see themselves as community catalysts taking a leadership role in getting things done (James and Cox 2007; Kemp et al 2009).

Institutional design for local government leadership

In Chapter 5 I suggested that there is a critical relationship between leadership and institutional design. Stated simply, the design of an organisation, or institution, can help or hinder the exercise of effective leadership. In this section I provide a brief summary of themes that could be of interest to those contemplating a redesign of their local government institutions in order to strengthen place-based leadership. I draw here on my experience of working with city authorities in a number of different countries, but I wish to stress that all the ideas and diagrams that follow are intended to be suggestive, rather than prescriptive.

Political cultures vary significantly and institutional design ideas that might be seen as attractive in one country, or locality, may be seen as unhelpful in another. In my view elected local authorities should have, to quote a phrase used by Sir Charles Carter in the UK context, the 'freedom to do things differently' (Carter 1996). In some countries, national governments impose few constraints on the way local authorities organise themselves, in others the central state (or state level in federal systems) is involved in specifying all manner of details relating to how cities organise themselves. The discussion here is focussed on the design of the representative system of local government. It is possible, indeed essential, to add public participation arrangements to all of the models presented here, and we will return to the theme of citizen empowerment shortly.

Where to begin a discussion of representative models? At the outset it is useful to clarify the responsibilities of those exercising political leadership. In many countries, a distinction is made between two basic roles that politicians fulfil – the exercise of executive power and the representative role involving holding executive power to account.[6] This is the classic 'separation of powers' model that city halls in many countries now employ. In this model those exercising strategic leadership of the city (let's call them the Executive) are identified, and their responsibilities are spelt out so that they can be held to account for the decisions they make. In this separation of powers model, the other politicians (let's call them the Assembly), while they may retain important decision-making powers in relation to their neighbourhoods, focus on representation, policy development and scrutinising the Executive. An illustration of a possible separation of powers is provided in Figure 7.1.

Figure 7.1: Illustrative responsibilities of an Executive and an Assembly

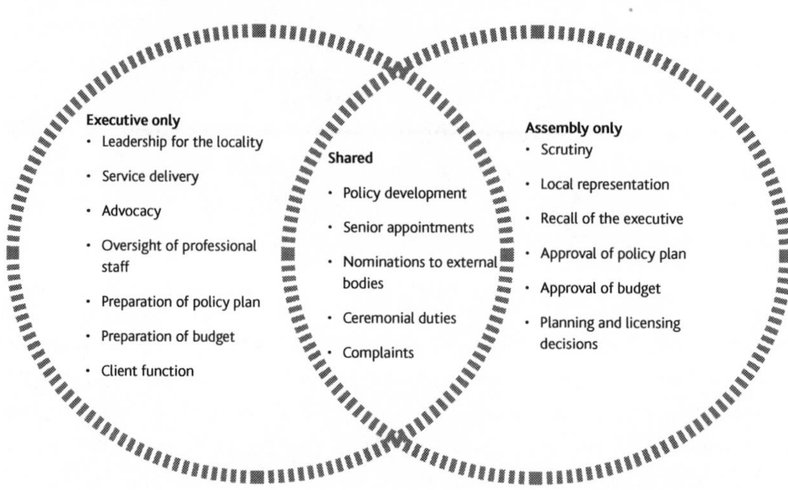

Source: Hambleton and Bullock (1996)

I wish to emphasise two points. First, this is an illustration. It is perfectly possible to shift elements around in this model. The balance of power between the Executive and the Assembly can be adjusted to reflect local political preferences – the Executive can be granted significant powers or very few. Second, it is important to stress that we are discussing here a local government model – it is not a pure parliamentary model. In central governments, in many democratic countries, the distinction between the Executive and the Assembly works tolerably well – the Executive makes decisions on policy, priorities and budgets, and the parliamentarians hold the Executive to account. Local government, and this is often misunderstood by central government officials, is different. It is perfectly possible, I would argue essential, for councillors in the Assembly of a local authority to be able to exercise executive power over a range decisions affecting the area that elected them. This can be accomplished by distinguishing between strategic decisions, which must be made by the Executive, and local decisions, which the Executive can delegate to local councillors and/or neighbourhood committees of various kinds.

In the British context, the Local Government Act 2000 introduced a separation of powers. Unfortunately, in some local authorities councillors who are not appointed to the Executive feel that their decision-making power has vanished. This is to misunderstand the model – the Executive has discretion to delegate powers to local councillors. I stress this point as successful place-based leadership is multi-level – it is not just those 'at the top' who need to exercise leadership. As mentioned earlier local councillors can exercise a vital community leadership role and this is perfectly possible in a local authority operating with a separation of powers model.

There is great diversity in approaches to local authority leadership and management across the world. In order to avoid sinking into a sea of confusing details, it is useful to simplify the debate by identifying a small number of alternative models. There are dangers in this approach – it is often the detail that is interesting. But, for the purposes of this discussion, I now put forward three models of local government organisation, all of which aim to support, albeit in different ways, effective place-based leadership. I am the first to recognise that there are other models, including models that do not involve a separation of powers. However, the three options I outline here are intended only to illustrate some of the alternative institutional forms now in use in cities around the world.[7]

The first point to stress is that in all cases we need to flip the organisation chart. The conventional management tree puts the politicians, the chief executive and the senior management at the top. In the inclusive city this is the wrong approach – it is the people who should be at the top. Everybody in the government of a democratic city – elected politicians and their officials – should see themselves as public servants.

In the first model – the Cabinet plus Council model – voters elect councillors – see Figure 7.2. The number of councillors on a council varies dramatically – in some cities there can be over 100 councillors, while in others there may be a much smaller number.[8] Once elected the councillors appoint an Executive (or Cabinet) – a small group of councillors charged with leading the local authority. In the UK the party political configuration of the council is a major factor determining who is appointed to the Cabinet. The Leader of the party with the most seats on the Council usually becomes Leader of the Council (and Leader of the Cabinet). The Assembly, called the Council in the UK, holds the Executive to account – it has a formal scrutiny role – and has the key role of agreeing the annual budget. The diagram shows how proposals flow to and fro between the Executive and the Assembly. At the bottom of the diagram we find the officers – the managerial and professional staff appointed by the councillors to provide advice and ensure cost-effective delivery of public services. Two features lie at the heart of the Cabinet model. First, the senior political leadership of the city is provided by a small group of people. Second, these individuals are indirectly elected – they are chosen by the elected councillors, not by the electorate.

Figure 7.3 provides an illustration of the Mayor/Cabinet plus Council model of city government. In this form of city government citizens vote both for the directly elected mayor and for their local councillor(s). As in the previous model there is: a separation of powers between the Executive and the Assembly with proposals flowing between the two; the Assembly scrutinises the work of the Executive; and officers provide support to both the Executive and the Assembly. The chief differences from the previous model are: the direct election of the most

Figure 7.2: The Cabinet plus Council model of city government

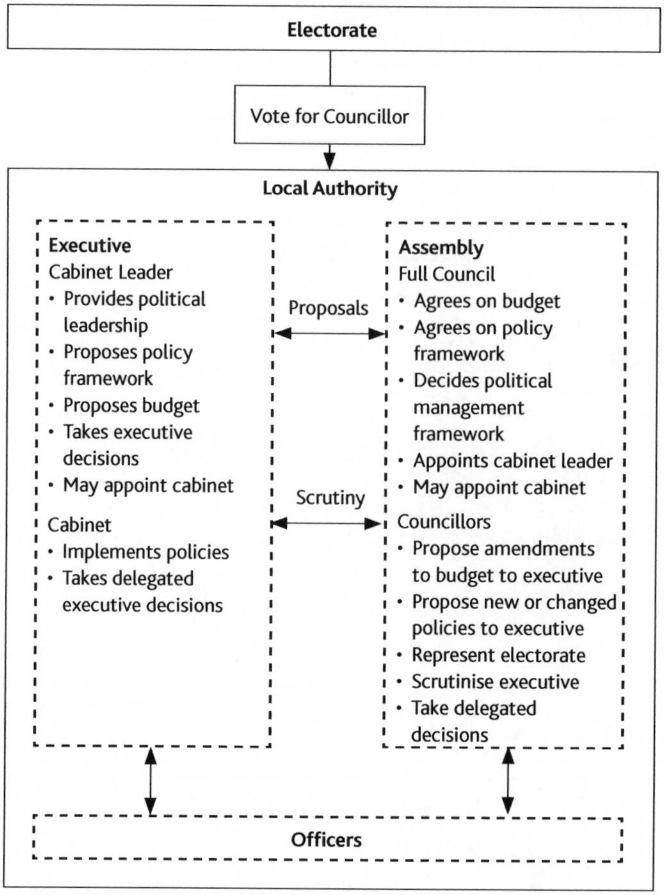

Source: Author

senior politician – the mayor – by the people of the city; the mayor normally appoints the people to serve in the Cabinet (and these politicians are sometimes called deputy mayors or assistant mayors); and the clear focus of power is on a single individual (the mayor).

Figure 7.4 illustrates our third option – the Mayor/City Manager plus Council model. The traditional American Council-Manager model does not have a mayor. However, in recent years, many of the cities employing this model have concluded that it is important to have strong political leadership working alongside the appointed manager (Svara 2009, 6–9; Svara and Watson 2010). In some of the larger Council-Manager cities the mayor has formal powers – for example, Cincinnati and Kansas City. In many ways the Mayor/City Manager plus Council model I present here resembles the Mayor/Cabinet plus Council model. Citizens vote both for the directly elected mayor and for their local councillor(s) and there is: a separation of powers between the Executive and the Assembly with proposals flowing between the two; the Assembly scrutinises the work of the Executive;

Figure 7.3: The Mayor/Cabinet plus Council model of city government

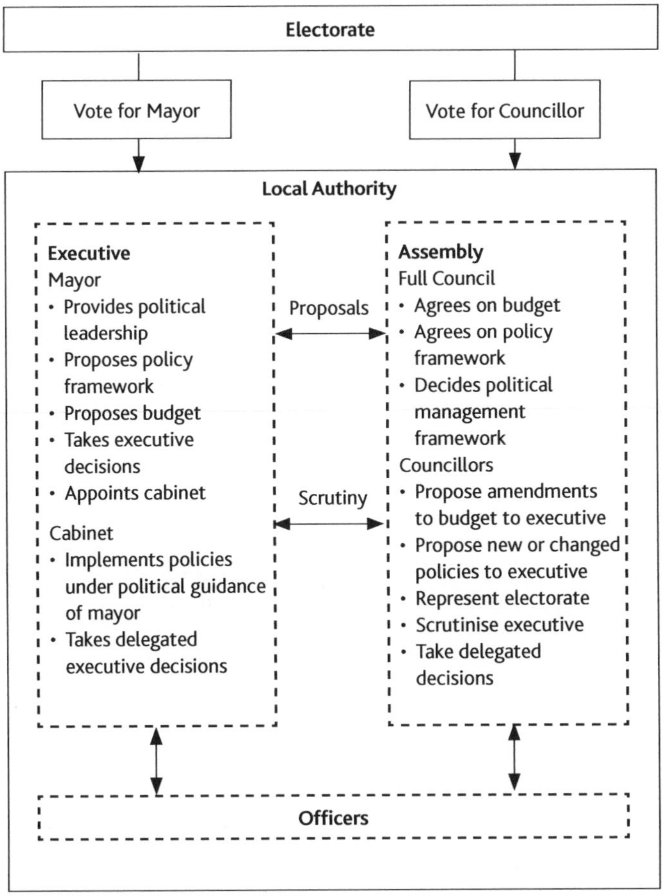

Electorate

Vote for Mayor

Vote for Councillor

Local Authority

Executive
Mayor
- Provides political leadership
- Proposes policy framework
- Proposes budget
- Takes executive decisions
- Appoints cabinet

Cabinet
- Implements policies under political guidance of mayor
- Takes delegated executive decisions

Proposals

Scrutiny

Assembly
Full Council
- Agrees on budget
- Agrees on policy framework
- Decides political management framework

Councillors
- Propose amendments to budget to executive
- Propose new or changed policies to executive
- Represent electorate
- Scrutinise executive
- Take delegated decisions

Officers

Source: Author

and officers provide support to both the Executive and the Assembly. The chief differences from the previous model are: there is no Cabinet of senior councillors working with the mayor on the strategic leadership of the city; and the mayor works very closely with an appointed officer – the City Manager.

The debate about directly elected mayors

Directly elected mayors have been a strong feature of American local government for more than a century. From an international perspective it is interesting to note that a growing number of countries, and cities, have decided to introduce versions of the directly elected mayor form of government in the last thirty years or so. The following are examples of European countries that have gone down this route: Slovakia (1990), Italy (1993), Germany (all Länder that did not already have directly elected mayors opted for mayors during the 1990s), Hungary (some cities in 1994, then all local governments in 1998) and Poland (2002). The German

Figure 7.4: The Mayor/City Manager plus Council model of city government

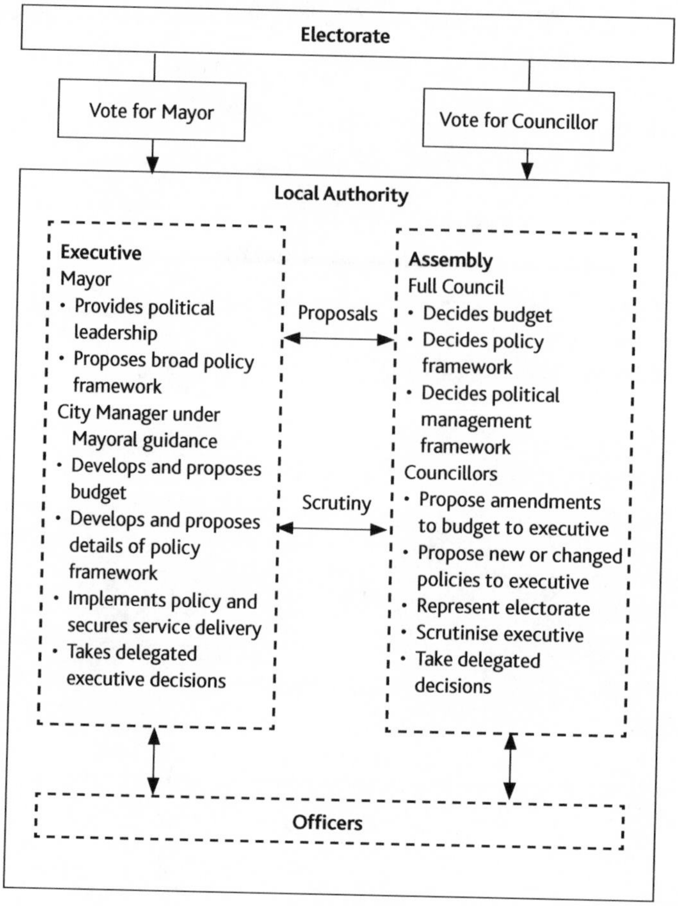

Electorate

Vote for Mayor

Vote for Councillor

Local Authority

Executive
Mayor
- Provides political leadership
- Proposes broad policy framework

City Manager under Mayoral guidance
- Develops and proposes budget
- Develops and proposes details of policy framework
- Implements policy and secures service delivery
- Takes delegated executive decisions

Proposals

Scrutiny

Assembly
Full Council
- Decides budget
- Decides policy framework
- Decides political management framework

Councillors
- Propose amendments to budget to executive
- Propose new or changed policies to executive
- Represent electorate
- Scrutinise executive
- Take delegated decisions

Officers

Source: Author

experience is intriguing as different Länder have introduced rather different models of mayoral governance (Wollmann 2014). Other countries are contemplating the introduction of directly elected mayors – for example Australia.

The English experience is likely to be of interest to those considering institutional reform because there has been extensive debate about mayoral models, and not a little experiment in the period since 2000. In Chapter 5 I noted that the Labour Government, elected in 1997, provided the legislation to underpin the introduction of the directly elected mayor for London in 2000, as well as legislation enabling other local authorities to introduce the model. And Innovation Story 2 discusses the introduction of Mayoral governance in Bristol in 2012.

The debate about elected mayors generates strong feelings. There are many arguments and counterarguments to consider. Here, by drawing on the literature relating to elected mayors and my experience of working with mayors in different countries, I summarise the main pros and cons as viewed in the UK context.

Arguments in favour of directly elected mayors:

- visibility – citizens and others know who the leader of the city is.
- legitimacy and accountability – arising from the direct election process.
- strategic focus and authority to decide – a mayor can make tough decisions for a city and then be held to account.
- stable leadership – a mayor holds office for four years and this can underpin a consistent approach to government.
- attract new people into politics – creative individuals may be able to stimulate innovation in citizen activism and business support.
- partnership working – a mayor is seen as the leader of the place, rather than the leader of the council. This can assist in building coalitions.

Arguments against directly elected mayors:

- celebrity posturing – the model could attract candidates more interested in self-promotion than sound policy making.
- wrong area – in the English context the Localism Act 2011 provides for mayors to be elected for unitary authorities (which form the central parts of the conurbations they are located in) when many consider that metropolitan mayors on the London model are needed.
- recipe for corruption – the model could place too much power in the hands of one person.
- weak power of recall – elect an incompetent mayor and the city is stuck with this person for four years.
- cost – having a mayor will cost more money.
- our over-centralised state remains – without a massive increase in local power to decide things the mayor will be a puppet dancing on strings controlled in Whitehall.

Another concern for those advocating the introduction of directly elected mayors is that, when viewed internationally, the vast majority of elected mayors are men. There are, of course, a number of female, directly elected mayors. American examples are Annise Parker in Houston, Jean Quan in Oakland and Nancy McFarlane in Raleigh. But critics of the mayoral model raise the argument that directly elected mayors tend to have a presidential style of leadership and this could be less appealing to potential women leaders, who may prefer a more collective approach to urban leadership (and leadership in general).

I set out some of the pros and cons of the mayoral model in a stark way in the hope that this can prompt fresh thinking. It is certainly inappropriate to prescribe a particular model of governance – in democratic societies citizens should decide how they wish to be governed. Also, as the previous discussion of democratic models has made clear, real choices are available. It is perfectly possible to design strong civic leadership models without introducing a directly elected mayor. As Innovation Stories 12 and 13 will show, Copenhagen and Melbourne provide world-class examples of urban leadership, but they do not have directly elected mayors. Equally, there is good evidence to support the argument that directly elected mayors can use their position to exercise bold, outgoing place-based leadership. For example, Innovation Stories 2 and 3 on Bristol and Chicago – show how directly elected mayors have been able to promote startling new initiatives. It is also worth noting that there are many different forms of mayoral governance. Cities and countries that do decide to introduce directly elected mayors have a good deal of scope to design in appropriate power relationships between the elected mayor and the assembly – some may opt for a strong mayor model, others may prefer a strong council model.

Redesigning metropolitan government in New Zealand

In 2007 the New Zealand Government, then controlled by the centre-left Labour Party, set up a Royal Commission on Auckland Governance to respond to growing concerns about the workability of local government arrangements in the city. Auckland is home to 1.5 million people – a third of New Zealand's population – and the success of the city is vital to national economic prosperity. There were concerns in government and elsewhere about the fact that the system of urban governance was weak and fragmented. Anxieties were also expressed about an absence of strategic planning, inefficient urban growth, infrastructure constraints, social disparity and poor urban design. Put bluntly the seven territorial authorities and the Auckland Regional Council were seen as not being up to the job.

Led by the Hon Peter Salmon QC, the Royal Commission carried out a very thorough investigation into the challenges facing the city and the city region, and developed a set of radical proposals for reform (Royal Commission on Auckland Governance 2009). In a startling move the Royal Commission recommended the dissolution of all the existing local authorities and the creation of a massive, new unitary authority called the Auckland Council.[9] The Commission also decided that this new 'super-city' (as it was dubbed by the media) needed an inspirational leader able to articulate a shared vision and deliver regional priorities decisively. The Commission recommended the introduction of a directly elected mayor to lead the new city. While elected mayors are well established in New Zealand, the Royal Commission proposed a significant strengthening of the powers of the proposed mayor for Auckland.[10]

The New Zealand government accepted many, but not all, of the recommendations of the Royal Commission. The governmental structure of Auckland was transformed and, in October 2010, citizens voted in Len Brown as the first directly elected mayor of the metropolis. Innovation Story 7 reports on the work of the Royal Commission, and discusses the approach Mayor Brown has adopted to the leadership of this vibrant multi-cultural city.

Creating a super-city: the reform of urban governance in Auckland

Aims

In a comparatively short space of time the governance of Auckland has been transformed. In 2010, in a radical move, the New Zealand government abolished the eight local authorities – seven territorial authorities and the Auckland Regional Council – that were then governing the city. It replaced them with what the press soon called a 'super-city' – a new, large, unitary authority, the Auckland Council, which is led by a directly elected mayor. The reform, which represents a bold effort to improve the leadership and management of urban development at the metropolitan scale, has attracted international attention.

In October 2010, against the expectations of the centre-right coalition government, the voters elected Len Brown as the first mayor of Auckland. Brown had a good track record as a community-oriented leader when he was mayor of Manukau City, one of the local authorities abolished by the reforms. As mayor of Auckland he has pursued policies to improve public transport, promote high-value economic development and build an inclusive city – an important consideration in a city of 1.5 million containing 180 ethnicities. In October 2013 he was re-elected for a second three-year term.

This Innovation Story aims to: outline the work of the Royal Commission on Auckland Governance, set up in 2007; summarise the government's response to the Royal Commission; and assess the impact of the mayoral form of governance on the city in the period since 2010.

Innovation Story outline

The review of metropolitan governance in Auckland was initiated by the centre-left government of New Zealand in 2007. The government felt that the existing fragmented system of local government was not delivering a cohesive approach to strategic, infrastructure and other planning. In order to address these concerns the government set up an independent Royal Commission on Auckland Governance to gather evidence, and report on how to improve the local government arrangements in order to achieve the future well-being of the region and it communities.

The Report of the Royal Commission on Auckland Governance, published in 2009, is, by any standards, an impressive document. It runs to over 1800 pages, and is one of the most thorough studies of metropolitan government carried out anywhere in the world. The report set out the case for change and suggested that existing arrangements scored badly on two counts: 1) Regional governance was weak and fragmented, and 2) Community engagement was poor.

The Commission considered a range of options and concluded that the establishment of a single, region-wide unitary authority – called the Auckland Council – would help to achieve strong and effective Auckland governance and overcome current fragmentation and coordination problems. This council would hold all council assets and employ all staff. The Commission stressed that there would be: '... one long-term council community plan, one spatial plan, one district plan, one rating system, one rates bill, one voice for Auckland' (Vol 2 para 30). In the media coverage this model came to be described as a super-city.

Overlooked, by at least some of the popular commentary on the Commission's proposals, is the fact that the Commission envisaged a lower level of government, below the level of the Auckland Council: 'In addition to the elected governing body of the Auckland Council, local democracy will be maintained through six elected local councils operating within the unitary Auckland Council' (Vol 2 para 33). The Royal Commission recommended that the new Auckland Council should be led by a mayor who is directly elected by all Aucklanders. This proposal excited a high level of public interest. The Royal Commission also made significant recommendations relating to Maori representation in the future government of the city region.

While the Commission was preparing its report, the New Zealand Labour-led social democratic government was replaced by a centre-right coalition. The government response to the Commission's report was, not surprisingly, to agree with the recommendations regarding governmental consolidation, but discard the suggestions the Commission made for enhancing local democracy. The Local Government (Auckland Council) Act 2009 created the new Auckland Council and the elections for the first mayor of Auckland took place in October 2010.

The Government recognised that there would have to be arrangements for decentralised management within the new Auckland Council and proposed the creation of 20 to 30 'local boards' across the region as a 'second tier of governance'. The Government rejected the proposal for Maori seats on the unitary council, and it also rejected most of the ideas the Royal Commission put forward for improving collaborative working between central government and the new Auckland Council.

Len Brown won the Auckland mayoral election and was sworn in as mayor on 9 October 2010. A lawyer by profession, Brown has a well established record of public service in the Auckland area, and enjoyed strong support from the less well-off in the city. Auckland Council now has three components: 1) The governing body, consisting of the directly elected mayor and 20 councillors elected on a ward basis; 2) 21 local boards, with members elected by local board area, looking after local matters; and 3) Council Controlled Organisations (CCOs) (like Transport and Watercare).

Mayor Brown has made improvements to public transport a priority, and has progressed plans to create a City Rail Link. Central government required the Council to prepare a Unitary Plan and Mayor Brown has steered the creation of a bold, 30-year Auckland Plan. This sets out firm planning and design rules for this expanding city. It envisages relatively high-density residential development around transport nodes. By improving urban design and creating a more compact city the aim is to make Auckland an even more liveable city. Mayor Brown has created a number of Advisory Panels to assist Auckland Council. Some of these are required by legislation – for example, the Ethnic People's Advisory Panel and Pacific People's Advisory Panel – but others stem from local initiative – for example, the Disability Advisory Panel, the Youth Panel and the Seniors Panel.

Some commentators feel that the super-city suffers from significant problems of internal communication. They argue that the previous decision-making based on geography (the seven territorial authorities) has been replaced by decision-making by function and that this is not, necessarily, an improvement. Others take the view that having a super-city is a significant step forward from the previous arrangements and that having a powerful directly elected mayor has strengthened the leadership of the city.

Leadership lessons

- Central governments in different countries could make more use of the Royal Commission, or similar, model of decision-making as they consider ways of improving local governance. Appointing an independent and experienced team to gather evidence, examine options and come up with imaginative recommendations can enlarge the way policy makers think about possible solutions.
- Central governments can take steps to transform metropolitan governance arrangements if the political will is there. It is misguided to believe that local vested interests within a metropolis will always be able to stymie radical reform. This Innovation Story shows how, in the New Zealand context, it has been possible to introduce radical change in a relatively short space of time.
- The Directly Elected Mayor (DEM) form of governance provides a high level of visibility to the leadership role. Mayor Len Brown is a far more visible public figure, both nationally and internationally, than the leaders of any of the pre-existing councils in Auckland. This prominence stems in part from the process of direct election, and partly from the efforts the mayor makes to be available to citizens and interest groups.
- Mayor Brown has been successful in furthering his aim of creating a more sustainable future for Auckland. The 30-year Auckland Plan will be of interest to other cities wishing to promote a strategy for urban growth that is not dominated by road building and low density residential development.

Sources

Cheyne, C, 2012, *Leading Auckland: Local political leadership in Australia and New Zealand's largest council*, Paper to the International Political Science Conference, Madrid, 12 July

Hambleton, R, 2009, Civic Leadership for Auckland: An international perspective, in *Royal Commission on Auckland Governance*. Vol 4, Part 11. pp 515–552, www.royalcommission.govt.nz
Royal Commission on Auckland Governance, 2009, *Auckland Governance Report*, Auckland, New Zealand: Royal Commission on Auckland Governance. www.royalcommission.govt.nz
Auckland Council: http://www.aucklandcouncil.govt.nz

Citizen empowerment and co-creation of solutions

In Chapter 3 I outlined three alternative strategies for public service reform – the introduction of market models into public services, the development of a customer orientation in public service bureaucracies, and the strengthening of citizen voice in the democratic process. These three alternatives are presented in Figure 3.1 and this shows how each strategy tends to treat people in different ways. The market model defines people as consumers, new managerialism pictures service users as customers, and democratic innovations respect people as citizens. These distinctions are often overlooked in public service reform debates – sometimes deliberately – and this creates much confusion. In this section I want to develop the discussion of citizen empowerment.

Sherry Arnstein, in her enormously influential article, 'A ladder of citizen participation', spurred fresh thinking about the nature of public participation in local decision-making, not just in the USA but internationally (Arnstein 1969). Her model, which was designed to encourage a more enlightened dialogue about the nature of participation, outlined eight stages of power sharing in ascending order – from 'manipulation', where participants are drawn into the process in order simply to give the appearance of consultation, through to 'citizen control', where there are varying degrees of shared planning and decision-making.

Danny Burns, Paul Hoggett and I attempted to build on her model to develop a ladder of citizen empowerment (Burns et al 1994, 160–79). Our ladder of citizen empowerment, which is reproduced as Figure 7.5, differs from Arnstein's model in two main respects. First, there are more rungs in the ladder – we wanted to distinguish more clearly between different degrees of control, particularly at the top of the ladder. Second, the rungs on the ladder are not equidistant. We noted that it is far easier to climb the lower rungs than to scale the higher ones. The ladder is divided into three bands – citizen non-participation, citizen participation and citizen control. The lower four rungs (citizen non-participation) are all fairly close together and amount to nothing more than pseudo-consultation. Higher up the ladder we find various forms of citizen participation and, within this band, we distinguish between informing, consulting, decentralised decision-making, partnership and delegated control. In the top two rungs we find examples of citizen control – here citizens have authority to take action without prior confirmation from a higher level.

Billie Oliver and Bob Pitt (2013, 14–21) discuss these and similar empowerment models, and note that they can be criticised for implying that the ladder must be climbed, with the upper rung being seen as the ultimate goal. This is a legitimate argument but it is certainly not what we, for our part, intended. We put forward our ladder of citizen empowerment 'to provide a conceptual framework which can help local authorities and others think through their empowerment strategies' (Burns et al 1994 p177). Oliver and Pitt understand this, and provide an excellent discussion of a variety of participation models, as well as a useful guide to further sources.

Figure 7.5: A ladder of citizen empowerment

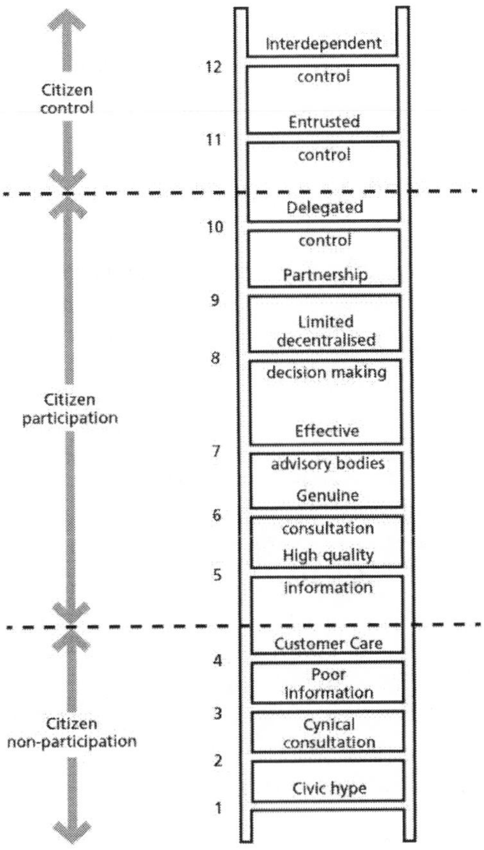

Source: Burns et al (1994, p 162)

In Chapter 3 I discussed the changing relationships between civil society, markets and the state. Figure 3.2 suggests that it may be helpful to imagine the relationships between civil society, markets and the state, not as a rigid triangle, but as three overlapping spheres of influence. The ladder of citizen empowerment highlights the significance of the area of overlap between citizens and the state. In many countries this relationship is being renegotiated, partly because public spending is being cut back, but also because the co-creation of services holds out great promise for improving the quality, responsiveness and cost effectiveness of public action. Stated simply, citizens are becoming more actively involved in meeting the needs of their community. In Chapter 6 I noted that, as new models of collaboration emerge – for example, co-governance, co-management and co-production (Brandsen and Pestoff 2006) – it seems likely that the innovation zones presented in Figure 5.3 will become increasingly important.

The literature on citizen empowerment is expanding rapidly, and these efforts to document and spread novel democratic practices are generating a wide array of opportunities for more ambitious approaches to public service innovation (Cornwall 2008; Fung 2004; Fung et al 2003; Oliver and Pitt 2013; Pearce 2010; Smith 2009). Here I would like to highlight two strategies that can be expected to become increasingly significant in the future: participatory budgeting and e-democracy.

Participatory budgeting

Participatory budgeting, which involves citizens deciding directly how public money is spent, is now in use in an expanding number of cities. Porto Alegre, Brazil should be credited with creating and implementing the first full participatory budget process in 1989. This empowerment strategy was seen to be highly successful. Capital spending in the city was redirected to focus on priorities identified by citizens – for example, sewer and water connections and schools. It was not surprising, therefore, that the approach spread rapidly to hundreds of Latin American cities. In more recent years, participatory budgeting has been taken up by cities in Europe, North America and elsewhere (Rocke 2014). Interestingly, the international trajectory of policy learning has been South to North, rather than the other way round. Hilary Wainwright (2003) provides a detailed analysis of the Porto Alegre experience, and shows how participatory budgeting, and similar experiments in popular democracy, form part of a wider movement for democracy in everyday life.

There are now many varieties of participatory budgeting (Smith 2009). A word of caution is needed. Some of the cities that claim to have adopted it have actually only introduced a pale imitation. For example, devolving comparatively small public budgets to neighbourhoods within a city can end up doing relatively little to enhance citizen power, and such action may even deflect public attention from more important matters. The original idea of participatory budgeting is radical. It involves citizens having a direct say in decisions relating to a significant part of a municipal or public budget. Processes vary but a typical Latin American approach might involve the following steps:

1. Area-based communities within the city are given budget briefings on how spending is currently allocated and the nature of the budget prospects
2. Area-based community representatives identify spending (or cutback) priorities (or projects) in an open, public process

3. Budget delegates from the areas develop spending plans with assistance from experts
4. Community members vote on proposals, and
5. The city or institution implements the top priorities.

Participatory budgeting, when it involves citizens having a direct say in significant spending decisions, is located well up the ladder of citizen empowerment shown in Figure 7.5.[11] Even modest efforts at participatory budgeting are likely to be at Rung 8 and radical models are on the boundary between citizen participation and citizen control – Rungs 10 and 11.

E-democracy

The rapid pace of change in information and communication technology (ICT) is having a dramatic impact on societies across the world. For example, more than half of adults in the UK now use social networking sites. Taking a wider view, the role of social media, like Twitter and text messaging, played a significant role in recent social uprisings – for example, the Egyptian revolution in 2011. Private sector companies, notably Facebook and Google, have been particularly effective in extracting personal information from users and then using it to develop highly targeted advertising. Some commentators suggest that, when it comes to ICT, governments are off the pace. For example, Smith (2009, 142), having noted the staggering changes in the commercial world, argues that: '... the potential for using ICT to increase and deepen citizen participation in political decision-making has lagged somewhat behind'.

The phrase 'e-democracy', a combination of the words electronic and democracy, refers to the use of modern information and communication technologies to enhance democracy. As such, it covers a bewildering range of initiatives (Coleman and Blumler 2009). A lively ongoing public debate is now unfolding between internet believers and cyber sceptics. Enthusiasts, like Clay Shirky (2008), appear to believe that we are entering a new era of direct democracy as a result of ICT. Critics point out that the Internet is changing the way we think, read and remember, and that it may be making us stupid (Carr 2010). And, while it holds great promise, there is a worrying digital divide between those with access to ICT and those who are, for one reason or another, excluded (Hindman 2009; Mossberger et al 2008). We will revisit this debate in Chapter 11 when we discuss how to go beyond the smart city.

Leaving aside the wider arguments about ICT, what kind of impact is e-democracy actually having on democratic urban governance? The three levels of citizen engagement shown in the ladder of citizen empowerment presented in Figure 7.5 can help us answer this question. First, at the lower end of the ladder, it is clear that there has been a massive expansion of e-non-participation. Many cities continue to view ICT as a way of pumping out web-based information about their achievements and activities – a one-way flow of city promotion. The critique of place marketing that I presented in Chapter 4 is relevant here. Those in charge of city hall ICT strategies need to avoid falling into the trap of alienating citizens by coming across as city boosters.

Second, and more positively, if we move up the ladder, we can note that initiatives are now taking place in many cities in efforts to enhance citizen participation using new technologies. For example, Innovation Story 3, in Chapter 6, documents the efforts of the City of Chicago to improve relationships between citizens and public servants via the use of a 311 non-emergency phone number and an Open311 online service. Initiatives of this kind use ICT to make service more convenient, citizen-friendly and responsive. Some cities are now promoting open data initiatives. The basic idea here is to open up access to unreleased public data so that social entrepreneurs, anyone for that matter, can develop apps to enhance the quality of life in the city. Such initiatives provide new opportunities for citizens to co-create solutions by collaborating with the state.

As we move up the ladder, heading in the direction of citizen control, what is the evidence suggesting that ICT can alter power systems in a fundamental way? We will return to this question in Chapter 11. Graham Smith (2009, 161) discusses e-democracy and concludes that: '... it is striking that ICT has not led to the emergence of new and interesting mechanisms for realising popular control...' In his view, much of the innovation that has been taking place so far has advanced the cause of e-government rather than e-democracy. ICT is delivering vast amounts of information to citizens but, it seems, not too much in terms of citizen power.

Looking ahead, ICT offers intriguing possibilities for both local representative democracy and participatory democracy. In relation to the former, Jane Scullion suggests that elected councillors have a choice between 'tweeting or retreating' (2013). In a perceptive analysis, she examines the choices facing those elected to local authorities and suggests that politicians who are early adopters of ICT can, perhaps, identify lessons for those considering how to be more effective in the new world of digital, urban politics. In relation to participatory democracy the central challenge is to develop really effective *place-based* ICT services – resources that serve local actors in a direct and helpful way. In ICT jargon this is sometimes described as 'situated software'. In Bristol, my own city, the Knowle West Media Centre provides an inventive example of this approach. In this instance, community-based workers have created a range of ICT services that relate to neighbourhood needs. For example, a user-friendly city dashboard presents data on how specific neighbourhoods within the city compare with the city as a whole.[12]

Multi-level leadership in an innovative Swedish city

In the early 1990s the bottom dropped out of the Malmö economy. The port city had grown to become the third largest city in Sweden. In the 1960s this successful industrial town had enormous shipyards that could rival any in the world. Now the docks and associated traditional industries have vanished. While the Malmö fall from economic grace mirrors the decline of many industrial cities it was probably more dramatic and more sudden than many. In the three-year period 1992–94 the city lost a third of its jobs.

Anders Rubin, Deputy Mayor for Housing and Urban Environment, who has been an elected councillor since 1985 and knows Malmö's industrial past very well, put it graphically: 'In three years we lost everything. We went from industrial town to no industry town.' [13] A decade or so later and Malmö is lauded as one of the most far-sighted cities in Europe for sustainable development. In an astonishing turn around the city has reinvented itself as an eco-friendly, multi-cultural city. Ilmar Reepalu, then Mayor of the City, and his colleagues decided to redefine the core purpose of the city, and backed their radical vision of a modern eco-city with innovative approaches to public service management, including the introduction of an entirely new decentralised way of running local services. Malmö has become a more ethnically diverse city in recent years, and it has made efforts to address issues relating to social sustainability as well as environmental sustainability. The Commission for a Socially Sustainable Malmö, which carried out an area-based analysis of health inequalities between 2010 and 2013, is an illustration.[14]

Innovation Story 8 outlines the radical changes made by place-based leaders in Malmö to turn their city around. As context for this story it is important to note that Sweden has one of the strongest systems of local government in the world. Most Swedish citizens pay their entire income tax to local government. Only the highest income earners – around 20 per cent of taxpayers – pay central government any income tax at all. Local authorities in Sweden raise around 70 per cent of their revenue from local taxes and they have great freedom to things differently. The Swedish central state is very small. Swedes ask: Why burden the citizens with the all the costs of a massive central state when local authorities can do most things for themselves? Within this legislative context local politicians in Malmö have exercised bold leadership and, in particular, the city has developed a way of responding to the diverse needs of the city by devolving power to localities within the city.

INNOVATION STORY 8

Malmö: from rust-belt to leading eco-city

Aims

In 1994 the newly elected political leaders of the City of Malmö were faced with a formidable challenge – in effect the long established economic structure of their city had collapsed. Malmö, the third largest city in Sweden, was a successful industrial city with a massive shipbuilding industry. But rapid deindustrialisation in the 1980s meant that the economic underpinnings of the city were ripped away.

Anders Rubin, then Deputy Mayor for Housing and Urban Environment, was part of the political leadership team that ushered in a new era: 'The disappearance of traditional industries was so fast and so complete that we had nothing to be defensive about. We simply had to come up with a new approach. And we decided that the way forward was to create a modern city that was at the very top when it comes to environmental issues.'[1]

The political leadership exercised by Ilmar Reepalu, then Mayor of the City, and his colleagues was not just bold and forward looking. As well as being strategic and anticipatory, it was backed by innovative approaches to management, including devolution of power to districts and neighbourhoods within the city.

Innovation Story outline

Civic leadership in Malmö is multilevel. At the level of the city region the construction of the magnificent Øresund Bridge linking Malmö and Copenhagen was a major strategic decision made by the central governments of Sweden and Denmark. But local leaders should be given credit for pressing for this investment. Opened in 2000 the bridge, with its international rail and road links, is contributing to a reshaping of the socio-economic geography of the whole Øresund region. In the period from the mid 1990s Malmö has switched from being a declining, former industrial town on the edge of Sweden to being at the heart of a buoyant Øresund knowledge economy.

Within this new regional context political leaders orchestrated the preparation and adoption of the Comprehensive Plan for Malmö 2000 (since updated in 2005 and 2012). This sophisticated urban strategy provides for mixed uses within the city. As Christer Larsson, the Director of City Planning, put it: 'The structure of the city is crucial to our approach to climate change. Through careful planning designed to ensure mixed-use developments close to railway stations we can reduce the need for car travel enormously.'[2]

In 1996, the City of Malmö was divided into ten geographical areas – each run by a City District Department. This model was modified in 2013 and there are now five geographical departments. The aim is twofold: to develop and strengthen local democracy; and to improve public service responsiveness. The decentralised system enables city government to gain a comprehensive view of the needs of the population in a given district and gives citizens enhanced influence over conditions in their area. The three main areas covered by the City District Departments now are: 1) health and medical care, 2) individual and family care, and 3) leisure and culture.

Devolution of decisions to the district level makes those decisions more responsive to local concerns and promotes citizen empowerment. Devolved management is particularly important in multicultural cities because neighbourhood needs can vary significantly. Malmö is a cosmopolitan city – some 28% of residents were born abroad and, in some parts of the city, more than half the inhabitants are non-Swedish-born.

Politicians in Malmö trust their officers to get on with the job of working with citizens to address community priorities. This is visible not just in the organisational design just referred to, but also in relation to a whole range of projects and initiatives. Three will be mentioned here to illustrate the argument.

The Västra Hamnen (the Western Harbour) is a stunning development where urban designers, architects, environmentalists, structural engineers and city planners have been very inventive. Even without mentioning the astonishing Turning Torso tower – a 54 storey mixed use skyscraper designed by Santiago Calatrava – the Västra Hamnen represents a breakthrough in sophisticated environmental design tuned to an urban context. Mayor Reepalu was very active in persuading reluctant developers to adopt a new approach, and building rights were only issued to developers who accepted the ambitious environmental goals. Here, people on foot and cyclists have priority over cars, walls and roofs are covered with plants, and green roofs of moss-stonecrop sedum carpet are found on a high proportion of the properties. The whole neighbourhood is carbon neutral, mainly because the district heating system stores heat down in the limestone beneath the neighbourhood in the summer and draws on it in the winter.

A second example, one that is more explicitly focussed on the aims of promoting an inclusive city, is provided by the transformation of a large, unfashionable housing estate into one of the greenest urban neighbourhoods in Europe. The story of Ekostaden Augustenborg (the Augustenborg Eco Neighbourhood) illustrates how community leadership at the neighbourhood level has had a significant impact.

Built in 1948–1952 Augustenborg, with a population of 3,000, was one of the first of the post-war Swedish housing estates. As Trevor Graham, project leader of the recent transformation of the neighbourhood, explains: 'At the time the new spacious homes with modern facilities and a high quality living environment were the foundation of the new Sweden, and Augustenborg became a leading symbol.' The area was a great success for the best part of twenty years. However, in the late 1960s and early 1970s things started to change. By then the housing units appeared small when compared with more modern developments and the area was subject to regular flooding – putting the laundrettes in the basements out of action and creating inconvenience and cost. Migration from Augustenborg left empty apartments and the area took on an abandoned feel.

In 1998, as part of the new political strategy outlined above, the Ekostaden Augustenborg project was launched with the aim of transforming the area into a sustainable neighbourhood. Local residents have been encouraged to take a leading role in idea development, design and implementation. A good example is provided by Morten Ovesen, a local resident, craftsman and water innovator – he helped to design a new open storm water system, one that now retains 70% of all rainwater. Examples of public innovation in Augustenborg include:

- There are now over 10,000 square metres of green roofs that are an important part of the storm water management process.
- Renewable energy is a key feature. Now over 400 square metres of solar collectors produce hot water (with excess production fed into the district heating system).
- Extensive façade renovation has improved the energy efficiency of the existing stock, reduced damp and ventilation problems and enhanced the attractiveness of the area.
- Open spaces and walkways have been redesigned and residents have reshaped public spaces into attractive communal gardens and playgrounds.
- Around 70% of waste is recycled or reused (with the rest being used for energy generation).
- A community based car pool, established in 2000, uses ethanol hybrid cars to further reduce environmental impacts

A third example of bold innovation in the city is provided by the Sustainable Rosengård initiative. Urban riots took place in this area in April 2010. Many residents of the district, which has a population of 20,000, felt that Rosengård was being neglected, that public funds were being channelled into middle class areas like the Västra Hamnen. Rosengård has a high level of ethnic diversity – for example, over 60% of residents were born outside Sweden – and the area is relatively poor.

Residents of a shared equity housing development, BRF Hilda, initiated a range of efforts to address issues relating to social sustainability as well as environmental sustainability. Malmö City Council has taken many steps to improve the quality of life for residents including, for example, constructing a train station and introducing measures to enhance bus services in order to improve links between Rosengård and surrounding parts of Malmö. Social sustainability has been enhanced by the creation of bicycle and pedestrian paths through the district. Local residents have been heavily involved in the planning and implementation of these paths as well as in the promotion of urban gardening and various social and cultural activities.

Leadership lessons

- Swedish local authorities are very powerful institutions. They enjoy constitutional protection and have the fiscal power and authority to take forward very bold initiatives. The Swedish system provides ample political space within which local leaders can innovate, and it is clear that local government can take on an emphatic role in shaping urban development.
- City leaders in Malmö have been radical in rethinking the raison d'etre for their city. The shock of rapid industrial decline did not disable place-based leadership. On the contrary it spurred fresh thinking and the development of practical strategies designed to create an entirely new future for their city.
- Bold political leadership can establish a vision for a city that can enable it to reinvent itself. In this case the leadership decided to transform Malmö into an internationally respected eco-city, and the progress made towards this objective is remarkable. In

recent years civic leaders have recognised the need to give more emphasis to social sustainability.

- Radical decentralisation of decision making to the district level can enhance public involvement and service responsiveness. The governance system of a city can be designed to tune into the needs and priorities of different area-based communities within a city.
- Recruit creative officers and give them authority to take risks and come up with new solutions. Professional staff, when given clear political guidance, can play an important leadership role in creating new kinds of sustainable urban development and community participation.
- At the grass roots, as exemplified by the transformation of the physical and social environment in the Ekostaden Augustenborg and the recent initiatives in Rosengård, it is community leadership at the very local level that can make a major difference. Senior figures in a city can set a tone that welcomes innovation. But it is local leaders who deliver improvements on a day-to-day basis.

Sources

The City of Malmö provides more information at: http://www.Malmö.se

Hall, P, 2013, *Good cities, better lives. How Europe discovered the lost art of urbanism*, Abingdon: Routledge, pp 238–247

Nylund, K, 2014, 'Conceptions of justice in the planning of the new urban landscape – Recent changes in the comprehensive planning discourse in Malmö, Sweden,' *Planning Theory and Practice*, 15, 1, pp 41–61

Reepalu, I, 2013, *Malmö: From industrial wasteland to sustainable city, Climate Leader Paper*: http://www.climateactionprogramme.org/climate-leader-papers

Endnotes

[1] All the quotations in this Innovation Story arise from personal interviews with stakeholders conducted by the author on 28 May 2008

[2] For a helpful analysis of justice themes in urban planning in Malmö, see Nylund (2014)

Conclusions

On 11 November 1947 Winston Churchill, in a speech in the UK House of Commons, made his famous statement about democracy:

> No one pretends that democracy is perfect or all-wise. Indeed, it has been said that democracy is the worst form of government except for all those other forms that have been tried from time to time.

In this chapter I have discussed the role of local democracy in modern societies and focussed, in particular, on urban democracy. Scan across the world and you will find many different forms of democratic urban governance. In line with the argument put forward by Churchill we can be confident that no city has come up with a 'perfect' model. But this is not to be discouraging. On the contrary the discussion has shown that ideas relating to the nature of democracy have advance dramatically during the last fifty years or so, and the chapter has shown that numerous innovations in democratic urban governance are taking place. I would like to highlight four points from the discussion.

First, it is clear that some interests in society do not care about what happens to place-based communities. Many large, multi-national companies and major financial institutions appear to view places as sites for commercial exploitation. These big firms and banks see the concerns of others as externalities – the needs of communities living in particular places do not figure in their calculations. Moreover, in too many companies business cultures have developed that focus narrowly on economic targets. Extreme self-interested behaviour in these organisations has been incentivised, with the granting of gargantuan bonuses to senior bankers being only the most obvious example of this trend. The creeping expansion of this greedy, exploitative culture led, of course, to the global financial collapse of 2008. Michael Sandel has shown that one of the defects of a market-driven society is that important non-market values, like solidarity and civic spirit, are crushed (Sandel 2012). The starting point for our discussion of local democracy is, then, that local government must now play a vital role in reclaiming power for place-based communities. Given the growth of place-less power in recent years, and the unequal societies it is creating, it is beyond doubt that a reassertion of place-based power is overdue.

This logic leads to our second theme. I have suggested that the purpose of local government is to provide place-based leadership for the common good. The discussion of the changing nature of local government has identified five dimensions of democracy. All have a part to play: inclusiveness; popular control; considered judgement; transparency and efficiency; and civic leadership. A distinction has been drawn between representative democracy and participatory democracy, and I have suggested that it is a mistake to believe that we have to choose between the two. The Innovation Stories presented in this book show that successful approaches to place-based leadership almost always combine representative and participatory approaches.

Third, the design of local government institutions makes a difference. It is not the whole story but it is clear that the design of an organisation, or institution, can help or hinder the exercise of effective leadership. As a prompt to fresh thinking about institutional arrangements I have suggested that many systems of urban government in use today incorporate a separation of powers between an Executive and an Assembly. This is not the only way to organise urban democracy, but it has some important advantages that reformers may wish to consider. To illustrate the possibilities I have presented three stylised models of city government: Cabinet plus Council; Mayor/Cabinet plus Council; and Mayor/City Manager plus Council. I have noted that the directly elected mayor form of government has grown in popularity in the last thirty years or so, and I set out the arguments for and against this model. To illuminate the debate about institutional design, and show how the directly elected mayor model can give place-based leadership a big boost, Innovation Story 7 describes the radical reshaping of metropolitan governance in Auckland, New Zealand.

The role of local government in fostering innovative approaches to citizen empowerment and the co-creation of solutions to community problems is the fourth major theme. A ladder of citizen empowerment was outlined to provide a conceptual framework for thinking about alternative empowerment strategies – see Figure 7.5. Two avenues that appear to hold out considerable promise for fruitful democratic innovation in the near future were outlined: participatory budgeting and e-democracy. A recurring theme in the discussion about modern civic leadership is that successful approaches cultivate leadership from the grassroots up. It is completely misguided to believe that electing, or appointing, a civic leader to the 'top job' comprises, in and of itself, an effective approach to urban leadership. As I explained in Chapter 5 leadership is dispersed and is multi-level. Malmö, Sweden provides an outstanding example of multi-level civic leadership and community empowerment. Innovation Story 8 draws attention not just to the way place-based leaders have transformed the city from an industrial wasteland into a path breaking eco-city, but also to the devolution of power within the city and to the high level of community activism at neighbourhood level.

Part 3
Experiences: Place-based leadership in action

CHAPTER 8

Leading the eco-city

The world is too much with us; late and soon,
Getting and spending, we lay waste our powers:
Little we see in Nature that is ours;
We have given our hearts away, a sordid boone!
William Wordsworth, 1807, *Poems in Two Volumes*

Introduction

In this chapter I present three Innovation Stories, drawn from different continents, to illustrate how civic leaders have taken bold steps to make their cities both more environmentally sustainable and fairer places to live in. The cities I have selected are: Curitiba, Brazil; Guangzhou, China; and Freiburg, Germany. The socio-political context for the exercise of place-based leadership in these three countries is very different. But, as we shall see, civic leaders in each city have pursued imaginative policies and practices that have integrated efforts to advance environmental objectives with a strong commitment to social equity.

These cities are not alone. Indeed, several Innovation Stories presented elsewhere in this volume, increase understanding of what it means to strive to create an inclusive eco-city. For example, Malmö, Copenhagen and Portland all provide fine examples of eco-city leadership. What does being an eco-city mean? This chapter offers a contribution towards an answer to this question. Fortunately other writers have covered this territory in much more detail. They explain how an eco-city is likely to be one that: supports an economy that works with the environment not against it; questions the primacy of economic interests over other considerations; is alert to the environmental impact of decisions relating to urban infrastructure (particularly transport, energy, water, waste and buildings in general); and is committed to the principles of sustainable planning and urban development (Beatley 2011; Jackson 2009; Hall 2013; Newton 2014).

The ultimate aspiration of many eco-cities is, then, for residents and businesses to eliminate carbon waste and to produce all needed energy through renewable resources. In this chapter I am using the phrase eco-city to refer to cities that have a demonstrable commitment to reducing carbon emissions alongside a political promise to reduce social inequality in society.

Why have a chapter on leading the eco-city in a book about the inclusive city? The answer to this question is set out in Chapter 1. There I suggested that any adequate definition of the inclusive city must embrace the way people interact with and value the natural environment. In public policy making awareness of the way decisions impact the natural environment should not be regarded as just 'another policy consideration'. Our relationship with nature is fundamental to the quality of life, and eco-thinking needs to be integral to public policy making for cities as elsewhere. The inclusive city I am advocating is, then, an all-encompassing concept embracing people and the environment in which they live. Inclusion is not usually envisioned in this way. In the past it has been seen simply as a socio-economic and/or a political concept. This is because, as explained in Chapter 1, there has tended to be an unhelpful divide in thought and action between those concerned with people and their life chances, and those concerned with the natural environment.

Wise civic leaders in a number of innovative cities rejected this compartmentalisation some years ago – and several of the Innovation Stories in this book, not just those in this chapter, illustrate this rather well. Over the years green activists and theorists have provided the intellectual underpinning for a move from anthropocentrism to eco-centrism (Eckersley 1992; Girardet 2008). In the 1960s and 1970s those who advocated green policies and practices were often caricatured as 'hug-a-tree' hippies who were out of touch with the mainstream. Most of the social policy and public management discourse ignored totally the environment and the ecological movement. Not any more.

Uniting social and ecological perspectives

Growing concerns about the existential threat that global warming poses to humanity has given eco-centric ideas a significant boost in public consciousness in many countries in recent years. Environmental activism, as well as a growing body of scientific evidence on the impact of climate change, has heightened political and public enthusiasm for inventing ways of living that tread much more lightly on the surface of the planet (Hopkins 2013). As Harriet Bulkeley (2013) explains, climate change is not simply happening *to* cities, giving rise to challenges that cities need to endure and/or overcome. Rather cities themselves are, in part, *producing* unwelcome changes in the climate.

For all these reasons a successful inclusive city is, as I explained in Chapter 1, a city in which civic leaders strive for just results while caring for the natural environment on which we all depend. In this chapter we discuss, albeit briefly, some of the key debates in what might be loosely described as eco-policy making for cities. The discussion in the early part of the chapter – on topics like urban and regional ecology, smart growth, urban resilience, and sustainable transport – is designed to set the scene for the Innovation Stories that follow.

While there is now a burgeoning literature on sustainable development, comparatively little has been written on the role of leaders and leadership in delivering sustainable policies and practices. For example, even highly respected books on the governance of sustainability do not even mention leadership (Adger and Jordan 2009). Planning theory is also pretty much silent on the topic – it is almost as if leadership is an intellectual no-go zone (Hambleton 2014). This is puzzling given that planning practitioners understand well enough the importance of leadership in delivering well-planned, sustainable cities.

There are some honourable exceptions to this neglect of leadership in the sustainable development literature. Sarah Parkin (2010), in her book on sustainability leadership, argues that an economy with low carbon use and high life satisfaction will require millions of exceptional leaders and, she sets out sound advice for practitioners and would-be leaders. Benjamin Redekop (2010) provides an intriguing edited volume suggesting that new theories of leadership, enlightened by modern biology and evolutionary theory, are needed. Judi Marshall and her colleagues provide a collection of essays that will be useful to those who are seeking to take on a role in pushing the sustainability agenda in organisations and communities (Marshall et al 2011). And Nicholas Stern (2010), now recognised as a world authority on climate change, concludes his book on how to save the planet by saying, 'Above all, we will need political leadership which is not only thoughtful and measured but also courageous and inspirational. That leadership must set out the compelling scientific and economic case for strong action' (Stern 2010, 209).

These various books drawing attention to the role of leadership in promoting sustainability are invaluable, but they are unusual in spotlighting leadership themes. I hope that this chapter can offer some additional insights on the importance of leadership, courageous and creative leadership, in taking on vested interests and promoting cities that are both more liveable and more just. Let's start by considering a classic example of successful environmental civic leadership.

You can't do that: mayoral leadership against the odds

In May 2000 Ken Livingstone, when he was elected Mayor of London, became the first directly elected political leader in UK history. In Chapter 5 I explained how the Labour Government, elected in 1997, in a bold and far-reaching move, provided the legislation to underpin the introduction of a new form of governance for the capital, one headed by a directly elected mayor. Livingstone, a very experienced left-leaning politician, had a reputation for daring initiatives and his approach to mayoral leadership in London reflected his willingness to push at the boundaries of what might be possible. In his autobiography, *You Can't Say That*, Livingstone provides his own account of a remarkable environmental initiative – the introduction of the London congestion charge (Livingstone 2011, 469–78). He notes that it was very challenging – even his own political advisers told him not to do it.

A congestion charge is a fee imposed on most motor vehicles operating within a designated zone within a city. Singapore deserves credit for being the first major city to introduce such a scheme in 1998, where the approach is known as electronic road pricing. But the London scheme, introduced by Livingstone is far larger, and his decision to take such a radical step has attracted interest from city leaders from across the world. The aims of the charge were to reduce traffic congestion, enhance the environmental quality of central London and raise funds to invest in major improvements to London's public transport system. The point I wish to emphasise here is that, in the period before the introduction of the charge, particularly during 2002, there was massive opposition to the idea. The *London Evening Standard*, the capital's newspaper, orchestrated a vitriolic campaign against Livingstone in general, and the congestion charge in particular.

Opposition also came from the Conservative Party, car users, petrol companies, motoring correspondents, theatre 'luvvies', various residents groups and numerous business interests, including Smithfield meat traders. As Tony Travers (2004, 191) noted, '... sections of the media became increasingly active in highlighting alleged unfairnesses, inconsistencies or, in some cases, potential evasion techniques'. As the pressures mounted Livingstone's political advisers concluded that it would be a foolish move to introduce the charge. They advised him that he would be finished politically if he went ahead because the media would portray him as: 'The Mayor who introduced a new tax'. They begged him to delay the idea until after he had won a second four-year term in 2004. To his lasting credit Livingstone ignored all of them.

Mayor Livingstone introduced the London congestion charge in February 2003. On the first day of operation, traffic in the congestion charge zone declined by 25%, a figure that shifted to around 15% to 20% less than pre-charge levels in subsequent weeks. Livingstone pumped the substantial income generated by the charge into public transport improvements. An independent evaluation of the policy concluded, '[It] is clear that the scheme has been a great success in its primary target of reducing traffic congestion within central London, and contributing to improving access by bus' (Richards 2006, 216)

Additional new buses were introduced and there were big improvements in bus reliability. The roads were made more attractive to cyclists, whose numbers increased significantly, and there was a 20% reduction in carbon emissions. Livingstone's central conclusion about the congestion charge was that: 'This was the only thing in my career that turned out better than I had hoped' (Livingstone 2011, 477). Within ten days Livingstone's opinion poll ratings were up 10%. The following year, in the May 2004 Greater London elections, Mayor Livingstone was rewarded for showing vision and courage in leadership. He was elected mayor for the period 2004–2008. Moreover, more people voted for him in 2004 than in his previous victory in 2000. He had imposed a new tax and become more popular than ever. This is because he used the funds generated to advance the public good, and voters appreciated the benefits.

This is an abbreviated outline of the story of the introduction of the London congestion charge. Other sources provide more detail and a good starting point for the interested reader is the book by Martin Richards (2006). We can note, however, that Boris Johnson, the incoming Conservative Mayor of London, did not discard the congestion charge. Indeed, no serious politicians are now advocating its abolition. It is clear that the main reason why London was able to make this major step towards a more sustainable city was the existence of powerful, place-based leadership in the capital. The introduction of the London congestion charge provides a classic example of civic leadership making a significant difference to the quality of life in a city.

Allow me a brief aside. A similar scheme for a congestion charge proposed for Greater Manchester was given the thumbs down in a public referendum in December 2008, despite the fact that a 'yes' vote would have brought a £3 billion package of transport funding to the city. The absence of strong, metropolitan leadership in Greater Manchester largely explains why the conurbation missed a terrific opportunity (Sherriff 2013). My point here is not to suggest that Manchester lacks talented civic leaders. I am, in fairness, probably biased in favour of Manchester as I was brought up in Stockport, which lies on the south side of the conurbation. Rather I am suggesting that, in line with the analysis I presented in Chapter 7, the institutional design of local government matters. The talented leaders in Greater Manchester were, unfortunately, saddled with a flawed model of metropolitan governance.

In simple terms we can note that the governance of Greater Manchester is fragmented, notwithstanding the recent creation of a Greater Manchester Combined Authority to improve joint working across the ten boroughs. No politician in Manchester had, or has for that matter, the legitimacy to offer the kind of bold civic leadership provided by Mayor Livingstone in London. It is reasonable to suggest, then, that, had Greater Manchester had a governance system like the one in London, with a conurbation-wide directly elected mayor committed to sustainable development, a congestion charge would have been introduced in 2008, and the city would today be a much greener, more liveable place than it currently is.

Environmentalism, climate change and civic leadership

In Chapter 1 I suggested that a concern for nature should be integral to urban policy-making, and Figure 1.1 highlights the relationships between the individual, society and nature. Until relatively recently the natural environment has not been seen as a top priority by many of those concerned with city leadership and urban management. Notwithstanding the efforts of green activists, city planners, landscape architects and professionals associated with public parks and open spaces, the natural environment has often been allocated a back seat behind topics like urban economic development, education, housing, transportation and social care. However, as various Innovation Stories in this book show, imaginative civic leaders recognise the role of nature in enhancing the enjoyment of living in the city. Innovation Story 1 on the High Line in New York City provides a good example of local community activists showing city hall leaders the way to go.

While it would be misleading to claim that awareness of environmental considerations now dominates city leadership across the world, it is pleasing to be able to record that urban ecology is now an expanding area for both urban practice and urban research (Douglas et al 2011). Following Bai and Schandl (2011) we can trace two main stages in the growing interest in urban ecology. First, scholars tended to focus on ecology *in* cities – a research domain that is concerned with the natural component of cities, meaning the flora and fauna within cities (Sukopp and Werner 1982). Here we find landscape designers, botanists and urban designers and, in more recent times, academics who study, for example, heat islands in cities, and the impact of green space on human health and wellbeing.

Second, there has been a growth of interest in the ecology *of* cities. This is a more fundamental approach that treats cities and city regions as distinctive ecological systems. It includes study of biogeochemical cycles and material and energy flows. Girardet (2008), in his study of urban development and climate change, provides a good example of this more holistic approach. Various urban scholars have contributed to our understanding of the interplay between socio-political and environmental considerations in the governance of cities and city regions (Beatley 2011; Boone and Modarres 2006; Bulkeley 2013; Flint and Raco 2012; Ravetz 2013).

Food policy should be mentioned in this context. It has emerged, in recent years, as an important topic for place-based leadership. In response to growing concern about 'food deserts' in parts of some cities, escalating obesity rates among children and the environmental degradation arising from big agricultural businesses, an increasing number of towns, cities and regions are creating Food Policy Councils (FPCs). These councils provide information and advice to support the development of community-based food systems (Raja et al 2008).

How does climate change fit into this discussion of urban and regional ecology? Are cities villains or visionaries when it comes to climate change? The answer is that cities can be both. Cities certainly cause a good deal of pollution and they are, to be sure, part of the problem. However, as William Meyer (2013) explains, the conventional wisdom, which claims that cities are bad for the environment, is misplaced. He shows how, largely unsung, cities offer environmental advantages arising, for example, from their compactness. The Innovation Stories in this chapter show how cities can play a leadership role when it comes to responding to the threat of climate change.

On the downside, evidence is accumulating that cities are making a major contribution to the growth of human induced (or anthropogenic) greenhouse gas (GHG) emissions. The UN Global Report on *Cities and Climate Change* shows that the proportion of GHG emissions resulting from cities is on the rise (UN-Habitat 2011). Recent reports from the Intergovernmental Panel on Climate Change (IPCC) reinforce the concerns presented in the UN-Habitat report. The IPCC was set up in 1988 to provide comprehensive scientific assessments about the risk of climate change caused by human activity and the options available for adaptation and mitigation. Drawing on the research efforts of thousands of scientists across the world the IPCC is the leading internationally accepted authority on climate change. The IPCC work is shared among three Working Groups, working on each of:

1. The physical science aspects of climate change
2. The assessment of the vulnerability of socio-economic and natural systems to climate change and options for adaptation, and
3. The options for mitigating climate change

All three Working Groups have reported recently (IPCC 2013; IPCC 2014a; and IPCC 2014b). At the time of writing a Synthesis Report is in preparation.

The three IPCC Working Group reports make for uncomfortable reading. Working Group 1 records that: 1) Warming of the atmosphere and ocean is unequivocal, 2) There is a clear human influence on climate change, and 3) It is extremely likely that human influence has been the dominant cause of observed warming since 1950 (IPCC 2013). Working Group 2 identifies a long list of vulnerable peoples, industries and ecosystems around the world that are exposed to significant danger (IPCC 2014a). Furthermore, Working Group 3 notes that greenhouse gas emissions grew more quickly between 2000 and 2010 than in each of the previous three decades, and urges a huge increase in green energy strategies (IPCC 2014b). The IPCC reports are almost certainly highly conservative. All IPCC publications have to be agreed by hundreds of scholars and reviewers, and this means that only the most robust statements survive the scrutiny process.

The findings of the 2013 report, which are consistent with the previous IPCC assessment published in 2007, record more evidence of temperature rises, melting glaciers and sea ice, rising sea levels and unsettling changes in weather patterns. George Monbiot (2013) claims that climate change and global warming are inadequate terms for what this IPCC report reveals: 'The story it tells is of climate breakdown'. Ban Ki-moon, the UN Secretary-General, has urged all countries to pay heed to the world's authority on climate change, and forge a new global deal to cut carbon emissions. In recent years national governments have, it has to be said, been slow to respond to these challenges, and a World Summit on Climate Change in Copenhagen in 2009 failed to agree binding carbon reduction targets. An enormous amount depends on the next World Summit on Climate Change to be held in Paris in December 2015.

In more positive vein we can note that cities can take, and are taking, significant action to mitigate and adapt to climate change. National governments may have faltered but cities are getting on with the job. For example, the UN-Habitat (2011) report identifies five main ways in which cities are mitigating climate change:

1. City planning to combat urban sprawl
2. Imaginative design and use of the built environment
3. Urban infrastructure initiatives focussing on energy efficiency
4. Transport planning and management
5. Carbon sequestration either through promoting natural carbon sinks (such as planting trees or protecting forests) or by technological means for carbon capture and storage.

Cities can also take steps to adapt the existing urban fabric to cope more effectively with climate change and new research is showing possible ways forward (Williams et al 2012). There are several international city networks committed to tackling climate change and promoting environmentally sustainable development, and they are doing excellent work.[1]

In Chapter 5 I discussed the nature of place-based leadership and the constraints on local agency. Various forces shape the political space available to local leaders – socio-cultural, economic, legal and environmental. In Figure 5.1 I show how place-based governance in any given locality is framed by these forces, and I explained how the environmental limits comprise the *only* side of the frame that is non-negotiable. The literature on environmental sustainability shows that we cannot continue to disregard the fact that the resources of the planet are finite (Berners-Lee and Clark 2013; Hopkins 2011; Jackson 2009). There are global limits in relation to fossil fuels, water, food, soil, forests and so on, and we disregard these limits at our peril. This is why the subtitle of this book is *Place-Based Innovation for a Bounded Planet*. The resources of the planet are not limitless.

Smart growth, urban resilience and sustainable transport

In Chapter 4 I discussed the important role that city development strategies can play in helping place-based leaders deliver progressive change. I explained how strong city planning focuses on coordinating and integrating the actions of different agencies and actors in a locality in order to achieve political objectives. City planning can shape the way the urban development market operates. It can orchestrate public and private investments in the urban infrastructure and, by shaping the physical development, can have a significant impact on living patterns, social inclusion and, of course, the overall sustainability of the built urban form. We will give further consideration to aspects of city planning and urban design in Chapter 9 when we consider efforts to create people-friendly cities.

Here I want to refer briefly to three inter-related concepts that are relevant, not just to the Innovation Stories on Curitiba, Guangzhou and Freiburg, but also to debates about how to plan and shape urban development. The three concepts are: smart growth, urban resilience and sustainable transport. Some may feel that these terms provide yet more evidence that debates about sustainable development are providing fertile soil for needless jargon. I will try to cut through the obfuscation.

Smart growth and urban design

Smart growth is a phrase used in the USA to describe an alternative to classic, low-density urban sprawl. It involves housing development that is, basically, dense enough to reduce the need for private car use. In some ways smart growth can be viewed as American architects, planners and landscape designers drawing inspiration from traditional European urbanism. For example, the Congress for the New Urbanism (CNU), set up in 1992, has actively campaigned for more sustainable development in US cities, and the banner often waved by champions of these ideas is smart growth.[2] It is important to state, however, that there is no agreed definition of smart growth.

As a general rule advocates of smart growth usually encourage increases in urban density, mixing of land uses, development close to public transport stations (transit-oriented development), a variety of housing types (including affordable housing), design of pedestrian and cycle routes separate from highways and protection of green space (Dittmar and Ohland 2004; Jenks and Jones 2010). Such developments are also sometimes described as sustainable communities or eco-neighbourhoods (Barton 2000; Condon 2010).

The UK Labour Government, led by Prime Minister Tony Blair recognised, in its early days, the importance of architecture and urban design in revitalising cities. In 1998 John Prescott, Deputy Prime Minister, set up an Urban Task Force '… to find out what has caused urban decline in England and to recommend practical solutions to turn our cities, towns and neighbourhoods into places where people actively want to live, work and play' (Urban Task Force 1999, 3).

An architect, Lord Rogers (formerly Richard Rogers) was appointed to lead the task force and its report, *Towards an Urban Renaissance*, remains a remarkable effort to integrate design thinking into city planning and urban management (Urban Task Force 1999). While the report does not use the phrase 'smart growth', as such, it comprises a comprehensive presentation of the benefits of compact urban development, high quality design and the idea of re-orienting transport public expenditure towards walking, cycling and public transport. Following the publication of the report a government body, the Commission for Architecture and the Built Environment (CABE), was set up to help raise the quality of urban design in the UK. For a short period CABE had a beneficial impact on urban design in the UK, and those involved deserve to be congratulated. But, as Rowan Moore explains, the hoped-for apparatus of strong leadership, skilled planners and democratic engagement never came to pass:

> [This] would have meant spending public money, and would also have implied a return to old Labour values, such as investing power and resources in local government, that were now vanquished. (Moore 2012, 235)

Moore is right to highlight the failure of the government to follow through on the recommendations of the Urban Task Force. But this does not, of course, undermine the value of the analysis presented in the report. Interestingly, in more recent times Sir Terry Farrell, another leading British architect, was asked by the UK Coalition Government to reenergise the debate about urban design in the UK, and his report, *Our Future in Place*, reaffirms many of the arguments presented by the Urban Task Force (Farrell 2014).

A central idea in all these efforts to design more sustainable ways of living is to move away from the predominant pattern of over reliance on car transport. Smart growth, which aims to provide for a healthy, community-oriented life style, is not to be confused with the similar-sounding notion of smart cities. The latter, as explained in more detail in Chapter 11, usually refers to cities that make extensive use of Information and Communication Technologies (ICT) to improve access to public services and to enhance the quality of life in the city. Smart growth and smart cities are not mutually exclusive concepts but it is perfectly possible to pursue one while ignoring the other.

Urban resilience

Urban resilience is a more complicated concept than smart growth. In everyday use the word resilience means springing back, or resuming an original shape after bending or stretching. The concept has been in use in the study of ecological systems for over forty years, although its meaning has evolved and is, even within ecological debates, contested. In more recent times efforts have been made to make connections between ecological and planning resilience research (Nelson et al 2006). For our purposes it is sufficient to note that the term resilience is often used to refer to the ability of an urban system to withstand, and recover, from shocks. This is, for example, the way the phrase is used in the annual conferences on *Resilient Cities* organised by ICLEI, the international organisation of local governments dedicated to sustainable development.[3]

The concept has enhanced understanding of urban vulnerability to disasters, like floods, storm surges or heat waves, and has been popularised by various writers (Lewis and Conaty 2012; Monaghan 2012; Newman et al 2009; Pearson et al 2014). Cathy Wilkinson (2012) explores the notion of socio-ecological resilience and suggests that planning theory should give more attention to ecological concerns. This is, in my view, a sound proposal. But I wish to suggest that scholars interested in resilience should be asking much more penetrating questions about the distributional consequences of being resilient. It is important to ask: Resilience for whom? Answering 'Resilient for everyone' is an unsatisfactory response because we know that steps taken in the name of the resilience agenda have distributional consequences.

For example, as I noted in Chapter 1, measures taken to make New Orleans more resilient to the risk of flooding have had an adverse impact on poor communities in the city (Goetz 2013). The environmental justice dimensions of fostering resilience seem to be getting displaced onto the margins of scientific discourse. Equally worrying, there is a risk that resilience will come to replace sustainability as the next spray-on term that vested interests may try to use to support the status quo of socio-political power relations in the modern city. In Chapter 1 I explained how various interested parties were able to redefine sustainable development to the point where, in some settings at least, it has become a virtually meaningless expression. Is urban resilience heading down the same path?

Perhaps we need to ask some more fundamental questions about the use of the word 'resilience' in the urban context. Has the academic fashion for studying resilience led to the concept being used in an inappropriate way? Do we always want urban systems to bounce back to how they were? Does the concept of resilience embody an inherently conservative political stance? This line of questioning implies that urban resilience may *not*, after all, be a desirable lodestar when it comes to creating the just city. Let's take an offensive example to give candour to the argument.

The apartheid system in South Africa was clearly a resilient socio-political system. The National Party, the ruling party in South Africa from 1948, was able to curtail the rights of the majority of black inhabitants for almost half a century. It was so resilient it was able to imprison articulate, political opponents, including Nelson Mandela, for decades. Dictatorships across the world are, right now, demonstrating that they can be resilient in the face of legitimate political pressures for change. The governmental systems dictators steer in these countries seem to manage, much of the time, to adapt creatively to perceived threats and shut them down. Resilience, then, describes a quality of a given system. It is not, in and of itself, a desirable objective for a social system. It describes a process – the ability to adapt to changing circumstances. Progressive politics requires the overthrow of oppressive power systems. Frankly speaking, we don't want these unjust systems to bounce back.

Some writers on urban resilience seem to recognise that we need to move *beyond* the notion of resilience and consider how to transform the systems that limit socio-environmental possibilities (Pelling 2011). But there is much confusion in the literature. For example, Satterthwaite and Dodman (2013) exhibit a tendency to collapse together resilience and transformation in their discussion of urban change. This approach fails to recognise that these words have *different* meanings. Transformation means making a thorough or dramatic change in form and/or character. It is *not* about bouncing back, it is about changing into something else. The Innovation Stories in this book suggest that progressive place-based leaders can take steps to change the way urban systems behave. The objectives of these civic leaders are, from beginning to end, political. The focus of attention is on who gains and who loses in the modern city, not some vague notion of urban resilience.

Sustainable transport

What about our third concept – sustainable transport? Wise city leaders recognise that affordable, swift and efficient public transport is essential to create an inclusive city and we have already touched on this topic in the discussion of smart growth and urban design. This realisation has important implications for urban planning. Too many cities are still being built in a way that perpetuates dependency on the private car for a high proportion of journeys. How has this situation come about? In the USA in the 1920s, as Girardet (2008, 134–6) explains, automobile industry interests were ruthless in expanding their market share, so much so that they orchestrated the closure of companies providing perfectly good, public transport.

Like their tramcar cousins in Europe, American streetcar companies were providing reasonably inexpensive public transport in the 1920s, but General Motors and Standard Oil saw them as a threat. The motoring, oil and tyre manufacturers bankrolled National City Lines to buy up streetcar companies and close them down. Streetcar tracks were ripped up from 85 US cities in a matter of a few years, and the 20th Century 'motor city' arrived. Robert Post (2010), who has examined the evolution of urban mass transit in the US, argues that marauders from the automotive world provide only part of the explanation. He suggests that: 'Many choices were involved in the triumph of "motorization", from minimising gasoline taxes to maximising investment in roads and highways' (Post 2010, 151). However, in a curious oversight, he fails to recognise that powerful vested private interests had a *direct* role in shaping these public policy decisions in America. In continental Europe, and this is a startling difference, the tramlines were expanded, not destroyed. This is partly because the car, oil and tyre companies were unable, despite their best efforts, to distort the urban transport policy agenda in Europe to the same extent.

It seems clear that, in the US, powerful private sector companies, driven by self-interested profit-seeking behaviour, were able to crush more sensible strategies. A consequence is that the US missed the opportunity to create sustainable transport systems on the European model. After World War II low density, car-dependent suburbs became symbols of urban progress – not just in the USA but also, it has to be said, in parts of Europe and other developed regions of the world. The passing of the 1956 US Federal-Aid Highway Act, which pumped billions of tax dollars into road construction, ensured that the USA became the world leader for urban sprawl. Today, and this is worrying, a good number of developing countries appear to be committed to spending truly vast sums of public money on building 21st Century versions of the motor city.

As Sir Colin Buchanan (1963) argued fifty years ago, any successful strategy for dealing with the expansion of traffic in towns needs to be based on the integration of land use planning, traffic and transportation planning. He noted that: '... in the long run the best way to keep a "ceiling" on private car traffic in busy areas is likely to be to provide good, cheap public transport, coupled with the public's understanding of the position' (Buchanan 1963, 240). In more recent times the Buchanan Report, as it came to be known in the UK context, was criticised for being too 'pro-car'. But Buchanan's recognition that trade-offs would have to be made between accessibility for vehicle users, the environment and financial costs was sound. The degree to which transport and land use planning has been integrated varies by country, and city. Peter Hall (2013, 39–55) provides an excellent overview of urban planning efforts, in Europe and elsewhere, designed to link people to places, and he highlights the importance of sustainable urban transport for the 21st Century mega-city region.

Katie Williams (2005) explores the relationships between travel patterns and the physical form of cities. She notes that almost all transport indicators worldwide suggest that cities and city regions are moving in an unsustainable direction. She considers whether compact urban form does, in fact, lead to the desired effects of reducing car-use and increasing walking, cycling and public transport patronage. To simplify her presentation, there is an ongoing debate here between those who favour different approaches to sustainable transport. For example, some advocate high density, compact cities while others argue that 'corridor developments' and multi-centred cities are more sustainable. Much depends on how you define sustainable transport and this debate is set to continue (Jenks and Jones 2010). From the point of view of delivering an inclusive city, it is clear, however, that efforts to enhance mobility for all residents of the city are essential, including the large numbers of people who do not have cars. The three Innovation Stories presented below all show, in differing ways, how place-based leaders have made their cities more inclusive by making a creative investment in public transport.

Radical public transport innovation in Curitiba

Located in southern Brazil, Curitiba has a track record of trying out bold new initiatives in relation to sustainable development and the management of urban growth. Clara Irazabal, in her comparison of urban governance in Curitiba and Portland, Oregon, notes that both these cities '... offer examples of urban planning processes that have aimed to holistically tackle major issues such as rapid population growth and its relationship to land use, transportation, and sustainability, with a relatively high degree of efficiency' (Irazabal 2005, 2). We return to examine aspects of sustainable development in Portland in Innovation Story 16 in Chapter 11. Here we focus on the remarkable achievements of civic leaders in Curitiba.

Jaime Lerner, former Mayor of Curitiba, led a team that prepared an imaginative master plan for the city in 1966. The plan rejected the, then prevalent, 'predict and provide' approach to analysing car ownership trends and road planning. It set out to integrate land use and transport planning, and prioritised the creation of a mass transportation system. Lerner, who later became a three-time mayor of the city, was the first to admit that Curitiba was poor, that it had slums and that it faced the same problems as other Brazilian cities. It did not, in truth, have the resources to build major motorways and rail transit systems.

Lerner made a virtue of these fiscal constraints and stressed that the new plan should be seen as an effort to foster citizenship and co-responsibility for the future. In a startling move Lerner's team proposed the creation of the first Bus Rapid Transit (BRT) system in the world. As described in Innovation Story 9 Curitiba introduced a highly integrated bus system to serve the entire city in 1974. The BRT concept involves the introduction of bus-ways – that is, road lanes that can only be used by express buses. Some describe a BRT as a 'surface subway' and that is a handy phrase – it points to the key ingredients of pre-payment of fares at the station, level access and large buses with multiple doors.

This approach to mass transit involves a radical redistribution of the use of existing road space and is far cheaper than alternative public transport solutions. As Herbert Girardet explains:

> Curitiba created a hierarchy of bus services, from those only serving local neighbourhoods to fast, articulated buses that run across the city on dedicated routes. By replacing conventional bus stops with so-called loading tubes, bus travel was greatly speeded up: as people enter the tubes they pay the resident conductor and when the bus arrives, everyone can get on and off instantly. (Girardet 2008, 143)

This radical innovation attracted international interest and many cities have sought to learn from the Curitiba experience. Over the years the city has acquired a reputation for being a well-planned city (Campbell 2012, 124–40). Political leaders and urban professionals have pushed forward green thinking and practices, and have also continued to make significant improvements to the innovative bus system. Civic leaders in Curitiba have, then, succeeded in integrating social and ecological perspectives. It is worth emphasising that the Curitiba strategy rejected expensive, technologically sophisticated solutions. The city has shown how labour-intensive solutions can substitute for capital-intensive approaches – and this strategy has helped to reduce unemployment. It is true, however, that Curitiba has now decided to develop a metro system to work in an integrated way with the BRT. And it is also the case that automobile manufacturing is a significant industry in the metropolis. Car ownership in 2010 was, at 680 vehicles per 1,000 inhabitants, relatively high for Brazil.

INNOVATION STORY 9

Creating a sustainable public transport system in Curitiba

Aims

The Brazilian city of Curitiba has a well-established reputation as an environmental and socially sustainable city.[1] What began in 1974 as the first Bus Rapid Transit (BRT) system in the world has evolved into an Integrated Transportation Network (*Rede Integrada de Transporte* or RIT).

The aim of the RIT is to provide affordable and environmentally sustainable public transport. It is a system that delivers high capacity, frequent, flexible, extensive and speedy public transport. The city sought to reduce reliance on car transportation by providing a high quality system of colour coded transport lines – regional, express, inter-neighbourhood, direct, feeder, downtown, circular, inter-hospital, school and tourist lines – to crisscross and circumnavigate the city. The RIT shares many features with rail rapid transit – including pre-paid tickets, speedy passenger loading and unloading secured through same-level access from the bus stations (the iconic tube shelters), plus the ability to transport very large numbers of passengers. But, a key point, the RIT is far cheaper than conventional rail transit, or subway, systems.

A flat fare system enables passengers to transfer across most bus routes for a single payment. A consequence of the exercise of bold civic leadership is that passengers spend considerably less of their income on travel costs than in other cities in Brazil.[2] Curitiba has developed a sophisticated bus system that benefits the population at large and it is not surprising that it has been emulated by other cities.

Innovation Story outline

Faced with significant population growth in the 1950's and 1960's, leading to rapid urbanisation and infrastructure pressures, municipal leaders instigated a national competition to revise Curitiba's master plan.[3] The 1966 plan, very innovative for its time, set out to integrate land use and transport planning. This approach contrasted with the prevalent 'car-led' approach to urban development of the 1960s, and prioritised the creation of a mass public transport system. Since its adoption, this Curitiba Master Plan (known as the Wilheim Plan) has played a critical role in shaping the city's development, and it was not revised until 1999.

Whilst a firm from Sao Paulo won the bid to prepare the plan, a significant feature of the process was the ongoing involvement of a group of Curitiban planners and urban development experts. This local group formed the Institute of Urban Research and Planning of Curitiba (IPPUC), an influential semi-autonomous planning implementation agency. This institute became a training ground for a number of the city's mayors, including Curitiba's internationally known, Jaime Lerner (a three-time mayor of the city) and Cassio Taniguchi (a two-time mayor).[4] The IPPUC enjoyed the support of the military dictatorship (1964–1985) and the institute continues to play an important role in urban planning in Curitiba.

Architect Jaime Lerner deserves credit, along with a group of planners and engineers, for developing Curitiba's BRT in the early 1970s. In his first period as mayor, he worked with interests across the municipal government and with the two organisations set up at the time of the development of the Curitiban Master Plan, the IPPUC and the URBS (Urban Development Agency of Curitiba), to develop the radical bus transportation proposals. Bearing in mind that Brazil was still a military dictatorship at this point, we can record that this was a largely technocratic process, rather than an exercise in participatory planning. Lerner's shift in role from architect/planner to politician, coupled with the mixing of staff between the municipal government, the IPPUC and the URBS, produced an elite actor group that had both a deep understanding of the city and considerable power and influence.

Keen to implement the Master Plan but with limited financial resources, Lerner and his associates pushed ahead with the BRT, rather than a planned subway system, on the grounds that it could be operational in a relatively short space of time, and that it was economically attractive because it made good use of the existing infrastructure. Confident of the technical capacity of the team of architects, planners and engineers around him, and with sufficient political stability and support, Mayor Lerner was comfortable progressing proposals without knowing all the answers ahead of time. For him getting things done, and learning from experience, was more highly valued than optimisation. In a presentation Jaime Lerner gave in Bristol in 2014 he put it this way:

> We don't have to have all the answers. Starting is important. I read the following on a sign in a public park in Mexico: "Better the grace of imperfection than perfection without grace". This is good advice. It is essential to try things out and this is why demonstration projects are so important[5]

Attention to implementation, a deep understanding of the city and its people by planners and politicians, a strong sense of mission and technical continuity, and a compatibility with the interests of the business elite of the city account for the approach pursued in Curitiba to meet transport and land use needs.

A commitment to cost effective innovation is a strong feature of Curitiba's BRT. Some of the striking features include: pre-payment boarding, a single fare, the introduction of articulated buses with a capacity of 250 passengers on express lines, the incorporation of a fleet of hybrid diesel and electric buses and, most recently, some 100% biofuel-powered buses running along Curitiba's sixth and newest bus transport corridor, the Linha Verde (Green Line). By 2016 the city's busiest BRT line is to be replaced by a subway – the Blue Line. This will enable increased passenger numbers and will extend transport links into the metropolitan area.[6]

It should be noted that in the 1960s and 1970s there was little tradition of community involvement in decision-making in Brazil. Thus, the planning and early implementation of the bus system progressed with little in the way of public consultation and participation. In the 1980s citizens protested about the cost of bus fares, an action that contributed to Lerner losing the 1983 mayoral election. Since the establishment of democracy in 1985 citizen engagement in public policy making has strengthened. However, the dominance of the mayor and the municipality remain strong. Recent protests in Curitiba and other Brazilian cities concerning an array of social and economic concerns, including affordable public transport, may herald a new phase of citizen engagement.

Leadership lessons

- Civic leaders in Curitiba rejected conventional wisdom and the idea of 'car-led' urban planning and development. Successive political and managerial leaders have pursued people-friendly rather than car-friendly approaches to urban decision-making
- Whilst having a clear vision, Mayor Lerner was comfortable embarking on the BRT initiative without having a comprehensive blueprint for its development. Confident leaders can try out ideas and learn from experience
- Professional planners, architects and engineers can contribute valuable insights and practical proposals for urban change. The professionals involved in designing the public

transport system used imagination and deployed 'green thinking' when eco-friendly approaches to urban development were in their infancy

- Getting a visionary plan approved can shape the trajectory of urban development in a city for decades. Overall direction can be maintained even if setbacks are encountered along the way
- The urban strategy for Curitiba has enjoyed the support of a wide range of interests in the city. Successive mayors have been successful in keeping various business leaders on board, as well as delivering significant improvements for all citizens in the city.

Sources

Campbell, T, 2012, *Beyond smart cities: How cities network, learn and innovate*, London: Earthscan, pp 124–140

Goodman, J, Laube, M, Schwenk, J, 2005, Curitiba's bus system is model for rapid transit, *Race, Poverty and the Environment* 12, 1, 75–6

Irazabal, C, 2005, *City making and urban governance in the Americas*, Aldershot: Ashgate Publishing

Moore, S, 2007, *Alternative routes to the sustainable city: Austin, Curitiba and Frankfurt*, Lanham: Lexington Books

Schwartz, H, 2004, *Urban renewal, municipal revitalization: The case of Curitiba, Brazil*, Alexandria: Higher Education Publications

Useful websites

http://www.curitiba.pr.gov.br/idioma/ingles: Curitiba municipal government website

http://www.ippuc.org.br/default.php?idioma=5: Curitiba's urban planning

http://urbs.curitiba.pr.gov.br/: Curitiba's transportation system

http://curitibainenglish.com.br/category/government/urban-mobility/: Curitiban English language website with a transport section

Endnotes

[1] Curitiba, capital of the State of Parana, is Brazil's seventh largest city with a population of 1.75 million (2010). Irazabal (2005) provides a useful overall analysis of the politics of urban and regional development in Curitiba focussing on planning and urban design practices in the city. See also Campbell (2012, 124–140).

[2] Reportedly they spend about 10 per cent of income on transport. See Goodman et al (2005).

[3] It is important to note that Brazil was a dictatorship until 1985.

[4] Prior to his first appointment as mayor, Jaime Lerner had been president of the IPPUC 1969–1970. He was appointed as mayor by the military for 1971–1974 and again for 1979–83. He was directly elected as mayor for 1989–1992 and, later, was elected as Governor of the State of Paraná (1995–1998, 1999–2000).

[5] Presentation on the *Future of Cities* at the Bristol Festival of Ideas, Watershed, Bristol. 24 May 2014.

[6] Curitiba in English – http://curitibainenglish.com.br/government/urban-mobility/curitibas-park-ways/

Pioneering Bus Rapid Transit in Asia

As discussed in Chapter 2 rates of urbanisation vary dramatically across the world. In some countries, and China provides a remarkable example, cities are expanding, and becoming more dense, at an astonishing rate. Here we will take a look at Guangzhou in southern China, a city that has grown very rapidly in the last thirty years to become a world megacity. It is difficult to be precise about population figures for the city, partly because there have been administrative reorganisations that have added territories to the original six city districts, and also because there is a high number of migrants, who stay and work in the city for over half a year but are not counted as permanent residents.

UN figures show that by 2000 the registered population was already 7.3 million. The current registered population of Guangzhou is around 12.7 million, a figure that is set to rise to 15.5 million by 2025. However, if we add in the migrant residents it is likely that Guangzhou already contains over 15 million people. Guangzhou is, then, one of the top 20 megacities in the world, and Figure 2.3 and Table 2.1 in Chapter 2 show how the size of the urban population is likely to compare with other megacities in 2025.

Rapid, spiralling growth in the urban population puts huge strains on any city, and Guangzhou is no exception. Jiang Xu and Anthony Yeh (2003) provide a useful analysis of the growth of the city, and document the many planning and infrastructure initiatives the city government has undertaken. Here I want to draw attention to the introduction of the Guangzhou Bus Rapid Transit (BRT) system in 2010. This is not the only investment in public transport that the city is making; the government is, for example, investing heavily in the construction of conventional metro lines. However, the BRT is of particular interest to other cities because it is an imaginative scheme that breaks new ground in urban transportation policy and practice. As mentioned earlier, a BRT involves dedicating lanes in a road system for bus use only. The Guangzhou BRT links astonishingly fast bus transport with the metro system, and it includes a popular bike sharing system.

A key measure of a BRT is the peak directional passenger flow – that is, the number of passengers per hour per direction. On this indicator the Guangzhou BRT, with a figure of more than 25,000, is the world's second highest capacity BRT after TransMilenio in Bogota. It is also the first high capacity BRT system in the world based on a 'direct service' operational mode in which BRT buses can enter and leave the BRT corridor without passengers needing to transfer vehicles. This operational mode results in a daily ridership of 850,000 average weekday passengers in the system, and the high capacity station design accommodates flows of nearly 30,000 passengers per hour in a single direction, which exceeds most metro systems worldwide.

Innovation Story 10 provides more details and highlights the way civic leaders were resilient in the face of opposition to the scheme. Earlier in this chapter I noted how Ken Livingstone, the first Mayor of London, had to overcome massive opposition to his plan to introduce a congestion charge in the city. In a similar way civic leaders in Guangzhou had to withstand considerable opposition from some influential official, academic, media and metro-aligned interests to the BRT scheme. The leadership listened to the concerns that were being expressed, but ultimately persevered with the proposals based on strong technical grounds rather than making compromises which could have weakened system performance. The outcome was an award-winning scheme.

INNOVATION STORY 10

Transforming public transport in Guangzhou

Aims

Guangzhou, with a registered population of around 12.7 million, is southern China's largest city. Known historically as Canton, it is the capital of Guangdong province. In the last thirty years, or so, the city has seen very rapid urban growth. The result is that Guangzhou is now one of the largest megacities in the world. Despite efforts to plan for and shape this urban expansion the city has experienced very severe traffic congestion. Civic leaders have taken on the challenge of improving public transportation in the city, and the government is investing significant sums in extending the metro rapid rail system.

This Innovation Story puts the spotlight on the Guangzhou Bus Rapid Transit (BRT) system introduced into the city in 2010. City leaders took a bold step when they introduced this, the first high capacity BRT system in Asia, with more than triple the one-directional passenger flows of any other BRT system in Asia, and second only to Bogota's TransMilenio system worldwide.

The aims were to allocate available road space more efficiently, provide well-designed, affordable public transport, cut journey times for travellers and reduce environmental pollution. As part of the strategy for achieving these aims the designers of the BRT set out to link the new bus services to the metro system, and to provide a high quality bike sharing programme as an integral part of the BRT. The Guangzhou BRT has had a major impact on public transport thinking and practice in Asia. This is partly because it is the first ever, high capacity 'direct service' BRT system, meaning a system in which BRT buses can enter and leave the BRT corridor so that many passengers do not need to transfer vehicles.

Innovation Story outline

Guangzhou is one of the oldest cities in southern China.[1] A thriving commercial port, the city already had a population of over one million by 1840. The communist takeover of Guangzhou in 1949 led to a fundamental shift in strategy for the city. The country as a whole retreated from engagement with the western world, although not developing countries. As a result the development of Guangzhou in the period from 1949 to 1978 was very slow – the southern gateway of China withered in the closed economy. The introduction of national economic reforms and 'open door' policies in 1978 transformed the prospects for the city. In a short space of time Guangzhou became a boom city.

Rapid economic development was accompanied by very fast population growth. The introduction of a land market in 1987 accelerated the pace of change. It triggered a spectacular redevelopment of the central area of the city as well as expansion into new areas. Guangzhou grew to become the commercial and business centre of the region. But the urban growth and redevelopment of the city led to horrendous traffic congestion, and residents were unimpressed with the city's development. A 1997 opinion poll suggested that 73% of residents were dissatisfied with Guangzhou's built environment.

In response to these problems the Guangzhou Government redefined its strategic objectives giving more emphasis to prosperity, efficiency and the idea of becoming a liveable, ecological city. This strategy has many elements. Here we focus on one specific initiative – the introduction of the largest Bus Rapid Transit (BRT) system in Asia, one that set high standards for design quality, customer service and capacity.

Zhang Guangning, mayor of Guangzhou from 2003 to 2010, deserves credit for recognising that radical action was needed to improve mass transportation in the city. City leaders were aware of the positive achievements of the BRT system in Curitiba (see Innovation Story 9) and, in late 2004, Zhang Guangning and government officials visited Bogota and Sao Paulo to see Latin America BRT Schemes for themselves.[2] The civic leaders were very impressed with what they saw and decided to develop proposals for a Guangzhou BRT system. The initial proposal, developed in 2005/06 by Institute for Transportation and Development (ITDP) and the Guangzhou Municipal Engineering Design and Research Institute (GMEDRI), under the auspices of the Construction Commission of Guangzhou, was for a 22.5 kilometre (14-mile) BRT 'corridor' leading from the centre of the city out to the east along Zhongshan Avenue. The idea was to link the new bus transportation directly to the metro system, provide well-designed bike parking at each BRT station, and make a major improvement in the speed and efficiency of passenger movements in the corridor.

In early 2007 the Guangzhou Urban Planning Bureau, who were in general staunchly opposed to the project during the design and planning stages, published information about the BRT proposals on its website, and in April that year the plan was approved by a national team of experts. The government started construction in November 2008 but, because this inevitably made the existing terrible traffic congestion much worse, there was a very high level of public dissatisfaction. This resistance was stoked by 'expert' academic opinion, and media coverage, proclaiming that the system would not function well, citing a lack of precedent worldwide for any 'direct service' BRT system on this scale. Earlier, in 2007/08, the proposal had teetered and came close to being abandoned. Mayor Zhang Guangning and city officials took great care to listen to the public, especially the representatives of the People's Congress.

One of the design features that met considerable resistance in the media was the proposal to ban left turns at many road intersections. It was argued that this would worsen traffic. In fact the opposite was true, and after implementation the intersections functioned much more smoothly. There was, of course, major disruption to traffic during the period of construction, and public complaints continued. But the BRT line, with high quality plazas, was built fairly swiftly and it opened in February 2010. Once the BRT started running the public response was very positive, largely because journey times in the corridor were slashed.

The Guangzhou BRT has, in fact, transformed Zhongshan Avenue from a nightmarish traffic jam into a remarkable public transportation route. The system carries an average of 850,000 passengers per day. This is a formidable number. At peak times the BRT carries more than 25,000 passengers per hour in a single direction, which is higher than most metro and all light rail lines worldwide.

Moreover, the scheme has the world's highest number of passenger boarding at BRT stations, the highest bus frequency, and some of the longest BRT stations (240 metres long in the city centre). In addition, the BRT has been praised for integrating a bike sharing system into the scheme. Opened in June 2010, and with bike stations located along the BRT corridor and in nearby commercial and residential areas, the system has 113 stations with 5,000 bikes. About 20,000 people use the bike share system every day, and surveys by ITDP revealed that more than two-thirds of these trips were by a motorised mode in the period before the BRT was created. The Guangzhou BRT has won several national and international awards relating to sustainable transport. There are serious plans to extend the BRT with several new lines.

Leadership lessons

- International city-to-city exchange can prompt fresh thinking and assist city leaders in developing novel solutions to pressing public policy challenges. In this case civic leaders and officials in Guangzhou took the time and trouble to visit Brazil and Colombia, and learn lessons from Sao Paulo and Bogota.
- Visits to other cities are arguably the single most important way that urban transport innovations have spread worldwide. Since it was opened in 2010 the Guangzhou BRT has been visited by hundreds of visiting delegations each year.
- City leaders faced opposition to the BRT proposals from various groups including some academics, the media, various 'experts', and some government bureaus. Instead of abandoning the approach they listened to the views being expressed, but persevered with design changes that had a strong technical basis. Public participation in decision-making improved the outcomes in many ways, for example through adjustments to station locations and access, and in the positioning of bike sharing stations.
- The city leaders showed resilience when the scheme ran into implementation difficulties. They kept the overall vision in focus and this enabled the scheme to be brought to fruition.

- Professional planners, engineers and architects developed creative urban design solutions, for example, in relation to the design of bus routes, bus stations and bike stations. Good use was made of external expertise.

Sources

Xu, J, Yeh, AGO, 2003, City profile, *Cities* 20, 5, 361–374

Xu, J, Yeh, AGO, 2005, City repositioning and competitiveness building in regional development: New development strategies in Guangzhou, China, *International Journal of Urban and Regional Research* 29, 2, 283–308

Useful websites

http://english.gz.gov.cn

http://www.lifeofguangzhou.com

The Institute for Transportation and Development Policy (ITDP) provides documents and films of sustainable transport, including Guangzhou: http://itdp.org

Streetfilms, founded in 2006, produces short films showing how innovative transportation design and policy can benefit cities, including film of Guangzhou: http://streetfilms.org

Endnotes

[1] The discussion here draws directly on Xu and Yeh (2003)

[2] The Institute for Transportation and Development Policy (ITDP) played an important role in facilitating this international learning and assisted the Guangzhou Government with the development of BRT proposals suited to Guangzhou. Founded in 1985 the ITDP promotes sustainable and socially equitable transportation worldwide.

Going green: the radical approach to local leadership in Freiburg

Imagine a city with a population of 220,000 where car ownership is going down, and the citizens are proud of it. From having no bike paths in 1970 the City of Freiburg now has a network of over 300 miles of bike lanes. The railway station has its own bike station with 1,000 supervised spaces, together with repair and bike hire services, a cycle shop, a café and a travel agency. Some neighbourhoods have been designed to achieve zero-energy or 'energy plus' development. Yes, that's right, here you will find solar powered houses contributing to the electricity supply – not taking from it.

Freiburg, Germany's southernmost city, can now claim to be a world leader when it comes to responding to climate change. Along with other eco-cities in, for example, Denmark and Sweden, it has set and achieved remarkable environmental standards. Urban designers in the UK have been so impressed with the achievements of the city that they published *The Freiburg Charter for Sustainable Urbanism* in an effort to identify guiding principles for good planning and design from the city (Academy of Urbanism 2012). Visitors from across the world flock to the city to learn about the many green innovations the city is now famous for – in public transport, solar energy, green jobs, urban design and the creation of communal forests and green spaces.

Many head for the Vauban district, on the south side of the city. Here they find a newly created, family-friendly neighbourhood full of green spaces and attractively designed homes. The energy to power this neighbourhood is 95% from renewable resources. Joan Fitzgerald, an American sustainable development expert, was astonished by what she found when she visited the area, saying:

> Vauban goes beyond anything we are thinking of in the United States under the banners of smart growth, transit-oriented development, or new urbanism (Fitzgerald 2010, 2).

By bringing together politicians, urban planners and residents in a highly constructive process of public participation the neighbourhood has raised the bar for modern, eco-friendly urban development. Many articles have now been published on Freiburg's high quality approach to city planning and urban design. Innovation Story 11 goes beyond these descriptive accounts to explain how this beautiful city has been created. It shows how leadership, inspiring place-based leadership by politicians, professionals and community activists, is the key factor explaining the Freiburg success story.

INNOVATION STORY 11

Going green: the Freiburg approach to local leadership

Aims

Freiburg, Germany, has established itself as a world leader in relation to sustainable development. The city, which has a population of 220,000, has been successful in promoting a culture that combines a very strong commitment to green values and respect for nature, with a buoyant economy built around, amongst other things, renewable energy. For example, the largest solar research institute in Europe – the Fraunhofer Institute for Solar Energy Systems (ISE) – is based here and solar technology has created hundreds of jobs in recent years. Freiburg is now one of the greenest cities in Germany. It has a high quality public transport system and it is very easy to move around the city either by tram or bicycle or on foot.

The Green City Office of the municipality and its official partners organise 'Solar Tours' to enable visitors to learn from the practical experience of some of the many solar projects that are now up and running in the city. Environmental policy, solar engineering, sustainability and climate protection are key features of public policy. The directly elected mayor of the city is a member of the Green Party. Mayor Dr Dieter Salomon, and the Freiburg City Council, are deeply committed to a green agenda for the city. The aim of this Innovation Story is to outline the main features of the Freiburg approach to sustainable urbanism.

Innovation Story outline

The origins of the community activism that underpins current innovations in Freiburg can be traced to the late 1970s. A successful, local and regional campaign against a proposal to locate a nuclear power station in nearby Wyhl provided the original impetus. Those involved recall that the campaign was both creative and inclusive – it united farmers and conservative businessmen, students and activists, old and young – in a new kind of political movement, a 'green' movement. A colourful coalition of anti-nuclear activists was born and, from small beginnings, success spurred further success. As early as 1986, the year of the Chernobyl disaster, the City Council declared the city a nuclear power free zone.

In 1992 Freiburg was chosen as Germany's 'Environmental Capital' for its pioneering achievements, such as the installation of an early-warning system for smog and ozone pollution, pesticide bans, recycling measures and its high quality public transport. The Green Party has strong roots here. In 2002 Freiburg became the first sizable city in Germany to elect a member of the Green Party as mayor. The population at large has a strong commitment to environmentalism, one that has stood the test of time. Many young people are now choosing to move to Freiburg not just because it has a well-respected university, but also because of the strong, green values it stands for. Moreover, the city has attracted a growing number of older people.

Freiburg is located within the state of Baden-Wuerttemberg and the local authority of Freiburg has two political institutions:

- **The City Council (Gemeinderat).** This has 48 members who are elected for a term of five years. They are elected 'at large' – they do not represent districts or wards within the city – and they are expected to serve the whole city. The City Council, which meets around twenty times each year, is the main policy-making body of the city – covering planning, the budget, legislation on how to carry out tasks on behalf of the federal and state levels of government and tasks carried out voluntarily by the city, as well as taxes and fees.
- **The mayor.** The mayor, who is elected for a fixed term of eight years, chairs the City Council and is the 49th member (and can vote). The mayor is also the most senior representative of the city and is the Chief Executive Officer of the city administration. In cities like Freiburg one or more deputy mayors support the mayor. There are four in Freiburg and they cover: budget and public housing; environmental politics, schools and youth; social and cultural affairs; and planning and development.

Local authorities in Germany are relatively strong. They have a constitutional right to local self-government. In addition, they have the authority 'to deal with all local matters affecting the municipality'. German local governments have, then, a general competence that is not restricted by higher levels of government. Furthermore, they have the competence to levy their own taxes to finance activities as they see fit.

This dispersal of power gives place-based leaders the freedom to act in radical ways. The Vauban district, an area of about 40 hectares, on the south side of the city, provides but one example of the way leaders have taken advantage of the political space available to them. It contains 5,200 people and around 600 jobs. The land was divided into relatively small plots, and preferences were given to private builders, households, social housing providers and co-operatives. Major house builders were banned. The outcome is a child-friendly, green suburb with an abundance of small-scale creativity. Sensitive, people-friendly design is central and building standards are demanding. Highlights of the neighbourhood include:

- a good tram service available in the development from an early stage giving frequent, fast and reliable service to the city centre and the city as a whole;
- a first class bike network encouraging cycling for longer and shorter trips;
- safe environments outside the homes, with children free to roam;
- extensive green spaces for recreation and social interaction;
- no parking in the car-restricted residential streets, except for unloading and/or dropping off frail or elderly people;
- multi-storey car parking in two garages on the fringes of the neighbourhood, providing space for cars for those that want them – but at a price;
- creative design of streetscapes, public spaces and community facilities.

In Freiburg, leaders from different realms of civic leadership have played a part in embedding radical innovation into the culture of local governance. First, the role of politicians has been critical in promoting and implementing green policies. As in cities across the world, the elected leaders set the direction and tone of local policy. A Social-Democrat mayor, Dr Rolf Böhme, was elected in 1982, and he encouraged many of the innovations that now make Freiburg famous. Mayor Dieter Salomon, who was elected in 2002, is strongly committed to the principle of sustainable development, and this principle guides his whole approach to the political leadership of the city.

Professional and managerial leaders have also played a vital role. For example, Wulf Daseking, who was Director of Planning and Building in Freiburg for an extended period before retiring in 2012, has provided imaginative, professional leadership to the planning and design work of the city. His efforts have been recognised internationally. For example, in November 2010 the British Academy of Urbanism gave the award of 'European City of the Year 2010' to Freiburg, and published *The Freiburg Charter for Sustainable Urbanism* to promote good planning and urban design.

Daseking believes professionals should 'stay put' in a given place for a reasonable length of time because this can enable professionals to have more impact. He says:

> It takes years to bring ideas to fruition. You must follow ideas through to the stage of implementation. We have too many young people who just run after a

career – whatever that is – and change jobs like changing shirts. No, a planner must work to make changes on the ground. This can be difficult as planning time horizons are long – and can be in conflict with political time horizons that tend to be short. Professionals have an important role in civic leadership – alongside other leaders – partly because they are able to take the longer view.[1]

Finally, community leaders operating at the grassroots are critical in the governance of Freiburg. Without the drive and energy of community-based activists it is difficult to see how significant change could have been brought about.

Leadership lessons

- The Freiburg story illustrates the value of having strong, independent local government. Local authorities in Germany enjoy constitutional protection. Local leaders, unconstrained by centrally imposed performance indicators, have developed a forward looking strategy and delivered on it.
- The community activism in the neighbourhoods within Freiburg is the key driving force behind the success of the city in becoming a world leader in relation to environmental awareness and action. The commitment to green values and collective purpose is highly developed, and this external grassroots pressure ensures year-on-year improvements in environmental performance.
- The officers and professionals appointed by the city to push at the boundaries of good practice have played a crucial role. Those involved in city planning, transport planning and urban design deserve to be recognised for their high quality contribution alongside the other professionals working for the City Council.
- Successive elected mayors and elected councillors have promoted ambitious thinking in the city, and their consistent commitment to green values coupled with an enthusiasm for trying out new approaches has set the tone for adventurous urban innovation.

Sources

Academy of Urbanism and Stadt Freiburg, 2012, *The Freiburg Charter for Sustainable Urbanism*, 2nd edition, London: Academy of Urbanism

Hall, P, 2013, *Good Cities, Better Lives. How Europe discovered the lost art of urbanism*, Abingdon: Routledge, 248–273

Hambleton, R, 2011, Place-based leadership in a global era, *Commonwealth Journal of Local Governance* Issue 8/9, May–November

For more information on Freiburg's approach: www.freiburg.de/greencity

Endnotes

[1] Personal interview, 2 March 2011

Conclusions

In this chapter I have suggested that effective approaches to creating an inclusive city unite social and ecological perspectives. In Chapter 1 I explained how there has, for the best part of a century, been an unhelpful divide in thought and action between those concerned with the 'city' and those concerned with 'nature'. This division has held back effective approaches to city leadership and urban management in many countries for decades. Sadly, there remains a divide in urban and environmental scholarship between those who study the socio-political dynamics of urban governance, and those who focus on analysis of the city and city region as an ecological system. Fortunately, imaginative city leaders do not allow their thinking to be constrained by disciplinary blinkers. Rather, as this chapter has shown, city leaders in London, Curitiba, Guangzhou and Freiburg, have taken action not just to lessen the carbon footprint of their city, but also to address social inequality.

In concluding this chapter I would like to highlight two important themes that have emerged. First, it is clear that place-based leadership can make a difference to the quality of life in a city. More than that, the evidence presented suggests that wise urban leadership can do much more than promote eco-friendly policies and practices. The civic leaders discussed in this chapter have a political commitment to social and environmental justice. They have taken political action to redistribute resources away from some interests and towards others – for example, away from the wishes of the car/petrol/road building industry and towards public transport. We have seen how senior leaders in a city can set the tone for public policy and urban management. And we have seen how this can tilt policy and practice in favour of progressive objectives and against market-driven forms of urban development.

Leaders occupying senior positions in urban governance, such as directly elected mayors, other senior politicians and their appointed chief officers, cannot solve current socio-environmental problems on their own. However, what they can do is set out a clear vision for their city, take a moral stance about equity and the environment, and spur other actors to advance the cause of creating an inclusive city. It is difficult to argue that the city leaders discussed in this chapter have failed to make a significant impact. Notwithstanding the pressures of place-less power that we discussed in Chapter 4 they have mapped out distinct, politically driven strategies for their cities and delivered on them.

The socio-political dynamics of urban governance varies internationally and the local political space available to place-based leaders in any given country evolves over time. However, even allowing for huge socio-cultural differences, we have seen how city leaders in four different cities in four very different countries – UK, Brazil, China and Germany – have exercised bold civic leadership. In particular, they have not backed down when multi-national companies and vested interests attempted to derail their efforts to create a more inclusive city. Civic leadership in all the cities we have discussed is multi-level. Leaders at the neighbourhood, district and borough levels, as discussed in some detail in Chapter 5, all make a significant contribution to the creation of the inclusive city. While recognising this fact it is, nevertheless, important to celebrate the achievements of senior leaders who, through their personal energy and commitment, have served their cities well. In this chapter we have come across four outstanding examples.

Ken Livingstone, the first Mayor of London, pushed through the introduction of a congestion charge in the capital against the wishes of the car/petrol/road building industry in 2003. He had to withstand all kinds of personal attacks, but was rewarded for his courageous decision by strengthened political support at the London elections in 2004. Similarly Jaime Lerner, when developing new sustainable development policies for Curitiba, was harshly criticised by motor industry interests when he suggested taking highway lanes away from car drivers and dedicating them for bus-only use. He took on the vested interests, introduced the first BRT in the world, and became a three-time Mayor of the city.

Zhang Guangning, when he was Mayor of Guangzhou, exercised bold civic leadership when he championed the introduction of the first high capacity BRT system in Asia in 2010. He had to contend with a good deal of opposition, but he resisted pressures to abandon what was to become an award-winning scheme. In Freiburg, Wulf Daseking, the Director of Planning and Building, demonstrated year-in and year-out civic leadership for over twenty years, insisted on very high quality urban development in the face of pressures to weaken environmental standards, and was recognised for his remarkable efforts by the British Academy of Urbanism in 2010. London, Curitiba, Guangzhou and Freiburg are all now more pleasant cities to live and work in because these place-based leaders exercised moral judgement, and worked hard to create a more environmentally friendly, inclusive city.

A second, and related theme, is that we have found that the vast literature on sustainable development, as well as the expanding literature on urban resilience, says next to nothing about the importance of public leadership, still less place-based leadership. We have noted a few honourable exceptions – for example, Sarah Parkin (2010), Benjamin Redekop (2010) and Judi Marshall and her colleagues (Marshall et al 2011). But the lack of attention paid to the role of leadership in creating sustainable, just cities is startling.

In Chapter 1 I noted that planning theory has virtually ignored leadership. I explained how, despite the fact that planning practitioners recognise the importance of leadership in bringing about sustainable urban development, planning theorists appear to regard leadership as an intellectual 'no-go' zone. Most planning theory books do not even mention leadership, still less offer an extended discussion of what it involves and how it might contribute to improving planning practice. This chapter can, perhaps, provide inspiration to those social scientists – in planning, sustainability, urban resilience, public management and related fields – who are interested not just to understand how urban systems operate but to throw new light on how to change the way urban systems behave.

The Innovation Stories in this chapter, and elsewhere in this book, do not pretend to offer full-blown explanations of the reforms that have taken place in the selected cities. In Chapter 1 I explained how an Innovation Story is not intended to provide ready answers but to prompt fresh thinking about the possibilities for place-based leadership and urban innovation. I noted that there are risks with this approach. In analysing the way some cities have pioneered new approaches to environmental and social justice we should *not* try to put them on a pedestal. Rather we should take account of the warning messages provided by Daniel Kahneman (2012). As I noted in Chapter 1, he draws attention to the 'narrative fallacy' – a tendency for those trying to explain events to ascribe too much weight to the role of talent in making things happen. In a sobering critique he argues that luck often plays a massive role. However, Kahneman's analysis is derived mainly from study of private sector decision-making. In my view Kahneman is too gloomy about the prospects for effective leadership, partly because he pays insufficient attention to the impact of wise public leadership in society.

Perhaps the Innovation Stories in this chapter can encourage scholars, policy makers and others to ask questions about why progressive change does happen in any given city. Is it all down to lucky breaks as Kahneman implies? Or can we unearth insights that might explain how reform was spurred along, indicate how opposing forces were outwitted, and reveal suggestions on how inclusive policies and practices can be sustained? Chapter 7 suggests that the way we design our systems of urban governance can help or hinder the exercise of bold civic leadership. In this chapter we have also discovered some insights on the way individual leaders can bring political skill, professional knowledge and emotional commitment to bear on current urban challenges.

CHAPTER 9

Creating people-friendly cities

What are our needs for happiness? We need to walk, just as birds need to fly. We need to be around other people. We need beauty. We need contact with nature. And most of all, we need not to be excluded. We need to feel some sort of equality.
Enrique Penalosa, former mayor of Bogota, UN World Urban Forum, Vancouver, 22 June 2006

Introduction

Not many urban leaders rush to proclaim that their city is unfriendly to people. A potential problem with the phrase 'people-friendly city' is, then, that, in and of itself, it signifies relatively little. Everyone can sign up to it. The discussion that follows attempts to move beyond bland claims, and identify the main building blocks that might be expected to feature in practical strategies designed to create people-friendly cities.

A quotation from William Shakespeare's *Coriolanus* was used at the beginning of Chapter 7 to highlight the importance of people in any sensible discussion of the city. Sicinius Velutus asks: 'What is the city but the people?' This famous dictum provided the prelude to a chapter focussed on the nature of democratic urban governance, and alternative ways of strengthening citizen power in the city. In this chapter we again focus on people and we will, again, refer to the vital importance of citizens having a central role in the decision-making processes that shape the urban environment and local life chances. However, our focus this time will be less on the process of democratic decision-making and more on the substantive outcomes effective place-based leadership aims to deliver.

A central theme that will emerge is that, to deserve the name, people-friendly cities have to be inclusive cities. Our starting point is human happiness. The literature on happiness, and the idea of developing public policies that promote happiness, has expanded in recent years (Ben-Shahar 2008; Layard 2011; Montgomery 2013). There are several strands here – some relating to personal growth and development, some relating to public policy and some relating to both.

In relation to public policy we can note that there is growing pressure to reconsider what we actually mean by improvements in 'living standards' (Sen 1984). As mentioned in Chapter 2 established measures of prosperity – like GDP and GDP-per-capita – have come under fire as they provide an inadequate basis for measuring the quality of life (Jackson 2009; Stiglitz et al 2009). Moreover, evidence is accumulating suggesting that, in the wealthy west, the acquisition of more and more material possessions appears to be leading, not just to a decline in human happiness, but to a growth in various kinds of mental illness (Montgomery 2013, 8–10).

In this chapter the discussion of people-friendly cities is divided into four parts. First, we discuss happiness and meaning in the people-friendly city. We explore what people's needs are, starting with the basic requirements of food, shelter, sanitation, health, education and safety. In addition to meeting these essential needs cities also offer the promise of a better quality of life – a life of rich and fulfilling experiences. To make headway here we need to explore a little further the notions of prosperity, happiness and feelings of identity. Second, we look at the way urban economies are changing and consider how place-based leadership can work to further the employment prospects of residents – long established and newly arrived. Third, we revisit the importance of governments developing inventive ways of working with markets and civil society to formulate new ways of creating and delivering public services. The old model of the state providing services to passive service users is being rethought in many localities. The fourth theme concerns urban place shaping – a concept introduced in Chapter 4. Here we examine the way city leaders in a number of progressive cities have adopted a proactive approach to urban development. Rather than waiting for private sector investors to bring forward proposals, civic leaders in these cities are actively expanding the public realm by shaping what happens in a very deliberate way.

This discussion sets the scene for two Innovation Stories illustrating outstanding place-based leadership. Innovation Story 12 highlights the transformation of Copenhagen from a car-clogged capital into a beautiful, welcoming city with extensive pedestrianised areas, cycle lanes, green spaces and public squares. Effective place-based leadership has made Copenhagen one of the most people-friendly cities in the world. In Innovation Story 13 we skip to the other side of the world and review another spectacular success story. In Melbourne civic leaders have, within the space of thirty years, transformed the central part of the city from a 'could-be-anywhere' soulless town centre into a people-friendly public realm at the heart of a major metropolis.

Happiness and meaning in the people-friendly city

It goes without saying that cities are not at the same starting line when it comes to meeting the needs of their residents. As discussed in Chapter 2, in developing countries very large numbers of people struggle to eke out a living in informal settlements. It follows that eradicating hunger and extreme poverty are the greatest challenges facing urban leaders in the rapidly expanding cities of the developing world. This is the first, and most important, message of the UN Sustainable Development Solutions Network in their recommendations for action to the United Nations (UN-SDSN 2013). Innovation Story 6, on pro-poor settlement upgrading in Langrug, South Africa provides a firm reminder that, in many cities, it is basic facilities like taps and toilets that matter most to local residents.

Designing people-friendly strategies for cities must, then, take account of the diversity of urban needs. Some seventy years ago, Abraham Maslow, the American psychologist, set out a framework for understanding human needs, which is still relevant today (Maslow 1943). Here I simplify his presentation. At the base of his hierarchy of five levels of need are physiological requirements: for example, breathing, food, water, sex and excretion. The next level up concerns safety involving security of: body, employment, resources, morality, the family, health and property. The third level relates to love and belonging – including friendship, family and sexual intimacy. A fourth level refers to self-esteem, confidence and respect of (and by) others. At his fifth level, self-actualisation occurs when individuals reach a state of harmony and understanding, because they are engaged in achieving their full potential.[1]

Maslow wrote that freedom of speech and freedom to express oneself were critical to the fulfilment of basic needs. True, Maslow's hierarchy of needs can be criticised for having a cultural bias – the values reflect, perhaps, a Western view of personal fulfilment. But, for the purposes of our discussion of how to create people-friendly cities, his typology reminds us that human needs vary dramatically. Measures that might be seen as deal-breakers in a wealthy western city – for example, car parking restrictions in a residential neighbourhood – will be regarded as profoundly unimportant in a city where needs for housing and sanitation are not being met.

In the quote at the beginning of this chapter, Enrique Penalosa, former mayor of Bogota, expresses eloquently the main dimensions of the people-friendly city. He highlights the need for contact with nature and with other people, the importance of beauty, and the need not to be excluded. Indeed, Penalosa's speech to the UN World Urban Forum in Vancouver in June 2006 is famous for both its imaginative content and it's emotional delivery. He noted, for example, that: 'If you base progress on per capita income, then the developing world will not catch up with rich countries for the next three or four hundred years'. Charles Montgomery (2013) offers an enthusiastic account of this speech, and also provides useful information on the back-story. Penalosa was mayor of Bogota from 1998–2001 and, in a short period of time, he reshaped public attitudes and boosted civic pride. By combining emotional appeals with radical innovations he altered the way people felt about their city:

> He was not going to make everyone richer. Forget the dream of becoming as wealthy as Americans... The dream of riches, Penalosa complained, only served to make Bogotans feel bad... No, the city needed a new goal. Penalosa promised neither a car in every garage nor a socialist revolution. His promise was simple. He was going to make Bogotans happier. (Montgomery 2013, 4)

Penalosa discarded the city's ambitious highway building programme and instead directed his budget into the creation of hundreds of miles of cycle paths, new parks and public squares, and a network of new libraries, schools and nurseries. He drew lessons from innovations taking place in other cities, particularly the remarkable Bus Rapid Transit (BRT) system in Curitiba – see Innovation Story 9. In 2000 he started a new BRT system for the capital. Known as the TransMilenio it comprises dedicated busways, articulated buses, specially designed stations, a smart-card fare collection system, a distinctive image as well as an affordable cost for low-income users. The TransMilenio, which has grown to become the biggest BRT system in the world, has delivered significant travel time savings, good levels of passenger satisfaction, reductions in accidents and carbon emissions and it operates without subsidy. This is, by any standards, impressive city leadership.

Penalosa undertook many bold innovations, and his legacy of people-friendly strategies for the City of Bogota has been a lasting one. In particular, his understanding of the value of public space in the city is sophisticated. He notes that the satisfaction we get from products purchased for private use tends to decrease over time, and often melts away completely. He argues that a '… great public space is a kind of magical good. It never ceases to yield happiness. It's almost happiness itself' (Quoted in Montgomery 2013, 5). Shortly, we will return to the theme of urban design, and the creation of convivial public spaces, when we discuss urban place shaping. But, first, a few words about identity and meaning.

Ben-Shahar (2008, 33) defines happiness as: 'the overall experience of pleasure and meaning'. There are, of course, other definitions, but most of them centre on the fact that happy people enjoy positive emotions. The evidence from research on happiness is unequivocal: how we feel is what matters, not how much stuff we've got. But happiness is about more than positive emotions – it is also about meaning. Viktor Frankl (2004) argues that meaning in one's life is the primary motivational force in people. Happiness depends, not on arriving at some tensionless state, but on striving to achieve a worthy goal. Peter Marris, the leading urban theorist, understood this well enough, and explained clearly what this means for civic leadership:

> The chances of achieving democratic, socially equitable planning depend… on creating a context of ideals and principles that articulate what most people want of their society and captures their imagination. The reformulation of social meaning is needed as urgently as any other kind of action. (Marris 1987, 162)

Inspiring city leaders, and Enrique Penalosa provides a good example, realise that appealing to citizen *feelings* is central to effective urban governance. In Chapter 4 I explained how place-based identity matters more than ever in our globalising world. Effective place-based leaders at the street level, the neighbourhood level, and the city/city region level assert the importance of place in public policy. Place has meaning for people and this should be respected, valued and cultivated.

Creating people-friendly urban economies

In Chapter 1 I referred to the argument set out by Michael Sandel (2012) in his book *What Money Can't Buy*. He shows how we have drifted, without realising it and without debating it, from having a market economy to becoming market societies. Sandel sees the market economy as a valuable tool for organising productive activity, but explains how a market society is an unhealthy one in which everything is up for sale. I built on his analysis and introduced an important distinction that we have revisited throughout this book – the distinction between place-less power and place-based power. Place-less leaders are people who are not expected to care about the consequences of their decisions for particular places and communities. We have seen how distant decision makers in many multi-national companies are more than ready to exploit local people and, where possible, avoid paying local taxes. Place-based leaders, on the other hand, are concerned with enhancing the prosperity of their place, and they exhibit a social commitment to local communities.

This distinction has profound implications for urban economic development strategy. In a globalising world successful city leaders are, all the time, negotiating with different kinds of private sector interests in order to enhance prosperity in their city. The wise city leader does not welcome every kind of economic investment. Some private sector businesses need to be turned away. This is because some companies, and multi-national companies fit this template far too often, can be unreliable partners. In Chapter 4 I provided a clear example to illustrate the problem with place-less power. In this case I noted that Kraft Foods, the big American-owned company (now renamed as Mondelez International), misled workers and wiped out a productive chocolate factory in Keynsham, near Bristol. This is not an isolated example. Place-less decision makers, are making decisions of this kind every day of the week. Ed Miliband, Leader of the UK Labour Party, while he may have simplified the argument to make his point more powerful, was correct when he identified two kinds of business: on the one hand, the wealth creators and producers and, on the other, the asset strippers or predators (Miliband 2011). Wise city leaders welcome wealth creators who are committed to their city, but take great care in how they interact with the predators.

Given this context, what strategies for local economic development fit well with the desire to create a people-friendly, inclusive city? This is a big subject, but it is possible to offer a few suggestions and signposts to the literature. The first point to stress is that all business is local. The global brands realise this and, with a variety of laughable slogans, strive to give the illusion that they offer 'authentic local appeal' (Quelch and Jocz 2012, 8). Naturally they fail because they are, of course, not local at all. Their very existence depends on exploiting differences between places, not supporting place-based initiatives and activities. In Chapter 4, in offering a critique of place-less power, I explained how distant decision-makers in multi-national companies often miss good business opportunities. Their knowledge of the local economy tends to be poor and this fact offers political space for local initiative. If all business is, indeed, local it may be that communities living in particular places have more power than the economic textbooks allow.

For example, in my city we have a local currency, the Bristol Pound. Launched in 2012 the new currency, which is not intended to replace sterling but to work alongside it, is expanding because of the values it stands for – building better community connections to local businesses, promoting shorter, eco-friendly supply chains, and preventing losses of local wealth to distant shareholders and offshore tax havens. Hundreds of Bristol businesses now accept the currency. Bristol businesses can now pay their business rates in Bristol Pounds and the City Council, as do a number of other large employers, give staff the option to take part of their salary in the currency. As explained in Innovation Story 2 George Ferguson, mayor of Bristol, takes his entire salary in Bristol Pounds.[2] A local currency in one city may appear a trivial initiative. But, as Rob Hopkins (2013) explains, the Bristol Pound is not some kind of weird one-off. His book is crammed with inventive examples of local communities taking action to recycle local wealth.

Secondly, city leaders committed to building an inclusive city can bolster local job opportunities by pursuing green initiatives of various kinds. As Innovation Story 11, on civic leadership in Freiburg illustrates, it is perfectly possible to blend sustainable development with an expansion of the green economy. In the Freiburg case literally hundreds of jobs have been created in the solar technology area alone. Joan Fitzgerald (2010) provides a helpful guide to ways of linking sustainability strategies to economic development. Her book is full of useful insights on how to grow jobs in renewable energy, green building, recycling – she has a chapter on 'Is there treasure in our trash?' – and transportation. More broadly, Tim Jackson (2009) provides a brilliant analysis challenging conventional economics. He shows how it is perfectly possible to make a transition to a sustainable economy.

Third, and I discuss this in more detail in Chapter 10, city leaders and their officials can develop creative strategies for responding to urban diversity. There are several components to equity-driven urban policy making but two should be mentioned in the context of a discussion of local economic development. First, city authorities are major employers so that the way they recruit staff is an important factor in the local economy. Fair, open procedures can enhance the ethnic and cultural diversity of city bureaucracies. Second, city authorities are major buyers of goods and services. They can examine their supply chains and consider whether the organisations they contract with are, or are not, furthering the interests of creating an inclusive city.

Stated simply civic leaders can ask: Are these companies producers or predators? The legislative framework provided to enable localities to resist the predators varies by country. It is clear, then, that national governments have an important role to play in shaping the rules of the game to advance the interests of local communities. In the UK, for example, the Public Services (Social Value) Act 2012 places a duty on all local authorities and public bodies in England and Wales to consider how they might improve the social, economic and environmental well-being – the 'social value' – of an area when they buy and commission goods and services. The idea is to shift the way value is measured in public service markets by adding in social considerations (Leighton and Wood 2010). In the UK this enables those contracting out public services to impose social requirements. They do not have to place contracts with the lowest bidder. For example, providers may be required to pay the living wage to all the people they employ and/or employ young unemployed people from the area. There are opportunities here, then, for locally based social enterprises or voluntary organisations to win contracts that may be able to reduce inequality by spending public money more wisely.[3]

Fourth, city leaders can work to create a new kind of civic economy – one that steps ahead of neo-liberal economics. A London-based company, aiming to promote sustainable places, has worked with partners to produce 25 case studies of civic entrepreneurship (Ahrensbach et al 2012). This compendium shows how it is possible to move towards more sustainable routes to shared prosperity. The civic economy is not, of course, a new idea. The Co-operative Movement advanced the intellectual and practical underpinnings for this approach in the 19th Century – and had a major impact. What is, perhaps, new is that new possibilities are emerging for conjoining the efforts of elected city leaders and values-driven private sector companies.

Cities have always been centres of invention and creativity. In recent times there has been growing recognition of this asset, and various writers have drawn attention to the fact that this should point towards a people-centred approach to urban economic development. For example, Richard Florida (2002) suggested that the traditional division of economic sectors into primary, secondary and tertiary industries was out of date. He argued that a fourth creative sector needed to be added. His influential book, *The Rise of the Creative Class*, suggests that companies increasingly go to where the talented and creative people are.

A consequence is that cities need to focus on creating the right people climate, rather than the right business climate. Other studies also suggest that the soft infrastructure, meaning a range of quality of life factors, is as important as hard infrastructure in fostering a buoyant urban economy (Landry 2006). Supporting local creative industries can, then, play an important role in building the inclusive city, but care is needed. As Peck (2005) explains, pandering to the requirements of a so-called 'creative class' can widen social divisions in a city. Catharina Thörn explores this theme in the Swedish context. In an insightful analysis she notes that various, highly praised eco-projects in Sweden do not score that well on equity considerations. They appear to be very successful in attracting so-called creative, middle class people but she notes that:

> ... a major risk with this kind of political choice is that the investments in these areas mainly serve those who are already "winners" in the new economy. At the same time, other parts of the city are being drained of finances, and abandoned by capital projects. (Thörn 2008, 54)

Creative industries have a great deal to contribute to every city, but civic leaders need to maintain a focus on inclusiveness.

Working with people

The idea of the state working *with* people rather than for people has been emphasised at various points in this book. Here I provide a brief recap of this theme. In Chapter 3 I discussed the changing relationships between civil society, markets and the state. Three overlapping spheres of influence are set out in Figure 3.2 and I suggested that effective place-based leaders work across these boundaries. I also drew attention to the importance of cultivating civic identity and place-based loyalty. In Chapter 6 I discussed the way the relationships between the citizen and the state are being renegotiated in many countries, and I explained how new approaches to the co-creation of services are being tried out. The following chapter explained at some length why inclusive cities have to be democratic cities, and I suggested that the purpose of local government is to provide place-based leadership for the common good. Figure 7.5 provides a ladder of citizen empowerment that can, I hope, be helpful to urban policy makers as they consider alternative approaches to working with people in their city.

An important theme, emphasised in all these chapters, is that the *way* civic leaders work with local people and various interested partners is critical. The Innovation Stories presented in this book illustrate a diversity of approaches to public and/or service user involvement in decision-making. But listening and collaborating are essential features of all of them. These ideas resonate with the notion of Asset-Based Community Development (ABCD), an approach that focuses on community assets rather than needs.[4] Alison Gilchrist and Marilyn Taylor put it this way:

> Every single person has capabilities, abilities and gifts. Living a good life depends on whether those capabilities can be used, abilities expressed and gifts given. If they are, such people will be valued, feel powerful and be well-connected to the people around them. And the community around the person will be more powerful because of the contribution that person is making. (Gilchrist and Taylor 2011, 22)

Critics of the ABCD approach argue that it fails to address the political reasons why community needs are so great in the first place. But such criticisms fail to recognise that there is no reason why an ABCD strategy rules out political activities. The distinctions made by Gilchrist and Taylor (2011) can help in this context. These experienced authors suggest that there are three different models of community development. First, radical models seek fundamental change in the way society operates. Second, pluralist models seek to rebalance the governmental system to make it fairer and more democratic. Third, the communitarian approach seeks to make existing structures work more smoothly. The ABCD strategy is sometimes associated with the third approach but it can, in fact, be adapted to play a role in any of these three models. For example, Innovation Story 6 describing pro-poor settlement upgrading in Langrug, South Africa could be described as a classic ABCD approach. But this does not mean that those involved are inactive in campaigning to change the situation that gives rise to the growth of informal settlements in and around South African cities.

Urban place shaping

Henry Shaftoe has produced a beautiful, well-illustrated book on *Convivial Urban Spaces* (2008). At one level it provides very practical guidance on how to design people-friendly public spaces in cities. But it is about much more than urban design. It covers the sociological and psychological dimensions of public space and also pays attention to management and maintenance. His starting point is that urban spaces need to be welcoming, sociable, festive – in a word convivial:

> Without such convivial spaces, cities, towns and villages would be mere accretions of buildings with no deliberate opportunities for casual encounters and positive interactions between friends or strangers. The trouble is that too many urban developments do not include such convivial spaces, or attempts are made to design them in, but fail miserably. (Shaftoe 2008, 5)

In Chapter 4 I discussed the role of place in public policy and drew distinctions between three approaches: place making, place marketing and place shaping. I provided a critique of the idea of place marketing. I suggested several reasons why the idea of marketing, or branding a place, is a misguided, even offensive, idea. The discussion that follows, therefore, concentrates on place making and place shaping. Stated simply Shaftoe's book is an excellent contribution to the literature on place making, by which I mean the planning and design of a people-friendly urban environment. Detailed urban design matters and Innovation Story 13 on Melbourne, appearing later in this chapter, illustrates this argument rather well.

Place shaping, in the way I am using it in this book, is a concept that is much broader than place making (Lyons Inquiry 2007). I define it as: Elected local authorities adopting a strategic role to shape the places they govern in order to promote the well-being of all the people who live there. As explained in Chapter 4 place shaping includes place making, but it also concerns the overall role of local government, and it includes activities that do not impact the physical environment. For example, Innovation Stories 3, 4 and 5 on Chicago, Swindon and Enschede promote the well-being of residents but are not focused on urban design at all.

As discussed earlier in this chapter, Enrique Penalosa, when he was mayor of Bogota, embarked on a bold and far-reaching place shaping effort. He employed transport engineers, city planners and urban designers to reshape the physical environment, but he also took steps to ensure the fiscal viability of the Bus Rapid

Transit system. Moreover, he kept bus fares low so that the transport improvements could advance the cause of equity in the city. Several other Innovation Stories in this book illustrate this kind of outgoing place-based leadership. For example, Innovation Story 9 on Curitiba provides another good example of a Latin American city being transformed by civic leaders who were willing to take forceful action to transform the public realm. Innovation Story 8 on Malmö provides a European example of imaginative place shaping, as does Innovation Story 11 on Freiburg.

In the next two Innovation Stories I wish to highlight the importance of the physical, public realm in advancing the cause of the inclusive city. As I explained in Chapter 4 gated communities are on the rise in cities across the world. By gated I mean a residential or commercial area with restricted access. Such areas involve privatisation of public space, restrictions on who can enter, and physical barriers to prevent unauthorised access. Gated communities or commercial areas are, by definition, exclusionary. They exclude people and, far from increasing safety in the city, they are cultivating a fantastical 'derivative fear' (Bauman 2006). Chapter 4 also discusses what I call the 'theft of public space'. I agree with the analysis presented by Anna Minton (2009) who sets out evidence to show that, in Britain, many cities are selling off the public realm. The Innovation Stories on Copenhagen and Melbourne, arguably two of the most liveable cities in the world, are doing exactly the reverse. In both cases place-based leaders have been *expanding the public realm* – to the benefit of business, residents and visitors alike.

Inviting people into the city: the Copenhagen experience

Place-based leaders have been reshaping the streets and public spaces of the City of Copenhagen for decades. A consequence is that the capital of Denmark is now a highly attractive city and is, arguably, one of the most people-friendly cities in the world. It wasn't always like this. In the late 1950s and early 1960s Copenhagen was as car clogged as any other European city. Jan Gehl, the famous architect/planner, who is from Copenhagen, offers a robust critique of the car-oriented planning he encountered in the 1960s:

> Modernism with its vision of the city as a machine, with its parts separated by function became highly influential. Also a new group, traffic planners, came gradually on the scene with their ideas and theories on how to ensure the best conditions – for car traffic. Neither the city planners nor the traffic planners put city space and city life high on their agenda, and for years there was hardly any knowledge about how physical structures influence human behaviour. (Gehl 2010, x)

Gehl's book, *Cities for People*, shows in meticulous detail how cities can be redesigned to celebrate city life. Gehl has contributed actively to city planning and urban design in Copenhagen, and his book draws extensively on work he has carried out in the city. Gehl notes that:

> In the period from 1962 to 2005 the area devoted to pedestrians and city life grew by a factor of seven: from approximately 15,000 sq m to a good 100,000 sq m... The many whole-hearted invitations to walk, stand and sit in the city's common space had resulted in a remarkable new urban pattern: many people walk and stay in the city... The conclusion from Copenhagen is unequivocal: if people rather than cars are invited into the city, pedestrian traffic and city life increase correspondingly. (Gehl 2010, 13)

Peter Hall (2013, 232–36) applauds the city planning achievements of the city. He notes how, since 1980, the city has put a strong emphasis on sustainable regeneration in the old harbour and industrial areas close to the city centre. Hall also explains how Copenhagen has established itself as a world leader in relation to climate change. It hosted the United Nations' Climate Change Conference in December 2009 and has a particularly good track record in relation to energy efficiency. Around 98% of Copenhagen residents are connected to a district combined heating and power (CHP) system. Many of these CHP plants are owned by cooperatives – a popular model in Denmark.

Innovation Story 12 focuses on the way city leaders in Copenhagen have, over a long period, worked to expand the public realm. The consistent drive to make cycling and walking much more attractive has paid off.

INNOVATION STORY 12

Expanding the public realm: developing people-friendly urban policy in Copenhagen

Aims

Copenhagen is widely recognised as one of the most liveable cities in the world. This Innovation Story is about the transformation of a car-clogged city into a lively people-oriented one, an incremental process that began in the 1960s. We will focus here on the way civic leaders have responded to social expectations and expanded the public realm by, amongst other things, taking public space away from vehicles and making it available for pedestrians, cyclists and fun activities.

Urban planners and academics have played a pivotal role in influencing the strategic direction of the municipal government and the setting of the ambitious targets to which the city aspires, such as being the world's best cycling city by 2015 and the world's first carbon neutral capital by 2025. In 2012, in recognition of Copenhagen's remarkable sustainability achievements, the city won the award of European Green Capital 2014. Driving this transformation is a Danish political culture that is deeply committed to collective public purpose, and recognition, by political leaders of Copenhagen, that city planning and urban design can play a key role in creating an inclusive city.

Central to Copenhagen's urban planning is the principle that a people-friendly city needs to be an inclusive city. Good urban design is valued not just because it enhances the visual experience of the city but because it can bring people together regardless of age, background, ethnicity and so on. As this Innovation Story will show, the creation of an urban environment that is attractive and, thus encourages people to walk, cycle and spend time in public outdoor spaces rather than being car dependent, are key tenets of Copenhagen's vision for a sustainable and inclusive city.

Innovation Story outline

Like many other cities in the 1960s, car traffic and congestion were dominant features of Copenhagen's city centre and contributed to deteriorating conditions for pedestrians. In 1962 Copenhagen City Council, responding to progressive movements in the city, became the first city in the world to remove vehicles from a major shopping street – Strøget was pedestrianised. What began as an experiment marked the onset of a series of step-by-step positive measures taken by political leaders to encourage a culture of walking and cycling rather than car dependency, an approach that is still ongoing today.

The closure of Strøget to vehicle traffic met with much scepticism on the part of both shopkeepers and the public. The former feared a decline in business, while the latter questioned whether street life could be promoted – many felt that the Danish climate, and a lack of tradition for using outdoor space for meeting and relaxing, would kill the initiative stone dead. But these initial concerns proved to be misplaced and the number of people using the streets increased. Jan Gehl, a Danish urban designer who has contributed a great deal to the reshaping of the public realm in Copenhagen, put it this way:

> The City of Copenhagen has been restructuring its street network for several decades, removing driving lanes and parking spaces in a deliberate process to create better and safer conditions for bicycle traffic ... The entire city is now served by an effective and convenient system of bike paths, separated by curbs from sidewalks and driving lanes... Bicycle traffic doubled in the period from 1995 to 2005, and in 2008 statistics show that 37% of personal transport to and from work and educational institutions was by bicycle.[1]

Pedestrianisation went hand in hand with a reduction in the number of parking spaces. Between 1962–1988 the number of car spaces reduced by two to three per cent each year whilst the amount of public space increased by three to four times. By 1992 there was six times more car-free space than in 1962 and by 1995 80% of traffic activity in the city centre was pedestrian. These radical changes amount to more than shifts in the mode of transport – a new people-friendly culture has been created with the result that people now spend much more time in the city centre. As benches and café seats replaced parking spaces in city squares people have chosen to spend more time in the city, enjoying a range of outdoor commercial, recreational and social activities.

A key feature in the leadership and management of the city has been the use of ambitious place-based targets coupled with rigorous monitoring of performance. In relation to cycling, for example, in 1996 the City Council introduced a system of bi-annual indicators (known as the Bicycling Account).[2] This process has provided the traffic department with rich data not just on bicycle use in the city, but also on Copenhageners' perceptions of cycling conditions. The insights derived from the Bicycling Account provide the basis for regular review of quantitative targets and investment plans.

The approach to planning is highly participatory – it involves widespread consultation with user groups and stakeholders. Regarding cycling conditions for example, the municipality invites cyclists and others to send in suggestions electronically for improving urban design. Changes which have stemmed from these consultation processes include: making cycle paths wider and providing better maintenance (snow removal and sweeping); changing the design of intersections to increase safety; reducing road space for cars on important bicycle arteries; bridges for cyclists and pedestrians; a system of bike routes through parks and green spaces; 2,500 free city-bikes (which can be borrowed for a returnable deposit); and establishing 'green waves' for cyclists (meaning synchronising traffic lights at rush hour times so that the movement of waves of cyclists is assisted).

The effect of these consultation-led changes has been most positive. In the 1970s about 10% of journeys to work and educational institutions were made by bike – this figure is now in the region of 37% and the target is to reach 50% by 2015. Cycling is now ingrained in the Copenhagen civic culture, with most children cycling by the time they start school. Many continue to cycle throughout their life, so much so that 68% of Copenhageners cycle at least once a week. These changes have not been made without conflict. For example, concerns have been expressed about inconsiderate riding by some cyclists. The municipality runs various education campaigns – for example, a 'Good Karma' campaign designed to ensure cyclists show a high level of concern for other cyclists and other users of the shared public space.

Cycling and pedestrian habits have combined to make for a highly liveable city, whilst a reduction in vehicle congestion has beneficial effects on air quality, carbon emissions and noise pollution. The contributions of planning professionals and academics have been significant. In 1968, urban planner and architect Jan Gehl and urban design academic Lars Gemzøe led a novel study designed to record how the city centre was actually used. This study was later repeated in 1986 and 1995 and provides a rich source of longitudinal data showing the relationship between the changes in Copenhagen's urban fabric and how people use the space.[3] This research was the first systematic study of pedestrian behaviour, the like of which had until then been the preserve of vehicle traffic research. In showing that initiatives focused on walking and cycling were leading to welcome improvements, such as increased street activities and a sense of safety, the research was instrumental in supporting politicians to continue a strategy of incremental enhancements to the urban environment, and the evidence-backed approach also helped to secure buy-in from the public at large.

Leadership Lessons

- Radical change can be achieved if civic leaders adopt an incremental but persistent approach to reform. Successive political administrations since the 1960s have continued a gradual approach to controlling car traffic in the city centre and creating quality public spaces. This step-by-step approach has given people time to get used to the changes and to adapt accordingly.
- Rigorous and ongoing research relating to the actual use of public space can provide a valuable underpinning for the development, implementation and review of policies. Copenhagen has introduced Bicycle Accounts and Green Accounts to monitor progress in a systematic way.
- An inclusive approach, emphasising open communication and involving a range of ways of learning from different interest groups in the city, means that policies can be modified to respond to changing perceptions.
- Civic leaders can be daring in trying out new approaches and then learning from the experience. When political leaders in Copenhagen took the decision to pedestrianise the main shopping street in the city they did not know, for sure, whether or not it would be a success. Copenhagen was one of the first cities to adopt an openly experimental approach to urban innovation and this ethos has paid off over the years.
- Urban design and planning professionals (operating both inside and outside the state) have contributed ideas and practical suggestions that have enabled Copenhagen to establish itself as a world leader in relation to being an inclusive city.

Sources

Copenhagen City Council – numerous strategies: http://subsite.kk.dk/sitecore/content/Subsites/CityOfCopenhagen/SubsiteFrontpage/LivingInCopenhagen/CityAndTraffic.aspx

Gehl, J, Gemzøe, L, 1999, *Public spaces – public life: Copenhagen 1996*, Copenhagen: The Danish Architectural Press

Gehl, J, 2010, *Cities for People*, Washington DC: Island Press

Nielsen TAS, Skov-Petersen, H, Carstensen, TA, 2013, Urban planning practices for bikeable cities – the case of Copenhagen, *Urban Research and Practice* Vol 6, 1, 110–115

Endnotes

[1] Gehl (2010, 11)

[2] This discussion of bicycle policies in Copenhagen draws on Nielson et al (2013)

[3] See Gehl and Gemzøe (1996)

Melbourne makeover: the transformation of a city centre

In the early 1980s the city centre of Melbourne was a dump. Private interests, concerned only with urban development profits, were busy taking advantage of weak political leadership and poor planning policies to manufacture a boring 'could be anywhere' town centre. In June 1978 the local newspaper, *The Age*, described Melbourne as having an 'empty, useless city centre' – and published pictures to prove it. From a place shaping point of view the centre was a disaster zone – totally dead at night and even pretty dreary in the day. Leap forward thirty years and we find that *The Economist* praises Melbourne as being the 'most liveable city in the world'. Indeed, Melbourne has now established itself as an international leader in how to create a people-friendly public realm at the heart of a major metropolis.

Some commentators attribute the change to the big urban projects that have attracted media attention and tourist visitors – for example, Federation Square, the new Museum of Victoria, and the Melbourne Exhibition Centre. Rob Adams, Director of City Design for the City of Melbourne, knows better. He played a critical leadership role in the transformation of the city centre, and is clear that the big projects alone could not account for the dramatic change:

> The change has been more subtle: the city is greener, more people live downtown, the footpaths are wider, paved with stone and featuring side walk cafes, flower stands and fruit stalls. There is more pedestrian space, as well as more bicycle routes and a better balance between the car and other forms of movement. (Adams 2005, 50)

In a more recent communication Adams notes that the central city residential accommodation rose from 650 dwellings in 1985 to 28,000 in 2013.[5] In the last thirty years place shaping in Melbourne has, and this is unusual for a major city, been design-led. Adams notes that activists with a design background and a love of Melbourne stood for election and won office at both state and local government levels. They then fostered the creation of an organisational culture that was committed to high quality urban design and the creation of a people-friendly city. Innovation Story 13 shows how strong political leadership coupled with a solid commitment to imaginative urban design has enhanced the prosperity of the city and created a public realm that all can enjoy.

Place-shaping: the Melbourne experience

Aims

In 1851 gold was found in the Yarra River about sixteen miles from Melbourne. Before the discovery the total population of Victoria was 77,000; seven years later there were half a million people living there. A massive gold rush ensured that Melbourne became the biggest city in Australia. By the 1890s the city was known as 'Marvellous Melbourne', the wealthy gold mining capital of Victoria, and the conurbation was one of the largest and most vibrant cities in the world.

Fast forward to the early 1980s and the outlook for Melbourne was increasingly grim. A soulless central business district was close to deserted at night and many of the well off had moved to distant suburbs. This Innovation Story outlines the way bold civic leadership was able, over a period of twenty years or so, to transform the central part of the Melbourne metropolis into an attractive people-friendly public realm.[1]

Innovation Story outline

First, let's take stock of the achievements. An excellent report, *Places for People*, published by the City of Melbourne in association with Jan Gehl in 2004, provides a thorough and detailed analysis of the changes that have taken place in the 'Central City' area.

It shows that residential accommodation, virtually nonexistent in the 1980s, rose from 738 units in 1994 to 9,895 in 2004. Bars, cafes and restaurants increased from 580 in 1998 to over 1,200 in 2004. Networks of arcades and pedestrian only streets now criss-cross the city centre, and new squares and public spaces are home to imaginative sculptures and artistic events. For example, the laneways in central Melbourne, a network of narrow alleys and streets, used to be devoted to car and delivery traffic. As part of the people-friendly strategy these were closed to vehicles and turned into pedestrian streets. Now, many deliveries to shops and residences are made by bike couriers rather than by trucks.

Yes, there are headline grabbing mega projects. For example, the famous, new Federation Square, at the corner of Swanston Street and Flinders Street, houses the National Design Centre, the Australian Centre for the Moving Image, a National Gallery of Australian Art and numerous cafes. The square is a magnet for visitors from near and far and the striking modern architecture has attracted international praise.

But the significant Melbourne place-shaping achievement is to be found elsewhere. The startling fact is that local leaders have transformed the *whole* of the city centre into a delightful, liveable and attractive district for residents, workers and visitors. As Rob Adams, Director of City Design for the City of Melbourne, explained to me an early step was to drop the term CBD – meaning Central Business District – and start talking about a Central Activities District.[2]

Thus, a key objective of the first Melbourne Strategy Plan of 1985 was to switch the whole area from a 12-hour pattern of activities to a vibrant 24-hour centre. The plan set out strong urban design principles and clear priorities for land use, built form, an increased central city residential population, community services and the streetscape.

Out went the previous 'laissez-faire' approach to urban development and in came very strong urban policies with firm requirements relating to design – for example, insisting on building up to the street frontage and requiring active frontage on the streets – as well as a very protective approach in relation to historic buildings and spaces.

How did they do it? Three features are striking. First, strong leadership – involving politicians and their officers collaborating closely on both agenda setting and delivery – has been crucial. Thus, praise is due to the far-sighted politicians elected to the Victoria State Government as well as Melbourne City Council in the early 1980s. They had an imaginative vision of what their city centre could be like and set about delivering it with ruthless effectiveness.

A new urban design subcommittee was created. Chaired by a councillor who was a strong advocate of the urban design agenda, this subcommittee was crucial in changing the engineering dominated culture of the local authority. As Rob Adams puts it: 'The subcommittee oversaw the introduction of design solutions that were based on requirements for a people-friendly city over any single-purpose requirement, such as traffic movement'.[3] The subcommittee also oversaw all major planning submissions insisting that the quality of the resulting street should take precedence.

City planners and urban designers can, then, make an invaluable contribution to place shaping but the institutional design of a city council needs to give political weight to the urban design agenda.

Second, the bold political leadership has been conjoined with a clear commitment to a strong design culture within city departments. After the adoption of the 1985 plan the council established a high-level urban design team. This team had the mandate to work to modify the traditional engineering approaches and sectional decision-making often found in city halls. Also, instead of farming out design work to private planning consultants and architects, a common practice in local government, the council built up a first class design and delivery department.

The original team of five has now grown to a division of nearly 60 professionals – planners, architects, urban designers, landscape architects and so on – who have, by working very closely with other council departments, built a capacity to shape and control development in the public interest. Development control, sometimes viewed as an unexciting backwater in local government is, without doubt, the key way in which Melbourne has delivered a high quality public realm in the central area.

However, the forthright approach to development control is only part of the design package. In 1993 the City invited Jan Gehl, a leading architect and urban designer based in Copenhagen, to work with them on a 'places for people' initiative. This enabled Melbourne to learn in a systematic way about high quality urban design in other countries. Action plans, streetscape plans, technical notes (right down to kerb design and paving details) were introduced to guide the behaviour of public utilities, council departments and the like.

The Melbourne approach to urban renewal is demonstrably financially viable. Create a truly attractive urban setting and developers will line up to invest. This, in turn, generates funding streams from property tax income. This funding can then be used to employ top city planners and architects who can insist on high quality urban design. It is the opposite of cutback management.

The third lesson relates to public private partnerships. Councillors in Melbourne created a city projects division capable of negotiating, designing and project-managing the delivery of public private partnerships.

The division has identified key sites for this model of development and has many success stories under its belt – for example, the transformation of the Queen Victoria site. In this instance the city purchased the property and then packaged up components of the site to attract private sector investment. This has led to a major mixed-use development combining 45,000 sq m of retail with car parking, child-care facilities and other uses. Some 20% of this site is public open space with 24-hour access and the development is clearly a positive addition to the public realm of the city.

Arguably the most successful element of the strategy was *Postcode 3000*. The 1985 Strategy Plan set a target of 8,000 new residential units in the central city by the year 2000. *Postcode 3000*, initiated in 1992, worked with private property owners to convert redundant office buildings and, later, new buildings to residential. This programme was spectacularly successful and has seen the residential numbers rise from 650 dwellings in 1985 to over 28,000 in 2013. This has been accompanied by a proliferation of bars, cafes, restaurants, art galleries, supermarkets and convenience stores.

In too many cities an out of date engineering culture remains and the importance of urban design is often undervalued. Melbourne shows how strong political leadership coupled with a bold approach to urban design can enhance the prosperity of the city as well as bring about a step change in the quality of the public realm.

Leadership lessons

- Strong leadership by councillors and officers working together can transform the entire culture of an organisation. In the Melbourne case it proved possible to embed a strong commitment to people-friendly design across city hall departments.
- The quality of the public realm that results from urban development should drive all planning decisions, not the attractiveness or otherwise of individual buildings. This requires high calibre professionals to articulate public purpose in their dealings with the private sector.

- Public private partnerships can bring about creative urban development but only if decisions are driven by public purpose. In Melbourne those wishing to develop property must demonstrate a community benefit if they are to win approval.
- A high level of attention to detail and a strong commitment to public participation is a strong feature of the way the City of Melbourne works with residents and other stakeholders in the city.
- Civic leaders in Melbourne engaged in systematic learning from other countries. In particular, the appointment of Jan Gehl Architects, from Copenhagen, as urban design consultants meant that the city was able to learn from examples of high quality urban planning in Europe.

Sources

Adams, R, 2005, Melbourne: Back from the edge, in E Charlesworth E, *City Edge: Case Studies in Contemporary Urbanism*. Oxford: Elsevier, 50–64

City of Melbourne, 2013, *Postcode 3000. A city transformed?* An exhibition, curated by Rob Adams, at the Melbourne City Galley, 22 August 2013–18 January 2014, http://melbourne.vic.gov.au/citygallery

City of Melbourne and Gehl Architects, 2004, *Places for People*, Melbourne: City of Melbourne

Endnotes

[1] The local governance system in Melbourne is unusual. The City of Melbourne, which has a population of around 100,000, lies at the heart of the Melbourne metropolis, which has a population of 4.1 million. While significant achievements are to be found in the conurbation as a whole this Innovation Story is focused on the City of Melbourne.

[2] Personal interview by the author on 2 November 2007.

[3] Adams 2005, 53.

Conclusions

In this chapter we have explored the concept of the people-friendly city and gathered together evidence from some of the most people-friendly cities in the world. At a conceptual level I suggested that a people-friendly city concerns itself not just with meeting the basic needs of residents, but also with efforts to lift the spirits of everyone in the city. We have seen how, once basic needs are met, inclusive city leaders focus sharply on what the city *feels* like. Does it feel safe? Is the environment welcoming? Do I feel happy here? Is this a fun place? Do my kids like it?

These are, of course, the kinds of questions that Jane Jacobs raised over fifty years ago in her visionary book, *The Death and Life of Great American Cities*. Time and again she stressed the importance of adopting a people-centred approach and, in particular, pleaded for city planning to focus on city vitality:

> Planning for vitality must stimulate and catalyse the greatest possible range and quantity of diversity among uses and among people

> throughout each district of a big city; this is the underlying foundation of city economic strength, social vitality and magnetism. (Jacobs 1961, 421)

Jacobs' analysis is a socio-economic one. She argued that social vitality and economic vitality go hand-in-hand. She was, of course, writing long before the emergence of the massively powerful, place-less businesses that now bestride the world. We have seen that these businesses are more than capable of making decisions without regard to the feelings or wishes of particular communities. It follows that her analysis needs to be updated to take account of this restructuring of private sector power. I explained that city leaders who wish to create inclusive cities would be wise to develop fresh thinking in relation to local economic development.

As part of this they might well find it useful to distinguish between two kinds of private sector interest: those that are place-less and those that are place-based. The former could well not have the interests of local workers and residents centre stage in their thinking. Indeed, place-less decision makers may care not a jot about the damage their actions cause for particular communities. Place-based companies, the multitude of small local businesses, are, on the face of it, more likely to have a commitment to the locality and the people who live there. Indeed, their success is intertwined with the fortunes of the locality in a way that is not the case for place-less companies. Added to this we can expect to see a growth in new kinds of civic businesses and socially and environmentally aware organisations in the years ahead.

The evidence presented in the chapter suggests that place-based leaders can play a critical role not just in setting a tone that favours the creation of a people-friendly, inclusive city, but also in spurring radical innovation. We have touched on the experiences of three remarkable cities: Bogota, Copenhagen and Melbourne. In each city political leaders have responded to community campaigns for a better quality of life by taking bold action designed to *change* the prevailing rules of the game.

Enrique Penalosa, former mayor of Bogota, and his colleagues altered the entire trajectory of their city – out went the urban highway plans and in came a much more people-friendly approach. Similarly civic leaders in Copenhagen set out an imaginative vision of a very high quality public realm and then set about delivering it. Likewise, place-based leaders in Melbourne transformed a semi-deserted city centre into a vibrant, exciting central area. These cities did not transform themselves by accident. Clearly, the political space for local initiative varies across these cities, and the nature of urban politics in these three countries differs considerably. It seems clear, however, that place-based leadership, bold and courageous leadership by local leaders, is the key reason why these cities now serve residents, workers and visitors so well.

CHAPTER 10

The diversity advantage

One of the most important challenges facing modern societies, and at the same time one of our most significant opportunities, is the increase in ethnic and social heterogeneity in virtually all advanced countries
Robert Putnam, *Diversity and Community in the 21st Century*, 2007

Introduction

For centuries, if not throughout human history, cities have grown and changed as a result of migration and immigration. A consequence is that all cities are, to some extent, multicultural or multiethnic.[1] In Chapter 2 I discussed the remarkable acceleration in the movement of peoples to cities in recent decades, and I also noted how the international movement of peoples has contributed to this trajectory of urban growth. In one sense this is nothing new – cities have always attracted migrants to them, including international migrants. As Peter Hall notes, in his review of creative cities in history, cultural diversity has been a key asset in the emergence and development of dynamic cities. His major study unearths insights from numerous innovative cities – from classical Athens, through industrial Manchester, and the dream factory of Los Angeles to social democratic Stockholm. His analysis suggests that: 'Creative cities were nearly all cosmopolitan; they drew talent from the four corners of their worlds, and from the very start those worlds were often surprisingly far-flung' (Hall 1998, 285).

Chapter 2 outlines how the interplay between globalisation and urbanisation has resulted in increasingly diverse cities. Some receiving cities, or immigrant gateway cities, now exhibit what Jill Gross and I have described as dynamic diversity. By this we mean the rapid arrival of large numbers of immigrants from a range of countries into a given city (Hambleton and Gross 2007, 218–20). Dynamic diversity does not refer simply to the swift pace of change and the numbers of immigrants, but also to the diversity in the origins of new arrivals.[2] We used the phrase to suggest that nuances at the local level are likely to be more complex than hitherto. Immigrants bring with them their own unique cultural heritage that shapes their expectations and actions, and it is fair to say that remarkable population shifts are now taking place in some cities. For example, in Toronto, as we shall see later in the chapter, foreign-born people now comprise the majority of the residents.

In major cosmopolitan cities, like London and New York, it is now the case that hundreds of different languages are in use on a day to day basis by residents. For example, a study of the languages of London's schoolchildren found that over 300 languages are now spoken in the capital (Baker and Eversley 2000). The increase in urban diversity poses important challenges for city leaders and public managers and for the systems of representation in urban governance. This chapter discusses these challenges. Attention centres on the task of leading and managing multicultural cities and, while the focus is on cultural and ethnic diversity, the aim here is to outline ideas and experiences that are relevant to the broader notion of the governance of difference.[3]

Chapter 1 explained how the inclusive city embraces diversity and strives for just results. This means giving active consideration to ways of advancing the 'right to the city' for all groups in society, and it involves working to remove discrimination motivated by race, ethnicity, gender, sexual orientation, religion, disability or age. This chapter refers to the experience of a number of cities that are trying out new approaches to what some describe as 'diversity management'. The general stance of this chapter is to focus on the advantages of diversity. I will not ignore the tensions that surround the governance of the multicultural city, but I take the view that to focus only on problems and conflicts can limit the imagination. Always putting the spotlight on troubles and concerns can blind us to opportunities, and it can also undervalue the remarkable achievements of innovative cities across the world.[4]

Understanding equal opportunities and diversity

Tiresome as it can be, it is important to clarify a few terms before we go much further. This chapter is concerned with equal opportunities and diversity in the modern city. But what do these terms mean? In practice these words are not only used in different ways in different countries and cultures, they are also contested. Moreover concepts and understandings shift over time. It follows that we need to exercise care and sensitivity as we explore this terrain.

Barbara Bagilhole (2009), writing from a UK perspective, provides us with a good starting point.[5] She notes that, when first introduced into UK public policy in the 1960s, 'equal opportunities' was driven by a desire to stop blatant discrimination – initially on grounds of race and gender. This original definition suggested that an effective equal opportunities policy would involve treating everybody fairly and equally regardless of background. Over the years this approach was expanded to cover a range of forms of discrimination going beyond the grounds of race and gender – for example, age, disability and sexual orientation. Similar policies have been, and are being, pursued in many countries.

However, this strategy for achieving equal opportunity – that is, by aiming to treat everyone in the same way – came to be questioned. Different treatment can be meted out, not only in an unjust way, but also in a way that advances the cause of equal opportunities. Bagilhole (2009, 49) notes that different experiences of disadvantage can occur between, and even within, social groups:

> For example, the experiences and consequences of racism and racial discrimination differ in important ways for black women and black men, and the experiences and consequences of sexism and gender discrimination differ in important ways for white women and black women.

It follows that 'treating everyone in the same way' might not be the most effective strategy. On the contrary, public policies and practices need to be tuned to meet the diverse needs of different communities and individuals.

The idea of 'diversity' entered the British, and European, public policy lexicon in the late 1990s. Bagilhole discusses the emergence at this time of a public debate in the European Union (EU) about 'living together with difference' – and she notes the increasing use of the term 'multiculturalism'. In this context, then, 'diversity' is not simply about 'being different' – it is concerned with the experience of being discriminated against. In EU policy diversity is explicitly linked to tackling discrimination. Thus, in 2003 the EU launched a publicity campaign, *For Diversity – Against Discrimination*, to inform the people of Europe of their rights and responsibilities under legislation introduced through the EU to combat discrimination. The campaign, which was organised by the, then, 27 Member States, highlights the benefits of diversity and makes people aware of the EU anti-discrimination legislation.

We should step back for a moment. Diversity policy and practice are not EU inventions. As Reeves (2005) explains the concept of 'diversity' originated in the USA in the 1970s – a country with a much more multicultural tradition than most countries. The point I wish to highlight here is that, in both the USA and Europe, there is a degree of confusion in the debate about diversity. In common usage diversity means 'being diverse'. The confusion arises because some aspects of 'being different' give rise to discrimination and disadvantage while some do not.

Reeves illustrates the important relationships between diversity and equality in the following way:

> Equal opportunities and diversity are not mutually exclusive. Equality should be the normative value underpinning diversity, giving it teeth and meaning. Equality means ensuring that people with different needs have equality of opportunity and outcome. Diversity without equality addresses only difference. Diversity with equality also addresses power. (Reeves 2005, 9)

Reeves highlights the problems that can arise when organisations think that, because they believe they have tackled equal opportunities successfully, they can now 'move on' to a 'diversity' approach. This is a misguided strategy as prejudice and discrimination are endemic in society. Reeves rightly stresses that it is essential not just to value diversity but also to tackle inequality on a continuing basis.

Bagilhole highlights another important concept that is now receiving more attention in equal opportunities policy-making, namely, intersectionality. Developed by feminist theorists, this concept draws attention to multiple layers of identity and to the intersection of factors. Some disadvantaged people experience several forms of oppression at one and the same time. Anita Lacey and her colleagues suggest that:

> Intersectionality is a means of seeing the ways in which many different aspects of what determines our lived experiences – including gender, race, class, age and ability – need to be taken into account in analysis, planning and programming. (Lacey et al 2013, 144)

The idea here is to recognise that simply adding up several types of oppression does not provide an adequate picture of the lived experience of someone suffering from multiple disadvantage – intersectionality attempts to provide a more integrated understanding.

Bagilhole rounds off her discussion of definitions by suggesting that the core purpose of equal opportunities and diversity policy is to achieve an equal society. She notes that the UK Equalities Review (Equalities Review 2007, 16) defines an equal society as one which 'protects and promotes equal, real freedom and substantive opportunity to live in the ways people value and would choose, so that everyone can flourish.'

An important theme in debates about equal opportunities and diversity relates to the invisibility of important groups. As Reeves (2005) explains, ethnicity and sex tend to be the most significant ways of categorising people in modern societies. In many countries discrimination on grounds of race and gender were the first kinds of discrimination to be outlawed by equal opportunities legislation. However, she notes that many other groups are victims of prejudice even if they may be less visible in society – for example, gay people, lesbians, disabled people, transgender people and so on. Her chapter on developing cultural competence outlines ideas that are useful in tackling all forms of discrimination.

This brief discussion of the relationships between equal opportunities and diversity policy has shown that the subject is complex and contested. Old prejudices around, for example, class and race, still exist. At the same time new forms of intolerance arise – for example, Islamophobia has emerged in a deeply troubling way in the period since the terrorist attacks on the USA on 11 September 2001. International organisations, like the United Nations and the EU, play a vital role in furthering human rights and tackling discrimination. So too do national governments that pass anti-discriminatory legislation and fund programmes to advance multicultural and intercultural understanding.

Often overlooked in these debates is the fact that place-based leadership has a vital contribution to make. The political leadership of a city may, depending on the constitution of the country, advance the cause of equality at a quicker pace than the national government. For example, Mexico City chose to legalise same-sex civil unions in the city in 2009 and, in 2010, the city became the first Latin American jurisdiction to legalise same-sex marriage. By 2013 over 2,500 same-sex couples were married under the recently approved legislation.

It is also the case that it is the very local dimension that really matters – the lived intercultural experience in workplaces, nurseries, schools, sports clubs, community centres and so on. As Ash Amin makes clear, in his insightful UK study of ethnicity in the multicultural city, it is the sites of everyday encounter that open up pathways to mutual understanding. He comments on British policy and notes that, while much of the UK debate about racial and ethnic relations was taking place at a national level, the really important negotiations of difference were taking place in urban neighbourhoods: 'The political implication is that the gains of interaction need to be worked at in the local sites of everyday encounter' (Amin 2002, 969). More recent research on sociality in, for example, primary school playgrounds in multicultural areas supports this conclusion (Wilson 2013).

This brings us back fairly swiftly to place-based leadership, and suggests that elected local authorities have a critical role to play in advancing the cause of equality and social inclusion (De Groot and Mason 2008). In successful multicultural cities community leaders – working at the grassroots and at the city level – are playing a critical role in building intercultural understanding. We will return to this theme of urban interculturalism shortly, and to its close cousin – transculturalism (Hou 2013). Next we turn to consider the impact of urban migration on cities.

The new cosmopolitans

Urban migrants bring different experiences and fresh energy to the city. In Chapter 2 I referred to globalisation and explained how it is helpful to define globalisation as 'the world becoming more interdependent and integrated' (Moynagh and Worsley 2008, 1). One consequence of globalisation is that more countries now host more migrants than ever before, and it is clear that most cities, certainly the dynamic ones, are increasingly cosmopolitan. In English the word 'cosmopolitan' has two main meanings. First, when used to describe a person, it implies that the individual is free from national limitations and prejudices – an appealing suggestion. Second, when used to describe a city or a neighbourhood in a city, it suggests an area containing people from many parts of the world. This is a simplification of a more complex debate, and some scholars suggest that 'cosmopolitanism' is a limited concept as it neglects 'class culture'. For example, Haylett (2006, 188) regards cosmopolitanism 'as a discourse which does not adequately describe working-class conditions of urban life or hold promise as a political project for working-class groups'. There is force in these arguments, and Haylett reminds us of the importance of building strong welfare states if we are to tackle inequality and secure social solidarity.

In the introduction to this chapter I suggested that dynamic, creative cities are, invariably, cosmopolitan. Richard Florida, in his research on the creative class –

through his writings and his advice to civic leaders in the US context – lends support to this view (Florida 2002). He suggests that creative cities are:

> … talent-harnessing places and places that are open to immigrants, artists, gays and racial integration. These are the kinds of places that, by allowing people to be themselves and to validate their distinct identities, mobilise and attract the creative energy that bubbles up naturally from all walks of life. (Florida 2005, 7)

In Chapter 2 I suggested that it is misguided to view migrants as helpless victims of global and political forces. On the contrary, it is often the case that migrants are relatively adventurous individuals willing to take on new challenges, even in very difficult circumstances. Added to this we can note that the vibrancy and excitement we experience in the modern city is often a direct consequence of the diversity of the city. Florida is not alone in suggesting that different kinds of people living and working together in close proximity can stimulate creativity and, with the right kind of place-based leadership, can provide cities with a diversity advantage (Wood and Landry 2008; Zachary 2000).

However, the governance of the multicultural city is not plain sailing. We now have more than a century of social scientific research documenting the experience of 'new arrivals' in cities.[6] Many studies have shown that the arrival experience is often not a happy one – migrants and immigrants often find themselves in conflict, sometimes violent conflict, with the established population (Bollens 2003). On occasions this discord stems from competition for urban services and jobs, but friction also results from huge gaps in understanding between host communities and newcomers.

In this context attitudes and perceptions are clearly critical, as evinced by a major survey of multiethnic American communities by Robert Putnam. This research suggests that residents of all races in ethnically diverse neighbourhoods tend, at first, to 'hunker down':

> Diversity does *not* produce "bad race relations" or ethnically-defined hostility... Rather, inhabitants of diverse communities tend to withdraw from collective life, to distrust their neighbours, regardless of the colour of their skin, to withdraw even from close friends, to expect the worst from their community and its leaders, to volunteer less... (Putnam 2007, 150–1, author's emphasis)

Putnam has been unfairly criticised for emphasising the downside of diversity. What his research shows, however, is that, in the longer run, successful US immigrant communities have overcome the initial 'hunkering down' phase by creating new, cross-cutting forms of social solidarity and more encompassing identities.

A unifying theme in scholarship on the multiethnic city, including work in the expanding field of intercultural studies, is that race relations are complex, dynamic and socially constructed (Ben-Tovim et al 1986; Landis et al 2004). Particularly important for this discussion, is that there is a growing body of literature suggesting that the negotiation of intercultural understanding occurs – if it occurs at all – at a very local level. Cities may well be sites of ethnic conflict, sometimes violent conflict, but it is also the case that urban neighbourhoods provide opportunities for intercultural encounter and engagement. Michael Maly, in his detailed and inspiring assessment of multicultural neighbourhoods in the US – including, for example, Uptown in Chicago – shows that many American neighbourhoods have achieved stable racial integration. Interestingly, he notes that place-based leadership is critical to sucess:

> Community leaders attend to neighbourhood quality by working to sustain positive intergroup relations and networks through the formation of parent-teacher associations, religious groups, interfaith groups, Chambers of Commerce, youth recreational leagues, political parties, and block clubs. These groups create an environment that promotes more positive associations among individuals and communal groups, especially across racial lines. (Maly 2005, 24)

We should refer here to the notion of transcultural placemaking. Jeffrey Hou (2013) and his colleagues have produced a useful collection of papers seeking to enhance our understanding of interculturalism. Hou suggests that transcultural placemaking sees cultures not as isolated from each other, but as cultures that are influenced and *transformed* through the process of urban place-making. This approach builds on the argument presented by Stuart Hall (2003) who suggests that cultural identity is a matter of 'becoming' as well as 'being' – culture and identity are, then, not fixed. If this argument is accepted we can suggest that place-based leadership can contribute to the process whereby communities discover new and constructive senses of identity.

Perspectives on urban diversity

Various writers have offered concepts to help us make sense of the dynamics associated with the international movement of people to cities and of the issues that then arise (Castles and Miller 2009; Saunders 2010; Spencer 2011). Amartya Sen (2006), in a brilliant analysis, suggests that in many societies we are becoming increasingly divided along lines of religion and culture. He notes that many of the conflicts and barbarities in the world ignore the *many* other ways in which people see themselves – for example, class, profession, morals and politics. He argues with passion that we need to recognise much more clearly that we are 'diversely different':

> The hope of harmony in the contemporary world lies to a great extent in a clearer understanding of the pluralities of human identity, and

> in the appreciation that they cut across each other and work against a sharp separation along one single hardened line of impenetrable division. (Sen 2006, xiv)

Useful ideas on how to frame and benchmark policies and practices designed to accommodate diversity have been provided by a variety of international organisations, as well as by individual cities. In this context I wish to highlight the efforts of EUROCITIES, a network of over seventy major cities in Europe. It is working with the European Commission to advance the cause of well-managed migration in Europe's increasingly diverse urban areas and I will refer to these efforts shortly. However, at this point, I want to introduce ideas presented by two scholars – Harm de Blij and Barry Checkoway – as they provide helpful frameworks for thinking about and responding to urban diversity.

Locals, globals and mobals

First, De Blij (2009), a highly respected geographer, offers suggestions derived from his analysis of the power of place in the modern world. He claims that it is helpful, in trying to understand the impact of globalisation on communities and places, to distinguish three kinds of people: 1) The locals – often the poorest people, who are least mobile and most susceptible to the impress of place; 2) The globals – the wealthy, advantaged classes to whom the world appears comparatively limitless; and 3) The mobals – the locals who have turned into transnational migrants and who are drawn by perceptions of opportunity and realities of need.

He acknowledges that there is a fourth category – refugees. Desperate migrants leave their homes in times of war and cross international boundaries to seek refuge. Refugees are driven out of their homes by conflict but hope to return – for example, the many Syrian people forced to flee their country in recent years because of violent conflict in their home environment. According to de Blij these are not mobals as their motives differ. Their suffering is immense and policies for refugees are far from adequate. Local authorities are found in a leadership role in providing assistance to asylum seekers – particularly in immigrant gateway cities – and this is likely to become an increasingly important challenge in the years ahead.

De Blij takes the view that it is the mobals who will be the great internationalisers of the 21st Century. He suggests that if their needs are not met the world order could be threatened, because:

> A sufficient number of them must see their hopes translated into reality, their local values accommodated, their efforts rewarded, to yield individual commitment to the order and stability that are the aims of the globals who will continue to exercise control. (De Blij 2009, 7)

It is worth noting that migrants are making a significant contribution both to their adopted countries and to their families back home. According to World

Bank figures the flow of 'remittance money' from migrants to their families has reached record levels in recent years. The amount has tripled in the last decade and, in 2012, it topped $530 billion – this 'is now more than three times the size of the total global aid budgets' (Provost 2013, 14).[7] In addition, we can note that political immigrants can play an important role in relation to the foreign policy of the country they have moved to. For example, immigrants to the USA from the middle east play a part in shaping American policy towards their home countries.

Monocultural, pluralist and multicultural change

Checkoway, an American community development scholar, is concerned with the implications of diversity for changing notions of democracy. He suggests that, 'If democracy is about the participation of the people, and if the people are becoming more diverse, then the future of democracy is inseparable from its diversity' (Checkoway 2007, 5).

He distinguishes three broad approaches to community change: 1) Monocultural change, 2) Pluralist change, and 3) Multicultural change. Here, for space reasons, I simplify his analysis. Monocultural change is based on the concept of a community whose people are relatively similar and are committed to a common purpose. In the USA, for example, immigrants are provided with information about the institutions of government, political parties and so on, which promote their assimilation and, according to this theory, they are able to join the 'melting pot', a powerful concept, or myth to some, in American social history.

Pluralist change is based on the idea that community is comprised of distinct groups, with their own social characterstics and interests. There are no single rules of order; there is no single melting pot. On the contrary, pluralist practice starts from how group members perceive themselves, how they perceive other groups and how they perceive other groups perceive them. Pluralist change contrasts with monocultural change in its emphasis on 'many' rather than 'one'. In Checkoway's presentation multicultural change – his third category – recognises the differences between diverse social and cultural groups but works to increase collaboration across group boundaries. It is neither monocultural nor pluralist, but rather conjoins difference and unity in the same effort. For some this concept may be better described as intercultural rather than multicultural change, and it is certain that this debate will continue.[8]

However, an argument about terminology may be a distraction. Checkoway develops a set of helpful suggestions relating to how to go about community change. It doesn't matter too much if some describe these approaches as multicultural change whilst others prefer the adjective intercultural, and yet others highlight transcultural processes. These strategies include: supporting everyday interactions, developing social and cultural competencies, finding common ground, building organisational capacity and so on. Some of these strategies feature in the work of the cities that we will refer to shortly. Here, however, I want to draw attention to Checkoway's simple conceptualisation, and to his suggestion that all three approaches to community change are often operating at one and the same time in a given locality.

A vital point needs to be highlighted. Amartya Sen (2006) notes, correctly, that an important distinction needs to be made between multiculturalism and, what might be called, 'plural monoculturalism' (Sen 2006, 156–60). Sen explains how plural monoculturalism is bad news:

> It is unfair to children who have not yet had much opportunity of reasoning and choice to be put into rigid boxes guided by one specific criterion of categorization, and to be told: "That is your identity and this is all you are going to get." (Sen 2006, 118)

Sen makes a passionate, and well informed, argument against 'faith-based' schools. The strategic argument he develops is that a 'federational' approach – the idea that there is a 'federation' of communities in Britain – is wholly misguided. We do not have, in Britain, a federation of communities, rather we have a collectivity of human beings living in Britain. This is a profound insight that needs to be projected into the centre of public policy debate.

Responding to urban diversity – insights from European cities

The European Union (EU) has a strong commitment to enhancing the economic, social and cultural benefits of migration in Europe.[9] As mentioned earlier it is the major cities that have led the way in developing successful approaches to migration, and the EUROCITIES network of cities has produced a range of useful materials for policy makers and practitioners. An important landmark in this context is the EUROCITIES *Charter on Integrating Cities* and the associated findings from the peer review project on diversity and equality in European cities (Maloney and Kirchberger 2010). City governments have, over the years, taken steps to respond to the changing needs of diverse population groups living within their boundaries. This can be quite a challenge because, as mentioned in the introduction to this chapter, dynamic diversity, involving the very rapid influx of large numbers of newcomers, has come close to overwhelming local public services in some cities. The EUROCITIES charter set out to develop a new strategy for accommodating diversity:

> The greatest challenge we face is polarisation and conflict between newcomers and established residents when integration fails.... Our vision of integration is one where all city residents can develop their full potential and have an equal chance of a life in safety and dignity.... This *Integrating Cities Charter* harnesses our duties and responsibilities as policy-makers, service providers, employers and buyers of goods and services to provide equal opportunities for all residents, to integrate

> migrants, and to embrace the diversity of the population that is a reality in our cities. (EUROCITIES 2010)

The study prepared to underpin this Charter documents three main strategies that progressive cities are using to promote diversity and equality: 1) Cities as policy makers and service providers, 2) Cities as employers, and 3) Cities as buyers of goods and services (Moloney and Kirchberger 2010). There are some overlaps between these categories but these headings can provide a helpful way of benchmarking performance in relation to diversity, and can stimulate fresh thinking in relation to what European cities call their 'local integration strategies' (meaning their efforts to embrace diversity, create equal opportunities and harness the benefits of a diverse population).

Cities as policy-makers and service providers

The first point to stress is that cities need to be committed to welcoming diversity and advancing equality. However, even when policy commitments are in place, there can be a gap between the commitment and the day-to-day practice carried out at street level. The EUROCITIES report has numerous suggestions on how to tackle this 'implementation gap'. These include: strong leadership and management systems to ensure consistency across local authority departments; requiring heads of departments to translate commitments into explicit guidelines for each staff position; consulting citizens with a migrant background; recording the experience of service users with a migrant background; adapting a variety of services – including education, housing, and employment support services – to the needs of populations with a migrant background; and introducing Equality Impact Assessments (EIAs) to ascertain compliance with anti-discrimination policy commitments.

The EUROCITIES report expresses some concerns about the preparedness of urban bureaucracies to respond to the diversity agenda:

> In some cities, the lack of a coherent system to register and treat complaints about discrimination is another challenge... cities do not always have the information that would allow them to assess how accessible their services are...This in turn means that the development of services cannot be based on a solid analysis of the needs. (Maloney and Kirchberger 2010, 10)

However, the main purpose of the report is to identify examples of promising innovation. It notes, for example, that the City of Amsterdam publishes a 'State of the City' report every two years. The data gathered to underpin these reports allows the city to understand if citizens with a migrant background have similar experiences to others. Cities across Europe, indeed across the world, are breaking new ground in how to advance policy and practice relating to urban diversity. For example, Sanchez de Madariaga and Roberts (2013) provide a helpful analysis of the way some cities are developing gender sensitive approaches to urban planning and management.

The language used to conceptualise and articulate these urban initiatives is, in itself, diverse. Some US cities have 'dismantling racism' initiatives (for example, Gainesville, Florida); Berlin has a 'Stadtteilmutter' (Neighbourhood Mothers) programme in neighbourhoods with a high migrant population to assist women with a migrant background understand the educational system; cities in the Gender Inclusive Cities Programme (GICP) (including Rosario, Argentina; New Delhi, India; Dar es Salaam, Tanzania; and Petrozavodsk, Russia) focus on 'women's safety and gender inclusion' (Viswanath 2013); and Rome has 'intercultural mediators' in schools in areas with a high percentage of people with a migrant background. The evidence suggests that it is unwise to search for a 'top down' solution or recipe for urban policy and service provision. It is essential to adopt a process of local social discovery and community engagement, and this is one of the reasons why local democracy and place-based leadership are so important.

Cities as employers

In addition to developing sound policies and responsive services cities can respond to multicultural challenges by using their power as employers. There are various elements to such a strategy. An important one in many multicultural cities involves attempting to employ a workforce that reflects the diversity of the population it serves. This is not only desirable from the point of view of social justice, it also enhances public service effectiveness as service providers are better placed to build up a good understanding of service user needs. The EUROCITIES report makes it clear that national legislation is critical in this area. In some countries cities are actively encouraged to achieve this 'mirror effect' between those working in and those being served by public services. In other countries the national legislation may actually prevent this – for example, some European countries do not allow non-EU nationals to be employed by public bodies. To advance the role of employment policy in responding to diversity city authorities adopt creative approaches to recruitment – for example, advertising positions in outlets read by ethnic minorities – and they also monitor the ethnic profile of their employees.

A second strand in relation to cities as employers is to increase the intercultural awareness of city administration staff. Efforts are taking place in some universities to develop courses relating to 'intercultural competencies' and many city halls have their own inhouse training programmes (Benavides and Hernandez 2007; Landis et al 2004). It is also the case that insights on cross-cultural communication drawn from the business world can be valuable (Maude 2011). However, there appears to be considerable uncertainty about the precise nature of intercultural skills and this has hindered the development of indicators that can be used in staff recruitment and promotion. Clearly it makes sense to draw in experts with a migrant background to provide intercultural training and development. Other steps can also be taken – for example, cities can record the experience of treatment of staff with a migrant background, build diversity and equality principles into job specifications, review the composition of interview panels, and encourage and support diversity role models.

Cities as buyers of goods and services

The third route to reform identified by the EUROCITIES report is to use diversity and equal opportunity principles in the public procurement process. This is an area of policy that is not highly developed and, in some countries, there may be legal obstacles to this approach. Cities pursuing this strategy assemble 'diversity information' about the firms they contract with or may contract with. Defenders of this approach argue that a city stands to gain benefits in economic growth and social cohesion if it can ensure that migrant-owned businesses have equal access to public contracts. For example, Leeds City Council in the UK examined the council's supply chain and its workforce in 2009, and the survey findings have helped the city assess how open and transparent its procurement practice is. The city has also developed a guide for prospective contractors to help them comply with their equality duties under the law and with the council's policy in this field. This strategy of advancing inclusion via procurement policy is more developed in the USA and Canada – and we explore the Toronto experience shortly.

Place-based leadership in the multicultural city

Having provided an overview of progressive practice in European cities I now want to set the scene for two Innovation Stories outlining inventive policy and practice in two other continents. The discussion in this chapter has made it clear that different countries are not embarking from the same departure point when they seek to address the challenges of our urban multicultural future. Some nations – and the USA is the classic example – have drawn on the strength of immigrants for centuries. Over the years, the awareness of the value of cultural diversity in urban America has become relatively advanced.[10] In other countries, history has resulted in a relatively homogenous society, and city leaders may have less experience of the challenges arising from immigration.

In the rest of this chapter I present two Innovation Stories providing insights drawn from two very different cities: Hamamatsu, Japan and Toronto, Canada. The aim here, as with all the Innovation Stories presented in this book, is to outline the role of place-based leadership in cities that are breaking new ground in their efforts to create inclusive cities. I have deliberately chosen cities operating in very different cultural settings because this can generate powerful lessons that, I hope, will be of interest to a wide range of cities.

Japan remains an ethnically and culturally homogenous society. However, urban leaders in cities like Hamamatsu are leading a process that could bring about innovation in national policy. The population of Japan is in an accelerating state of decline, and it can be argued that the country needs to welcome new immigrants if it is to prosper. However, this argument goes against the grain of the national political discourse.

As Yamanaka (2008) argues, the Japanese central government appears to be resistant to foreigners wishing to move permanently to Japan. However, she notes that, since the 1980s, Japan has received an influx of immigrant workers and that, by 2006, over two million foreigners, from many nationalities, had made Japan their home.[11] She concludes by suggesting that Japan has an opportunity to transform itself from being '... an homogenous and exclusionary nation into a heterogeneous and inclusive one, and in the contemporary world of global competition, that transformation is likely to be a beneficial one' (Yamanaka 2008, 194). In this context Innovation Story 14 offers a glimpse of what local leaders can do to advance ideas relating to multiculturalism, even in a country where the central government has very restrictive immigration controls.

INNOVATION STORY 14

Advancing intercultural understanding: the Hamamatsu approach

Aims

In the period since the 1990s Hamamatsu City has pursued a range of policies and practices designed to integrate foreign residents into the life of the city. The Japanese government has very restrictive immigration controls with the result that, even today, Japan is one of the most ethnically and culturally homogenous societies in the world. Local government leaders have taken a lead in promoting multicultural co-existence (*tabunka kyōsei*) and Hamamatsu has been particularly active in pursuing this agenda.

Despite the fact that Japan has a relatively low fertility rate and an ageing population, national policy relating to immigration is very restrictive. Historically, Japanese legislation has banned unskilled foreign labour. However, the Immigration Act 1990 resulted in a change – it allows third generation *Nikkeijin* (Japanese descendants) from Brazil, Peru and elsewhere to move to and work in Japan on the basis of their Japanese ethnicity – the *teijusha* visa. Hamamatsu City aims not just to develop effective policies and practices relating to newcomers to the city, but also to influence the national policy relating to foreign residents. By working with other localities in Japan the city aims to promote change in national migrant integration policy so that the country can adapt to the growing realities of an increasingly multicultural society.

Innovation Story outline

Hamamatsu City is an industrial city in central Japan that is well known for its manufacture of musical instruments, motorcycles and textiles. The city, which has a population of 821,000, is home to a number of company headquarters – for example, Yamaha Corporation and Suzuki Motor Co. The industries that have grown up in the city have high labour demands, and this is one reason why Hamamatsu City was one of the first to welcome foreign residents.

In 2010, Japan had 2.1 million registered foreigners, representing 1.7% of the total population. In Hamamatsu the number of registered foreigners in 2012 was 25,138, which is 3.1% of the city population. This is not a high proportion of foreign residents when compared with immigrant gateway cities in other countries, but in the Japanese context this is a sizable minority. For example, Hamamatsu is home to the largest Brazilian population in Japan and, to a lesser extent, a significant Peruvian population.

In Japan local authority involvement in international exchange has been growing since the 1970s, moving from an initial focus on cultural exchange programmes to a situation in which, by the 1990s, 'international policy' became an established feature of Japanese local government. The Japanese constitution guarantees local autonomy for local government, and this has provided space for place-based innovation to flourish.

Yasuyuki Kitawaki, who was the directly elected mayor of Hamamatsu City from 1999–2007, took the view that foreign residents should not be viewed as temporary guest-workers. Rather, in common with other cities experiencing a rapid growth in newcomers, he realised that many foreign residents wanted to stay and settle down. This would mean that existing policies and practices would need to be modified to adapt to changing circumstances.

In 2000 Hamamatsu City took on a leadership role by fostering the creation of a Council of Municipalities with a Large Migrant Population. In 2001 this Council brought together 13 cities in the Tokai and Northern Kanto regions – all of them localities experiencing common problems arising from a sudden influx of foreign newcomers. The Council adopted the 'Hamamatsu Declaration', which aspired to the creation of a new society consisting of indigenous peoples and newcomers – a society with a strong commitment to intercultural understanding and respect for each other's cultures. Mayor Kitawaki and his colleagues developed a range of policies and practices designed to value diversity.

One example of these place-based policies is provided by the creation of new consultative structures at the level of the city. A problem for local governments in Japan is that, while foreign residents have rights relating to access to public services (like education and social services), foreigners do not have any political rights. National legislation does not grant foreign residents the right to vote in local elections. Clearly, local authorities cannot violate national election law, but Hamamatsu City has been creative. Like other cities, for example Kawasaki, it has set up a Foreign Residents Council. This provides a way of gathering inputs from foreign residents into the governance of the city, and other Japanese cities have introduced innovations along these lines.

In 2007 Yasutomo Suzuki was elected mayor of Hamamatsu, and he continues to pursue a range of diversity initiatives. For example, in 2010, a Hamamatsu Foreign Resident Study

Support Centre was opened to provide language lessons in Japanese and in Portuguese (for Japanese school teachers and Japanese residents interested in supporting Brazilian families).

Mayor Suzuki has promoted international dialogue in a variety of ways, for example, through membership of the international organisation United Cities and Local Governments (UCLG). An outcome of the 2010 regional meeting of the Asia Pacific UCLG in Hamamatsu was a declaration promoting multiculturalism and diversity.

In 2012, Mayor Suzuki hosted the Asia-Europe Intercultural Cities Summit and this inspired the city to adopt the Hamamatsu Intercultural City Vision. The vision, which is guided by three 'c's – collaboration, creation and comfort – seeks 'An intercultural city built together where creativity and development continues based on mutual understanding and respect'. Progress on the vision is reported to the Hamamatsu City Intercultural Integration Promotion Council, the Foreign Residents Council and the public.

Leadership Lessons

- Elected local authorities are directly involved in dealing with the experience of the multicultural city and deserve to be listened to. Local leaders can articulate the value of creating inclusive cities and can provide central governments with valuable insights. They can be particularly effective if like-minded local authorities band together around a shared agenda.
- The Japanese constitution guarantees autonomy for elected local authorities and this means that locally elected leaders can try out new approaches, and break new ground.
- In Japan all municipalities have directly elected mayors who serve for four-year terms. This electoral arrangement provides political legitimacy to the mayors and enables them to pursue policies that might not, at first sight, be popular with the electorate as a whole. The model can underpin risk taking and enable elected mayors to challenge established patterns of thinking.
- In addition to foreign resident support being implemented by non-profit organisations (NPOs), such as Japanese language classes, foreign residents in the city have independently formed organisations to provide support for other foreign residents of the same nationality. Also, empowerment and partnership support for these NPOs takes place at the Hamamatsu Intercultural Centre and the Hamamatsu Foreign Study Support Centre.
- International exchange in relation to diversity management can be very productive for all involved.

Sources

Aiden H, S, 2011, Creating the 'Multicultural Coexistence' Society: Central and local government policies towards foreign residents in Japan, *Social Science Japan Journal* 14, 2, 213–231

Kitawaki, Y, 2010, A Japanese approach to municipal diversity management: The case of Hamamatsu City, http://www.coe.int/t/dg4/cultureheritage/culture/Cities/Publication/BookCoE12-Kitawaki.pdf

Sharpe, MO, 2010, When ethnic returnees are de facto guest-workers: What does the introduction of Latin American Japanese Nikkeijin (Japanese descendants) suggest for Japan's definition of nationality, citizenship, and immigration policy? *Policy and Society* 29, 357–69

Yamanaka, K, 2008, Japan as a country of immigration: Two decades after an influx of immigrant workers, in S Yamashita, M Minami, DW Haines, JS Eades (eds) *Transnational Migration in East Asia. Senri Ethnological Reports* 77, 187–196

Useful websites

Hamamatsu Intercultural City Vision 2013–2017: http://www.city.hamamatsu.shizuoka.jp/admin/policy/kokusai/icc_vision/iccvision_en.pdf

Hamamatsu City information website for foreign residents including some information about the Foreign Residents Council: http://www.city.hamamatsu.shizuoka.jp/hamaEng/index.html

Hamamastu Foreign Resident Support Centre: http://www.hi-hice.jp/u-toc/en/

Hamamatsu Foundation for International Communications and Exchange: http://www.hi-hice.jp/HICEeng/aboutus/business.html#1

In the introduction to this chapter I mentioned that most of the residents of Toronto are foreign-born. As noted in Chapter 2, in the discussion of dynamic diversity, Toronto is one of the most multicultural cities in the world. Lucia Lo calls Toronto 'Canada's premier immigrant gateway' (Lo 2008, 97). She notes that, in 2001, the Toronto Census Metropolitan Area (CMA) was home to 4.65 million people, including more than two million immigrants from 169 countries.[12] Her analysis shows how Toronto's immigrant population is concentrated in the central part of the metropolis but, as might be expected, it is not evenly distributed.

Lo shows how, during the last three or four decades, there have been significant changes in the composition of those migrating to Toronto, and she provides maps to show the settlement patterns of immigrants. Immigrant groups, such as the Chinese, Greeks, Italians and Portuguese, that arrived prior to the 1970s, tended to settle in the inner city. Lo (2008, 103) describes these areas, with a nice turn of phrase, as the 'smaller gateways within the larger gateway city'. In these ethnic neighbourhoods immigrants from a particular group tended to concentrate and create their own cultural and religious institutions, businesses and services. The spatial assimilation model predicts that, over time and with growing prosperity, these groups would move to the suburbs and become more spatially integrated with long-established residents. Lo outlines a more complex picture. In the period since the 1970s, affluent immigrants have tended to settle in the outer suburbs, and the more disadvantaged ones have moved into the inner suburbs. She concludes that the overall pattern of immigrant settlement in Toronto is one of increasing spatial separation, although she believes that residential segregation by race is less marked than in many US cities.

City leaders in Toronto celebrate the diversity of the city and the slogan, 'Diversity Our Strength', was adopted back in 1997. The city has a strong track record of addressing issues arising from diversity – issues relating to access, equity and human rights. Going back over a period of more than twenty years the city has established a reputation for progressive policy making and urban management. Kristin Good (2009) provides an excellent analysis of these developments and highlights the important, and largely unacknowledged work, of municipal officials, civil society leaders and others to integrate immigrants. Innovation Story 15 highlights some of the achievements of civic leaders as the city has moved towards the creation of an inclusive city. Rob Ford, a right wing politician, was elected as mayor of Toronto in 2010. In recent years he has sought to reverse many of the progressive policies pursued by David Miller, the previous mayor. Ford is, to put it mildly, a controversial figure. A court found that he violated the Ontario conflict of interest law and, following accusations that he was caught on film smoking crack cocaine, the political leadership of the city has attracted national and international publicity for all the wrong reasons. The Innovation Story presented here covers the period before the election of Mayor Ford.

INNOVATION STORY 15

Place-based leadership in the multicultural city: the Toronto experience

Aims

In the 1970s the Toronto Board of Education noted the increase in the diversity of school children and parents, and began to address the barriers faced by 'new' Canadians. A school community relations department was established, and school community advisers were appointed to open up the system to parents whose first language was not English. A decade or so later the municipal government of Toronto adopted a proactive role in responding to the needs of its increasingly diverse and rapidly growing immigrant population, and many bold innovations have resulted in the years since then.

According to the Canadian National Household Survey 2011 the population of the city was 2.6 million. Over half (51%) of those living in Toronto were born outside Canada, and the residents of the city come from 230 different ethnic groups. City leaders consider the diverse population to be a major asset, and this is reflected in the City of Toronto's motto, 'Diversity Our Strength' (adopted in 1998). However, the volume and diversity of immigrants arriving in the city also presents employment, social integration and communication challenges. This Innovation Story shows that the City of Toronto has pioneered a range of imaginative social, economic, cultural and political initiatives that embrace Canada's official policy of multiculturalism. The period covered in this presentation ends in 2010. In that year Rob Ford, a right wing politician, was elected as mayor of Toronto and he has chosen to adopt a divisive approach to urban leadership – one that is in danger of impairing the achievements of previous civic leaders in relation to equality and diversity.

Innovation Story outline

In Canada, the official position is that the federal government in conjunction with the provinces is responsible for immigration policy, but responsibility for multicultural policy is less clear. Municipalities, like the City of Toronto City, are charged with providing services in line with provincial policy. Toronto is not alone in being home to a large number of immigrant communities, and several Canadian cities have developed progressive policies in relation to diversity management. However, compared to other cities Toronto has pursued a particularly active and comprehensive approach to multiculturalism, going well beyond issues related to service provision.

In 2001, for example, Toronto was the first municipality to adopt an immigration and settlement policy framework to enable newcomers to fully participate economically, culturally, socially and politically in day-to-day city life. In April 2003 the City Council set out a bold Vision Statement on Access, Equity and Diversity. This committed the City to: '...implement positive changes in its workforce and communities to achieve access and equality of outcomes for all residents to create a harmonious environment free from discrimination, harassment and hate'.

The *Plan of Action for the Elimination of Racism and Discrimination* designed to accomplish the vision has seven strands: political leadership; advocacy; economic participation; public education and awareness; service delivery; building strong communities; and accountability. This plan is full of intelligent and practical recommendations on how to advance the cause of diversity management and community engagement. Furthermore, the city lobbied the province to pass the City of Toronto Act in 2007. This demonstrates the city's keenness to increase its autonomy to develop and implement policies tailored to meet the needs of Toronto's diverse population.

The business community and private foundations have played an important part in supporting organisations representing immigrants and ethnocultural minorities. For example, Alan Broadbent, a leading Toronto businessman and philanthropist, established the Maytree Foundation in 1982. The Foundation has influenced change in Toronto by providing grants to community organisations, offering management training to employees of community organisations, and developing community leaders in partnership with York University through its Leaders for Change programme.

The municipality has responded to these pressures from civil society striving to create a more inclusive city. The mayoral role is particularly interesting. Whilst the Canadian mayoral model of local government is traditionally described as a 'weak' form of leadership (using the conventional political science way of describing the balance of power between a mayor and a council), in Toronto we can identify a succession of mayors who have exercised strong leadership. For example, following the amalgamation of six neighbouring municipalities into Metropolitan Toronto, the new City Council, under the leadership of Mayor Mel Lastman (1998–2003), established a Task Force on Access and Equity.

The role of this Task Force was to harmonise the policies and structures of the pre-existing governments, and the work led to the creation of five Community Advisory Committees covering: Aboriginal affairs; disability issues; status of women; race and ethnic relations; and lesbian, gay, bisexual and transgendered issues. Many innovations stemmed from the creative work of these committees. For example, a Community Partnership and Investment Programme was set up to provide resources – advocacy, research, public engagement activities and so on – to address issues relating to race relations.

Highlights from Mayor David Miller's term in office (2003–2010) include the expansion of an employment mentoring scheme to professional immigrants, and the strengthening of multilingual access to city services. Today the city's web pages can be browsed in more than 51 languages and the City's 311 information service is offered in 180 languages. For more than a decade now the City has provided an annual diversity report card based on identified indicators of performance relating to access, equity and diversity.

Dating back to the late 1970s Toronto City Council has worked with community leaders to pioneer initiatives to systematically address issues concerning equity, access, racism, and discrimination in relation to its diverse communities. Leading on such initiatives for the Council today is the Equity, Diversity and Human Rights division (EDHR), formerly the Diversity Management and Community Engagement Unit (DMCEU). The EDHR division is centrally located in the City Manager's office, and is responsible for ensuring that the City's services, programmes and policies are responsive to the needs of Toronto's diverse communities.

Ceta Ramkhalawansingh, Manager of the DMCEU until 2010, draws attention to four features of the Toronto approach: comprehensive, integrated, collaborative and having an advocating role.[1] A striking feature of the Toronto approach is the strong commitment to annual monitoring and auditing. This process holds various stakeholders to account and helps to integrate anti-racist, non-discriminatory, equity and accessibility policies and programmes across a wide range of services. More recently (2009), a multi-sectoral Roundtable on Access and Equity, has developed an Equity Lens to assess policy and practice. The Equity Lens, which incorporates an Equity Impact Assessment, is used by the City Council in policy development and implementation to identify and remove barriers and reinforce good practices across council services.

The City Council has been proactive in commissioning research to inform policy development. The 2003 Action Plan referred to above, originated from a piece of research commissioned by the Council from one of the city's academic institutions. In addition, Toronto is fortunate to house the Centre of Excellence in Research on Immigration and Settlement (CERIS). This is part of a project, the Metropolis Project, funded by the federal government to foster collaboration between academics and not-for-profit agencies. The work of CERIS provides an extensive evidence base upon which to develop policy. In addition, the centre has been instrumental in fostering and maintaining strong networks between community stakeholders.

Leadership lessons

- The School Board, or Education Committee, of a city can play a vital role in responding to the needs of diverse communities. In Toronto it was the School Board that led the way on showing how municipal programmes needed to adapt.
- Business leaders and private foundations, like the Maytree Foundation, can make a major contribution by supporting community based organisations and developing the knowledge and skills of community leaders.
- The City of Toronto took advantage of the absence of direction from higher levels of government, regarding immigration settlement and integration issues, to develop its own approach to pursuing its vision of an inclusive city strengthened through its diversity. Civic leaders can claim political space for progressive policy making.
- Directly elected mayors, by working with the City Council and other agencies, can set a bold and positive tone relating the value of diversity in a city.
- Drawing community-based leaders into the policy making process, via Task Forces and various consultation mechanisms, has helped to create a multi-sectoral alliance committed to advancing equity in the City (including local activists and academic institutions).
- Locating the Equity, Diversity and Human Rights (EDHR) division at the heart of the municipal organisation and providing it with adequate resources gives the diversity agenda visibility and prominence.
- Regular annual monitoring of progress in reaching diversity objectives and standards provides an excellent way of holding stakeholders to account.

Sources

The City of Toronto Office of Equity, Diversity and Human Rights: http://www.toronto.ca/diversity

Tossutti, L, 2012, Municipal roles in immigrant settlement, integration and cultural diversity, *Canadian Journal of Political Science* 45, 3, 607–633

Good, K, 2009, *Municipalities and multiculturalism. The politics of immigration in Toronto and Vancouver*, Toronto: University of Toronto Press

Ramkhalawansingh, C, 2012, Multiculturalism by other names: Sketching four decades of evolving practice in Toronto, *Canadian Journal for Social Research/Revue Canadienne de Recherche Sociale* 2, 1, 77–83

Endnotes

[1] Presentation by Ceta Ramkhalawansingh on 'Workforce planning and diversity in the workplace' to a Conference on *Towards a Representative Bureaucracy*, Zeppelin University, Friedrichshafen, Germany, 1–3 July 2010.

Conclusions

In this chapter I have provided an overview of current debates about equal opportunities and diversity in modern society. Clearly international bodies, notably the United Nations, and nation states play a critical role in advancing the cause of equal opportunities – with the 1948 Universal Declaration of Human Rights providing crucial underpinning for public policy across the world. My focus in this chapter has not, however, been on the international and national laws designed to counter discrimination and advance the cause of equality. While I have referred to this broader context, my main aim has been to signal that city, or place-based, leadership has a critical role to play in advancing social justice and fairness in the city.

This is because intercultural relations between people with different backgrounds and beliefs are advanced, or set back, by lived experience at the very local level. It is the sites of everyday encounter, often in the city, that really matter. In Chapter 1 I explained how central governments tend to 'see like a state' – this produces 'silo-based' knowledge that is designed to assist top down government. This approach leads, in many countries, to a national discourse relating to immigration and equal opportunities that lacks sophistication. Public debate often fails to draw on the experience of local government managers and local activists and, as a result, neglects the contribution that place-based leadership can make. Luckily, cities themselves are not sitting around waiting for national guidance on how to advance equality and promote prosperity. Changes in society, including the rapid movements of peoples across international frontiers, mean that cities, and particularly immigrant gateway cities, are in the front line in relation to diversity management and the creation of the just city. I have attempted to convey something of what this involves in this chapter.

Some readers may be disappointed with the coverage of the various dimensions of diversity. Where is the detailed discussion of the lived experiences of disabled people? How come LGBT groups only get a brief mention? What about Islamophobia, and the growing urban obsession with security and surveillance? And how come issues that concern women and girls, travellers, and indigenous peoples are not given more attention? These are all legitimate criticisms. My defence, and I alluded to this in the introduction to the chapter, is that I have chosen to focus on cultural and ethnic diversity for two reasons. First, because of the impact of globalisation and the upsurge in urban migration I described in Chapter 2, the governance of the multicultural city is now a massively important public policy challenge – and it seems clear that many cities see this as a very high priority. Second, I hope that the discussion of equal opportunities and diversity, presented in this chapter, will stimulate fresh thinking in relation to the broader challenge of the governance of difference. The focus in this chapter has been on urban migration and cultural diversity but, when we 'see like a city', it is clear that inventive approaches to meeting the needs of newcomers can stimulate innovation in how to reach other groups who experience processes of social exclusion.[13]

In closing this chapter I make three points. First, a key theme to emerge from this discussion is that local leadership matters – it can promote community capacity-building to advance the cause of equal opportunities. By this I mean promoting the ability of local people to address problems, generate new resources of energy and commitment, and accomplish real change in their communities. The two Innovation Stories presented in this chapter – on Hamamatsu and Toronto – are both inspiring. Here we find place-based leaders, not just elected politicians but also committed public servants and community activists and campaigners, breaking new ground in how to create the inclusive city. Their efforts are to be admired. But, more important, they are not alone. Cities across the world are leading the way in creating intercultural cities.

Second, as civic leaders work to advance the cause of equal opportunities and inclusion, concepts developed by urban scholars can be useful. In this chapter I have highlighted ideas presented by Harm De Blij and Barry Checkoway. De Blij (2009) distinguishes 'locals, globals, and mobals' and reminds us that they all have a part to play in the creation of the inclusive city. Checkoway (2007) develops a number of very practical suggestions on how to bring about multicultural change in the modern city – his ideas on how to frame challenges are helpful as well as his emphasis on the importance of developing intercultural competencies. He notes how democratic societies need both to recognise differences and build bridges across cultural boundaries. In addition, I would like to draw attention to an intriguing analysis of 'why we hate' by Jack Levin and Gordana Rabrenovic. These American sociologists, who have studied hate and prejudice in many countries, suggest that leadership can play a critical role in shaping a culture of tolerance and understanding (Levin and Rabrenovic 2004, 205- 12).

Finally, as so much of the debate about equal opportunity and diversity is influenced by perceptions, it is helpful to draw attention to the insightful analysis provided by the art critic John Berger in his revolutionary book, *Ways of Seeing* (Berger 1972). In a short television series broadcast by the BBC in 1972, and in his accompanying book, Berger shows how what we see and experience is always influenced by what we know or believe. His analysis concerns painting and art criticism. But his refreshing and accessible approach to how we see the world around us is relevant to the debate about equality and diversity. Do we see diversity as an undesirable threat to our sense of identity? Or can diversity be welcomed as a source of new possibilities? Berger invites us to bring a critical eye to what we see and experience – and encourages us to think more deeply about what is before us.

Part 4
Lesson drawing: Insights and international learning

CHAPTER 11

From smart cities to wise cities

What we urgently need today is a more inclusive view of what it means to be a scholar – a recognition that knowledge is acquired through research, through synthesis, through practice, and through teaching
Ernest L. Boyer, *Scholarship Reconsidered*, 1990

Introduction

Digital enthusiasts argue that smart cities are a panacea. They claim that the current revolution in communication technologies will transform cities in the 21st Century in the way that electricity changed them in the last. For sceptics these claims are frothy hype. Many will argue that somewhere in between these extremes there is an emerging consensus. This consensus claims that advances in information and communication technologies (ICT) are ushering in a new era in which pervasive electronic connections are making cities more liveable and more democratic. In this chapter I want to question this consensus. I do this not to be contrary for the sake of it, but because the evidence that smartness is building more inclusive cities is fragile.

I am not here arguing against the imaginative use ICT in modern city management. Indeed, I have already shown that new technology, when deployed by well-trained and talented staff, can boost the quality of public services. Innovation Story 3 in Chapter 6 provides a good practical example to support my argument. It illustrates how new technology can be used not only to enhance access to services, but also to bring about significant improvements in the internal management of City Hall departments. In this case we can see how the Chicago 311 and Open311 service provides an astonishing level of service responsiveness to citizens. As in many other US cities, any resident can dial 311 at any time and receive immediate assistance. This level of responsiveness would be impossible in the absence of ICT to provide up to the minute information to front line staff, and to route requests electronically to the relevant departments.

However, having super-responsive services is not enough to create an inclusive city. Smart technology, including recent advances in social media, can enhance the performance of public services, but a troubling question remains: Are these technologies strengthening local democracy and giving voice to the have-nots in society?

The argument in this chapter is presented in five steps. First, I try to unpack what being a 'smart' city might mean. Because the word smart is now used in a fairly indiscriminate way this task is more difficult than might, at first, appear. I will suggest that there are, in fact, at least three sets of ideas competing for attention in the ongoing smart cities discourse, and I label these: 1) Digital cities, 2) Green cities and 3) Learning cities. It may be possible to unite these perspectives around a common policy agenda in a given city. But this is likely to be challenging because core values underpinning the different approaches appear to be in tension.

In the following section I identify five digital danger zones, or questions, for the digital enthusiasts to consider. It may be that these five concerns can be addressed through super-enlightened ICT strategies, but I have my doubts. In the third section I therefore outline a new way forward. The argument presented here is that we should attempt to move *beyond* the limiting confines of the smart city debate to develop a deeper understanding of the nature of public learning and democratic innovation in the modern city. Some of the most successful cities in the world may not use this language, but I believe that they have already embraced the idea of what I call the **wise city**. By this I mean a city in which values relating to justice, democracy and care of the natural environment guide the creation of the inclusive city. Leaders of wise cities recognise the value of new technology as a servant of public purpose, nothing more. They know that advocating being 'smart' is vacuous.

In the fourth step in the narrative I turn to examine the role of the university in the city. In some ways universities are the sleeping giants of place-based leadership. However, as the nature of modern scholarship comes to be redefined, we can see that a growing number of universities now recognise that active engagement with the politics of place has enormous two-way benefits. The intellectual and other resources of the university can be deployed to help improve the local quality of life, and engagement with the city can boost the quality of academic endeavour. In order to illustrate the value of 'engaged scholarship' I present two Innovation Stories. Innovation Story 16 explains how Portland State University is working closely with the City Council and other partners to make Portland into an even more sustainable and more inclusive city. Innovation Story 17 discusses the role of the CEPT University in working with the Ahmedabad Municipal Corporation to plan and design the Ahmedabad Bus Rapid Transit system.

Unpacking smart city rhetoric

The literature on smart cities has mushroomed in recent years, and the adjective 'smart' is now used widely in public debates about city government, urban development, and modern architecture. Enthusiasts claim that we will all be better off if we live in smart cities, with smart buildings and smart places to loiter in and use the free Wi-Fi. But will we? What does this increasingly popular term actually mean? Does being 'smart' represent a breakthrough in how to understand and improve the city? Or is it just another spray-on term that has already been so misused that it is now devoid of meaning? More specifically, for the purposes of this book, can smart thinking and practice advance the cause of creating the inclusive city?

The adjective 'smart' is, it must be said, rather beguiling. Unfortunately this may, in itself, be problematic. It has the troubling effect of implying that doubters must be in favour of ignorance. It is, then, worth sparing a moment to consider what smart means. In English the word has, in fact, several meanings, not all of them flattering. On the one hand, a smart person may be seen as clever and well groomed, even stylish. But they might also be seen as slick and shallow, even obnoxious. For example, the phrase smart alec, or smart ass, refers to someone who displays ostentatious or smug cleverness. Today the phrase smart city, possible because it is rarely defined clearly, continues to divide opinion. Some believe it can provide profound insights on how to govern cities. Others take the view that it is a superficial marketing concept designed to promote the interests of the major ICT companies, who have a vested interest in selling their products and capturing personal data about citizens. The argument becomes even more complicated when the word is translated into other languages.

Lena Hatzelhoffer and her colleagues provide an introduction to the notion of the smart city in practice (Hatzelhoffer et al 2012). Their analysis suggests that the phrase smart city came into common usage in the 1990s. At that time, there was considerable excitement about the potential for using ICT to improve urban planning and city management. In those days a city could be considered smart if it actively used information technologies to improve the living and working conditions of people living in the city and the city region. With the growth of new electronic devices – PCs and tablets, simple mobile phones and high-performance smartphones – and the expansion of high-speed landline and mobile connections the availability of ICT services has become virtually ubiquitous. This expansion of availability, plus the wider growth of the digital economy, has led many city leaders to believe that improved use of ICT is essential to enhance their city's economic competitive position.

However, over the years, this focus on technical capacities has come to be questioned. Various writers have argued that concentrating on the availability and quality of ICT was misguided, and that a city should be regarded as smart only if the urban society had learned to be adaptable and innovative. Mark Deakin and Husam Al Waer (2012) assemble a collection of essays discussing this shift in thinking. Their book focuses on the role of ICT, but, like other writers, for example, Townsend (2013), these authors suggest that it is the integration of digital technologies into everyday social life that is the most significant development. The claim is made that linking the two – the technical and the social – can create opportunities for more intelligent decision-making in cities by government and governed. Clay Shirky (2008, 196) heralded this approach when he argued that cyberspace is an out of date concept:

> The internet augments real-world social life rather than providing an alternative to it. Instead of becoming a separate cyberspace, our electronic networks are becoming deeply embedded in real life.

At risk of oversimplification we can suggest that ICT-oriented approaches to smart cities have evolved through three main phases: 1) Provision of online information via city websites (1990s), 2) City portals for online information services and a growing number of transactions (2000s), and 3) Open data and social media initiatives creating new opportunities for government and citizens to work together to use ICT to meet community needs (2010s). Part of this most recent phase involves the use of, forgive the jargon, 'Big Data', meaning the capture, analysis, mapping and interpretation of truly vast amounts of data about people and their behaviour. Initiatives to take advantage of Big Data are now proliferating. For example, in 2013 the UK government launched a Future Cities Catapult, meaning a well-funded organisation set up to help UK cities become smarter and more forward thinking.[1]

So far, so good. However, and this undoubtedly causes confusion, there are at least two other discourses vying for space in smart cities thinking. First, some commentators and practitioners use the term smart city to describe what many would prefer to call a sustainable city. For example, the 'smart growth' movement has gained support in North America in recent years. As discussed in Chapter 8, smart growth involves the creation of more compact and integrated urban development. It encourages increases in urban density, mixed-use development, a variety of housing types, transit-oriented development, protection of open space and so on. It is, of course, perfectly possible to pursue a smart growth strategy without bothering about ICT at all. Indeed, some radical, green activists prefer to remain off-grid arguing that the hardware, cables, copper wire, telecommunications masts and all the rest of the technical equipment needed to support digital cities means that they cannot possibly be regarded as eco-friendly. However, some cities are attempting to integrate digital and green initiatives. In these cities the use of the word smart signals an effort to blend an eco-friendly approach to urban development with a commitment to making intelligent use of ICT.[2]

Another major theme concerns what we might describe as the learning city. Tim Campbell (2012) has provided a helpful discussion of this perspective. The subtitle of his book headlines his focus of interest: 'How cities network, learn and innovate'. He is critical of what might be called traditional, smart cities thinking:

> Building up a knowledge economy of highly educated talent, high-tech industries and pervasive electronic connections are only the trappings of smartness and cannot guarantee the outcomes that policy makers hope to achieve. Though global talent and seamless connections are important, they can also amount to the dressing of a pauper in prince's clothing. (Campbell 2012, 5)

Campbell argues that useful learning takes place in the heads of people who care about and take action to affect the cities where they live. We will return to his argument when we discuss international lesson drawing in Chapter 12. Here we can note that Cambell's analysis is consistent with the argument put forward by

Zachary Neal (2013) who discusses the connected city. Neal draws on a wide literature to present a thoughtful analysis of the role of networks across a variety of geographical scales. He highlights the role of networks of communication between cities as well as within them.

This discussion suggests that the term 'smart cities' is both confusing and contested. Figure 11.1 provides a simple diagram to highlight the way three overlapping perspectives are contributing to the current smart cities discourse. Some civic leaders want their cities to be digital cities, others prioritise smart growth and picture their cities as green pioneers, yet others prefer to focus on building rich networks to facilitate learning and innovation. The diagram shows how a given city may work to advance two, or even all three, agendas. I hope that this effort to draw distinctions between different approaches will help city leaders identify strategic choices.

Figure 11.1: Perspectives on smart cities

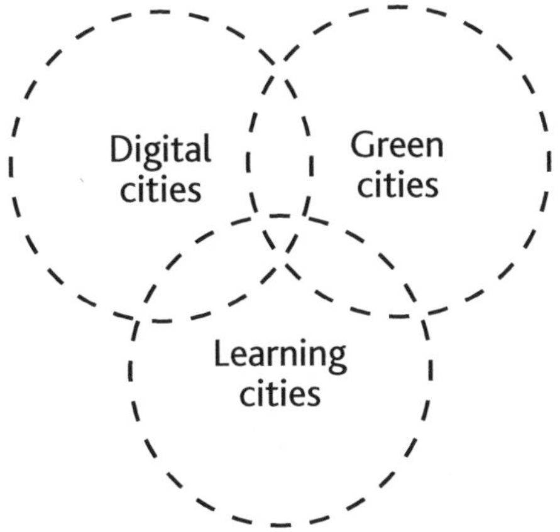

Source: Author

Digital danger zones

Having outlined the contours of the discourse about smart cities I want, in this section, to raise a few doubts about ICT-driven approaches to smart cities. Figure 11.1 could be taken to imply that the three perspectives on smart cities carry equal weight. This is not intended and this is certainly not the case. The dominant voices in the smart cities discourse are the digital enthusiasts – the big ICT companies, who have a clear vested interest, but also the civic hackers discussed by Townsend (2013). There is not space here to develop a full critique but, since the vast bulk of writing on digital cities is self-congratulatory in tone, it serves a useful purpose to raise a few concerns. My aim here is to encourage those involved in ICT-based approaches to smart cities to consider whether or not their activities are leading to the creation of more inclusive cities. Is digital power reducing inequality in the city? Are excluded voices now listened to in a way that did not happen before? If the answer to these questions is 'No', can ICT be employed to tackle social exclusion and bolster citizen power? I raise five points for consideration.

First, it is reasonable to ask: Where is the evidence that ICT is enhancing the quality of urban democracy? We discussed e-democracy in Chapter 7 and noted that, while there is evidence to suggest that e-government is delivering benefits – for example improved public access to services – solid findings relating to the way e-democracy is strengthening citizen empowerment appear to be thin on the ground. It is right to celebrate ICT advances, like the electronic citizen cards introduced into cities like Zaragoza and Gijon in Spain. In these cities, with some variation in the details, a single citizen electronic card enables the owner to pay for public transport, unlock a bike-share, borrow a book from a library, access Wi-Fi, and pay for things like entry to a swimming pool and car parking. This is prize-winning, high quality e-government (or service delivery). But do these electronic cards enhance citizen power in relation to the governance of their city? In Chapter 7 I set out a ladder of citizen empowerment – see Figure 7.5. Those involved in the development of ICT strategies for cities might want to consider afresh how to develop innovations that move citizen power much higher up the ladder.

Second, we have the acute problem of the digital divide. On the whole poor families and communities suffer a double, digital disadvantage. They tend to have poor access to the Internet and, in addition, they tend to lack the skills needed to make use of online resources (Mossberger et al 2008). Previous chapters have suggested that the inclusive city needs to be a democratic city in which all residents are able to participate fully in society. It follows that a useful test of 'smartness' concerns the degree to which any given innovation furthers this democratic end. The creative development of ICT to enhance the quality of life in the city for all residents is full of possibilities. But, unfortunately, the evidence suggests that online services and processes are bolstering inequality. It follows that a central question for the smart city debate is: 'Smart for whom?' Answering 'Everyone' is not a convincing response given that we know that many smart-city efforts are failing to tackle social exclusion.

A third concern relates to the fact that there is now a substantial body of evidence suggesting that digital empowerment is a myth (Hindman 2009). This is because there are, not surprisingly, powerful hierarchies shaping a medium that continues to be celebrated for its openness:

> This hierarchy is structural, woven into the hyperlinks that make up the Web; it is economic, in the dominance of companies like Google, Yahoo! and Microsoft; and it is social, in the small group of white, highly educated, male professionals who are vastly overrepresented in online opinion. (Hindman 2009, 18–19)

In an incisive analysis Hindman shows how the Internet has served to level some existing political inequalities, but it has also created new ones. He points out, in line with the argument I presented in Chapter 7, that true participation requires citizens to engage in direct discussion with other citizens. But ICT is not doing too well on this score. His research shows that, whilst more citizens than ever before are contributing views via the Internet, this does little to enhance democracy if hardly anyone reads these outpourings:

> From the perspective of mass politics, we care most not about who posts but about what gets read – and there are plenty of formal and informal barriers that hinder ordinary citizens' ability to reach an audience. Most online content receives no link, attracts no eyeballs, and has minimal political relevance. (Hindman 2009, 18)

The fourth problem, and this was identified by Hatzelhoffer et al (2012, 204–5), is that many people are sceptical about the benefits of ICT. Disadvantages of ICT identified by respondents in their study of smart city policies in Friedrichshafen, Germany include: 1) It leads to less physical exercise, 2) It competes with face-to-face social and cultural activities, 3) The information provided is often perceived as false, 4) Use of the Internet can become addictive, 5) The cost of Internet and mobile usage is very high, and 6) There is too much advertising and spam. It is possible that some of these complaints are not that well founded, but it would be foolish to believe that they can all be dismissed out of hand.

A fifth concern relates to the invasion of privacy. The large scale sensing of data about people creates profound civil liberty concerns. The arrival of Big Data in urban management only amplifies this worry. Enthusiasts for the use of Big Data claim that sophisticated data gathering tools can provide useful information that will enable governments to advance the public good (Williams 2013). Some advocates go further and claim that: 'Big data is poised to reshape the way we live, work and think... The ground beneath our feet is shifting... Soon big data will be able to tell whether we're falling in love' (Mayer-Schonberger and Cukier 2013 192–4). These writers betray an astonishing lack of awareness of the potential downsides of Big Data. Carried away by the possibilities of manipulating truly vast amounts of information about us, these believers fail to provide a forensic analysis of the safeguards that need to be introduced to protect our rights to privacy. To be fair, the authors just cited do refer to the risks associated with Big Data, and note that there is a 'dark side of big data' (Mayer-Schonberger and Cukier 2013, 170). But, they fail to provide any clear and actionable suggestions on how to stop the dark side taking over. Vague suggestions about holding data users to account do not match the dangers we face.

What is to prevent governments from misusing the rich resources provided by smart city information systems? In Chapter 4 I referred to the insidious growth of a kind of urban militarism. Stephen Graham (2010) documents the growth in the use of CCTV and electronic surveillance in many cities in recent years, and he draws attention to the erosion of civil liberties. In the past concerns about the stealthy, secret construction of an electronic police state in countries like the USA and the UK were often dismissed as alarmist. Not any more.

Edward Snowden, a former contractor to the US National Security Agency (NSA), has shown that these concerns are well founded. Following his decision to release details of the NSA mass surveillance programmes to responsible newspapers in June 2013, we now know of the existence of PRISM. This is an American, clandestine data-gathering system that has been assembling enormous amounts of data about the civilian population in the USA since 2007. This is a frightening revelation, one that has shocked US citizens and been drawn to the attention of the judiciary. On 16 December 2013 Judge Richard Leon declared that this mass collection of so-called metadata probably violates the fourth amendment of the US Constitution, which bans unreasonable search and seizure. Leon noted the utter lack of evidence that a terrorist attack has ever been prevented because searching the NSA database was faster than other investigative tactics.

In a stinging judgement he described the NSA data gathering technology as 'almost Orwellian' and granted a preliminary injunction to plaintiffs Larry Klayman and Charles Strange, because he believed that a constitutional challenge was likely to be successful.[3] The public pressure to rein in NSA use of mass surveillance was mounting and President Obama was forced to act. On 17 January 2014 he announced important reforms, although civil liberty activists regard his statement as only a first step to restoring privacy. The Snowden revelations have stunned Americans, but citizens living in countries that share information with the NSA are equally shocked. A key question for ICT-driven smart cities initiatives that emerges from this discussion of privacy concerns is: How can smart city enthusiasts guarantee that governments will not misuse the innovative data systems they create?

Moving beyond the smart city

The discussion presented above is not an attempt to undermine the value of smart cities thinking or to discourage smart cities experiments. Rather I am hoping to encourage a more critical approach to the subject and, in particular, to stimulate a more penetrating consideration of the question: Who is gaining? The distributional effects of smart cities policies are not being given the attention they deserve. Unfortunately much of the literature on smart cities is dominated by case studies that appear to be little more than place-marketing literature, almost in the category of 'Look how good we are'. Worse than that, some academic studies are overly technical in emphasis, and fail to examine how smart cities policies relate to the politics of power in the cities concerned. A current example is provided by a major European Union funded study of 'Smart cities of the future'. The international team of eight scholars carrying out this massive international study offer the evidence-free statement that:

> Smart cities are equitable cities.... We believe that... the sort of infrastructure, expertise and data that will characterise the smart city will enable equity to be easily established and such cities to improve the quality of urban life. (Batty et al 2012, 516)

Claims of this kind are deeply troubling. The suggestion that smart cities are equitable is, of course, pure assertion, and the belief that equity is 'easily established' in smart cities betrays political naivety. Granted, it is possible to imagine a future in which ICT makes a contribution to the development of inclusive, democratic cities. However, I have drawn attention to some of the significant challenges that ICT-focussed efforts at urban innovation will need to address if such aspirations are to be realised. Scholarship on digital cities that fails to deal head-on with the five danger zones I have outlined can be expected to produce findings that are of limited value.

In the rest of this chapter I want to make a case for developing a deeper understanding of the nature of public learning and democratic innovation in the modern city. I will argue that we need to go well beyond the confines of the limiting smart city discourse. Spectacular advances in ICT, including revolutions in social media and crowd-sourcing, are not going save our cities. It is the exercise of judgement that matters, not technological advance. It is possible that innovations in ICT can contribute to making cities more inclusive, but only if these developments are driven by public purpose. In democratic societies such public purpose must stem from democratic deliberation, and I reviewed various ways of enhancing urban democracy in Chapter 7.

In previous chapters I have suggested that place-based leaders are central to the effective performance of democratic cities and that they can promote the development of inclusive cities. Such leaders articulate public purpose and exercise well-informed, value-based judgements in their decision-making to advance it. This line of reasoning leads me to suggest that, when it comes to civic leadership, the focus of attention should be on wisdom, not smartness. Put bluntly, being smart is not going to cut it. It is not enough to be clever, quick, ingenious, nor will it help even if Big Data is superseded by Even Bigger Data. Acquiring zettabytes, or even yottabytes, of data about human and technical interactions in cities is not going to enhance the quality of life in cities in the absence of judgement.

In Chapter 5 I discussed the nature of leadership in modern societies and, in particular, I suggested that leadership requires far more than intellectual dexterity. In that chapter, following Keohane (2010), I suggested that leadership involves broadening your perspective to take account of the views of others affected by your judgements. It involves making an emotional connection – and the **New Civic Leadership** I outlined in that chapter is, of course, values based. I now want to suggest that wisdom lies at the heart of this **New Civic Leadership**. What is wisdom? The simple answer is the judicious application of knowledge. The key word here is judicious. Knowing a vast amount is *not*, in the end, what matters – it is being able to exercise judgement that is critical. Sir Geoffrey Vickers, one of the best writers on the art of judgement, has written extensively about the application of knowledge in decision-making (Vickers 1965). He offers profound insights and returns, time and again, to the nature of values in the policy process:

> Learning what to want is the most radical, the most painful and the most creative art of life. (Vickers 1970, 76)

Sir Geoffrey signals an important message for modern civic leaders. Forget about data for a moment and ask: What kind of city do we want to create? The idea of the city as an advanced learning system offers potential. Such a city draws insights from a range of forms of knowledge, not just data that can be captured by electronic surveillance and presented on a computer screen. Information about how people *feel* about living in the city is of critical importance. This more rounded social knowledge is in people's heads.

In Chapter 1 I suggested that it is helpful to make a distinction between 'explicit' knowledge (sometimes described as formal, scientific or professional knowledge) and 'tacit' knowledge (meaning knowledge stemming from personal and social experience). Tacit knowledge is often undervalued in public policy making and this is clearly misguided. Tacit knowledge embodies understanding of what it is like to live in the city and it embraces emotions – it includes, as discussed in Chapter 3, an appreciation of loyalty and civic identity. Successful civic leadership pays attention to how the city feels. Wise city leaders build their understanding by drawing on both kinds of knowledge. The soft evidence derived from tacit knowledge is blended with the hard evidence proffered by explicit knowledge.

Redefining scholarship

As part of this presentation I want to suggest that universities are a neglected resource in many cities. Reflecting their origins many fine universities are located slap bang in the middle of their city and, simply by virtue of their presence, they have an impact on urban and regional developments as well as the local civic culture (Goddard and Vallance 2013). However, many universities do not see themselves as key players in improving the quality of life in their city. On the contrary, the traditional university still tends to view its campus as being a space that is, somehow, detached from the surrounding area – a separate reflective place devoted to learning, research and study. Increasingly, and we will return to this theme shortly, universities are recognising that this attempt to cut academic life off from society not only creates town-gown tensions, but also misses significant opportunities for student learning, practice-oriented research and innovation in theory building. The disconnected campus is an outdated view of the role of the modern university.

In Chapter 1 I introduced the idea of engaged scholarship, a phrase used to describe a process in which the academic and civic cultures communicate with each other in a creative way. I defined engaged scholarship as the co-creation of new knowledge by scholars and practitioners working together in a shared process of discovery. For the purposes of this definition a practitioner is anyone who is not a scholar. Figure 1.2 illustrates how practice and academe are brought together in engaged scholarship. In some of the most innovative cities in the world universities see themselves as place-based leaders and play an active role in, for example, urban development (Perry and Wiewel 2005; Wiewel and Perry 2008). Later in this chapter I will present two Innovation Stories to illustrate this argument. First, however, we need to reflect on the changing nature of scholarship in the modern world.

In 1862 Abraham Lincoln signed into US law the famous Morrill Act. This heralded, not just a startling expansion of higher education in the US, but also a reframing of the very purpose of a university. The Act, later called the Land Grant College Act, provided grants of federal lands to the states for the creation of public universities and colleges. Using proceeds from the sale of the land these 'land-grant' universities were to provide for 'the liberal and practical education of the industrial classes in the several pursuits and professions of life'. This was a breath taking innovation that lead to the establishment in every state of a distinctively American kind of university, one that attempted to fuse scholarly inspiration with a strong commitment to practical application. Some 150 years later the US continues to benefit from the foresight shown by Representative Justin Smith Morrill and his colleagues as the vision he espoused was of an 'engaged university', not an ivory tower.

Ernest Boyer, in his insightful book *Scholarship Reconsidered* (1990), built on the land grant tradition to articulate a more rounded view of the nature of modern scholarship than the one that still prevails in many universities today. He felt that it was time:

> ... to move beyond the tired old "teaching versus research" debate and give the familiar and honorable term "scholarship" a broader, more capacious meaning, one that brings legitimacy to the full scope of academic work. (Boyer 1990, 16)

Boyer distinguishes four overlapping kinds of scholarship:

- The **scholarship of discovery** comes closest to what is meant when academics speak of research. It contributes not only to the stock of human knowledge but also to the intellectual climate of a college or university.
- The **scholarship of integration** gives meaning to isolated facts, putting them in perspective. It places discoveries into their larger scientific, social and political context. It is serious disciplined work that seeks to interpret, draw together, and bring new insights to bear on original research.
- The **scholarship of application** applies knowledge to consequential problems. Boyer does not see this as a one-way process in which knowledge

is first 'discovered' and then 'applied'. He stresses that new intellectual understandings can arise from the very act of application.
- The **scholarship of teaching** keeps the flame of scholarship alive by sharing knowledge not just with students in the lecture theatre or seminar room but also by disseminating insights and research findings in the public sphere.

Boyer stresses that what we urgently need today is a more inclusive view of what it means to be a scholar: '… a recognition that knowledge is acquired through research, through synthesis, through practice, and through teaching' (Boyer 1990, 24). In Figure 11.2 I provide a visual illustration of Ernest Boyer's taxonomy of scholarship. This shows that all four kinds of scholarship overlap one another.

Boyer argues that the interactions between the different kinds of scholarship enhance the performance of the whole. In effect Boyer presents a strong argument against the disengaged university. Indeed, according to Mathew Flinders (2013, 629), he offers a 'damning and far-reaching critique of the gradual withdrawal of academics from the public sphere'. Boyer's ideas had a significant impact on US higher education. Many universities took account of his analysis and revised their academic promotion and evaluation criteria to take account of his wider definition of scholarship.[4]

Figure 11.2: Enlarging the definition of scholarship

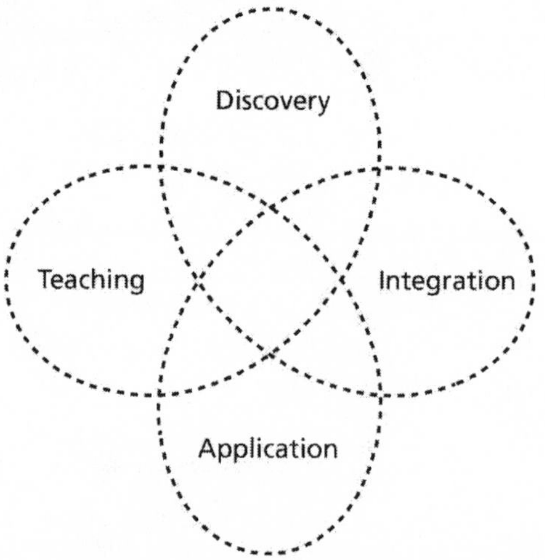

Source: Concepts (Boyer, 1990, pp 15-25) Diagram (Author)

The triangle of engaged scholarship

By building on Boyer's analysis, and my own experience of working in British and American universities, I have identified a 'triangle of engaged scholarship'

(Hambleton 2007b). In this model the familiar pillars of research and education, long established in the European tradition, are linked to a third pillar: policy and practice. This conceptualisation is shown in Figure 11.3. It is my contention that it is the *sides* of the triangle that hold out exciting possibilities for intellectual and practical advance. The triangle suggests that the talents and resources of a university can be conjoined in a creative way with the world of policy and practice to the benefit of all stakeholders. The Innovation Stories presented in this book provide examples of interaction on the left hand side of the triangle. In this case, the process involves researchers and practitioners co-creating plausible accounts of urban innovation. Turning to the right hand side of the triangle, well-managed student projects can benefit policy and practice in a city as well as enhance the learning experience of the students involved. Innovation Story 6 provides an example of this approach. In this case the settlement upgrading project in Langrug, South Africa was assisted by more than one student project. This approach is well established in American urban planning programmes – see, for example, the edited collection provided by Lorlene Hoyt (2013).[5] Along the bottom side of the triangle academics feed insights drawn from research into course content and they work with students to co-create new insights.

Figure 11.3: The triangle of engaged scholarship

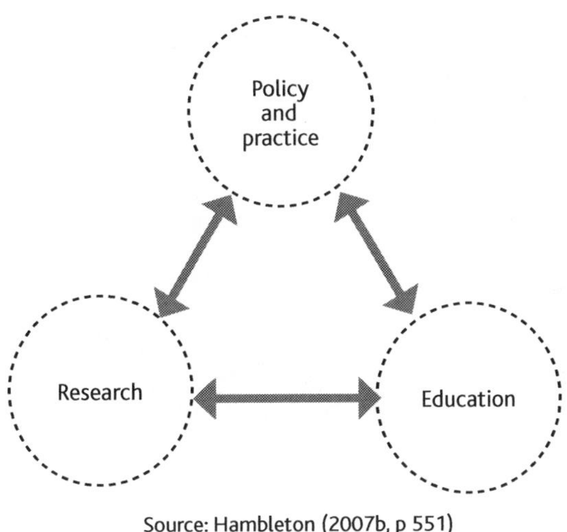

Source: Hambleton (2007b, p 551)

Ernest Boyer was a visionary thinker and he now has a growing number of followers. Certainly the notion of 'engaged scholarship' has flourished in recent years. This surge of interest in strengthening the societal relevance of universities can be seen in efforts to promote 'knowledge exchange' and university 'public engagement' in many countries. Many scholars across the world are breaking new ground in changing the relationships between their university and their city. Not all of them will use the language of 'engaged scholarship' but the significance of their efforts for the future of higher education is difficult to overestimate.

Because of the land grant tradition the culture of civic engagement is particularly well developed in many US public universities.[6] But, even in America, there is room for improvement. A study by the Pew Partnership notes that:

> Many colleges and universities articulate a commitment to the public good but too often fail to bear witness to that commitment intellectually, structurally, institutionally, or behaviorally. (Pew Partnership 2004, 2)

The same could be said of colleges and universities in just about any country. The Pew Partnership report presents evidence from the US of university innovations in civic engagement, and concludes that higher education has a vital role to play in helping to address national and community problems, and in preparing students for engaged, responsible citizenship.

It is encouraging to note that academic interest in civic, or public, engagement has grown in recent years. For example, in the UK, the Academy of Social Sciences has set out advice on how learned societies can become more active in knowledge exchange and public engagement (Benyon and David 2008). Moreover, a National Coordinating Centre for Public Engagement (NCCPE) was created in 2008 to help inspire and support universities to engage with the public.[7] Added to this, the Talloires Network is working hard to build up an international network of universities committed to public and civic engagement.[8]

This discussion of the changing nature of scholarship can be located within a wider conversation about the role and purpose of universities in modern times. Ronald Barnett (2011), in an imaginative exploration, asks: 'What is it to be a university?' He examines how the nature of being a university has unfolded over time – simply stated, from being a metaphysical university, to a research university and now an entrepreneurial university. He offers a robust critique of the latter, which he describes as a 'for-itself', competitive institution driven by neo-liberal patterns of thinking, one in which the collective academic community fades. Barnett then outlines various 'feasible utopias', meaning futures for universities that have a relatively realistic potential of actually happening. His favoured model is the 'ecological university' by which he means a university that is both authentic and responsible. This notion, which balances the tensions between the inner and the outer callings of the university, is in line with the scholarship of engagement that I have presented here:

> This is a university that takes seriously both the world's interconnectedness and the university's interconnectedness with the world. (Barnett 2011, 451)

John Brewer (2013) takes the view that social science can play a crucial role in the creation of such public-facing universities. He believes that the social sciences are under threat from, inter alia, external forces seeking to marketise higher education, and narrow thinking within the social scientific community. He argues for the development of a 'new public social science' and notes that:

> ... social science teaching and learning has civilizing, humanizing and cultural effects in addition to whatever use and price value the new public social science might have. (Brewer 2013, 169)

He notes, correctly, that university civic engagement is about much more than dissemination of research findings to different audiences. Rather, as I have argued here, it requires a reformulation of research and teaching activities in ways that can bring different publics into the process of discovering and applying new knowledge.

Universities as place-based leaders

In this chapter I have suggested that civic leaders and their advisers might find it helpful to move beyond notions of the smart city and consider ways of creating the wise city. Universities can, in my view, make a significant contribution to this process. The 'engaged university' is rooted in the locality and makes a respected contribution as a place-based leader. It puts time and resources into the cultivation of a local civic culture that welcomes study, analysis and public learning. It supports research on and for the city, values community development and fosters action-oriented student learning. A growing number of urban universities see themselves in this way. They have rethought the nature of modern scholarship, taking account of ideas like those put forward by Ernest Boyer (1990), and they give serious backing to the notion of 'engaged scholarship' in their recruitment and promotion procedures. I was fortunate to work in one such university – the University of Illinois at Chicago (UIC) – for a period.[9] In this instance the university as a whole is deeply committed to 'engaged scholarship' and this strategy is furthered through an initiative known as the Great Cities Commitment. Made by UIC in 1993 this commitment aims to promote urban research to improve the quality of life in Chicago and other cities around the world.

In the remainder of this chapter I present two Innovation Stories providing illustrations of the work of two very different urban universities: Portland State University, Oregon, USA and the CEPT University, Ahmedabad, India. I have chosen these two universities because they illuminate, in very different settings, what engaged scholarship can do. Moreover, they are both strongly committed to the creation of the kind of inclusive city I outlined in Chapter 1. One is operating in a highly developed country – the USA – while the other is making an important contribution in a developing country – India. It is helpful to juxtapose the experience of these two innovative universities not least because the stories show how the notion of 'engaged scholarship' makes sense for any modern university.

The discussion earlier in this chapter shows how, ever since the Morrill Act of 1862, American universities have established themselves as world leaders in relation to 'engaged scholarship'. Portland State University (PSU) provides an admirable example of the way an urban university can interact in a creative way with interests beyond the campus. Innovation Story 16 sketches the way PSU is contributing, right now, to efforts to build a more equitable and a more sustainable Portland city and city region.

INNOVATION STORY 16

University engagement with the city: the experience of Portland State University

Aims

Portland, Oregon has acquired a reputation as one of the USA's most liveable and progressive urban areas. A city of 588,000 in a metropolitan area of 1.8 million, Portland has a long-established commitment to sustainable urban development. American urban planning scholars celebrate the quality of policy-making and governance in the city, not least because, over a long period, political leadership has secured an integrated approach to land use and transport planning. This brings together the state, metropolitan and local governments in a unified process.[1] These interlocking relationships have enabled the development of farsighted policies that have succeeded in, amongst other things, restricting urban sprawl, promoting eco-friendly urban design and creating an extensive network of public parks.

Citizen involvement in decision making through, for example, a system of neighbourhood associations, coupled with a strong appreciation of the natural environment, means that the city is now regarded as, arguably, the greenest city in the USA. For example, Portland has the highest percentage of bicycle commuters in the country, and it was the first US municipality to adopt a firm position on climate change – it set out ambitious targets for the reduction of greenhouse gas emissions in 1993.

In 2012 the City Council adopted a new plan for the city – The Portland Plan. This is innovative as it puts advancing equity at heart of the strategy. The City is attempting to build on its successful approach to sustainable development by building in a stronger commitment to social justice in the period through to 2035. Within this context of progressive city leadership, this Innovation Story highlights the role that the city's university – Portland State University (PSU) – is playing, in partnership with the City of Portland, other public agencies, community groups and the private sector, to make Portland a more sustainable and a more inclusive city.

Innovation Story outline

PSU is the only comprehensive public university in Portland, Oregon's largest city. It has 30,000 students and is located on a campus in the heart of the Portland business district. The university is committed to tackling urban problems and to improving the quality of life for the citizens of Portland and other cities as reflected in its motto *Let Knowledge Serve the City*. Central to achieving this commitment is the University's vision for engaged and innovative scholarship that 'contributes to the economic vitality, environmental sustainability, and quality of life in the Portland region and beyond'.[2] In pursuit of this vision, since 2001, the University has attempted to embed sustainability into all teaching and research programmes, and into its campus management and development. A PSU goal is 'for students to graduate with a degree and with a basic knowledge of what sustainability means, and how it can be applied, no matter what their field of study'.

PSU promotes a tri-partite understanding of sustainability, one that combines social, environmental and economic dimensions. Accordingly the University organises its activities to engage with these three spheres. In addition to studying sustainability, the University seeks out opportunities for its students to advance their understanding of sustainability through engagement in the field. In 2012–13 PSU students performed 1.02 million service hours in the community.[3] Portland's participatory culture is an enabling factor in this regard.

Spearheading PSU's commitment to sustainability through applied scholarship is the University's President, Wim Wiewel. Building on the approach of previous presidents, notably Judith Ramaley, he is strongly committed to the notion of an engaged university. He believes that PSU should be seen as a community asset with a significant contribution to make to public policy and practice relating to both sustainability and equity in the city region and beyond.

For more than twenty years faculty in the university have played important civic leadership roles in the city and the city region. Here there is space only to mention two current initiatives to illustrate how PSU actively engages with the city and local partners to find innovative solutions to public policy challenges – one focussing on environmental sustainability, and one addressing equity.

Launched in 2011, Electric Avenue is a joint research and development initiative of PSU, the City of Portland and Portland General Electric, and a number of other partners. The aim of the initiative is to learn about the performance of charging stations for electric vehicles, and driver preferences relating to charging and travel patterns. This action/research project is very hands on – it has provided seven charging stations for electric vehicles on a public street in the PSU campus and is monitoring usage. This study, which is designed to throw new light on the practical aspects of providing electric charging services for vehicles, ties in well with the idea of promoting the export of green technological innovations from the region. The Greater Portland Export Plan, for example, has a marketing campaign, *We Build Green Cities*, to promote clean-tech companies and products.[4]

In 2009 PSU built on an idea, first developed in Cincinnati, to develop a comprehensive approach to supporting the success of every child from Cradle to Career – meaning from pre-school through college. Many partners are involved in this initiative – the Leaders Roundtable, the Mayor and the City, Multnomah County, social service providers, community organisations and others. The strategy has involved the development of a set of agreed educational and social performance indicators relating to a child's readiness for kindergarten through to post-secondary education and into a career. The aim is to identify the stages at which a child needs support and then to co-ordinate efforts to deliver that support.

The initiative has led to the creation of a new crosscutting partnership known as All Hands Raised. This orchestrates the process of collaboration and shares progress and early results generated by the collaborative efforts. The underlying idea is that community leaders can achieve high *collective impact* if they abandon their individual agendas for change and work towards a collective approach to improving student achievement.[5] Through the concept of collective impact, PSU is seeking to improve the educational system by aligning often different initiatives, funding sources and organisations around a set of common goals and their shared measurement. All Hands Raised, aims to reduce the educational achievement gaps between different social groups, and improve the economic health of Portland and the Metro area. President Wiewel is clear that the initiative can contribute to the creation of a more inclusive city: 'This initiative has equity written all over it. There is widespread agreement on the need to target resources on under served groups and poor performing schools. We are very much in favour of the equity agenda.'[6]

These examples show that, by bringing together academics, students, politicians, business people, community activists and citizens, the PSU is playing an important role in the place-based leadership of the city, the city region and the state as a whole.

Leadership lessons

- A university can play an important leadership role in the area where it is located. Across the world a growing number of urban universities are recognising that they can make a significant contribution to place-based leadership, and Portland State University provides an excellent example of this outgoing approach
- Strong commitment to this agenda from successive university presidents and faculty as a whole, coupled with a highly participatory culture in the City of Portland, has enabled a very wide range of strategic initiatives to be pursued. This ethos of engagement permeates the work of the faculty and the way students see their education. This enhances the performance of the university in academic terms and, at the same time, delivers significant benefits for local communities

- The Portland Plan, published in 2012, is a sophisticated urban plan. It integrates three strategies to advance the cause of equity in the city: 1) thriving educated youth, 2) economic prosperity and affordability, and 3) healthy connected city. PSU was an active partner in the preparation of the plan and is now actively engaged in working to implement it.
- Working with partners in the locality enables PSU to advance knowledge in innovative ways. Whilst the university is seeking to contribute to scholarship that has global relevance, its approach to achieving this is to focus on understanding and learning from its immediate place setting – the City of Portland, the Metropolitan area and Oregon State.

Sources

Kania, J, Kramer, M, 2011, Collective Impact, *Stanford Social Innovation Review* Winter, 36–41

Katz, B, Bradley, J, 2012 *The Metropolitan Revolution*, Washington DC: Brookings Institution Press

Irazabal, C, 2005, *City making and urban governance in the Americas: Curitiba and Portland*, Aldershot: Ashgate

Ozawa, C, P, (ed), 2004, *The Portland Edge: Challenges and successes in growing communities*, Washington DC: Island Press

Portland State University, 2011, *Opportunity and Competitiveness for the Region: Portland State University Strategic Plan 2011–2014* http://www.pdx.edu/president/sites/www.pdx.edu.president/files/Portland%20State%20University%20Strategic%20Plan%202011-2014_1.pdf

Useful websites

Portland State University: http://www.pdx.edu/
Electric Avenue: http://www.pdx.edu/electricavenue/
All Hands Raised: http://allhandsraised.org/

Endnotes

[1] See, for example, Irazabal (2005) and Ozawa (2004)
[2] http://www.pdx.edu/portland-state-university-mission
[3] Official PSU service hours statistics
[4] See, for example, Katz and Bradley 2012, 156–159
[5] Kania and Kramer (2011)
[6] Personal interview by the author 26 April 2012

In Chapter 2 I adopted a global perspective and outlined the spectacular growth of the urban population in the world as a whole. I noted that the global urban population is set to rise from around 3.6 billion in 2011 to around 5.0 billion in 2030 – that's close to a 40 per cent increase in less than twenty years. The evidence presented there suggests that most of this extraordinary urban growth is going to take place in developing countries. Can universities in developing countries help city leaders shape urban strategies? The answer is 'yes' – provided academics can engage directly with the wide range of stakeholders shaping the public policy agenda.

Here I introduce an example drawn from India. Ahmedabad, the largest city in Gujarat, provides an intriguing illustration, not just of the tensions that arise when a city expands rapidly, but also of the kinds of strategies that might be pursued in order to make the burgeoning metropolis more livable than might otherwise be the case. Ahmedabad established itself in the early 20th Century as the home of the expanding textile industry, and earned the nickname 'Manchester of the East'. The population of the city grew from 274,000 in 1921, when Mahatma Gandhi moved to the city, to over 6.3 million in the metropolitan area in 2014. This figure is expected to jump to 12.5 million by 2030.

In his detailed history of the city Howard Spodek (2011) describes Ahmedabad as the 'shock' city of 20th Century India. He suggests that this capacity to shock has several dimensions. For example, on the upside the city made a startling economic recovery following the collapse of the textile industry in the city in the 1980s. On the downside the city acquired world notoriety for public conflict between Hindus and Muslims, with truly horrendous outbreaks of violence in 2002 (Spodek 2011, 248–70). CEPT University, founded in 1962, has played an active role not just in educating students who have gone on to have careers in Ahmedabad but also in contributing actively to public policy making for the city. Innovation Story 17 outlines the role of CEPT in the planning and design of the award winning Ahmedabad Bus Rapid Transit system.

INNOVATION STORY 17

University engagement with the city: the experience of CEPT University, Ahmedabad

Aims

Ahmedabad, the former capital of the Indian state of Gujarat, is the largest city in the state and is a rapidly expanding metropolis. In 2011 the population of the city was already 5.6 million and in Greater Ahmedabad it was over 6.3 million. Population projections show that Greater Ahmedabad is expected to grow to 12.5 million by 2030. This is a spectacular rate of urban growth and it inevitably poses major challenges for city leaders.

The aims of this Innovation Story are to illustrate the role of professional staff and scholars at the Centre for Environmental Planning and Technology (CEPT) University in contributing to, and critiquing, the development of the city. The university supports city planning and urban management activities in the metropolis in a variety of ways. For example, scholars at CEPT have made important contributions to policy relating to jobs and employment opportunities in the city.[1] Academics have offered thoughtful commentaries on urban development projects and pointed to flaws in urban mega-projects – for example, the Sabarmati Riverfront Development project.[2] In addition, CEPT educates large numbers of architecture, planning, design, and management students, many of whom take up careers in the city. Here we focus on one example of CEPT activities – the role of academic staff in relation to the planning and design of the Bus Rapid Transit (BRT) system introduced into the city in 2009. This policy innovation has won national and international awards in the field of public transport, and provides an interesting example of a serious effort to further the aims of sustainable mobility and equity in a rapidly expanding Indian city.

Innovation Story outline

First – some background. In history Ahmedabad has been called the 'Manchester of India' mainly because the 19th Century industrial growth of the city was, like Manchester in the UK, largely based on a massive expansion of the textile and garment industries. The Indian independence movement developed strong roots in the city when Mahatma Gandhi established two ashrams in 1915 and 1917. Sadly, following independence in 1947, the city suffered intense communal violence between Hindus and Muslims. The Ahmedabad Municipal Corporation (AMC) was established as the institution of local government in 1950, when the population had reached around 770,000.

In a respected book about the history of the city Howard Spodek describes it as the 'Shock city of 20th Century India'.[3] In his presentation the 'shock' effect has several aspects but two stand out. First, there is the startling physical and economic development of the city with burgeoning businesses, industries and urban development. Second, and very troubling, are the disturbing outbreaks of communal violence that have seen the city in the international news for all the wrong reasons. For example, in 2002 there was a repeat of the 1969 outbreak of violence between Hindus and Muslims, and over a thousand, mainly Muslim, people were killed.

CEPT University was established in 1962 with the creation of a School of Architecture, and the School of Planning was established in 1972. Now CEPT is a university and has five faculties – Architecture, Planning, Technology, Design and Management. Teaching programmes focus on building professional capacities and are centred on 'studios' or 'labs'. Here students engage with real problems and challenges. Practising professionals contribute to courses and the university works as a collaborative of academics and practitioners.

Professionals from CEPT were involved in preparing the detailed plans for both Phase 1 (2006–2007) and Phase 2 (2008) of the Bus Rapid Transit (BRT) system. Two centres at CEPT were involved. The Centre for Urban Equity was involved from the beginning, and the Centre for Excellence in Urban Transport is now the principal consultant to the AMC for planning and designing BRT routes and stations. Supported by the Indian Ministry of Urban Development (MoUD) and the AMC, the Centre provides ongoing advice to Janmarg (which means 'people's way'), the company created to run the BRT. Recent research on BRT systems in India suggests that Ahmedabad is exceptional in that it now has in place about 60km of a rapid transit network, whereas other cities seem, so far, to have been unable to expand their initial 'pilot' BRT corridors.[4]

Evaluation research on BRT systems in India suggests that they are far cheaper than rail-based transport systems.[5] For example, the Delhi Metro Rail Corridor cost $29.5 million per kilometre whereas a BRT costs $1.93 million per kilometre. Research on the impact of the Ahmedabad BRT suggests that the system has, indeed, been very cost-effective when compared with rail-based options. In the first three months of operation the system was free to use, and this resulted in a high level of positive feedback from the public and the media. BRT stations are neat and clean, the frequency of buses is maintained and support staff is always available. Survey research suggests that 12% of BRT passengers have shifted their travel from private motorised modes.

The same research suggests, however, that the BRT in Ahmedabad has, at present, some limitations. First, the original plans for well-designed walking and cycling facilities linked to the BRT stations have not been implemented. The buses run on central median lanes and are not linked adequately into urban neighbourhoods. Second, the fares are too high for low-income households with the result that the urban poor, and especially women among them, are not receiving the hoped-for benefits.

Leadership lessons

- Central governments can stimulate city–university collaboration by providing grants and incentives. The Indian Ministry of Urban Development (MoUD), through a national level programme, called the Jawaharlal Nehru National Urban Renewal Mission (JNNURM), provided a valuable spur to local innovation.
- A university can contribute knowledge and expertise to urban planning and policy making in the city where it is located. Faculty at CEPT University are making an important contribution to public policy making in two ways: 1) Providing professional advice and guidance to city leaders and public managers, and 2) Offering independent scrutiny of the performance of public policies.
- A university can act as a 'critical friend' in the way it relates to city leaders and urban stakeholders. By offering independent analysis of policies and projects scholars can prompt fresh thinking in relation to who is gaining and who is losing as a result of policies and practices.
- In relation to sustainable transport planning it seems clear that strategic 'network' thinking is needed, rather than 'corridor' thinking. Whilst far from complete, Ahmedabad has succeeded in developing a bus rapid transit network, rather than a corridor, and CEPT University is clearly playing a constructive role in urban transport planning.

Sources

Desai, R, 2012, Governing the Urban Poor: Riverfront development, slum resettlement and the politics of inclusion in Ahmedabad, *Economic and Political Weekly* Vol XLVII, 2, 14 January, 49–56

Mahadevia, D, 2012, *Decent work in Ahmedabad: An integrated approach*. Report of the International Labour Organisation (ILO) Regional Office for Asia and the Pacific. June. Bangkok: International Labour Organisation

Mahadevia, D, Joshi, R, Datey, A, 2012, *Low-carbon mobility in India and the challenges of social inclusion: Bus Rapid Transit (BRT) case studies in India. policy summary*. Roskilde: UNEP (United Nations Environment Programme) and Technical University of Denmark

Mahadevia, D, Joshi, R, Datey, A, 2013, Ahmedabad's BRT system. A sustainable urban transport panacea? *Economic and Political Weekly* Vol XLVIII, 48, November, 56–64

OneWorld Foundation India, 2012, *Efficient solution for urban mobility. Documentation of best practice*. January.

Spodek, H, 2011, *Ahmedabad: Shock City of Twentieth-Century India*, Bloomington: Indiana University Press

Useful websites

CEPT University, Ahmedabad: http://www.cept.ac.in

Official website of Ahmedabad Janmarg Ltd: http://www.ahmedabadbrts.com/web/index.html

Endnotes

[1] Mahadevia (2012).

[2] Desai (2012).

[3] Spodek H. (2011).

[4] Mahadevia et al (2012).

[5] This and the following discussion draws on Mahadevia et al (2013).

Conclusions

In his book, *The Shallows*, Nicholas Carr has shown how the Internet is changing the way we think, understand and remember. His book is not a manifesto for Luddites who dislike all things technological. Rather he invites us to note that research shows that, 'people who read linear text comprehend more, remember more, and learn more than those who read text peppered with links' (Carr 2010, 127).

Carr assembles a substantial body of scientific research on the effects that the Internet is having on the way we discover new information, transfer it from working memory to long-term memory and weave it into our conceptual schemas. Carr argues that there is nothing wrong with skimming across sources and picking up new ideas. Rather he points out that eye-tracking experiments have revealed how the Internet has an important impact on attention and cognition. Basically, he is concerned that cognitive overload short circuits deeper thought processes and numerous studies confirm this. A consequence is that, while the Internet provides vast amounts of information, it is actually diminishing our ability to know, in depth, a subject for ourselves. It may actually be making us stupid.

In this chapter I have presented an argument that can, perhaps, be seen as a parallel to the presentation provided by Carr. His book examines mental processes, whereas the discussion in this chapter has been concerned with social processes. I have suggested that advances in communication technologies have benefits but the gains may be more superficial than might, at first, appear. On the plus side, it is clear that innovations with ICT can enhance access to public services and improve the ability of public servants to respond to requests from citizens. Moreover open data and social media initiatives can provide opportunities for social entrepreneurs to create new apps to meet social needs. Smart city initiatives that bring together digital experts with non-technical people can be expected to lead to significant improvements in public service responsiveness in the years ahead.

However, I have suggested that, when it comes to efforts to deepen democracy and strengthen citizen participation, the evidence that ICT can make a big difference is thin on the ground. The arrival of e-democracy has been underwhelming. It has certainly not led to a surge of effective innovations in citizen empowerment. The discussion in this chapter has reinforced the argument presented in Chapter 7. There I suggested that, while ICT is delivering vast amounts of information to citizens, it does not appear to be doing that much to advance the creation of democratic, inclusive cities.

This chapter has identified five weaknesses in ICT-driven approaches to smart cities. I have called these danger zones, rather than fundamental flaws. It is possible that ICT experts can work with others to find ways of navigating safe and fruitful paths through these danger zones. At this point, however, the route maps across this minefield have yet to be constructed. It is clear, then, that technologically driven approaches to urban governance have serious limitations. This is why I have argued that we need to develop a deeper understanding of the nature of public learning and democratic innovation in the modern city. My central suggestion is that decision-making in and for cities should be led by sound judgement, not technological advance. From the point of view of public policy ICT innovations that fail to serve public purpose are a distraction. Hence my headline argument that future thinking about cities should focus not on developing smart cities but on creating wise cities.

How do we do this? There are many ways, but one possibility is to tap into the resources of local universities. In many cities, universities are the sleeping giants of place-based leadership and social innovation. However, the giant is waking up. Across the world higher education is undergoing significant change and, as part of the rethinking of the role of universities in modern society, the very nature of scholarship is being reconsidered.

In this chapter I have suggested that the notion of 'engaged scholarship' has much to commend it. I have outlined what it means, and provided two Innovation Stories to show how universities can make an important contribution to the creation of the inclusive city. Innovation Story 16 outlines the way Portland State University is playing an active part in the governance of the City of Portland and the wider city region. Innovation Story 17 describes the way CEPT University is contributing to public policy making in the Ahmedabad metropolitan area. These two universities are not alone in demonstrating a strong commitment to 'engaged scholarship'. It is encouraging to note that a growing number of scholars in a wide range of disciplines now see active engagement with the city as a splendid way to advance knowledge and understanding, as well as contribute to public purpose.

CHAPTER 12

International lesson drawing

We don't want nobody nobody sent.
Chicago Ward Committeeman to Abner J. Mikva, 1948

Introduction

I am British so it was a steep, cross-cultural learning curve for me when I was appointed as Dean of the College of Urban Planning and Public Affairs at the University of Illinois at Chicago (UIC) in 2002. Luckily I had great colleagues – faculty, staff and students – who helped me learn a little, certainly not enough, about American higher education in general, and Chicago politics in particular. Very early on I struggled with Abner Mikva's famous account of the reaction he received when he tried, as a student, to volunteer to help with local political activity in Chicago. He was told: 'We don't want nobody nobody sent'. For a start, I did not understand what it meant.

I needed a lesson in Illinois history and UIC colleagues were generous in their assistance. Abner Mikva, who was later to become a senior adviser to President Obama, studied at the Chicago Law School in the late 1940s. He was already an enthusiastic Democrat supporter when, walking home one night in 1948, he dropped into the ward headquarters of the Democratic Party and said: 'I'd like to volunteer to work for Adlai Stevenson and Paul Douglas'. The quintessential ward committeeman took the cigar out of his mouth and said: 'Who sent you?' Mikva said: 'Nobody'. The committeeman put his cigar back in his mouth and said: 'We don't want nobody nobody sent'.

Here, then, is an illustration of the classic blow-off that newcomers received when they tried to get involved in Chicago Democratic politics back in the machine era. In those days it was not what you cared about or what you could offer that mattered. It was whom you knew. Hopefully, these nepotistic prejudices are long gone. But the story is a powerful allegory of tribalism and narrow thinking. Here we see, in full flow, the view that you are an outsider, you don't belong here and we don't want you. Interestingly, the committeeman did not put the lively law student off politics. Mikva was to serve in the Illinois House of Representatives before being elected to the US Congress and becoming an influential national figure in the Democratic Party. I introduce this chapter with this illuminating story because, in our rapidly globalising world, we *do* want nobody nobody sent.

Modern progressive city leaders understand this. They are enthusiastic about learning from other cities and, in particular, discovering insights from cities in other countries where very different approaches are being applied. They are keen to exchange ideas on policies and practices, build new relationships, benchmark their performance against innovative cities on an international basis, and develop long-term city development strategies. In this chapter we will discuss this idea of city-to-city learning and consider ways of improving the effectiveness of international policy exchange.

We start out by noting that international city-to-city exchange is nothing new. What is new, however, is the rapid expansion and intensification of international dialogue. Scholars studying comparative government and politics draw attention to different levels of analysis and we consider the relationship between three levels of analysis in the second section below. This is followed by a discussion of international lesson drawing. Much of the discourse relating to international policy transfer refers to the idea of 'best practice'. I provide a section arguing that there is no such thing. 'Best practice' is a wholly unhelpful concept that is holding back public service innovation. The chapter then examines knowledge exchange in a little more detail, and a framework for understanding international lesson drawing is put forward. The chapter closes with a discussion of elements that we might want to see developed in the emerging grammar of place-based leadership.

International learning and exchange

International learning relating to city government is nothing new:

> Aristotle dispatched his assistants to collect the constitutions of over one hundred city-states, which he then compared to derive general political principles. (Heidenheimer et al 1990, 7)

The practice is also long established in city planning and architecture. Visit the stunning urban space lying at the heart of the beautiful hill town of Pienza in Tuscany and you will encounter an early example of cross-national policy transfer. In 1459 Pope Pius II decided to redevelop the central area of the town in order to create an ensemble of buildings and spaces to exemplify Renaissance perfection. While Pius turned to Rossellino, a famous Florentine architect who worked closely with Leon Battista Alberti, to lead the design effort, it is clear that Pius was the prime mover.

Before he was elected to the papacy in 1458, Pius travelled extensively in Europe and it is clear that he brought his international experience to bear on the designs for Pienza. Thus, for example, the aisles in the new cathedral are the same height as the nave. This architectural design – untried in Italy at the time – follows the model of the Hallenkirchen Pius had encountered in northern Europe. The result is a Tuscan cathedral with an unusually light, airy interior. Outside the cathedral the harmony of space and volume created by the new buildings is breathtaking. Not surprisingly planners and architects from all over the world continue to make the pilgrimage to Pienza to learn from a classic example of how to create people-friendly urban spaces that integrate effortlessly with the existing urban fabric.

As I will explain later, the planning and design of Pienza in the fifteenth century benefited from a process that I describe as informal, international policy transfer – more of this shortly. The point I wish to highlight here is that, throughout urban history, cities have engaged in city-to-city learning. However, this process of international exchange has received a rocket boost in recent times. As discussed in Chapter 2, over the last thirty years or so, globalisation has led to a spectacular increase in the intensity and velocity of international exchange in all spheres of life – from art, literature, film, music, ballet and culture, through commerce, business and crime, to public policy and city management.

It is now the case that, as Tim Campbell (2012) explains, forward-looking city leaders are keen to acquire new knowledge from cities in other countries, and the international transmission of ideas, and the values behind them, is now an inextricable part of effective urban innovation. The rapid expansion of the Internet has, of course, enabled cities to share information about practices and initiatives on an international basis in a way that would have been impossible only a few years ago.

We should step back, for a moment, and situate this discussion of international lesson drawing relating to urban policy and practice in a broader context. As a first step we should distinguish between coercive policy transfer and voluntary transfer (Dolowitz et al 2000; Evans 2004). Some policy transfer arises as a result of specific mechanisms of harmonisation, such as international or supranational agreements, deliberately formed by the parties in multilateral negotiations. Such arrangements, following international negotiation, impose, or coerce, change in the countries that have agreed to participate. For example, policy transfer in Europe has been strongly influenced by the European Union for more than sixty years, so that it is now possible to study and discuss the 'Europeanisation of public policies' (Saurugger and Radaelli 2008). Voluntary transfer, on the other hand, stems from a process that parties (nations, states, cities, local authorities etc) enter into of their own free will. There is no higher-level protocol requiring policy modification. In this book, including the discussion in this chapter, our focus is on *voluntary* policy exchange.

Linda Hantrais (2009) provides a good introduction to international comparative research. She discusses the nature of 'international' or 'cross-national' research and explains how these different words, and others, like 'transnational', imply different academic approaches. At one level most social scientists agree that international comparative studies involve comparison of specific issues or phenomena in two or more countries, societies or cultures. However, there is much less consensus about what it is that should be compared, whether nation states provide a sensible unit for comparison, the degree to which contextual variables should figure in analysis and so on.

Hantrais distinguishes between macro and micro levels of analysis:

> Macro-level studies concentrate on groups of individuals, systems, structures and processes, whereas micro-level analysis focuses on

> individual activities or behaviour. This dichotomy has come to be associated with different methodological approaches and perspectives. (Hantrais 2009, 54–5)

She makes an important point about linking levels of analysis. Drawing on Michel Lallement's work she suggests that:

> … the actual level of analysis selected is less important than the researcher's ability to make sense of the findings by unravelling the interactive relationship between different levels, more especially in multidisciplinary studies. (Hantrais 2009, 55)

This linking of levels of analysis is important for our purposes. In Chapter 5 I discussed the nature of place-based leadership and explained how various forces constrain the power of place. Figure 5.1 shows how place-based governance can only be understood within the context of the various forces that frame the political space available to local actors. I will take just one simple example to illustrate the point. The remarkable achievements of place-based leaders in the City of Freiburg, set out in Innovation Story 11, cannot properly be understood in the absence of at least some knowledge of the constitutional protection enjoyed by local authorities in Germany. Freiburg has, because it is in Germany, the constitutional right to do things differently, and civic leaders have taken advantage of this local autonomy to engage in bold innovation. By comparison local authorities in, say, the UK are working in an ironclad straitjacket imposed by central government. Here, imaginative place-based leadership is hemmed in by an obsessive culture of 'we know best' centralism. It follows that understanding the attitudes and practices of higher levels of government to local government matters a great deal when considering urban policy transfer possibilities.

International exchange: three levels of analysis

In 2009 Christine Cheyne and I examined the nature of cross-national exchange relating to local governance between the UK and New Zealand over the last twenty years or so (Cheyne and Hambleton 2011). In an attempt to make sense of what seemed to be happening in the international exchange process we suggested that it was helpful to consider three overlapping levels, or spheres, of influence: 1) Ideological and political forces, 2) Ideas in good currency, and 3) The role of scholars in cross-national exchange. In the discussion presented here I adapt this approach and, setting aside the role of scholars for a moment, I suggest that international lesson drawing can benefit from distinguishing between three levels of analysis as follows:

- ideological and political forces
- ideas in good currency
- agency exercised by place-based leaders.

Ideological and political forces

First, there is an ideological level. Without embarking on a wide-ranging review, we can note that ideological frames of reference shape patterns of thinking and generate a prevailing view that often goes unquestioned. In Chapter 1 I discussed the role of power in modern society and, following Lukes (2005), I drew attention to the way powerful interests manipulate group values and edge alternative perspectives out of the public discourse. The so-called Washington Consensus provides a good example of such a frame of reference. This neo-liberal perspective asserts that world development will be advanced by downscaling the role of government, by deregulation and privatisation. As Will Hutton (2006) reminds us, this is only one perspective. He outlines the contours of the so-called Beijing Consensus – an approach to development that embraces technological innovation, stresses equity and sustainability and promotes values-led experimentation (Hutton 2006, 206–7). Much international policy exchange, and the international management consultants and place branding companies can be criticised in this context, fails to critique the neo-liberal ideological cargo that is often being shipped as part of the policy transfer process.

This ideological framing is often deeply embedded in political and professional practice with the result that flawed 'ways of seeing and doing' flow across frontiers in a way that almost goes unnoticed. Take city planning. In Chapter 2 I explained how, in the coming period, there will be a massive expansion of urban growth in developing countries. In many of the countries that will be affected by this seismic population shift the urban planning systems are unsuited to the challenge. Vanessa Watson elaborates this point in an analysis derived from the experience of the global South:

> ... the planning systems in place have been either inherited from previous colonial governments or have been adopted from Northern contexts to suit particular local political and ideological ends. The need for planning systems to be pro-poor and inclusive has therefore not been given much consideration. (Watson 2009, 2260)

She explains how there is now a fundamental tension between the logic of governing and the logic of survival. She urges scholars working in the fields of urban planning and development studies to expose the 'conflict of rationalities' now arising between, on the one hand, current managerial and marketised systems of government administration and, on the other, marginalised and impoverished populations surviving largely under conditions of informality.

It is clear, then, that ideologies matter. However, it would be wrong to conclude that international policy transfer is destined to be the servant of ideological domination. The Innovation Stories presented in this book illustrate, as often as not, an imaginative capacity on the part of progressive civic leaders to escape the limits of, or at least challenge, prevailing ideological mind-sets.

Ideas in good currency

Second, we can drop down from ideology to the level of ideas in good currency. This is a notion developed and deployed by Donald Schon (1971). He explains how governments learn and adapt to changing events and, in particular, he focuses on the role of ideas. The ideologies, just discussed, shape the discourse about which ideas receive attention and which are neglected. Ideas in good currency rise and fall. From the point of view of wanting to see the creation of more inclusive cities some of these ideas will be welcome. For example, evidence has been presented to show that the idea of investing in public transport can clearly advance the cause of the inclusive city. Innovation Stories 9, 10 and 11, on Curitiba, Guangzhou and Freiburg, show how imaginative approaches to public transport have transformed life styles and life chances for citizens.

However, some ideas that attract international attention may actually be thoroughly bad ideas. For example, in Chapter 3 I explained how **New Public Management** became an idea in good currency in many countries in the 1990s. This belief system, stemming from private sector thinking, has done great damage to the public service ethos. This is because these ideas have helped market, or quasi-market, models and ways of thinking to penetrate into areas of life where they have no place (Sandel 2012). Fortunately, however, **New Public Management** is now being widely questioned. New understandings relating to how the state can co-create solutions with actors in civil society are, instead, on the rise. But, before getting too enthusiastic about these relatively new ideas, we should guard against jumping on the next fashionable bandwagon. Maybe co-creation will have a downside.

The point I wish to stress here is that ideologies, and ideas in good currency, are just ways of thinking. They may be backed by evidence, but maybe not. They are certainly not fixed and immutable. It follows that scholars adopting a critical approach to urban studies and city governance can play an invaluable role in helping us understand the nature of these ideas and, more specifically, can highlight whose interests are being served by their deployment (Brenner et al 2012; Imbroscio 2010). Enlightened civic leaders pay attention to critical scholars, even if the arguments they present can be very challenging.

In Chapter 3 I explained how Joseph Chamberlain, when he was mayor of Birmingham, UK, in the 1870s, blew apart the prevailing belief system about the role of local government, and pioneered an entirely new way of leading cities and meeting human needs – the democratic, municipal gospel was born. In a similar way, many of the place-based leaders featured in the Innovation Stories presented in this book reject the Washington Consensus and head off in an entirely different direction. Civic leaders in, for example, Copenhagen, Malmö and Curitiba have little time for neo-liberal ways of thinking. Indeed, as discussed in Chapter 1, the global financial crash of 2008/09 has raised major question marks about market-driven ideas and approaches. A consequence is that more and more city leaders are promoting strategies that do not rely on a belief in so-called free-market ideology. They know that there is no such thing as a 'free market' and they are re-asserting community based values against the aggressions of place-less power.

Agency exercised by place-based leaders

Third, if we move down one more level, we arrive at individuals, small groups, social movements, local activists, artists, radicals and entrepreneurs. Here we find free spirits who take action believing it to be right regardless of dominant patterns of thinking. The environmental movement provides many examples of lively activists who think for themselves and have the courage to take action – these are the positive deviants celebrated by Sara Parkin (2010). The evidence is accumulating that such activists, simply by getting on and doing things differently in particular places, are changing attitudes more broadly (Hopkins 2013; Jackson 2009; Parkin 2010). Bringing independent, socially informed thinking to the table is, perhaps, one of the most important functions of progressive, place-based leaders. Certainly, the Innovation Stories in this book illustrate how innovative urban leaders have a strong tendency to reject so-called 'best practice' and to break new ground in how they go about improving the quality of life in cities and localities.

We have seen how place-based leaders have, in some situations, shown great courage by taking decisions that fly in the face of powerful interests. The introduction, in 2003, of a congestion charge on motorists driving into central London by Mayor Ken Livingstone provides a classic example – see Chapter 8. From Melbourne to Portland we have seen that, with the backing of their local populations, progressive place-based leaders have rejected neo-liberal ways of thinking. These leaders have moved policy and practice towards the creation of the inclusive city despite, not because of, prevailing neo-liberal thought patterns. Interestingly, these place-based efforts are, not surprisingly, developing into new ideas in good currency. For example, the co-creation of new solutions, the emphasis on eco-friendly behaviour and the commitment to tackling social inequality are gaining growing numbers of adherents, particularly in younger age groups, in all continents. It is possible to suggest that, in the future, these new ideas in good currency will come to dislodge the prevailing neo-liberal ideology and replace it with a more enlightened one. Let us hope so.

International lesson drawing for policy and practice

Having considered the interplay between different levels of analysis we now explore the nature of international lesson drawing for policy and practice. Why should cities bother about developments in other countries? What is international lesson drawing anyway?

Richard Rose (2005) offers some helpful advice on how to go about, what he calls, instrumental learning from other countries. By building on and extending the presentation provided by Rose I identify five main reasons why forward-looking city leaders recognise that it is important to engage in international exchange.

- First, as Rose (2005) observes, learning can focus on actual accomplishments in another setting. This, he argues, can provide a better basis for policy innovation than merely making up ideas and speculating about what might happen if they were adopted.
- Second, in a rapidly globalising world, citizens expect professionals to be up to date with the latest developments – wherever they take place. Information, people and money now flow almost effortlessly across national frontiers in the worlds of science, business, the arts and culture. Why should public policy be walled into national enclaves?
- Third, as explained in Chapter 10, city leaders, public service managers and NGOs operate in an increasingly multi-cultural world. Examining experience in other countries can enhance the cultural competence of both politicians and professionals by exposing individuals to different ways of doing things.
- A fourth reason for studying experience in other countries is that common problems do *not* produce an identical response. It is the *differences* in the responses that governments make to common problems that can offer powerful and compelling insights for both theory and practice.
- Fifth, through international exchange cities can build connections with other cities that can lead to all kinds of relationship benefits. Such relationships can be binary pairing (as in sister-city links), or clusters focussing on a particular theme (for example, the C40 group of cities concerned to tackle climate change), or more extended networks (for example, UCLG, the global network of cities, local and regional governments).

Rose (2005) suggests that policy makers do not seek fresh ideas from other countries for their own sake but to promote political satisfaction. This lays down a significant challenge for academics. Comparative research on public policy, including comparative research on urban governance and city planning, is an expanding field (Carroll and Common 2013; Dolowitz et al 2000; Evans 2004). But when this work is limited to advancing understanding – the traditional focus of scholarship – it falls short of instrumental learning. Cross-national lesson drawing requires investigators to go beyond description and analysis and offer evidence-based advice to policy makers. We can make a connection here to the notion of engaged scholarship. Introduced in Chapter 1, where I defined it as the co-creation of new knowledge by scholars and practitioners working together in a shared process of discovery, it can be argued that engaged scholarship can play an important role in international lesson drawing. I discussed the concept of engaged scholarship in some detail in Chapter 11 and the Innovation Stories presented in this book provide practical examples.

In 1991, Marilyn Taylor and I worked with the UK Harkness Fellowships programme in an attempt to co-create improvements in transatlantic urban policy transfer. At that point in time the UK Harkness programme offered fellowships for outstanding mid-career public policy professionals, from the UK, Australia and New Zealand, to visit and study in the USA for a short period. We developed a checklist of factors for fellows to use during their visit, held a conference with the fellows on their return and encouraged them to write up their experiences. This process led to the creation of an edited book on *People in Cities. A transatlantic policy exchange* (Hambleton and Taylor 1993).

A key finding that emerged from this relatively early study of cross-national policy transfer, one that has been reinforced by more recent research, was the importance of taking account of the policy setting. We concluded that it is important for visitors seeking new insights from another country to focus not just on the policy (or practice), and whether it was successful or not (as viewed from different vantage points), but also to examine what aspects of the policy setting appeared to be crucial to policy success or failure (Hambleton and Taylor 1993, 240–3). The fellows were very positive about their international learning experience and, perhaps surprisingly, they welcomed the discipline imposed by having to write up the lessons they had learned as chapters for a book.

True, there are pitfalls to avoid in cross-national learning and, again, Rose (2005) provides a helpful outline of the main danger zones. First, mindless copying of an innovation is a classic error – local culture and context vary. It follows that policies that may perform well in one location may be a disaster if transplanted across frontiers without adaptation. Sensitivity to local history, traditions and power structures is critical – sensitivity to place, if you will. Second, it follows that a search for so-called 'best practice' is a thoroughly foolish enterprise – we need processes that lead to the discovery of relevant practice. We will return to examine why the notion of 'best practice' is so misguided in a moment. Third, so-called 'successful' policies may not actually be 'successful'. With most cities now practicing some form of place marketing, if not outright civic boosterism, it is essential that policies being considered for transfer require some kind of evaluation before they are placed in the 'For export' shopping cart. Fourth, and this is a point not given adequate consideration by Rose, there is an ideological dimension to policy exchange that we neglect at our peril. As mentioned earlier, the ideological context shapes any conversation about international policy transfer, and those involved in international exchange need to be alert to this dimension.

Escaping from the lazy language of 'best practice'

Management consultants, policy advisers, professional experts and, sad to say, some academic researchers often suggest that they have identified 'best practice' when they report on policies and practices they have examined. In speeches and interviews with the media Government ministers will sometimes assert that they have identified 'best practice' that all should attempt to emulate. Indeed, some private consulting firms specialise in 'best practice' and claim to be able to offer ready-made templates to organise procedures, approaches to bench marking and so on. I want to suggest that there is, in fact, no such thing as 'best practice'. In my view, the use of the phrase 'best practice' is almost certainly unhelpful in any area of policy making, and it has no place in intelligent approaches to cross-national policy transfer relating to cities, urban governance and community development.

These are strong words. It is, of course, possible for particular industries or professions to develop guides to action that, in specific technical areas, could be described as 'good practice' or, even, 'required practice'. For example, engineering guidance on sound bridge construction probably qualifies as an area where the profession is able, on an international basis, to agree on 'good practice'. Even here, however, I take the view that the use of the phrase 'best practice' would be unwise. This is because it promotes convergent thinking – the idea that there is a single 'best' solution.[1] If engineers had stuck to copying 'best practice' in the past the suspension bridge would never have been invented.[2]

There are five main reasons why 'best practice' should be discarded from the lexicon of international lesson drawing for public policy. First, as Snowden and Boone (2007) explain, 'best practice' is, by definition, past practice. A key theme in this book is that the world is changing fairly rapidly, and this is one of the main reasons why public innovation is so important. In such a world hindsight no longer leads to foresight. It follows that emulating what worked in the past may not be shrewd.

Second, it is a denial of the richness and diversity of modern life to claim that a practice can be described as the 'best' in all cases. Recall that 'best' is the superlative of 'good' – it means matchless, unequalled, unsurpassable. As explained at some length in this book, and particularly in Chapters 4 and 11, places vary and cultures vary. It follows that any judgements about a practice need to be related to the spatial and socio-cultural context. To say that a particular practice is 'best' regardless of context betrays a serious lack of cultural awareness. There is, for example, no reason to believe that the 'best' British practice, were such a thing to exist, would be viewed as the 'best' in Brazil or China.

Third, and this is a development of the second point, decisions in public policy have distributional consequences. For example, the utopian vision of an inclusive city that I set out in Chapter 1 provides a value-based statement of what I think cities should strive to be. It stresses the importance of local democracy, justice and caring for the natural environment on which we all depend. People holding other values will disagree with this view. They may, for example, prefer to see the quality of life in cities shaped by uncontrolled market forces. What this person thinks is 'best' for the city will differ from my view of what is 'best'. In public policy making different people will, and should, have differing views about what is the most desirable way forward. Legitimate political differences mean that there can be no such thing as the 'best' way to run a city. Those advocating 'best practice' need to answer the question 'Best for whom?' There is a broader point here. The language of 'best practice' can, at times, signal an attempt to bring about a managerialisation of politics, one that seeks to disguise conflicts in society. 'Best practice' is often, then, used as a subtle instrument of domination by powerful vested interests.

A fourth problem with the use of the phrase 'best practice', and it is a fundamental one, is that in a complex world, one that is unpredictable and in flux, it is unwise to believe that a 'best' course of action can be identified and followed.

> Most situations and decisions in organisations are complex... That is why, instead of attempting to impose a course of action, leaders must patiently allow the path forward to reveal itself. They need to probe first, then sense, and then respond. (Snowden and Boone 2007, 5)

Chapter 6 provides an extended discussion of the role of leadership in creating the conditions within which bold innovation is valued and encouraged. By drawing insights from jazz music it highlights the value of improvisation in public policy, of experimentation. The discussion there shows how innovation is a process of local social discovery, not a search for some kind of mythical 'best practice'.

My fifth concern about the use of the phrase 'best practice' is that it pushes intellectual effort in the wrong direction. It creates the false impression that the 'best' answer is out there – someone else has already discovered it for us. It conjures up the depressing picture of hard working civil servants desperately scanning the world to unearth, often at short notice, examples of practice in other countries that ministers, mayors and other senior figures can use to guide their decisions or, worse still, support their pre-conceived ideas of what ought to be done. All the Innovation Stories in this book show that, while learning from abroad can stimulate fresh thinking, the process of successful innovation stems from a process of place-based social invention.

A knowledge utilisation perspective

So far in this chapter we have discussed various approaches to comparative policy analysis and international lesson drawing. It is time to dig a little deeper. What, exactly, is the nature of the international exchange process? What is being exchanged?

Stated simply international lesson drawing is a form of knowledge exchange. This, in itself, does not take us very far. How is this knowledge acquired and used? Rich (1997) makes a helpful contribution by distinguishing three kinds of knowledge utilisation: information pick-up; information processing; and information application. These are all important in the international lesson drawing process.

- **Information pick up** refers to how users receive information. This can range from scanning the Internet, searching databases, contacting relevant authorities, holding webinars, phoning up the local university through to organised field visits to other countries and city-to-city exchanges.
- **Information processing** can be described as interpretation or sense making. The newly discovered knowledge needs to be tested for validity and compatibility with existing knowledge and values. This stage is central to the learning process. It is, invariably, a collective process and the organisational environment within which the knowledge is reviewed and considered becomes critical. The arguments presented in Chapter 6 are relevant here. If leaders are open to new ideas and experiment they will foster a culture of innovation. This will mean that new ideas from another country can be expected to receive a fair hearing and could well stimulate the creation of fresh solutions. If the organisational culture is cautious and defensive the information processing stage will be used to dilute or kill off challenging insights.
- **Information application** refers to using the information in decision-making. Rich (1997) distinguishes four elements to application: use, utility, influence and impact. 'Use' only refers to receiving and reading the information – not, in itself, significant. 'Utility' is rather more important – it involves the user making a judgement about the relevance of the information and formulating proposals for action. 'Influence' and 'Impact' arise when the knowledge contributes to a decision and a consequential result.

Ettelt et al (2012) have applied these concepts in an analysis of international policy learning in relation to health policy making in UK central government. They conclude that the process, for a central government department at least, is more difficult than might at first appear. This is partly because of the hierarchical forms of management that shape behaviour in Whitehall departments. Typically the international learning is 'delegated to junior policy colleagues or analysts' (Ettelt et al 2012, 497). Here, then, is a fundamental problem with a large amount of academic international policy analysis – it focuses on *central* governments, *not local* governments. As we shall see shortly, city-to-city knowledge exchange networks are far more hands-on, vibrant and effective than lumbering state-to-state exchanges. It is often the mayor, not some junior official, who takes the lead on an international exchange initiative. When it comes to effective international lesson-drawing city halls are not disabled by the long chains of command that hamper the efforts of their colleagues in central governments. This gives innovative cities a major advantage, particularly when it is recognised that a key challenge for modern public policy is to learn quickly, be creative, experiment with new approaches and learn from experience.

A framework for international lesson drawing

In Figure 12.1 I set out a framework for understanding international lesson drawing for public policy.[3] The framework distinguishes two kinds of policy transfer: informal and formal.[4] **Informal policy transfer** arises when individuals take notice of experience in another country and use the insights they have gained to influence their practice. Earlier I mentioned how Pope Pius II employed a process of informal learning from abroad when he arranged for the redevelopment of Pienza, Tuscany in 1459. A modern example of informal urban policy transfer is provided by the waterside, or marina, approach to urban renewal. In the 1960s and the 1970s urban planners tended to neglect the decaying harbours and canals located in the central areas of many cities. These 'eyesores' were seen as relics of a bygone era and, surprising to say nowadays, new urban development often turned its back on the water.

Donald Schaefer, when he was mayor of Baltimore from 1971 to 1986, deserves credit for seeing the hidden potential of the run down docks as a focus for urban regeneration. The successful reinvention of the Inner Harbour, under Mayor Schaefer and, subsequently, Mayor Kurt Schmoke, as a major leisure and tourist destination is now something of an urban planning legend. Certainly the Baltimore experience had a major impact not just on planning practice in other US cities, but also in the UK. Indeed, waterside renewal became an international idea in good currency. For example, the creative and successful redevelopment of both the Bristol Floating Harbour and Cardiff Bay owe much to informal lesson-drawing from Baltimore. High quality urban design, attention to the shaping of public spaces, ensuring access to the waterfront, mixing uses within buildings, bringing public and private stakeholders together, renovating important old buildings in a creative way – all features of the approach adopted in Baltimore – are concepts that have been exported to many cities in other countries.

Figure 12.1: A framework for understanding international lesson drawing

Source: Author

Formal policy transfer is more systematic than the informal approach. It involves an entity explicitly setting out to examine experience in one or more countries in order to generate specific lessons that the organisation can act on. The entity could be a government (national, state, or local), an international organisation, a Non Governmental Organisation (NGO), a university (or group of universities), a private sector company and so on. In some cases different kinds of entities might combine their efforts. For example, in Europe the European Commission regularly funds comparative research projects, usually carried out by universities, research institutes and consultants, on public policy topics of pressing interest to member states.

Informal and formal are, then, the two layers of policy transfer shown in Figure 12.1. Sure, there are overlaps between them, and this is why the cells are marked out with dotted lines. These categories are, to some extent, porous. Across the top of Figure 12.1 I distinguish three categories of transfer: technical measures; policy and practice; and governance change.[5] Again, the dotted lines signal permeability.

International technical exchange

If we turn to the first column we can see that, in its simplest form, international lesson drawing may focus on technical measures. Exchange on nitty-gritty issues of this kind may not hit the headlines, but it can lead to significant improvements in governmental effectiveness. Cell 1 in the diagram relates to informal policy transfer relating to technical matters. An enormous amount of international technical exchange is taking place all the time. Commercial companies facilitate this process by putting on international trade shows and conferences to showcase new technical advances that public authorities might want to purchase. In addition, professionals working in public services are constantly on the lookout for new technologies that might improve their performance, and there are many professional associations facilitating technical learning on an international basis. A good example is the International Fire Service Training Association (IFSTA), which shares ideas on fire fighting techniques.

Initiatives falling in Cell 2 of Figure 12.1 involve systematic evidence gathering to advance international knowledge relating to new techniques. Again commercial companies play a valuable role, as do networks of local authorities and universities. In addition, a large number of international organisations now seek to draw insights from scientific advances and translate research findings into technical guidance for practice. Set up in 1948 as a specialised agency of the United Nations, the World Health Organisation (WHO) provides a well-known example. The WHO exists to promote the highest possible levels of public health and, as part of its' work, it provides international guidance on topics like nutrition, polio eradication and a wide range of health topics.[6]

The Innovation Stories in this book have not focussed on technical measures. This is because, as I have explained at some length, successful moves towards the creation of inclusive cities require more significant changes than technological advance can provide. It follows that the next two columns in Figure 12.1, which focus on policy and practice and governance change, are more important than technical measures. However, if managed creatively technology can help leaders move towards their political objectives. Innovation Story 3 on the 311 service in Chicago provides an example. Here we saw how advances in computer technology, when coupled with a well-trained team of city hall staff, have been able to make services much more accessible to everyone in the city.

International exchange relating to policy and practice

Transferring ideas relating to policy and practice – the second column in Figure 12.1 – is more difficult than exchange of technical measures because established core values about what is appropriate are more likely to be questioned. As a result there are more obstacles in the path of effective knowledge utilisation. Nevertheless, we have seen how, at various points in this book, city-to-city international exchange relating to policy and practice has proved to be inspirational. Initiatives in Cell 3 involve informal policy transfer. Innovation Story 10 on the creation of the Bus Rapid Transit (BRT) system in Guangzhou provides a good example of this kind of international learning. In this case Mayor Zhang Guangning and his colleagues visited Bogota and were inspired by the achievements of the TransMilenio. This kind of city-to-city policy exchange is now accelerating at an exponential rate, and Campbell (2012) discusses various approaches and maps some of the patterns.

Cell 4 of Figure 12.1 refers to systematic evidence gathering leading to change in policy and practice. As with initiatives in Cell 3 activity of this kind is expanding rapidly. Individual cities may choose to gather evidence from other countries in a systematic way by bringing in outside help. Innovation Story 13, on place shaping in Melbourne, provides an example. Here civic leaders wanted to learn about imaginative approaches to urban design in other countries. In order to ensure that their remaking of the centre of the city would be on the cutting edge, they turned to the Copenhagen architect and urban designer Jan Gehl for advice and support. Gehl's team drew on a range of international experiences to offer excellent guidance to the city.

International exchange relating to governance

On the right side of Figure 12.1 we encounter the most demanding kind of transfer – that relating to governance change. Here policy makers ask whether the design of the institutional arrangements they have in place to govern society need to be reconsidered. Thus, for example, leaders may ask: 'How are cities and metropolitan regions planned and governed in other countries? Can we learn lessons for the institutional design of urban and regional government in our own country by examining foreign experience?'

A good example of informal policy transfer relating to governance (Cell 5) is the introduction of directly elected mayors into British local government.[7]

Debates relating to the institutional design of local governance are discussed in Chapter 7, including the arguments for and against introducing directly elected mayors. In the period 1999–2011 the British government introduced various statutes enabling localities to adopt a mayoral form of governance, if they so wished. Innovation Story 2 documents how Bristol citizens chose to introduce the mayoral form of governance into the city in 2012, and provides a preliminary assessment of the impact of the new model. The Bristol innovation in urban governance would not have been possible if central government had not drawn lessons from other countries and decided to pass legislation to permit the use of the mayoral model in the UK.

Finally, in the bottom right hand corner of Figure 12.1 we find formal policy transfer relating to governance change. The Royal Commission on Auckland Governance (2009) provides a good example of this approach. As explained in Innovation Story 7 the Royal Commission commissioned an analysis of urban governance models in other countries as part of its' research. The recommendations the Royal Commission made to the New Zealand Government drew on the analysis. In due course, the government decided to transform the governance of the city and the new system, notably the introduction of a metropolitan mayor for the new super-city, was influenced by international research and analysis.

Reflections on the international lesson drawing framework

International dialogue and exchange in all six cells of Figure 12.1 is on the rise. Perhaps this is not surprising given that we now live in a rapidly globalising world. From the point of view of place-based leaders wanting to create more inclusive cities several strategies and pathways to discovery are available. First, it is clear that cities wanting to improve their performance are becoming increasing active in creating new, city-to-city networks focussing on specific policy topics. Often referred to as 'communities of practice' these networks usually depend heavily on the Internet to exchange ideas, policies and practices. An Appendix provides more details of some of these international city networks. Second, recognising the impact of global forces, the institutions funding policy relevant research have become more international in their outlook, and are actively funding cross-national urban research projects in a way that was not the case twenty years ago. There are many examples of a move towards comparative research, including in national governments, nationally based research foundations and research councils. International organisations, like the European Commission, the OECD, the UN, and the World Bank provide many other examples of efforts to gather evidence on a systematic, cross-national basis. Third, many universities have, themselves, become more enthusiastic about cross-national comparative research – partly as a way of enhancing the quality of scholarship and partly from a desire to be more engaged in society in the sense used in Chapter 11.

This presentation of alternative approaches to international lesson drawing for cities is intended to provide a simple way of mapping the terrain.[8] As mentioned earlier, there are some areas of overlap between the categories. However, I hope that Figure 12.1 provides a way of making sense of a complex field – and it is one that we can expect to become more complex in the years ahead. City leaders may, perhaps, find the framework a useful input to the way they think through their international city-to-city learning strategies.

I would like to highlight three points from this discussion. First, all the approaches to international lesson drawing shown in Figure 12.1 are legitimate, and can lead to significant benefits for governors and governed alike. Second, the challenges for bringing about successful policy transfer increase as the ambition moves from technical measures (comparatively uncontroversial), through policy and practice (more challenging) to governance change (very challenging). This is because changes in policy and practice may require significant modification in behaviour, while governance change invariably involves a restructuring of local power.

Third, it seems clear that cities are much better placed than national governments to engage in international policy transfer of whatever kind. Benjamin Barber (2013) in his book on mayoral leadership supports this argument by drawing attention to 'dysfunctional nations' as compared to 'rising cities'. Certainly the research carried out for this book suggests that place-based leaders, as demonstrated by the many Innovation Stories presented in earlier chapters, are close to the ground, know their communities, and can make things happen quite quickly. The pace at which place-based leaders can move is mesmerising when compared with the glacial speed of decision-making one often encounters in central governments. It follows that nation states that have strong local governments will continue to enjoy an innovation advantage. The implications for academic, comparative research are far reaching. Scholars who are intrigued to understand the major drivers of international policy exchange in the coming period need to switch their attention from nation states to cities. Academic journals concerned with comparative public policy have hardly begun to address this challenge.

City futures and the inclusive city

In 2004, on behalf of the European Urban Research Association (EURA) and the Urban Affairs Association (UAA), I was part of a team that organised an international, academic conference on *City Futures*.[9] Held in Chicago, and administered by the University of Illinois at Chicago (UIC), the conference set out to explore alternative scenarios for cities.[10] In 2003, to spur fresh scholarly thinking about future possibilities, we set out two alternative futures for cities in the call for papers:

- **The alarming scenario**. This envisaged globalisation threatening local jobs, widening social divisions and leading to social disintegration. The city becomes a balkanised world with consumers living isolated lives in separate fortified enclaves. Political tensions draw forth the erosion of civil liberties as governments struggle to manage the 'ungovernable' city.

- **The uplifting scenario**. This saw global awareness growing in leaps and bounds. Transnational migrants would continue to refresh the culture, economic vitality and politics of increasingly lively urban areas. In many cities tolerance between different ethno-religious groups improves as diverse communities come to understand each other and work out ways of living together. Local democracy is revitalised, the public realm expands and cities re-establish themselves as enlightened centres of culture and civilised living.

It is not difficult to identify the preferred scenario. I revisit these scenarios in this closing part of the book to remind us of the stakes involved.

On the downside it can be argued that, in some respects, the prospects for cities are now considerably worse than they were in 2004 – there is evidence to suggest that the alarming scenario is winning out. For example, social inequality within cities has increased during this period, gated communities designed to exclude people are proliferating, and there are far too many examples of new urban developments that are uninspiring, if not very poor. Moreover, national governments have made insufficient progress in relation to climate change and environmental justice issues. It would not be difficult to add to this list of urban woes.

However, as explained at the very beginning of this book, my aim is not, simply, to provide an international examination of urban trends and emerging problems. On the contrary the central purpose of this book is to draw attention to the spectacular achievements of place-based leaders in different countries and continents who have moved policy and practice towards the creation of inclusive cities. While it is essential to understand the complex nature of modern urban problems, it is wise, at the same time, to pay attention to the efforts of civic leaders who have responded in a creative and imaginative way to these challenges. These place-based leaders should be praised because, notwithstanding the pressures of place-less power, they have taken positive steps to create more liveable, child-friendly, inclusive towns and cities.

The seventeen Innovation Stories presented in this volume provide strong evidence to support the claim that place-based leadership can make a significant difference, that market-dominated ways of thinking can be challenged and that local actors can shape urban fortunes. Moreover, the seventeen cities featured in the Innovation Stories are not the only ones breaking new ground. Progressive leaders in thousands of cities across the world are striving to move cities in the direction of the uplifting scenario identified above, and there are many exceptional achievements. Viewed from this perspective it is possible to identify many signs of progress since the *City Futures* Conference of 2004.

Conclusion: the grammar of place-based leadership

In the Preface I indicated that this book does not attempt to spell out solutions for cities. Rather, in a spirit of contributing to a process of co-creation of new possibilities, the book, by drawing on the work of David Cooper (1976), has attempted to hint at a grammar that the reader can revise and develop in the light of her or his own experience. The Opening section of the book identifies five components to this grammar, or potential grammar, and I revisit them here.

First, place matters. This is not to argue that other sources of identity and meaning are unimportant. Globalisation and, in particular, the arrival and expansion of the Internet, enable us to communicate with, and form relationships with, people who reside far away from where we live. This ability to communicate instantly over vast differences is full of progressive potential and, if used wisely, can be a liberating force. But, as we explore these new possibilities, we should never forget that most of us live in a particular place – and, for a variety of reasons, this place is likely to remain important to us. It is a source of community empowerment and it may even be that, in terms of our ontological security, place matters more today than it ever did before.

Second, civic leaders need to build inclusive, sustainable cities – not one or the other. We have, at various points in the narrative, noted the gap that too often exists between social and environmental reformers. My definition of the inclusive city, put forward in Chapter 1, attempts to unite two reform discourses that have, at times, ignored one another:

> The inclusive city is governed by powerful, place-based democratic institutions. All residents are able to participate fully in society and the economy, and civic leaders strive for just results while caring for the natural environment on which we all depend.

Third, civic leadership should assert the power of communities living in particular places. The book has shown that place-less power has expanded its' reach dramatically in the last thirty years or so. Place-less institutions, meaning organisations that disregard the consequences of their decisions for communities living in particular places, are not serving society well. Their power needs to be diminished and the power of place, meaning the power of local democracy, needs to be strengthened.

Fourth, we have discovered that there is great diversity in approaches to civic leadership, city planning and urban governance across the world. Sharing stories on an international basis about efforts to create inclusive cities can provide a source of inspiration to communities in other places. It is hoped that the seventeen Innovation Stories set out in this book offer practical lessons, or suggestions, for place-based leaders who may not have heard of them before.

Fifth, it is clear that academics can make a useful contribution to urban policy-making and public management. To be really effective, however, scholars need to embrace the idea of engaged scholarship – an approach which involves academics and practitioners co-creating new knowledge and understanding.

I would like to conclude by turning to the wisdom of a poet who became a president. Born in Prague, Vaclev Havel was a playwright, poet, dissident and politician. He was the last president of Czechoslovakia (1989– 92) and the first president of the Czech Republic (1993– 2003). He played a critical role in bringing about the dissolution of the Warsaw Pact, a Cold War power block linking eight communist states in Central and Eastern Europe. Havel never wanted to be a political leader and this makes his insights on democratic leadership all the more compelling:

> I am convinced that we will never build a democratic state based on rule of law if we do not at the same time build a state that is – regardless of how unscientific this may sound to the ears of a political scientist – humane, moral, intellectual and spiritual, and cultural. The best laws and the best-conceived democratic mechanisms will not in themselves guarantee legality or freedom or human rights – anything, in short, for which they were intended – if they are not underpinned by certain human and social values. (Havel 1992, 18)

In line with Havel's advice the place-based leadership I have described and analysed in this book strives to advance the cause of moral judgement in public policy and practice. It is the exercise of judgement – by all of us – that will create the inclusive city.

Notes

Preface

1 I use the word 'mainland' because there has been extensive urban unrest – known as 'The Troubles' – in Northern Ireland since the 1960s. These troubles involved conflict between elements of Northern Ireland's nationalist community (who mainly self-identified as Irish and/ or Roman Catholic) and its unionist community (who mainly self-identified as British and/ or Protestant (Bew et al. 2002). It should also be noted that urban disorder had occurred in mainland Britain before 1980. For example, the riots, which took place in the summer of 1958 in the St Ann's district of Nottingham and in the Notting Hill area of London, were shocking attacks on black communities by crowds of white racists. But, when compared with the Bristol riots and subsequent urban disturbances, there was little physical damage and nobody was killed.

2 The Scarman Report (Scarman, 1981) identified two main causes of the disturbances that took place in Brixton, London in April 1981: 1) oppressive policing over a period of years, and in particular the harassment of young blacks on the streets of Brixton, and 2) deeply frustrated and deprived people feeling the need to protest against society to draw public attention to their grievances. Harrison (1983, 369) amplifies our understanding by providing a moving account of the existential plight of people living in deprived inner city areas at the time. He predicted, correctly, 'a steady rise in the climate of fear and the society of barricaded self-defence, and a steady erosion of civil liberties'.

3 The Ouseley Report (2005) responded to the riots that took place in Bradford, West Yorkshire in July 2001. Lord Ouseley, former Chairman of the Commission for Racial Equality, led a Review Team, and his report argued that growing divisions among the population - along race, ethnic, religious and social class lines – had created a culture of fear in the city. His report suggested that strengthening civic leadership was critical, and that the top priority for municipal and community leaders was to create a 'can do' culture and to eliminate the culture of fear. The fact that, ten years later, urban riots did not break out in Bradford in August 2011, despite the widespread outbreaks of disorder elsewhere in the country, has led some to conclude that good civic leadership in Bradford has been successful in building multi-cultural understanding in the city.

4 Tesco, the biggest supermarket chain in the UK, is criticised for the way it offers loss-leading prices on convenience items in order to erase competition from locally based shops. Clement (2012, 87) argues that the April 2011 bout of public disorder in Bristol – known locally as the 'Tesco riot' – had been shaken into being 'by provocative policing on behalf of a giant corporation against the local community'.

5 The 2011 riots spread to 66 areas, lasted for four days, caused five deaths and millions of pounds of damage. An Independent Panel was set up by the government to study the causes of the 2011 riots. Chaired by Darra Singh, it concluded that the social unrest stemmed from a range of factors including: a lack of opportunities for young people, poor parenting, a failure of the justice system to rehabilitate offenders, a rise in materialism and distrust of the police (Riots, Communities and Victims Panel, 2012). The panel argued that the key response must be to 'give everyone a stake in society'. The Government published a response to the report of the Independent Panel in July 2013 (DCLG 2013). The Government chose not to have a Minister present the response to Parliament, which would have enabled a public debate. Instead, the Government issued the response, without an accompanying Press Release, during the Summer Recess (when Parliament is not sitting). Critics suggested that the Government was trying to

minimise public discussion of its failure to address issues raised by the Panel, and noted that the response indicates that, over a year after the report of the Independent Panel was published, only 11 of the 63 recommendations have been acted upon.

6 Barber (2013) argues that leadership approaches developed in cities are illuminating for public leadership in general for two reasons: 1) city mayors are well used to working on 'interdependent challenges' and are less likely to fall into 'silo' thinking when compared with national governments; and 2) city mayors are becoming increasingly effective in collaborating across international borders.

7 I draw this idea of developing a grammar, or series of grammers, from Cooper (1976).

Chapter 1

1 The literature on urban and environmental studies is an expanding one. I provide citations to various sources throughout this book. The following texts provide useful overviews of the challenges now facing cities: Benton-Short and Short 2013; Boone and Modarres 2006; Bridge and Watson 2011; Dannenberg et al 2011; Davies and Imbroscio 2010; De Blij 2009; Fainstein 2010; Friedmann 2002; Gehl 2010; Girardet 2008; Nightingale 2012; UN-DESA 2012; and UN-Habitat 2010; 2011; and 2012.

2 Over thirty years ago Dearlove (1979, 259) offered a robust critique of scholars who engage in problem solving and policy analysis. He suggested that a 'practical and relevant orientation to those in power has meant that [scholars in institutions adopting this approach] have tended to engage in a special kind of research which, because of its starting brief and assumptions, is objectively deficient and ideological'. This position should not be dismissed, and more recent scholarship in urban studies – for example, a collection assembled by Davies and Imbroscio (2010) – reminds us that researchers need to study the 'unexamined' and 'taken for granted'. In this book I attempt to bridge the worlds of academe and practice by drawing on US ideas relating to 'engaged scholarship' and this approach is explored in more detail in Chapter 11.

3 Recent debates about the role of research in universities in the UK, and elsewhere, have revealed conflicts of view about whether scholars should be required to demonstrate that their research has 'impact' or not. The Higher Education Funding Council for England has, for example, now introduced a Research Excellence Framework (REF) to replace the Research Assessment Exercise (RAE). Under the REF the evaluation of research efforts of all research active scholars in the country includes an assessment of their research impact. A 2009 consultation paper put it this way: 'Significant additional recognition will be given where researchers build on excellent research to deliver demonstrable benefits to the economy, society, public policy, culture and quality of life' (HEFCE 2009). In the UK, at least, national policy for universities encourages researchers to demonstrate 'impact' and we will discuss this development further in Chapter 11.

4 The evidence to support the argument that cities and societies are becoming more unequal is substantial. See, for example: Davis 2006; Dorling 2011; Hamnett 2003; Nightingale 2012; OECD 2008; Piketty 2014; Sassen 2001; and Wilkinson and Pickett 2010.

5 Numerous other scholars have contributed to the discussion of social equity in cities. See, for example: Brenner et al 2012; Friedmann 2002; Iveson and Fincher 2011; Nightingale 2012; Sandercock 1998 and 2003; and Young 2000.

6 At this stage of the discussion I am introducing themes relating to the leadership of localities. The arguments apply to rural and semi-urban areas as well as cities. At times the phrases 'urban leadership', 'city leadership', 'civic leadership' and 'local leadership' are used to refer to the same idea – they are all versions of 'place-based leadership'. Chapters 4 and 5 examine the nature of place-based leadership in more detail.

7 In his speech to the Labour Party Annual Conference in 2011 Ed Miliband, the Leader of the UK Labour Party, made a similar distinction between different kinds of business. He argued that the main political choice today is not between parties who are pro-business or anti-business – all parties must be pro-business. He suggested that the real choice now facing citizens is: 'Are you on the side of the wealth creators or the asset strippers? The producers or the predators? Producers train, invest, invent, sell.... Predators are just interested in the fast buck, taking what they can out of the business....We must learn the lesson that growth is built on sand if it comes from our predators and not our producers' (Miliband 2011). In the period since this speech was made the leaders of other UK political parties have developed similar rhetoric, often referring to the need for a more responsible form of capitalism. Meanwhile, Sassen (2014) has elaborated a theoretical framework to explain the growth of 'predatory formations'.

8 As Saskia Sassen explains, large corporate firms work actively to skew decision-making in their favour. She notes that the extensive lobbying efforts of US companies receive virtually no attention in the mainstream news. For example, GE spent $39.3 million just on Washington lobbying in 2010, more than $73,000 per senator and representative (Sassen 2014, 269). The point I want to highlight here is that centralisation of power within nation states suits *big* business. While the sums of money involved in lobbying central governments may appear huge, the big companies know that this is excellent value for money. It would be impossible for corporate power to be able to exercise the same amount of influence across the decision-making of the hundreds of thousands of local governments (that now exist across the world) were they to gain a significant expansion in their political power.

9 As an aside we can note that, within both the sciences and the social sciences, there has been a remarkable growth in interdisciplinary studies in recent years. Interdisciplinarity involves combining two or more academic disciplines in a single study. Subjects such as global warming, the epidemiology of AIDS, and social inequality require insights to be drawn from different disciplines. In the sciences we see the emergence of new interdisciplinary fields, such as bioinformatics and synthetic biology.

10 This idea of 'seeing like a city' rather than 'seeing like a state' derives from work by Scott (1998).

11 The UK *Total Place* initiative morphed into *Community Budgets* during 2011/12. The *Community Budgets* approach focuses attention on new ways of meeting the needs of families with multiple problems. We examine a pioneering example of this approach, the Family LIFE Project in Swindon, in Innovation Story 5 in Chapter 6.

12 Problems of rampant departmentalism in central government are nothing new. The *Total Approach* of the 1970s encountered many of the problems that now confront *Total Place* and *Community Budgets* initiatives (Hambleton 2010).

13 Michael Heseltine, a leading Conservative politician, was the UK Secretary of State for the Environment in the early 1990s. In that role he floated the possibility of introducing directly elected mayors into local government in order to strengthen local leadership in England (Department of the Environment 1991). Tory MPs attacked the idea, fearing it would lead to high-profile place-based politicians who would become rival forces in their constituencies. Quick as a flash, the policy was dropped. In Chapter 5 we discuss how the Labour Government, and in particular Prime Minister Tony Blair, reinvigorated the debate about place-based leadership in England.

14 The paper claims to use the UK as an example of 'city oriented national policies and initiatives that seek to marry local leadership with national frameworks in a global system' (Clark and Clark 2014, 5). The text, however, is more than misleading when it suggests that a major shift in power from central government to UK cities is taking place. It omits any reference to the unprecedented cuts in local government spending (around a 30 per cent reduction in total

annual revenue spending over the three-year period 2012/13 to 2014/15), nor to the fact that the so-called Localism Act 2011 contains over 140 centralising measures, still less to the fact that elected local authorities, even now, cannot set their own levels of local taxation. Local leaders in the UK continue to be hamstrung by a massively over-centralised state, and we will revisit this debate in Chapter 5.

15 The movement from 'government' to 'governance' is now a familiar theme in urban and local government studies. See, for example: Denters and Rose 2005; Goss 2001; Haus et al 2005; Heinelt et al 2006; Hambleton and Gross 2007.

16 This is consistent with the managerial literature on innovation – see, for example, Tidd et al (2005, 66)

17 The literature on power is extensive, and I am only introducing a few important ideas at this point. The interested reader may wish to refer to Flyvbjerg (2001), Foucault (1979), Lukes (2005) and Scott (2001).

18 The literature on social inclusion, social exclusion and inequality is expanding. See, for example: Askonas and Stewart 2000; Byrne 1999; Craig et al 2008; Dorling 2011; Taket et al 2009; and Young 2000. For disability policy see: Fleisher and Zames 2001; and Roulstone and Prideaux 2012.

19 We discuss the meanings of place, space and territory in Chapter 4. At this point I am using the word 'place' to signal elements of all three.

20 My colleagues at the University of the West of England have contributed valuable insights in relation to this theme within the UK context (Smith et al 2007). An excellent American study of uneven neighbourhood outcomes is provided by Levy et al 1974.

21 See, for example, Doran et al 2004

22 Marshall was writing about the advance of citizenship rights in the British context, and this sequence of achievements will depart, in timing at least, from the evolution of citizenship rights in other countries. Nevertheless, his separation of citizenship into three parts is helpful. Marshall's lectures are reproduced in a more recent volume in which Tom Bottomore adds in a discussion of how the ideas have fared 'forty years on' (Marshall and Bottomore 1992). Bottomore draws attention to the significant impact of post-war migrations, especially of workers from poorer countries to more developed countries. In his prescient analysis he notes the significance of 'a new debate about formal citizenship, as well as organisations campaigning for more liberal policies in the conferment of citizenship on long-term residents (and on the other side nationalist, not to say xenophobic, movements which aim to exclude or expel foreign workers).' (Marshall and Bottomore 1992, 83)

23 Welfare states have been successful in delivering a wide range of important services but gains are always under threat. For example, social housing is under attack in the USA (Bennett et al 2006; Goetz 2013)

24 The 'right to the city', which gained United Nations (UN) recognition at the World Urban Forum in Barcelona in 2004, has its origins in the writings of Henri Lefebvre – notably Lefebvre 1996 (originally published in 1968). It has gained momentum in recent years – see, for example, Mitchell 2003, Brown and Kristiansen 2009, Soja 2010 and Harvey 2012.

25 The brutal gang rape of a woman on a bus in Delhi, India on 16 December 2012 provides disturbing, high profile evidence to support the analysis Whitzman and her colleagues make (Whitzman et al 2013) for improving public safety for women. Shackle (2013) argues that India is not unique in failing to implement laws designed to protect women, and advocates a serious and sustained discussion of rape, and the myriad factors that allow it to happen. Sanchez de

Madariaga and Roberts (2013) provide an extensive analysis of the impact of gender on urban planning in Europe, and explore the links between environmental sustainability and gender-sensitive urban development.

26 The LGBT acronym is well established in the UK and the USA but it may not be familiar in all countries. In use since the 1990s, the term refers to the lesbian, gay, bisexual and transgender community. There are variations in different countries, but the term has gained some acceptance as a self-designation by many sexuality and gender identity-based groups. See, for example, Hirshman (2012) and Stein (2012).

27 Various writers have drawn attention to the importance of embedding an understanding of diversity in the planning and management of the modern city – see, for example, Watson 2006, and Fincher and Iveson 2008.

28 Cornwall (2008) provides a helpful international analysis of inclusive democratic practices, and Taylor (2011) provides an extended examination of the nature of 'community' and 'community empowerment'. Fraser (2004) also offers useful insights on this theme.

29 A growing number of writers have drawn attention to the unfortunate consequences of this divide in thought and practice. Here I draw, in particular, on Boone and Modarres (2006), Benton-Short and Short (2013), Newman et al (2009) and Parkin (2010).

30 Even Susan Fainstein in her excellent book *The Just City* neglects ecological considerations: 'The question of sustainability will also be raised, but this will be a subsidiary discussion – not because of its lack of importance but simply because it is too difficult to encompass within a single book' (Fainstein 2010, 20–1)

31 For example, the goal of 'sustainable development' was endorsed by the leaders (including Prime Minister Thatcher of the UK and President Reagan of the USA) of the G7 group of industrialised nations at the Toronto summit of 1988. An attempt was made to disguise the conflicts between environmental protection and economic development: 'The term sustainable development appears like a magic wand to wave away such conflicts in a single unifying goal. We can have our cake and eat it, it seems to say' (Jacobs 1991, 59)

32 This framework departs from the familiar presentation of sustainable development in the literature and in policy circles. The established model of sustainable development also comprises three overlapping spheres – but these are usually labelled as environmental, economic and social. Policy prescriptions stemming from this conceptualisation often advocate thinking in terms of 'a triple bottom line' – achieving economic prosperity, environmental quality and social justice (Elkington 1997). As we have seen, however, while many companies and governments may espouse these principles, actual performance in implementing the principles often leaves a lot to be desired.

33 Richard Rees and I spoke at a conference on *Places in Transition* in London on 21 January 2010 organised by the UK Resource for Urban Design Information (RUDI). I draw here, with his permission, on his presentation titled *Re-thinking places: The individual, society and nature in city design*.

34 Spurred on by concerns about climate change, the wasteful consumption of vast quantities of fossil fuels, fears about food and water shortages, and in recognition of the need to develop renewable energy strategies and a steady state economy, the literature on urban resilience is expanding. A number of useful texts are now available – see, for example, Berners-Lee and Clark 2013; Bulkeley 2013; Droege (2006), Flint and Raco (2012), Hopkins (2011), Jackson (2009), Lewis and Conaty (2012), Monaghan (2012) and Newman et al (2009). For overviews of the city as an eco-system see Girardet (2008) and Newman and Jennings (2008).

[35] Ford (2013, 48–9) explains how guerrilla gardening is an umbrella term covering a range of activities – from individuals and small groups, who make seed bombs or plant flowers and herbs in small public patches of earth, through to highly motivated groups who illicitly adopt abandoned or neglected land and cultivate it for the benefit of all.

[36] It is worth noting that in recent years scholars have created new academic journals that are attempting to advance interdisciplinary analysis of cities and urban development – ones that span socio-political and socio-environmental perspectives. For example, the European Urban Research Association (EURA) launched an international journal – *Urban Research and Practice* – in 2008; and *The International Journal of Urban Sustainable Development* was first published in 2010.

[37] I draw this idea of developing a grammar, or series of grammars, from Cooper (1976). His presentation invites the reader to break the 'rules' and invent new possibilities.

[38] In another publication Friedmann (2000) provides a brillant defence of utopian thinking in relation to cities. This pro-utopian position also gains support from Anthony Giddens who suggests that policy relating to climate change should be seasoned with a dash of utopian thinking: 'Why? Because however it happens, we are moving our way towards a form of society that essentially will be quite different from the one in which we live today' (Giddens 2009, 13)

[39] It may be important to note that 'just result' has a particular meaning in this context. Iris Young outlines a process of public deliberation in which the conditions of equal opportunity to speak, and freedom from domination, encourage all to express their needs and interests: 'Knowing that they are answerable to others, and that they are mutually committed to reaching agreement, means that each understands that his or her best interests will be served by aiming for a just result' (Young 2000, 30)

[40] A parallel can be drawn with community development practice. Participatory approaches often encounter friction around the question: Whose knowledge counts? Eversole (2012) discusses how to blend 'expert' knowledge with 'indigenous knowledge' in community development practice.

[41] The Anglo-Dutch study develops three Innovation Stories and each story is presented under the following headings: 1) Introduction and overview, 2) Aims and objectives, 3) Urban governance context, 4) Unfolding the Innovation Story, 5) Understanding the impact of the innovation, and 6) Explaining the role of leadership in the innovation (Hambleton and Howard 2012). In this book I use a less elaborate framework.

[42] Kahneman explains that Taleb (2007) developed the 'narrative fallacy'; and that the 'halo effect' was presented in a book by Rosenzweig (2007).

Chapter 2

[1] In the following discussion of population growth and change I draw on the work of the United Nations Department of Economic and Social Affairs (DESA) and, in particular, their analysis of world urbanisation prospects (UN-DESA 2012). More: http://esa.un.org/unup

[2] These figures are inevitably broad brush. De Blij (2009, 184–6) explains how the definition of 'urban' varies by country. For example, in Canada any settlement that has a population that is larger than 1,000 is a 'town', whereas in India a place can have up to 5,000 residents and still be designated a 'village'. In Japan, a settlement cannot be officially designated as 'urban' until it has 30,000 inhabitants or more. This definitional variety, quite apart from the speed of change and the limitations of census data, mean that we should not expect precision when discussing global urban trends.

3 For example, the United Nations Human Settlements Programme (UN-Habitat) assembles invaluable data on global urbanisation, produces regular reports on the state of the world's cities and offers many ideas on how to improve policies for cities – see, for example, UN-Habitat (2012).

4 United Cities and Local Governments (UCLG) deserves special mention in this context. Headquartered in Barcelona, UCLG represents the interests of local governments across the world, regardless of the size of the communities they serve. UCLG's members represent over half of the world's population and the organisation is active in carrying out comparative research on local governance and in promoting the values of local self-government. More: http://www.uclg.org

5 The adjectives used here – minor, small, medium-sized, large – are my own, not those of the UN. They assist with communication and are consistent with Birch and Wachter (2011, 9–15)

6 These figures refer to the metropolitan area of Mexico City. In 2012 Mexico City itself had a population of 8.9 million. However, if the 60 or so municipalities that surround the city are included, the Metropolitan Area of the Valley of Mexico (as it is called) had a population of 20.1 million in 2012. This example reminds us that, as we discuss 'shrinking' cities, it is very important to be clear about the geographical areas being considered. The distinction between the 'central city' and the 'metropolitan area' is critical in this context.

7 The text that follows draws directly on the analysis provided by Brugmann in Chapter 3 'The Great Migration' (Brugmann 2009, 33–54)

8 The term 'dynamic diversity' is close to, but different from, 'hyper-diverse'. The latter is used in urban studies scholarship to refer to communities that are very multiethnic. For example, Price and Benton-Short (2007, 112) suggest that a population is hyper-diverse if: 1) at least 9.5% of the total population is foreign-born, 2) no one country of origin accounts for 25% or more of the immigrant stock, and 3) immigrants come from all regions of the world. Our term dynamic diversity draws attention to the rapid pace of change towards a much more diverse population in a given locality – a process that has important implications for the maintenance of effective democratic governance.

9 Dynamic diversity in Toronto is discussed in more detail in Innovation Story 15

Chapter 3

1 This quote is from Joseph Chamberlain's speech to the City Council on his third election as mayor. Chamberlain served three one-year terms (Hennock 1973, 143)

2 A typical pattern is that local activists break new ground by trying out new approaches. These experiments form the evidence base for reform campaigns and a responsive state is able to take up the ideas and build them into local and/or national policy. For example, Robert Owen, a Welsh social reformer, was active in promoting improvements in the health and working conditions of factory workers in the UK in the early 19th Century. Widely regarded as the founder of infant child-care in Britain, the sensitive approach to workers and their families introduced under his leadership at the New Lanark mill and community had a national, even European, impact. The UK Factory Act 1819 was, for example, influenced by his efforts. Jane Addams, a social and political activist, provides a good American example of inspirational local leadership. In 1889 she co-founded Hull House, Chicago, the first settlement house in the US. By demonstrating how radical ideas could work, she pioneered a range of social services for mothers and children in the 1890s. Her local initiatives and campaigning had a major impact on the trajectory of US policies for health and welfare.

3 An early version of this diagram was presented in Burns et al (1994, 22). I have used it extensively in training and development workshops with civic leaders and public managers in numerous countries. It can be very helpful in assisting leaders and managers think through the kind of relationship they wish to see developed between the state and society in their locality. In any given city it is possible to have a mix of empowerment strategies; arriving at an appropriate balance between these options is a critical matter for place-based leaders to consider.

4 Private sector management books are crammed with advice on how companies should not just get close to their customers but should develop a customer obsession. Many are now using social media not just to find out enormous amounts of personal information about customers, but also to turn gullible customers into salespeople. For example, many Internet websites designed to sell products now invite buyers, often in a not so subtle way, to recommend purchases to their friends via social networking sites.

5 New Public Management emerged in the 1980s and involves the use of private sector management practices in the public sector. In essence, it stems from the belief that government should be run like a private business. Pollitt (1990) identified the contours of managerialism in public services that emerged at the time. A useful overview is provided by Denhardt and Denhardt (2003, 12–24); see also Hood (1991).

6 At the time of writing Nesta has, surprisingly, refused to disclose how much they have paid for their share in the new business, and the financial details of the new arrangements have yet to be shared with the public.

7 The letter is discussed by Jamie Doward in The Observer (Doward 2014).

8 I draw here on an analysis I presented in a previous book to illustrate this shift (Hambleton 2007, 164–5).

9 There are different ways of interpreting the movement from government to governance and Jill Gross and I discuss these at some length elsewhere (Hambleton and Gross 2007). We note that the movement is not, necessarily, benign. Two of the chapters in our book offer a robust critique of urban governance models. Judd and Smith (2007) argue that governance in some American cities has gone too far in the sense that private stakeholders have taken over the reins of civic power. Davies (2007) offers a similar critique of UK local governance and suggests that the regeneration partnerships developed in many localities are designed to orchestrate a neo-liberal agenda. It follows that the design of governance arrangements and, in particular, the arrangements for democratic accountability are enormously important.

10 There is a substantial literature relating to various aspects of civil society. Taylor (2011) provides a good introduction. Other useful texts on the following topics are: social capital (Putnam 1993); communitarianism (Etzioni 1995); and community development (Ledwith 2011). We return to these themes in Chapter 7.

11 There is a growing literature on network governance that is beginning to throw new light on the interactions between actors in policy making and policy delivery networks. Davies (2011) provides a good overview as well as a robust critique of network governance theory and practice.

12 The idea of creating a 'Big Society', as set out by Prime Minister David Cameron in various speeches in 2010, seeks to encourage volunteerism in society (Norman 2010; Tuddenham 2010). The concept has been criticised for its vacuity, and many claim that it is merely a rhetorical device to provide cover for major cuts in public spending.

13 The idea of public value, first presented in a book by Mark Moore, has attracted interest in public policy circles in the USA and the UK (Moore 1995; Benington and Moore 2011). However, the term has never been defined clearly with the result that it becomes a vague, disembodied

concept – one that conceals conflicts of view and, as a result, diminishes the vital role of politics in public service reform discussions (Rhodes and Wanna 2007).

14 Hoggett (2009, 61–77) provides an incisive analysis of the dynamics of conflict in modern societies, and notes how some communities can become heavily 'defended' to the point where their boundaries become increasingly rigid and impermeable.

15 The origins of community development as a recognisable paid activity can be traced back to the early 1950s. The field blossomed in the 1960s, partly because of the growth of the civil rights movement in the USA, but also because of similar pressures for more participatory approaches to public policy making in Europe and elsewhere. The *Community Development Journal (CDJ)* was launched in 1965. A useful collection of key texts on community development is provided in Craig et al (2011)

Chapter 4

1 We should note that some feminists have offered a critique of the notion that 'home' is, necessarily, a secure and peaceful place. In simple terms the argument they present is that, for women, the home may be a place of work, a place of conflict and even an arrangement for women's oppression. For a discussion of space, place and gender see Massey (1994).

2 I offer just one example, drawn from my own experience. While working for the Chief Executive of Stockport Metropolitan Borough Council in the 1970s I was honoured to be involved in setting up a comprehensive system of area management in the borough. Stockport was the first English authority to devolve powers to place-based area committees of councillors, a system that is now embedded in the political structure of the borough. To handle decision-making the bureaucracy developed a form of matrix management with some officers having dual accountability – to departmental and area-based sources of authority. An examination of the creation of the scheme is provided in Hambleton (1978).

3 There is some evidence to suggest that business thinkers are beginning to recognise that this is an unsatisfactory state of affairs, even when viewed from a narrow profit seeking point of view. This is because all business is local (Quelch and Jocz 2012). Many global companies now strive to present themselves as locally oriented and eco-friendly. For example, IBM claims it creates 'Solutions for a Small Planet' and HSBC marketing literature claims that it is 'The world's local bank'. Assertions of this kind may, of course, be just spray-on coatings designed to mask a global machine that remains unresponsive to the needs of particular places. Much depends on whether decision-making power in such companies is devolved in a massive way to managers working in particular localities.

4 The Oxford English Dictionary definition of 'brand' is: a) a particular make of goods, or b) an identifying trademark, label etc. Either way it is a commercial concept. Inevitably, therefore, the use of the word brand in the context of cities or places involves a commodification of these places. A particular trademark has to be defined and communicated. Much city branding and place marketing activity therefore involves the manipulation of information and imagery about a given place in order to present a desired message (Anholt 2010; Dinnie 2011; Go and Govers 2013; Zavattaro 2013).

5 The discussion here simplifies a complex set of debates relating to the changing nature of city and regional planning. For more extended treatments please see: Adams and Tiesdell 2013; Haughton et al 2010; Morphet 2010; and Rydin 2011.

6 Evan McKenzie, a professor at the University of Illinois at Chicago, maintains an insightful blog on the growth of private government in the USA: http://privatopia.blogspot.co.uk

7 The tragic killing of a black teenager in a gated community in the USA in 2012 illustrates, in an alarming way, Bauman's argument about the effects of a pervasive culture of fear. Trayvon Martin, a 17-year-old unarmed, African American student, walked into a gated community in Sanford, Florida on 26 February 2012. George Zimmerman, a local resident, shot him dead. Zimmerman was charged with second-degree murder, but was acquitted because the prosecution were unable to prove their case beyond a reasonable doubt. When Zimmerman was acquitted in July 2013, there was a national outcry.

8 In the USA the legal arguments around what is a public space and what is not continue to this day. Kohn (2004) explains that, in the landmark decision *Lloyd v. Tanner* (1972), the Supreme Court found that the right to free speech only extends to activity on public not private property. However, in a subsequent decision, *Pruneyard v. Robbins* (1980), the Supreme Court indicated that a shopping mall, unlike a home or a private club, issues an invitation to the general public and therefore opens itself up to certain kinds of regulations. This means that free speech in privately owned places, although not protected by the US Constitution, can, potentially at least, enjoy protection by state legislation, if the place is publicly accessible. Plenty of work for lawyers here, you might say.

Chapter 5

1 The notion of political space is well established in urban studies and social geography. For example, Lefevre (2010) discusses the process of building metropolitan areas as political spaces. Following Cox (1998) he defines political space as a space of involvement of political, economic and social players where a legitimate collective action is produced, an action necessary to address existing issues and orient the future. We discuss this shaping of place-based collective action later in the chapter.

2 The extraordinary centralisation of power within the British state is deeply troubling for those of us who live in the UK. Prime Minister Thatcher – through the introduction of the Rates Act 1984 – took the power to set the level of local taxation over the heads of local voters. Known originally as 'rate capping' (as the single local tax available to local authorities in those days was a property tax called rates), this centralised approach was, despite promises to the contrary, retained by the Labour Government in the period from 1997–2010. The Coalition Government, elected in 2010, has also retained capping. In various lectures I have described the dramatic shift of power within England from localities to Whitehall in the last thirty years as 'centralisation on steroids'. Film available at: www.urbananswers.co.uk

3 The Woodrow Wilson International Centre for Scholars deserves praise in this context. The Centre has done much to promote research and analysis of urban governance in developing countries, and has produced a series of useful publications – for example: Ruble et al 2001; Tulchin et al 2002; Eyoh and Stren 2007. More information: www.wilsoncenter.org

4 Research on the performance of US city mayors lends support to this claim. For example, Ferman (1985, 197) shows how '...leadership strategies must be examined in the context in which they are executed'. And Flanagan (2004), in the light of his examination of the performance of nine American city mayors, highlights how timing is critical – the political space available to civic leaders, the relationship between structural forces and the power of agency, varies over time.

5 I have found the following texts to be particularly helpful: Bungay 2011; Burns 1978; Gardner 1990; Grint 1997; Heifetz and Linsky 2002; Keohane 2010; Parkin 2010; and Pendleton and Furnham 2012.

6 The literature on public leadership is still relatively young but some useful texts have appeared recently: Brookes and Grint (2010); and Joyce (2012). A useful commentary on public leadership literature is provided by Liddle (2010).

7 There are many leadership books focussing on the personal qualities and skills of leaders – see, for example, Nicholson (2013) and Taylor (2002)

8 Early on in my career I worked for several different local authorities within England and can confirm that, in the 1970s, I encountered a number of political leaders who saw themselves as the council 'boss'. There was no mistaking their autocratic view that they knew best what the people in their city needed. This perspective was, of course, born from their experience, and explains, in part, the paternalistic styles of leadership and management that we discussed in Chapter 3. Chicago was not the only city to be run by a 'boss' in the 1960s and 1970s (Royko 1971).

9 As an aside we can note that recent academic work is starting to throw new light on the changing nature of leadership. For example, Drath et al (2008) discuss the ontology of leadership and note that modern leadership is likely to involve dialogue and sense-making, which involves a shift away from leader-follower conceptualisations. Sun and Anderson (2012) highlight the links between transformational leadership and civic capacity and advocate integrative public leadership.

10 I recognise that leadership is a contested concept. Discussion of the nature of leaders and leadership should always take account of historical processes and the social context. Nevertheless there is, for the purposes of this book, virtue in a ten-word definition because it provides a reasonable degree of clarity about how I am using this slippery term.

11 The idea of realms of civic leadership was first developed in work the author carried out on leadership for the Royal Commission on Auckland Governance (Hambleton 2009). These ideas were further developed in a scoping report for the UK Local Authority Research Council Initiative (LARCI) (Hambleton et al 2009); and in a report the author co-authored with Jo Howard for the Joseph Rowntree Foundation (Hambleton and Howard 2012).

12 I am grateful to Katherine Rossiter, Managing Director of the Society of Local Authority Chief Executives and Senior Managers (SOLACE), for this insight, provided at an Anglo-Dutch Workshop on Place-based Leadership that Joanna Howard and I co-organised on 9 November 2011. SOLACE would like to acknowledge the source of this concept as The Cranfield School of Management. For further information and to read Dr Catherine Bailey's discussion of the 'ZOUD', go to: http://www.som.cranfield.ac.uk/som/dinamic-content/media/knowledgeinterchange/topics/20110404/Article.pdf

Chapter 6

1 Swindon and Enschede participated in an international action research project led by the author and Jo Howard in 2011/12. The two cities shared their experiences on how to deliver radical public innovation to tackle social exclusion. Longer versions of the Innovation Stories presented in this chapter are provided in the final report of that research project (Hambleton and Howard 2012). I am grateful to the Joseph Rowntree Foundation for permission to reproduce material from this research report in this chapter.

2 In the policy studies literature these kinds of problems are, following Rittel and Webber (1973), sometimes described as 'wicked' problems and they are contrasted with 'tame' problems. Tame problems may be complicated but they can probably be resolved in a step-by-step fashion because there is only a limited degree of uncertainty. A wicked problem is altogether more complex. This is because there is no clear relationship between cause and effect and the various

stakeholders in the policy process will have competing ideas about how to solve the problem. Grint (2010) suggests that tame problems are akin to puzzles that can be solved whereas wicked problems require leaders to ask questions so that collaborative problem solving can take place. The conceptual distinction between complicated and complex problems is most helpful. However, I find the adjectives 'wicked' and 'tame' to be needless and distracting jargon and prefer to avoid using these terms.

[3] Adner (2012) uses the phrase 'innovation ecosystem' repeatedly. This is confusing as an ecosystem is a biological community of interacting organisms and their physical environment. His book does not discuss the environment at all and a better description of the system he is describing is 'innovation system'.

[4] In many countries the public telephone network has a single emergency telephone number to give the caller instant access to emergency services. The first emergency number to be introduced anywhere in the world was in London in 1937 using the number 999, and this was quickly extended to the whole of the UK. In North America and some South American countries, the emergency number is 911. In the European Union, Russia, Ukraine and Switzerland 112 was introduced as the emergency number in the 1990s.

[5] This section and Innovation Story 5 draw directly on the analysis of the Social GP programme provided by Bas Denters, Pieter-Jan Klok and Mirjan Oude Vrielink. This appears as Chapter 4 in *Public Sector Innovation and Local Leadership in the UK and the Netherlands* (Hambleton and Howard 2012). I am most grateful to them for giving me permission to draw on this material in this chapter.

[6] Informal settlements provide accommodation for an expanding number of poor people in the developing world. A number of respected organisations have grown up to speak out on behalf of shack/slum dwellers and to promote citizen-led poverty reduction. Satterthwaite and Mitlin (2014) provide a helpful overview of these efforts. There are numerous national shack/slum dwellers federations. Shack/Slum Dwellers International (SDI) is the leading international association. More: http://www.sdinet.org

[7] I wish to acknowledge here the following for their very important contributions to the discussion that is presented in this chapter: Jo Howard, Bas Denters, Pieter-Jan Klok and Mirjan Oude Vrielink. We are, in turn, more than grateful to the practitioners in Bristol, Enschede and Swindon, who provided the practical wisdom that underpinned our study. A longer version of our thinking is provided in Hambleton and Howard (2012). I am grateful to the Joseph Rowntree Foundation for permission to reproduce diagrams from our research report as well as edited sections of text from the report.

[8] This idea of a 'Zone of Uncomfortable Debate' (ZOUD) was used in the Anglo-Dutch research project in 2011. Kathryn Rossiter of SOLACE introduced the concept and cited the source for this notion as Dr Catherine Bailey, Director of the Cranfield Business Leaders Programme: http://www.som.cranfield.ac.uk/som/dinamic-content/media/knowledgeinterchange/topics/20110404/Article.pdf

[9] Barrett (2012, 43) highlights the importance of imperfection and forgiveness and quotes Miles Davies, the legendary trumpeter, bandleader, and composer, who had a favourite saying about jazz musicians: 'If you're not making mistakes, it's a mistake'. This reminds me of a similar comment made, some years ago, when I attended a circus skills class. Our tutor, Haggis, an outstanding seven-club juggler would shout out: 'If you are not dropping the clubs you are not improving!'

[10] Scharmer and Kaufer (2013, 184–9) provide a helpful discussion of the role of prototype initiatives in promoting innovation, and refer to prototyping as 'exploring the future by doing' (p188).

11 Yapp argues that the ability to use metaphors and stories is important in innovation. In line with the analysis presented here, he suggests that the innovation capacity of public service organisations would be improved if their senior managers possessed more developed narrative skills.

12 This quotation has been attributed to Malcolm Muggeridge, an English journalist and author. However, he acknowledged that it was a saying he had discovered informally from someone in Manchester in the 1960s – see *Radio Times,* 9 July 1964.

Chapter 7

1 There is a growing body of literature addressing this theme. See, for example, Jackson (2009), Chang (2010), Esteva et al (2013) and Piketty (2014).

2 In a famous speech on 20 October 1850 the Chartist leader, Ernest Jones, urged his followers to 'Organise, Organise, Organise'. A century later Saul Alinsky, the influential American community activist, used very similar ideas in his approach to political campaigning in Chicago (Alinsky 1969). And, in more recent years, Barack Obama in his years as a community organiser on the South Side of Chicago, was to employ many of the same techniques. Wolffe (2009, 60–64) argues that Alinsky-inspired organising in Chicago enabled the future President of the US to find his racial identity, develop a worldview and a real understanding of the importance of community-based action.

3 I set out these ideas in a public lecture – 'What is local government for?' – to the Bristol Festival of Ideas Mayor's Conference, The Watershed, Bristol, 15 May 2013. Available at: http://urbananswers.co.uk

4 King John of England signed the Magna Carta at Runnymede on 15 June 1215. This required the King of England to accept that his will was not arbitrary, and it is widely recognised, in the English-speaking world, as a significant step forward for the introduction of constitutional law in England and beyond.

5 As a personal aside, in May 1988 I visited the US Senate to watch the national debates. At that point there were, out of 100 Senators, only two women – Nancy Kasselbaum, a Republican from Kansas, and Barbara Mikulski, a Democrat from Maryland. On the day I visited the Senate these two women, and this is no criticism, were absent from the chamber. The overwhelmingly uncomfortable feeling of maleness – and it is not a good feeling – in a major political assembly has never left me. I wrote about this at the time (Hambleton 1988).

6 The discussion that follows draws directly on Hambleton and Bullock (1996). There may be a need to clarify the use of terms here as local government systems in different countries use different words to describe various roles and responsibilities. In some countries the Executive – the senior group of politicians leading the city – is called the Cabinet. As we shall see in some cases the Executive is a single person – for example, a directly elected mayor. The Assembly of politicians is often called the Council.

7 Each country has its own legislative arrangements setting down the powers of local government and arrangements relating to the design of local government institutions. It follows that there are significant opportunities for international exchange and learning relating to the strengths and weaknesses of alternative governmental forms. The following sources provide useful overviews of some of the models: Svara (2009), Svara and Watson (2010) and UCLG (2008).

8 There are significant variations between countries, and between localities in particular countries, in what political scientists call the representative ratio – meaning the average number of citizens per councillor. In some continental countries, for example, Germany the number is around 250

and in France it is lower still. The UK expects councillors to represent, on average, much larger numbers of people – the average number of citizens per councillor is over 2,600. In the USA the number each councillor is expected to represent can be very large indeed and, in some cities, it is over 100,000 – for example, Phoenix, Arizona

9 I should declare an interest. In 2008 I was appointed by the Royal Commission to provide the Commission with strategic advice in relation to civic leadership and I wrote a Research Paper, *Civic Leadership for Auckland. An International Perspective* (Hambleton 2009).

10 In recent years the Auckland reforms have had an impact on local governance in the rest of New Zealand. For example, in 2012 the government announced legislative changes designed to strengthen the formal powers of all directly elected mayors in the country and these came into effect in November 2013 (Cheyne 2013).

11 A number of organisations now provide resources for those interested to pursue the idea of participatory budgeting. For example, in the UK an independent body backed by the charity Church Action on Poverty, provides advice and support: www.participatorybudgeting.org.uk In North America there is a non-profit organisation providing advice to communities: www.participatorybudgeting.org And many individual cities provide web-based resources relating to their own way of doing participatory budgeting

12 The Knowle West Media Centre (KWMC) is a highly respected community-based organisation based in Bristol. Founded in 1996 it is an arts organisation and charity devoted to supporting communities to get the most out of digital technologies. More: http://kwmc.org.uk

13 Personal interview 28 May 2008

14 In 2010 Malmö City Council appointed Professor Emeritus Sven-Oluf Isacsson to chair a commission to assemble evidence relating to health inequalities in the city. The final report identifies a number of helpful policy recommendations (Gavriilidis et al 2013)

Chapter 8

1 Two international networks should be mentioned in this context. Founded in 1990, ICLEI (International Council for Local Environmental Initiatives) is a well-established network of cities and local governments dedicated to sustainable development: http://www.iclei.org Convened by Mayor Ken Livingstone of London in 2005, the C40 Cities Climate Change Leadership Group is a network of some of the world's largest cities, and including some smaller cities, that are taking action to reduce greenhouse gas emissions: http://www.c40.org

2 In the USA the Congress for the New Urbanism (CNU) should be recognised as making a significant contribution to the 'smart growth' movement. The Charter of the New Urbanism, originally published in 1992 and since updated, sets out the principles: http://www.cnu.org/charter

3 ICLEI has been running international conferences on Resilient Cities since 2010. More: http://www.iclei.org In addition, we can note that, in 2013, The Rockefeller Foundation launched a 100 Resilient Cities Challenge to encourage cities to better address the increasing shocks and stresses of the 21st Century. More: http://100resilientcities.org

Chapter 9

1 Developmental psychology has advanced understanding of a person's self-concept considerably in the years since Maslow wrote his influential analysis. See, for example, Kegan (1982)

2 For more information on the Bristol Pound: http://www.bristolpound.org

3 For more information visit: http://www.socialenterprise.org.uk

4 Somewhat confusingly there are two uses of the ABCD acronym. Here we are discussing Asset-Based Community Development. This is not to be confused with a model for evaluating community development efforts known as Achieving Better Community Development. Gilchrist and Taylor (2011) provide more details of both approaches.

5 Personal communication 5 February 2014

Chapter 10

1 A note on definitions may be helpful. I use terms in the following way: 'multicultural' and 'multiethnic' to refer to groups of people comprising individuals from several cultures and/or ethnic groups (including individuals who ascribe themselves to more than one group); the term 'diversity' (in a social, cultural and demographic sense) to refer to a society made up of individuals from different national, racial or ethnic backgrounds; and the term 'equality' to refer to an absence of discrimination motivated by nationality, race and/or ethnic origin, religion, gender, sexuality, physical ability or age.

2 A similar concept to dynamic diversity is super diversity, a phrase used by Vertovec (2007). He uses this phrase to describe the wholly new, and increasingly complex, social formations that have arisen in some cities in the last twenty years or so as a result of the movement of more people from more places to more places. The concepts of dynamic diversity and super diversity emerged in parallel, and describe, essentially, the same phenomenon.

3 The governance of difference in localities is a major topic and we cannot do it justice in a single chapter. However, other scholars have addressed this theme, for example: Amin (2002); Beebeejaun (2010); Crowder (2013); Fincher and Iveson (2008); Hoggett (2009); Reeves (2005); Sandercock (2003); Watson (2006); and Wood and Landry (2008).

4 This idea of focussing on the advantages of diversity rather than on the drawbacks is consistent with the approach adopted by Wood and Landry (2008, 11). They explain that the way you look at a challenge determines how you address it, and they outline two reasons why the narrative about diversity should be much more positive: 'First, there are enormous untapped resources, which our societies can scarcely afford to forgo, available from the creative power of heterogeneity and dissonance. Our second conviction is that a positive impulse to intercultural exchange is vital to encourage cross-fertilisation from which innovation can proliferate'. Whitzman et al (2013, 11) in their discussion of the lives of women and girls in cities also argue for a focus on positive possibilities: 'It is common to talk about challenges, but less common to think in terms of the opportunities that cities and city life offer... It is in placing women and girls as active and important participants in decision-making around urban futures that we can focus on the opportunities, not just the challenges'.

5 I draw here on Bagilhole (2009, 27–55).

6 It is true that immigrants sometimes relocate to rural areas in the country they have moved to – this could be to secure employment in agriculture (eg crop picking). However, the vast majority of immigrants set out to start a new life in a foreign city. This is partly for economic reasons and partly because it is in the city that they are more likely to be able to find others with a similar ethnic background. This notion of 'chain migration' is discussed in Chapter 2.

7 Bilsborrow (2011, 80) notes that: 'On a global scale, the total annual value [of financial transfers from migrants back to their households in developing countries] now greatly exceeds the

Overseas Development Assistance (ODA) from all multilateral and bilateral sources combined, and indeed rivals that of total private overseas capital investment in developing countries'.

8 In the European context it is possible that some practitioners involved in equal opportunities will take the view that Checkoway is describing intercultural rather than multicultural change. In the UK, for example, policy relating to minority ethnic immigration started out as assimilation – involving the merging of differences into the dominant culture. As suggested earlier in this chapter, this approach shifted towards multiculturalism in the 1990s – this new ethos emphasised understanding and accepting different minority ethnic cultures. However, a third stage has been reached because the limits of multiculturalism have been exposed. As Bagilhole (2009, 220) explains, multiculturalism can come into conflict with universal human rights: 'In the UK, debate arose in particular around issues of multiculturalism and women's rights. This centred on the 2003 Genital Mutilation Act, "forced" versus arranged marriages and so-called "honour" killings'. The third stage involves intercultural deliberation – an approach that respects minority viewpoints, involves minorities in decision-making, but draws the line at permitting practices that violate the values embodied in international human rights standards.

9 There are several components to EU policy for migration. A key factor is that the European workforce is decreasing because of demographic change, and the EU will not be able to meet its economic and employment targets if migrants face barriers to employment. The EU has a European Agenda for Integration not just for migrants who hold citizenship of a Member State, but also for migrants coming from outside the EU (European Commission 2011).

10 I draw here on my personal experience of being an immigrant from the UK to the USA in 2002–07. During this period I was Dean of the College of Urban Planning and Public Affairs at the University of Illinois at Chicago, a campus with 28,000 students – one of the most diverse student bodies in the country.

11 This was 1.6% of the Japanese national population of around 128 million.

12 We should note that more recent data is now available. The Canadian National Household Survey of 2011 suggests that the Toronto CMA had a population of 5.52 million and the immigrant population was 2.53 million (46% of the metropolitan area total).

13 It is worth celebrating the remarkable expansion, in recent decades, of both academic analysis and policy advance in relation to issues of fairness in modern societies. Spurred on by social movements, critical academics, political activists and others there is now a vast literature on social, economic and ecological justice – and I have attempted to provide citations to some of this literature at various points in this book.

Chapter 11

1 For more information on the work of Future Cities Catapult visit: http://futurecities.catapult.org.uk

2 This linkage of ecological and digital agendas is, for example, a feature of urban policy making in Bristol. Jo Howard and I have examined this digital+green initiative elsewhere (Hambleton and Howard 2013)

3 On 27 December 2013 US District Judge William Pauley contradicted Judge Richard Leon and ruled that the NSA's mass surveillance programme was legal. Two different judgements from the district courts can be expected to result in the issue going to an appeal court and eventually the US Supreme Court.

4 The traditional university evaluates scholars according to two main criteria: research and teaching. A university committed to the scholarship of engagement adds other criteria designed

to assess the societal relevance of academic efforts (Elman and Marx Smock 1985). This aspect of scholarship is often called professional service in US universities but other terms are used – for example, societal impact and/or influence on policy and practice.

5 This approach overlaps with educational practices that are sometimes described as community or service learning. A note of caution is needed. Tanja Winkler (2013b), writing from a South African perspective, notes that community–university engagements of this kind may not always deliver sufficient benefits to the communities involved.

6 There is an extensive literature on US higher education engagement in public policy and practice. Two associations of universities provide valuable online resources. The Coalition of Urban Serving Universities (USU) is a network of more than 40 large, public, urban research universities: www.usucoalition.org The Coalition of Urban and Metropolitan Universities (CUMU) includes a number of smaller urban universities and publishes a quarterly journal – *Metropolitan Universities Journal*. More: www.cumuonline.org A small but influential research and action institute focussing on how to use analysis to advance equity and social justice is PolicyLink: www.policylink.org

7 The National Coordinating Centre for Public Engagement (NCCPE) defines engagement as a two-way process, involving interaction and listening, with the goal of generating mutual benefit. It has an excellent website providing useful resources and links relating to university public engagement: www.publicengagement.ac.uk

8 The Talloires Network, created in 2005, is an international association of institutions committed to strengthening the civic roles and social responsibilities of higher education: http://talloiresnetwork.tufts.edu

9 The University of Illinois at Chicago (UIC) is a leading public research university. With 28,000 students it is the largest university in the Chicago area. I was honoured to serve as Dean of the College of Urban Planning and Public Affairs at UIC from 2002-07, and learned a great deal from students, community partners, faculty and members of UIC administrative staff about the value of engaged scholarship.

Chapter 12

1 Convergent thinking uses reasoning to converge on the 'right' answers. Divergent thinking uses reasoning to think fluently and tangentially. This distinction is well established in psychological research on human intelligence (Hudson 1967). De Bono (1971) develops this analysis and distinguishes vertical thinking from lateral thinking. Both forms of reasoning – convergent and divergent – are vital to achieve social advance. However, in times of rapid change and uncertainty the ability to use divergent (or lateral) thinking becomes absolutely critical. This psychological distinction resonates with the distinction made in Chapter 1 between organisational approaches that focus on improvement (achievement of specified targets) and innovation (invention of new solutions). 'Best practice' holds back the imagination by giving the impression that there are 'best answers' out there when there are, in reality, many possible answers.

2 There is widespread agreement that the Tibetan saint, Thangtong Gyalpo, invented the suspension bridge in the 15th Century, and he built many such bridges in Tibet and Bhutan. It was not, however, until the 19th Century that western engineers picked up on the idea that hanging the deck of a bridge from suspension cables opened up entirely new possibilities for bridge design.

3 Figure 12.1 is based on my own experience of international lesson drawing in relation to urban policy and practice over the last thirty years or so, including the work of my company *Urban Answers*. More available at: http://urbananswers.co.uk

4 This distinction between informal and formal approaches to cross-national policy transfer was first set out in Hambleton (2007c)

5 I should note that I am using the word 'policy' in two different ways in this diagram. In the vertical axis on the left I am using the word in a generic way to embrace technical measures, policies, practices and governance change. I am using it as an over-arching term to cover what governments do. In the horizontal axis I am trying to be more specific about the meaning of policy. Here it is distinguished from measures, which are more specific than policy and may relate to quite technical matters, and governance change, which is a broader concept than policy.

6 The WHO does much more than facilitate the international transfer of technical measures. Much of its' work is, in practice, focussed on international exchange relating to policy and practice. However, one of its' strengths is the technical know-how it brings to global public health challenges.

7 The author was an Academic Adviser to Ministers in the UK Department of Communities and Local Government (1997–2002) and assisted Ministers in their examination of mayoral models of urban governance in other countries.

8 Other more elaborate frameworks are available – see, for example, Dolowitz et al (2000, 10).

9 This international conference on City Futures attracted 250 participants from 36 countries. Because the conference was seen as a success the European Urban Research Association (EURA) and the Urban Affairs Association (UAA) have followed this up with further City Futures Conferences at five-yearly intervals. City Futures II was held in Madrid in 2009 and City Futures III was held in Paris in June 2014. More information is available on the EURA website: http://www.eura.org

10 The core academic team organising the conference comprised Jill S. Gross, City University New York, Janet L. Smith, University of Illinois at Chicago, and the author. The administration of the conference was organised by Jodi White Jones, University of Illinois at Chicago. The scenarios presented here are drawn from the Call for Papers for the conference issued in 2003.

APPENDIX

International city networks and resources

This appendix lists international urban networks and websites that provide useful resources for those concerned with city and regional governance and city-to-city learning. The list, which is in alphabetical order, is not comprehensive. Rather it is intended to provide a starting point for the interested reader.

100 Resilient Cities

The Rockefeller Foundation launched the *100 Resilient Cities Challenge* in 2013 to enable 100 cities to better address the increasing shocks and stresses of the 21st Century. Each successful applicant must commit to developing a citywide resilience plan. More: http://100resilientcities.rockefellerfoundation.org

C40 Cities Climate Leadership Group

First convened by London Mayor Ken Livingstone in 2005, the *C40 Cities Climate Change Group* is a network of some of the largest cities that are taking action to reduce greenhouse gas emissions. More: http://www.c40.org

Cities Alliance: Cities without slums

Founded in 1999, the *Cities Alliance* is a global partnership for urban poverty reduction and the promotion of the role of cities in sustainable development. More: http://citiesalliance.org

Citiscope Global News

Launched in 2013 *Citiscope* is a global news resource for all those interested in city leadership and urban management. It uses the power of professional journalism to draw reader attention to factual accounts of innovation in cities across the world. More: http://www.citiscope.org

City Mayors: Running the world's cities

Established in 2003 the *City Mayors Foundation* is an international think tank dedicated to promoting strong and prosperous cities, as well as good local government. More: http://www.citymayors.com

CITYNET

Established in 1987, CITYNET promotes cooperative partnerships and links among cities in Asia and the Pacific in order to improve the sustainability of cities. More: http://citynet-ap.org

CLAIR – Council of Local Authorities for International Relations

Founded in 1988, the Council of Local Authorities for International Relations (CLAIR) is a network of Japanese cities and regions working together to promote global learning and partnerships, particularly around revitalization of local areas and solutions for low carbon and ageing societies. More: http://www.clair.or.jp/e

Commonwealth Local Government Forum (CLGF)

The Commonwealth Local Government Forum (CLGF) works to promote and strengthen local government across the Commonwealth. The Forum has more than 160 members in 40 Commonwealth countries. More: http://www.clgf.org.uk

DELGOSEA

Launched in 2010 DELGOSEA is a network of cities and municipalities in Southeast Asia set up to promote exchange of information on innovative approaches to democratic local governance. More: http://www.delgosea.eu

EUROCITIES

Founded in 1986 EUROCITIES is a network of over 130 major European cities. The network, which seeks to influence European Union (EU) policy relating to cities as well as foster international exchange relating to urban policy making, aims to reinforce the important role of local governments in the multilevel governance of Europe. More: http://www.eurocities.eu

European Urban Research Association (EURA)

Launched in Brussels in 1997 the European Urban Research Association (EURA) is an international network of scholars set up to encourage international exchange and cooperation in relation to urban research, and to offer contributions to urban policy debates. More: http://www.eura.org

Global Network on Safer Cities (GNSC)

Launched in 2012, the Global Network on Safer Cities (GNSC), an initiative of UN-Habitat, has the goal of equipping local authorities and urban stakeholders to deliver urban safety. More: http://unhabitat.org/urban-initiatives-2/global-network-on-safer-cities/

ICLEI Local Governments for Sustainability

Founded in 1990, ICLEI (International Council for Local Environmental Initiatives) is a well-established network of cities and local governments dedicated to sustainable development. More: http://www.iclei.org

Metropolis

Metropolis is the world association of the major metropolises, meaning cities and metropolitan regions with more than one million inhabitants. Created in 1985, the association, which now has more than 130 members, manages the metropolitan section of United Cities and Local Governments (UCLG) (see separate entry). More: http://www.metropolis.org

Shack/Slum Dwellers International (SDI)

Launched in 1996, *Shack/Slum Dwellers International (SDI)* is a network of community-based organisations of the urban poor in 33 countries in Africa, Asia and Latin America. More: http://www.sdinet.org

Sister Cities International

Founded in 1956 by US President Eisenhower, Sister Cities International aims to promote peace through mutual respect, understanding and cooperation. The network unites tens of thousands of citizen diplomats and volunteers in programmes in 140 countries. More: http://www.sister-cities.org

The Global Urbanist

Created in 2009 by alumni of the urban policy and international development programmes at the London School of Economics and Political Science, *The Global Urbanist* is an online magazine reviewing urban affairs and urban development issues across the world. More: http://globalurbanist.com

United Cities and Local Governments (UCLG)

United Cities and Local Governments (UCLG) represents and defends the interests of local governments on the world stage, regardless of the size of the communities they serve. With headquarters in Barcelona, the organisation aims to be the united voice and world advocate for local self-government. More: http://www.uclg.org

Urban Affairs Association (UAA)

Based in North America, the Urban Affairs Association (UAA) is an interdisciplinary, professional organisation for urban scholars, researchers and public service professionals. It fosters international exchange relating to urban life and city planning and urban management. More: http://urbanaffairsassociation.org

World Cities Culture Forum

Launched in 2012, the World Cities Culture Forum is a collaborative network of over 20 world cities that share a belief in the importance of culture for creating thriving cities. The network brings together senior policymakers and thought leaders. More: http://www.worldcitiescultureforum.com

World Cities Network

Launched in 2012, the *World Cities Network* is an independent body created to improve the resilience of cities. It facilitates sharing of ideas and experiences across the real estate, technology, design and urban infrastructure industries. More: http://www.worldcitiesnetwork.org

World Urban Forum (WUF)

Organised by the United Nations Human Settlements Programme (UN-Habitat), the *World Urban Forum (WUF)* is hosted in a different city every two years. It brings together a large number of policy makers, practitioners, activists and scholars to examine the most pressing issues facing human settlements across the world. More: http://wuf7.unhabitat.org

Acknowledgements

The idea for this book began when I carried out a study of civic leadership for the Royal Commission on the Governance of Auckland in 2008. The Commissioners were enthusiastic about gaining insights from urban governance in other countries. The experience suggested to me that it could be fruitful to extend my work on place-based leadership into an international comparative book. I thank the Royal Commission for inviting me to contribute to their study.

The momentum needed to embark on a book-length project was provided by an Anglo-Dutch study of public service innovation. Carried out in 2011/12 this action/research project involved the co-creation of three Innovation Stories examining bold examples of place-based leadership in three cities. I wish to thank the Joseph Rowntree Foundation for funding this Anglo-Dutch study, and to thank all those involved. I learned an enormous amount from the innovative leaders in the three cities – Bristol, Enschede and Swindon. In particular I thank Jan Ormondroyd, Gavin Jones and Hans Weggemans for their support for this work.

Special thanks go to Jo Howard, who co-led this research project with me, and to our Dutch academic colleagues: Bas Denters, Pieter-Jan Klok and Mirjan Oude Vrielink, of the University of Twente, who made major contributions to this project.

I have benefited from stimulating exchanges with scholars in many different countries as this book has taken shape. In particular, I would like to thank members of two international networks – the European Urban Research Association (EURA) and the Urban Affairs Association (UAA). Both these interdisciplinary associations are active in encouraging the development of engaged urban scholarship, and I have found it invaluable to present emerging ideas at EURA and UAA conferences and receive comments and criticisms.

Carmel Conefrey, then a PhD student in my faculty at the University of the West of England (UWE), deserves special praise. In 2012/13, funded by a small grant from the Joseph Rowntree Foundation, she helped me research many of the Innovation Stories presented in this book. She brought a fresh eye to the idea of an Innovation Story, first developed in the Anglo-Dutch project, and she was a great colleague to work with.

I have been fortunate to receive academic help and encouragement from friends and colleagues here in Bristol. I would like to record my personal thanks to Jo Howard and David Sweeting. We have worked closely on several action/research projects studying aspects of civic leadership and local democracy in recent years, and collaborating with them is a delight. The Bristol Civic Leadership Project, started in 2012, provides an example. This study is examining the impact of introducing the directly elected mayor form of governance into the city, and I would also like to thank Alex Marsh, Director of the School for Policy Studies, University of Bristol, who is the fourth member of our research team.

I offer special thanks to Katie Williams, the Director of the Centre for Sustainable Planning and Environments at UWE. She leads our Centre in a most creative way, and is a great supporter of interdisciplinary research. I thank all my colleagues at UWE for their ideas, suggestions and comments: Rob Atkinson, Michael Buser, Marcus Grant, Stephen Hall, Paul Hoggett, David Ludlow, Katie McClymont, Graham Parkhurst, Danni Sinnett and Andrew Tallon.

A large number of practitioners and academics assisted in the construction of the seventeen Innovation Stories that appear in this book. I include information on sources at the end of each Innovation Story. But many people not mentioned gave freely of their time and advice, and I am most grateful to all of them.

Colleagues from a number of countries have contributed to the ideas set out in this book – through informal conversations, as well as by reacting to specific drafts. In particular, I would like to thank Rob Adams, Sy Adler, Nevin Brown, Christine Cheyne, Wulf Daseking, Bas Denters, Lars Engberg, Karl Fjellstrom, Arturo Flores, Kristin Good, A. V. Goodsell, Trevor Graham, Carolyn Hassan, Hubert Heinelt, Clara Irazabal, Rutul Joshi, Cathy Kenkel, Joy Kennard, Ineke Kleine, Pieter-Jan Klok, Aditya Kumar, Jacob Norvig Larsen, Su Maddock, Darshini Mahadevia, Phil McDermott, Peter McKinlay, Ali Modarres, Henrik Nolmark, Britt Olofsdotter, Ceta Ramkhalawansingh, Johru Robyn, Anders Rubin, Andrew Stephens, Richard Stren, Nazem Tahvilzadeh, Yoichi Takimoto, Adiam Tedros, Ron Vogel, Mirjan Oude Vrielink, Sue Wald, Vanessa Watson, Bob Whelan, Wim Wiewel, Tanja Winkler, Keizo Yamawaki, Lin Ye, and Xuduo Zhao. Closer to home I have benefited from insights provided by Jaya Chakrabati, Dave Clarke, George Ferguson, Stephen Hilton, Helen Holland, Barbara Janke, Mike Leigh, and Paul Taylor.

I am fortunate to work in a university with outstanding research support staff. The research underpinning this book has benefited from contributions from Jane Newton, Carolyn Webb and Julie Triggle. Chris Wade, our graphic designer, has made a major contribution to this book by turning my rough sketches into the figures you see in this volume.

I would like to thank the anonymous referee who reviewed this manuscript for Policy Press for their sound advice, particularly in relation to ideas about the changing nature of the modern university.

Policy Press has provided a friendly, helpful and creative service to me as an author. In particular, I would like to thank my editor Emily Watt, for her encouragement and thoughtful advice, and I would also like to acknowledge Susannah Emery, Laura Greaves, Jessica Miles, Jennifer Rivers Mohan, Alison Shaw, Laura Vickers and Dave Worth for their many professional contributions.

This book would not have been possible without the support of my family. I thank Jake and Beth for their insights and, in particular, I want to thank Pam for her many comments, inspiring ideas and constant encouragement.

References

Academy of Urbanism, Stadt Freiburg, 2012, *The Freiburg Charter for sustainable urbanism*, 2nd edn, London: Academy of Urbanism

Adair, J, 2002, *Inspiring leadership*, London: Thorogood Publishing

Adams, D, Tiesdell, S, 2013, *Shaping places: Urban planning, design and development*, Abingdon: Routledge

Adams, R, 2005, Melbourne: Back from the edge, in E Charlesworth (ed) *City edge: Case studies in contemporary urbanism*, 50–64, Oxford: Elsevier

Adebowale, M, 2008, Understanding environmental justice: Making the connection between sustainable development and social justice, in G Craig, T Burchardt, D Gordon (eds) *Social justice and public policy: Seeking fairness in diverse societies*, 251–75, Bristol: Policy Press

Adger, WN, Jordan, A (eds), 2009, *Governing sustainability*, Cambridge: Cambridge University Press

Adner, R, 2012, *The Wide Lens. A new strategy for innovation*, London: Portfolio Penguin

Agranoff, R, 2012, *Collaborating to manage: A primer for the public sector*, Washington, DC: Georgetown University Press

Agranoff, R, McGuire, M, 2003, *Collaborative public management: New strategies for local governments*, Washington, DC: Georgetown University Press

Ahrensbach, T, Beunderman, J, Fung, A, Johar, I, Steiner, J, 2012, *Compendium for the civic economy*, Produced by 00:/, 2nd edn, The Netherlands: Transcity/Valiz

Alinsky, S, 1969, *Reveille for radicals*, New York: Vintage Books (First published in 1946)

Allmendinger, P, 2009, *Planning Theory*, 2nd edn, Basingstoke: Palgrave

Amin, A, 2002, Ethnicity and the multicultural city: Living with diversity, *Environment and Planning A* 34, 6, 959–80

Anguelovski, I, 2013, New directions in urban environmental justice: Rebuilding community, addressing trauma, and remaking place, *Journal of Planning Education and Research* 33, 2, 160–75

Anholt, S, 2010, *Places: Identity, image and reputation*, Basingstoke: Palgrave

Argyris, C, Schon, DA, 1978, *Organisational learning: A theory of action perspective*, Reading, MA: Addison-Wesley

Arnstein, S, 1969, A ladder of citizen participation, *Journal of the American Institute of Planners* 35, 4, 216–24

Askonas, P, Stewart, A (eds), 2000, *Social inclusion: Possibilities and tensions*, Basingstoke: Palgrave

Atkinson, R, Blandy, S (eds), 2006, *Gated communities: International perspectives*, Abingdon: Routledge

Bachrach, P, Baratz, MS, 1970, *Power and poverty: Theory and practice*, Oxford: Oxford University Press

Bacon, N, 2013, The social flow, *Journal of the Royal Society of Arts*, 3, 27–9

Bagaeen, S, Uduku, O (eds), 2010, *Gated communities: Social sustainability in contemporary and historical gated developments*, London: Earthscan

Baghai, M, Quigley, J, 2011, *As one: Individual action, collective power*, London: Penguin

Bagilhole, B, 2009, *Understanding equal opportunities and diversity: The social differentiations and intersections of inequality*, Bristol: Policy Press

Bai, X, Schandl, H, 2011, Urban ecology and industrial ecology, in I Douglas, D Goode, MC Houck, R Wang (eds) *The Routledge handbook of urban ecology*, 26–37, Abingdon: Routledge

Baker, P, Eversley, J (eds), 2000, *Multilingual capital: The languages of London's schoolchildren and their relevance to economic, social and educational policies*, London: Battlebridge

Balducci, A, Mantysalo, R (eds), 2013, *Urban planning as a trading zone*, New York: Springer

Banner, G, 1996, The next steps: Future options for local government, in P McDermott, V Forgie, R Howell (eds) An agenda for local government: Proceedings from the New Local Government Conference, 23–8, *Local Government Studies Occasional Paper 2*, Palmerston North, New Zealand: Massey University

Barber, B, 2013, *If mayors ruled the world: Why they should and why they already do*, New Haven, CT: Yale University Press

Barber, BR, 1984, *Strong democracy: Participatory politics for a new age*, Berkeley, CA: University of California Press

Barnett, R, 2011, The coming of the ecological university, *Oxford Review of Education* 37, 4, 439–55

Barrett, FJ, 2012, *Yes to the mess: Surprising leadership lessons from jazz*, Boston, MA: Harvard Business Review Press

Barton, H (ed), 2000, *Sustainable communities: The potential for eco-neighbourhoods*, London: Earthscan

Barton, H, Grant, M, Guise, R, 2010, *Shaping neighbourhoods*, 2nd edn, Abingdon: Routledge

Bason, C, 2010, *Leading public sector innovation: Co-creating for a better society*, Bristol: Policy Press

Batty, M, Axhausen, KW, Giannotti, F, Pozdnoukhov, A, Bazzani, A, Wachowicz, M, Ouzounis, G, Portugali, Y, 2012, Smart cities of the future, *The European Physical Journal Special Topics* 214, 1, 481–518

Bauman, Z, 2006, *Liquid fear*, Cambridge: Polity Press

Beatley, T, 2011, *Biophilic cities: Integrating nature into urban design and planning*, Washington, DC: Island Press

Beebeejaun, Y, 2010, Do multicultural cities help equality? in JS Davies, DL Imbroscio (eds) *Critical urban studies: New directions*, 121–34, Albany, NY: State University of New York Press

Bell, DA, de-Shalit, A, 2011, *The spirit of cities: Why the identity of a city matters in a global age*, Princeton, NJ: University of Princeton Press

Benavides, AD, Hernandez, JCT, 2007, Serving diverse communities: Cultural competency, *Public Management*, July, 14–18

Benington, J, Moore, MH (eds), 2011, *Public value: Theory and practice*, Basingstoke: Palgrave

Bennett, L, Smith, JL, Wright, PA, 2006, *Where are poor people to live? Transforming Public Housing Communities*, Armonk, NY: ME Sharpe

Ben-Shahar, T, 2008, *Happier: Can you learn to be happy?* New York: McGraw-Hill

Benton-Short, L, Short, R, 2013, *Cities and Nature*, 2nd edn, London: Routledge

Ben-Tovim, G, Gabriel, J, Law, I, Stredder, K, 1986, *The local politics of race*, Basingstoke and New York: Palgrave

Benyon, J, David, M, 2008, *Developing dialogue. Learned societies in the social sciences: Developing knowledge transfer and public engagement*, London: Academy of Social Sciences

Berg, R, Rao, N (eds), 2005, *Transforming local political leadership*, Basingstoke: Palgrave

Berger, J, 1972, *Ways of seeing*, London: Penguin

Bernard, E, Osmonbekov, T, McKee, D, 2011, Customer learning orientation in public sector organisations, *Journal of Nonprofit and Public Sector Marketing* 23, 2, 158–80

Bernays, E, 1928, *Propaganda*, Brooklyn, NY: Ig Publishing

Berners-Lee, M, Clark, D, 2013, *The burning question. We can't burn half the world's oil, coal and gas: So how do we quit?*, London: Profile Books

Bew, P, Gibbon, P, Patterson, H, 2002, *Northern Ireland 1921–2001: Political forces and social classes*, London: Serif

Bilsborrow, RE, 2011, Global patterns of migration, sources of data, and the new policy consensus, in TN Maloney, K Korinek (eds) *Migration in the 21st century: Rights, outcomes and policy*, 79–97, Abingdon: Routledge

Binney, G, Williams, C, Wilke, G, 2012 (3rd edition), *Living Leadership: A practical guide for ordinary heroes*, Harlow: Pearson Education Limited

Birch, EL, Wachter, SM (eds), 2011, *Global urbanisation*, Philadelphia, PA: University of Pennsylvania Press

Bissinger, B, 1997, *Prayer for the city*, New York: Vintage Books

Blair, T, 1998, *Leading the way: A new vision for local government*, London: Institute for Public Policy Research

Blakely, E, 2007, Gated communities for a frayed and afraid world, *Housing Policy Debate* 18, 3, 475–80

Blakely, E, Snyder, MG, 1997, *Fortress America: Gated communities in the United States*, Washington, DC: Brookings Institution and Lincoln Institute for Land Policy

Bollens, SA, 2003, Managing urban ethnic conflict, in R Hambleton, HV Savitch, M Stewart (eds) *Globalism and local democracy*, 108–24, Basingstoke and New York: Palgrave

Boone, CG, Modarres, A, 2006, *City and environment*, Philadelphia, PA: Temple University Press

Boyer, EL, 1990, *Scholarship reconsidered: Priorities of the professoriate*, Princeton, NJ: Carnegie Foundation for the Advancement of Teaching

Boyer, EL, 1996, The scholarship of engagement, *Journal of Public Service and Outreach* 1, 1, 11–20

Brandsen, T, Pestoff, V, 2006, Co-production, the third sector and the delivery of public service, *Public Management Review* 8, 4, 493–501

Brenner, N, Marcuse, P, Mayer, M (eds), 2012, *Cities for people, not for profit: Critical urban theory and the right to the city*, Abingdon: Routledge

Brewer, JD, 2013, *The public value of the social sciences*, London: Bloomsbury

Bridge, G, Watson, S (eds), 2011, *The new Blackwell companion to the city*, Chichester: Wiley-Blackwell

Brookes, S, Grint, K (eds), 2010, *The new public leadership challenge*, Basingstoke: Palgrave

Brown, A, Kristiansen, A, 2009, *Urban policies and the right to the city*, Nairobi and Paris: UN-Habitat and UNESCO

Brown, K, 2009, Human development and environmental governance: A reality check, in WN Adger, A Jordan (eds) *Governing sustainability*, 32–51, Cambridge: Cambridge University Press

Brugmann, J, 2009, *Welcome to the urban revolution: How cities are changing the world*, Noida, India: HarperCollins

Buchanan, C, 1963, *Traffic in Towns: The specially shortened edition of the Buchanan Report*, Harmondsworth: Penguin

Bulkeley, H, 2013, *Cities and climate change*, Abingdon: Routledge

Bungay, S, 2011, *The art of action: How leaders close the gaps between plans, actions and results*, London: Nicholas Brealey

Burdett, R, Sudjic, D (eds), 2011, *Living in the endless city*, London: Phaidon

Burns, D, 2007, *Systemic action research: A strategy for whole system change*, Bristol: Policy Press

Burns, D, Hambleton, R, Hoggett, P, 1994, *The politics of decentralisation: Revitalising local democracy*, Basingstoke: Palgrave

Burns, JM, 1978, *Leadership*, New York: Harper and Row.

Byrne, D, 1999, *Social exclusion*, Buckingham: Open University Press

Byrne, J (ed), 2012, *The occupy handbook*, New York: Hachette Book Group

Campbell, T, 2012, *Beyond smart cities: How cities network, learn and innovate*, London: Earthscan

Canter, D, 1977, *The psychology of place*, London: Architectural Press

Caro, R, 1975, *The power broker: Robert Moses and the fall of New York*, New York: Vintage

Carr, N, 2010, *The shallows: How the internet is changing the way we think, read and remember*, New York: WW Norton

Carroll, P, Common, R (eds), 2013, *Policy transfer and learning in public policy and management*, Abingdon: Routledge

Carter, C, 1996, *Members one of another: The problems of local corporate action*, York: Joseph Rowntree Foundation

Castello, L, 2010, *Rethinking the meaning of place: Conceiving place in architecture-urbanism*, Farnham: Ashgate

Castells, M, 1989, *The informational city: Information technology, economic restructuring and the urban–regional process*, Oxford: Blackwell

Castles, S, Miller, MJ, 2009, *The age of migration: International population movements in the modern world*, 4th edn, Basingstoke: Palgrave

Chang, H, 2010, *23 things they don't tell you about capitalism*, London: Penguin

Checkoway, B, 2007, Community change for diverse democracy, *Community Development Journal* 44, 1, 5–21

Cheyne, C, 2013, *The Auckland effect, 'disaster capitalism' and the future of local governance in New Zealand*, Paper to the Urban Affairs Association Annual Conference, San Francisco, 3–6 April

Cheyne, C, Hambleton, R, 2011, The Kiwi connection: Reflections on local governance policy transfer between the UK and New Zealand, *Journal of Comparative Policy Analysis* 13, 2, 215–31

Clark, G, Clark, G, 2014, *Nations and the wealth of cities: A new phase in public policy*, London: Centre for London

Clement, M, 2012, Rage against the market: Bristol's Tesco riot, *Race and Class* 53, 3, 81–90

Cochrane, A, 2007, *Understanding urban policy: A critical approach*, Oxford: Blackwell

Cochrane, A, 2012, Making up a region: The rise and fall of the South East of England as a political territory, *Environment and Space C: Government and Policy* 30, 1, 95–108

Cohen, A, Taylor, E, 2000, *American Pharaoh*, Boston, MA: Little Brown

Coleman, S, Blumler, JG, 2009, *The internet and democratic citizenship*, Cambridge: Cambridge University Press

Collinge, C, Gibney, J, Mabey, C (eds), 2011, *Leadership and place*, Abingdon: Routledge

Colomb, C, 2012, *Staging the New Berlin: Place marketing and the politics of urban reinvention post-1989*, Abingdon: Routledge

Condon, PM, 2010, *Seven rules for sustainable communities: Design strategies for the post-carbon world*, Washington, DC: Island Press

Cooper, D, 1976, *The grammar of living: An examination of political acts*, Harmondsworth: Penguin

Cooper, S, 2011 (2nd edition), *Brilliant Leader. What the best leaders know, do and say*, Harlow: Pearson Education Limited

Copus, C, 2006, *Leading the localities: Executive mayors in English local governance*, Manchester: Manchester University Press

Cornwall, A, 2008, *Democratising engagement: What the UK can learn from international experience*, London: Demos

Cox, K, 1998, Spaces of dependence, spaces of engagement and the politics of scale, *Political Geography* 17, 1, 1–23

Cox, KR, 2013, Territory, scale, and why capitalism matters, *Territory, Policy, Governance* 1, 1, 46–61

Craig, G, Burchardt, T, Gordon, D (eds), 2008, *Social justice and public policy: Seeking fairness in diverse societies*, Bristol: Policy Press

Craig, G, Mayo, M, Popple, K, Shaw, M, Taylor, M (eds), 2011, *The community development reader: History, themes and issues*, Bristol: Policy Press

Cresswell, T, 2004, *Place: A short introduction*, Oxford: Blackwell

Crowder, G, 2013, *Theories of multiculturalism: An introduction*, Cambridge: Polity Press

Cullen, G, 1961, *Townscape*, London: Architectural Press

Dahl, RA, 1961, *Who governs? Democracy and power in an American city*, New Haven, CT: Yale University Press

Dannenberg, AL, Frumkin, H, Jackson, RJ (eds), 2011, *Making healthy places*, Washington, DC: Island Press

Davies, B, 1968, *Social needs and resources in local services: A study of variations in provision of social services between local authority areas*, York: Joseph Rowntree Foundation

Davies, JS, 2007, Against 'partnership': Toward a local challenge to global neoliberalism, in R Hambleton, JS Gross (eds) *Governing cities in a global era: Urban innovation, competition and democratic reform*, 199–210, Basingstoke: Palgrave

Davies, JS, 2011, *Challenging governance theory. From networks to hegemony*, Bristol: Policy Press

Davies, JS, Imbroscio, DL (eds), 2010, *Critical urban studies: New directions*, Albany, NY: State University of New York Press

Davis, M, 1990, *City of quartz: Excavating the future of Los Angeles*, London: Verso

Davis, M, 2006, *Planet of slums*, London: Verso

DCLG (Department for Communities and Local Government), 2013, *Government response to the Riots, Communities and Victims Panel's: Final report*, July, London: Department of Communities and Local Government

De Blij, H, 2009, *The power of place: Geography, destiny and globalisations rough landscape*, Oxford: Oxford University Press

De Bono, E, 1971, *Mechanism of mind*, Harmondsworth: Penguin

De Groot, L, Mason, A (eds), 2008, *How equality shapes place: Diversity and localism*, London: SOLACE Foundation Imprint

Deakin, M, Al Waer, H (eds), 2012, *From intelligent to smart cities*, Abingdon: Routledge

Dearlove, J, 1979, *The reorganisation of British local government: Old orthodoxies and a political perspective*, Cambridge: Cambridge University Press

Denhardt, JV, Denhardt, RB, 2003, *The new public service: Serving, not steering*, Armonk, NY: MESharpe

Denters, B, Rose, LE (eds), 2005, *Comparing local governance: Trends and developments*, Basingstoke: Palgrave

Detroit City Council, 2012, *Detroit future city: Detroit framework plan*, December, Detroit: Detroit City Council

Dijk, MP van, 2006, *Managing cities in developing countries*, Cheltenham: Edward Elgar

Dinnie, K, 2011, *City branding: Theory and cases*, Basingstoke: Palgrave

Dittmar, H, Ohland, G (eds), 2004, *The new transit town: Best practices in transit-oriented development*, Washington, DC: Island Press

DOE (Department of the Environment), 1991, *The internal management of local authorities in England*, London: The Stationary Office

Dolan, P, Hallsworth, M, Halpern, D, King, D, Vlaev, I, 2010, *Mindspace: Influencing behaviour through public policy*, January, London: Cabinet Office and Institute for Government

Dolowitz, DP, with Hulme, R, Nellis, M, O'Neill, F, 2000, *Policy transfer and British social policy: Learning from the USA?* Buckingham: Open University Press

Donaghue, B, Jones, GW, 1973, *Herbert Morrison: Portrait of a politician*, London: Weidenfeld and Nicholson

Doran, T, Drever, F, Whitehead, M, 2004, Is there a north–south divide in social inequalities in health in Great Britain?, *British Medical Journal* 328, 7447, 1043–45

Dorling, D, 2011, *Injustice: Why social inequality persists*, Bristol: Policy Press

Dorling, D, 2013, *Population 10 billion*, London: Constable and Robinson

Douglas, I, Goode, D, Houck, MC, Wang, R (eds), 2011, *The Routledge handbook of urban ecology*, Abingdon: Routledge

Doward, J, 2014, Lords challenge No 10 to prove value of 'nudge' unit, *The Observer*, 27 July p 20

Dowding, K, John, P, 2009, The value of choice in public policy, *Public Administration* 87, 2, 219–33

Drath, WH, McCauley, CD, Palus, CJ, Van Velsor E, O'Connor, PMG, McGuire, JB, 2008, Direction, alignment, commitment: Toward a more integrative ontology of leadership, *The Leadership Quarterly* 19, 635–53

Droege, P, 2006, *The renewable city*, Chichester: Wiley

Drucker, PF, 1954, *The practice of management*, New York: Harper and Row

Drucker, PF, 1989, *The new realities*, New York: Harper and Row

Duany, A, Plater-Zyberk, E, Alminana, R, 2003, *The new civic art: Elements of town planning*, New York: Rizzoli International Publications

Eckersley, R, 1992, *Environmentalism and political theory: Toward an ecocentric approach*, London: UCL Press

Edwards, M, 2009, *Civil society*, 2nd edn, Cambridge: Polity Press

Egan, J, 2004, *Skills for sustainable communities: The Egan review*, April, London: Office of the Deputy Prime Minister

Elkington, J, 1997, *Cannibals with forks: The triple bottom line of 21st century business*, Oxford: Capstone Publishing Limited

Elman, SE, Marx Smock, S, 1985, *Professional service and faculty rewards: Toward an integrated structure*, Washington, DC: National Association of State Universities and Lan-Grant Colleges

Equalities Review, 2007, *Fairness and freedom: The final report of the Equalities Review*, London: Justice

Esteva, G, Babones, S, Babcicky, P, 2013, *The future of development: A radical manifesto*, Bristol: Policy Press

Ettelt, S, Mays, N, Nolte, E, 2012, Policy learning from abroad: Why it is more difficult than it seems, *Policy and Politics* 40, 4, 491–504

Etzioni, A, 1995, *Spirit of community: Rights, responsibilities and the communitarian agenda*, London: Fontana

EUROCITIES, 2010, *Charter on integrating cities*, Brussels: EUROCITIES, www.integratingcities.eu

European Commission, 2011, *European agenda for the integration of third-country nationals*, COM, 2011, 455 final, July, Brussels: European Commission

Evans, M (ed), 2004, *Policy transfer in global perspective*, Aldershot: Ashgate

Evers, A, Laville, JL, 2004, Social services as social enterprises: On the possible contributions of hybrid organisations and a civil society, in A Evers, JL Laville (eds) *The third sector in Europe*, Cheltenham: Edward Elgar

Eversole, R, 2012, Remaking participation: Challenges for community development practice, *Community Development Journal* 47, 1, 29–41

Eyoh, D, Stren, R (eds), 2007, *Decentralisation and the politics of urban development in West Africa*, Washington, DC: Woodrow Wilson Centre

Fainstein, SS, 2010, *The just city*, Ithaca, NY: Cornell University Press

Farrell, T, 2014, *Our future in place: The Farrell review of architecture and the built environment*, London: Farrells

Feldman, MS, Khademian, AM, 2007, The role of the public manager in inclusion: creating communities of participation, *Governance: An International Journal of Policy, Administration and Institutions*, 20, 2, pp 305–24

Ferguson, G, 2013, *State of the city address*, First Annual Lecture by the Mayor of Bristol, Presented at the Wills Memorial Building, University of Bristol on 18 November

Ferman, B, 1985, *Governing the ungovernable city: Political skill, leadership and the modern mayor*, Philadelphia, PA: Temple University Press

Fincher, R, Iveson, K, 2008, *Planning and diversity in the city*, Basingstoke: Palgrave

Fitzgerald, J, 2010, *Emerald cities: Urban sustainability and economic development*, Oxford: Oxford University Press

Flanagan, RM, 2004, *Mayors and the challenges of urban leadership*, Lanham, MD: University Press of America

Fleisher, D, Zames, F, 2001, *The disability rights movement: From charity to confrontation*, Philadelphia, PA: Temple University Press

Flinders, M, 2013, The politics of engaged scholarship: Impact, relevance and imagination, *Policy and Politics* 41, 4, 621–42

Flint, J, Raco, M (eds) 2012, *The future of sustainable cities: Critical reflections*, Bristol: Policy PressFlorida, R, 2002, *The rise of the creative class*, New York: Basic Books

Florida, R, 2005, *Cities and the creative class*, Abingdon: Routledge

Flyvbjerg, B, 1998, *Rationality and power: Democracy in practice*, Chicago, IL: University of Chicago Press

Flyvbjerg, B, 2001, *Making social science matter: Why social inquiry fails and how it can succeed again*, Cambridge: Cambridge University Press

Ford, A, 2013, *Mindfulness and the art of urban living: Discovering the good life in the city*, Lewes: Leaping Hare Press

Forester, J (ed), 2013, *Planning in the face of conflict: The surprising possibilities of facilitative leadership*, Chicago, IL: American Planning Association

Foucault, M, 1979, *Discipline and punish*, New York: Vintage Books

Frankl, VE, 2004, *Mans search for meaning*, London: Random House

Fraser, N, 2004, Institutionalising democratic justice: Redistribution, recognition and participation, in S Benhabib, N Fraser (eds) *Pragmatism, critique, judgement: Essays for Richard J Bernstein*, 125–48, Cambridge, MA: The MIT Press

Frederickson, HG, 2005, Transcending the community: Local leadership in a world of shared power, *Public Management* 87, 10

Friedman, TL, 2005, *The world is flat*, New York: Farrar, Straus and Giroux

Friedmann, J, 2000, The good city: In defence of utopian thinking, *International Journal of Urban and Regional Research* 24, 2, 460–72

Friedmann, J, 2002, *The prospect of cities*, Minneapolis, MN: University of Minnesota Press

Fung, A, 2004, *Empowered participation: Reinventing urban democracy*, Princeton, NJ: Princeton University Press

Fung, A, Wright, EO, Abers, RN, 2003, *Deepening democracy: Institutional innovations in empowered participatory governance*, London: Verso

Gardner, JW, 1990, *On leadership*, New York: The Free Press

Gavriilidis, G, Natarajan, N, Ostergren, P, 2013, *Empowerment evaluation of policies towards a socially sustainable Malmö*, Malmö: Malmö City Council

Gehl, J, 2010, *Cities for people*, Washington, DC: Island Press

Gehl, J, Gemzøe, L, 2000, *New city spaces*, Copenhagen: Danish Architectural Press

Gibney, J, Copeland, S, Murie, A, 2009, Toward a 'new' strategic leadership of place for the knowledge-based economy, *Leadership* 5, 1, 5–23

Giddens, A, 2009, *The politics of climate change*, Cambridge: Polity Press

Gilchrist, A, Taylor, M, 2011, *The short guide to community development*, Bristol: Policy Press

Gillinson, S, Horne, M, Baeck, P, 2010, Radical efficiency: Different, better, lower cost public services, Research paper, London: NESTA

Girardet, H, 2008, *Cities, people, planet: Urban development and climate change*, 2nd edn, Chichester: John Wiley

Girouard, M, 1985, *Cities and people: A social and architectural history*, New Haven, CT: Yale University Press

Glaeser, E, 2011, *Triumph of the city*, New York: PenguinGlaser, E, 2013, The west's hidden propaganda machine, *Guardian*, 17 May

Glasze, G, Webster, C, Frantz, K (eds), 2006, *Private cities*, London: Routledge

Go, FM, Govers, R (eds), 2013, *International place branding yearbook 2012*, Basingstoke: Palgrave

Goddard, J, Vallance, J, 2013, *The university and the city*, Abingdon: Routledge

Goetz, EG, 2013, *New deal ruins: Race, economic justice and public housing policy*, Ithaca, NY: Cornell University Press

Goleman, D, Boyatzis, R, McKee, A, 2002, *The new leaders: Transforming the art of leadership into the science of results*, London: Time Warner

Good, KR, 2009, *Municipalities and multiculturalism: The politics of immigration in Toronto and Vancouver*, Toronto: University of Toronto Press

Goss, S, 2001, *Making local governance work: Networks, relationships and the management of change*, Basingstoke: Palgrave

Goss, S, Tarplett, P, 2010, Partnerships: Rhetoric or reality?, in S Brookes, K Grint (eds) *The new public leadership challenge*, 263–79, Basingstoke: Palgrave

Graeber, D, 2013, *The democracy project: A history. A crisis. A movement*, London: Allen Lane

Graham, S, 2010, *Cities under siege: The new military urbanism*, London: Verso

Graham, S, 2011, The new military urbanism, in G Bridge, S Watson (eds) *The city*, 121–33, Oxford: Blackwell

Gramsci, A, 1971, *Selections from the Prison Notebooks of Antonio Gramsci*, New York: International Publishers

Gratz, RB, Mintz, N, 1998, *Cities back from the edge: New life for downtown*, New York: Wiley

Grint, K (ed), 1997, *Leadership: Classical, contemporary and critical approaches*, Oxford: Oxford University Press

Grint, K, 2005, *Leadership: Limits and possibilities*, Basingstoke: Palgrave

Grint, K, 2010, Wicked problems and clumsy solutions: The role of leadership, in S Brookes, K Grint (eds) *The new public leadership challenge*, 169–86, Basingstoke: Palgrave

Grogan, PS, Proscio, T, 2000, *Comeback cities: A blueprint for urban neighborhood renewal*, Boulder, CO: Westview Press

Gross, JS, 2007, Diversity and the democratic challenge: Governing world cities, in R Hambleton, JS Gross (eds) *Governing cities in a global era: Urban innovation, competition and democratic reform*, 73–91, Basingstoke: Palgrave

Gross, JS, 2012, Diversity, democracy and space: The governance of migration in the metropolis, Paper presented to the *Governing the Metropolis: New Directions for Research Conference*, Paris, November.

Gyford, J, 1991, *Does place matter? Locality and local democracy*, London: Local Government Management Board

HM Treasury, 2010, *Total place: A whole area approach to public services*, March, London: HM Treasury

Hall, P, 1988, *Cities of tomorrow: An intellectual history of urban planning and design*, Oxford: Blackwell

Hall, P, 1998, *Cities in Civilisation*, London: Weidenfeld and Nicholson

Hall, P, 2013, *Good cities, better lives: How Europe discovered the lost art of urbanism*, Abingdon: Routledge

Hall, S, 2003, Cultural identity and diaspora, in JE Braziel, A Mannur (eds) *Theorising diaspora: A reader*, 233–46, Malden, MA: Blackwell

Hambleton, R, 1978, *Policy planning and local government*, London: Hutchinson

Hambleton, R, 1988, The American gender gap, *Times Higher Education Supplement*, 12 August, 13

Hambleton, R, 1998, Strengthening political leadership in UK local government, *Public Money and Management*, January–March, 41–58

Hambleton, R, 2004, Leading localities in a partnership era, *Local Governance* 30, 1, 4–13

Hambleton, R, 2007a, New leadership for democratic urban space, in R Hambleton, JS Gross (eds) *Governing cities in a global era: Urban innovation, competition and democratic reform*, 163–76, Basingstoke: Palgrave

Hambleton, R, 2007b, The triangle of engaged scholarship, *Planning Theory and Practice* 8, 4, 549–53

Hambleton, R, 2007c, *Cross-national lesson drawing for planning: Taking advantage of globalisation*, Paper to the Association of European Schools of Planning (AESOP), Naples, 11–14 July

Hambleton, R, 2009, Civic leadership for Auckland: An international perspective, in *Royal Commission on Auckland Governance* 4, Part 11, 515–52

Hambleton, R, 2010, New wine in old bottles?, *Municipal Journal*, 18 February, p 16

Hambleton, R, 2013, Elected mayors: an international rising tide?, *Policy and Politics* 41, 1, 125–8

Hambleton, R, 2014, Place-based leadership: A new agenda for spatial planning and local governance, *Borderlands: The Journal of Spatial Planning in Ireland*, 4, April, 11–32

Hambleton, R, Bullock, S, 1996, *Revitalising local democracy: The leadership options*, London: Association of District Councils/Local Government Management Board

Hambleton, R, Gross, JS (eds), 2007, *Governing cities in a global era: Urban innovation, competition and democratic reform*, Basingstoke: Palgrave

Hambleton, R, Howard, J, 2012, *Public sector innovation and local leadership in the UK and the Netherlands*, York: Joseph Rowntree Foundation

Hambleton, R, Howard, J, 2013, Place-based leadership and public service innovation, *Local Government Studies* 39, 1, 47–70

Hambleton, R, Sweeting, D, 2004, US-style leadership for English local government?, *Public Administration Review* 64, 4, 474–88

Hambleton, R, Sweeting, D, 2014, Innovation in urban political leadership: Reflections on the introduction of a directly elected mayor in Bristol, UK, *Public Money and Management* 34, September, 315–22

Hambleton, R, Taylor, M (eds), 1993, *People in cities: A transatlantic policy exchange*, Bristol: Policy Press

Hambleton, R, Taylor, M, 1994, Transatlantic urban policy transfer, *Policy Studies* 15, 2, 4–18

Hambleton, R, Howard, J, Buser, M, Taylor, M, 2009, *International insights on civic leadership and public service innovation*, Report for the Local Authority Research Council Initiative (LARCI), Swindon: LARCI

Hambleton, R, Howard, J, Marsh, A, Sweeting, D, 2013, *The prospects for mayoral governance in Bristol*, The Bristol Civic Leadership Project, March, University of the West of England, Bristol: Bristol, http://bristolcivicleadership.net

Hamnett, C, 2003, *Unequal city: London in the global arena*, London: Routledge

Hantrais, L, 2009, *International comparative research: Theory, methods and practice*, Basingstoke: Palgrave

Harrison, P, 1983, *Inside the inner city: Life under the cutting edge*, Harmonsdworth: Penguin

Harte, P, 2013, Investing in peace: Reflections on the work of the International Fund for Ireland from 1986–2011, *Borderlands: The Journal of Spatial Planning in Ireland* 3, January, 9–26

Hartley, J, 2011, Public value through innovation and improvement, in J Benington, MH Moore (eds) *Public value: Theory and practice*, 171–84, Basingstoke: Palgrave

Harvey, D, 1973, *Social justice and the city*, London: Edward Arnold

Harvey, D, 2012, *Rebel cities: From the right to the city to the urban revolution*, London: Verso

Haslam, SA, Reicher, SD, Platow, MJ, 2011, *The new psychology of leadership: Identity, influence and power*, Hove: Psychology Press

Hatzelhoffer, L, Humboldt, K, Lobeck, M, Wiegandt, CC, 2012, *Smart city in practice: Converting innovative cities into reality*, Berlin: Jovis Verlag GmbH

Haughton, G, Allmendinger, P, Counsell, D, Vigar, G, 2010, *The new spatial planning: Territorial management with soft spaces and fuzzy boundaries*, Abingdon: Routledge

Haus, M, Heinelt, H, Stewart, M (eds), 2005, *Urban governance and democracy: Leadership and community involvement*, Abingdon: Routledge

Havel, V, 1992, *Summer meditations on politics, morality and civility in a time of transition*, London: Faber and Faber

Haylett, C, 2006, Working-class subjects in the cosmopolitan city, in J Binnie, J Holloway, S Millington, C Young (eds) *Cosmopolitan urbanism*, pp 187–203, Abingdon: Routledge

Hayward, CR, Swanstrom, T (eds), 2011, *Justice and the American metropolis*, Minneapolis, MN; University of Minnesota Press

Healey, P, 2010, *Making better places: The planning project in the 21st century*, Basingstoke: Palgrave

Heidenheimer, AJ, Heclo, H, Adams, CT, 1990, *Comparative public policy*, 3rd edn, New York: St Martin's Press

Heifetz, RA, Linsky, M, 2002, *Leadership on the line*, Boston, MA: Harvard Business Press.

Heifetz, R, Grashow, A, Linsky, M, 2009, *The practice of adaptive leadership*, Boston, MA: Harvard Business Press

Heinelt, H, Sweeting, D, Getimis, P (eds), 2006, *Legitimacy and urban governance: A cross-national comparative study*, Abingdon: Routledge

Held, D, 1987, *Models of democracy*, Oxford: The Polity Press

Hennock, EP, 1973, *Fit and proper persons: Ideal and reality in nineteenth-century urban government*, London: Edward Arnold

Hersey, P, 1984, *The situational leader*, New York: Warner Books
Heseltine, M, 2012, *No stone unturned in pursuit of growth*, London: Department of Business, Innovation and Skills
Heynen, N, Kaika, M, Swyngedouw, E (eds), 2006, *In the Nature of Cities. Urban political ecology and the politics of urban metabolism*, Abingdon: Routledge
HEFCE (Higher Education Funding Council for England), 2009, *Research excellence framework: Second consultation on the assessment of funding of research*, September 2009/38, Bristol: HEFCE
Hindman, M, 2009, *The myth of digital democracy*, Princeton, NJ: Princeton University Press
Hirschman, AO, 1970, *Exit, voice and loyalty*, Cambridge, MA: Harvard University Press
Hirschman, AO, 1971, *A bias for hope: Essays on development and Latin America*, Newhaven, CT: Yale University Press
Hirshman, L, 2012, *The triumphant gay revolution*, New York: HarperCollins
Hodgson, L, 2004, Manufactured civil society: Counting the cost, *Critical Social Policy* 24, 2, 139–64
Hoggett, P (ed), 1997, *Contested communities: Experiences, struggles, policies*, Bristol: Policy Press
Hoggett, P, 2009, *Politics, emotion and identity*, Boulder, CO: Paradigm
Hollis, L, 2013, *Cities are good for you: The genius of the metropolis*, London: Bloomsbury
Hood, C, 1991, A public management for all seasons?, *Public Administration* 69, Spring, 3–19
Hopkins, AG (ed), 2002, *Globalisation in world history*, London: Pimlico
Hopkins, R, 2011, *The transition companion: Making your community more resilient in uncertain times*, Totnes: Green Books
Hopkins, R, 2013, *The power of just doing stuff*, Cambridge: UIT/Green Books
Hou, J (ed), 2013, *Transcultural cities: Border-crossing and placemaking*, Abingdon: Routledge
Howard, J, Lever, J, 2011, New governance spaces: what generates a participatory disposition in different contexts? *Voluntary Sector Review*, 2, 1, 77–95
Hoyt, L (ed), 2013, *Transforming cities and minds through the scholarship of engagement: Economy, equity and environment*, Nashville, TN: Vanderbilt University Press
Hubbard, P, Kitchin, R, Valentine, G (eds), 2004, *Key thinkers on space and place*, London: SAGE
Hudson, L, 1967, *Contrary imaginations*, Harmondsworth: Penguin
Hunt, T, 2004, *Building Jerusalem: The rise and fall of the Victorian city*, London: Weidenfeld and Nicolson
Hutton, W, 2006, *The writing on the wall: Why we must embrace China as a partner or face it as an enemy*, New York, NY: Free Press
Hutton, W, Giddens, A (eds), 2000, *On the edge: Living with global capitalism*, London: Jonathan Cape

Illsley, B, Jackson, T, Curry, J, Rapaport, E, 2010, Community involvement in the soft spaces of planning, *International Planning Studies* 15, 4, 303–19

Imbroscio, DL, 2010, Keeping it critical: Resisting the allure of the mainstream, in JS Davies, DL Imbroscio (eds) *Critical urban studies: New directions*, 89–103, Albany, NY: State University of New York Press

IPCC (Intergovernmental Panel on Climate Change), 2013, *Working group 1. Climate change 2013: The Physical science basis*, September, Geneva: IPCC Secretariat

IPCC (Intergovernmental Panel on Climate Change), 2014a, *Working group 2. Climate change 2014: Impacts, adaptation and vulnerability*, March, Geneva: IPCC Secretariat

IPCC (Intergovernmental Panel on Climate Change), 2014b, *Working group 3. Climate change 2014: Mitigation of climate change*, April, Geneva: IPCC Secretariat

Irazabal, C, 2005, *City making and urban governance in the Americas*, Aldershot: Ashgate Publishing

Iszatt-White, M (ed), 2013, *Leadership as emotional labour. Management and the 'managed heart'*, Abingdon: Routledge

Iveson, K, Fincher, R, 2011, 'Just diversity' in the city of difference, in G Bridge, S Watson (eds) 2011, *The new Blackwell companion to the city*, 407–18, Chichester: Blackwell

Jackson, T, 2009, *Prosperity without growth: Economics for a finite planet*, London: Earthscan

Jacobs, J, 1961, *The death and life of great American cities*, New York: Vintage

Jacobs, MJ, 1991, *The green economy: Environment, sustainable development and the politics of the future*, London: Pluto Press

James, S, Cox, E, 2007, *Ward councillors and community leadership: A future perspective*, York: Joseph Rowntree Foundation

Jenks, M, Jones, C (eds), 2010, *Dimensions of the sustainable city*, London: Springer

Johnson, JC, Galea, S, 2011, Urban health in low- and middle-income countries, in AL Dannenberg, H Frumkin, RJ Jackson (eds) *Making healthy places*, pp 350–65, Washington, DC: Island Press

Jones, BD (ed), 1989, *Leadership and politics: New perspectives in political science*, Lawrence, KS: University Press of Kansas

Joyce, P, 2012, *Strategic leadership in public services*, Abingdon: Routledge

Judd, DR, Smith, JR, 2007, The new ecology of urban governance: Special-purpose authorities and urban development, in R Hambleton, JS Gross (eds) *Governing cities in a global era: Urban innovation, competition and democratic reform*, 151–60, Basingstoke: Palgrave

Kahane, A, 2004, *Solving tough problems: An open way of talking, listening and creating new realities*, San Francisco, CA: Berrett-Koehler Publishers

Kahneman, D, 2012, *Thinking, fast and slow*, Penguin: London

Kaika, M, 2005, *City of flows. Modernity, nature and the city*, Abingdon: Routledge

Kantor, P, Lefevre, C, Saito, A, Savitch, HV, Thornley, A, 2012, *Struggling giants: City-region governance in London, New York, Paris and Tokyo*, Minneapolis, MN: University of Minnesota Press

Kegan, R, 1982, *The evolving self: Problem and process in human development*, Cambridge, MA: Harvard University Press

Kemp, R, Kemp, E, Eldridge, C, Maxwell, B, 2009, *Cabinet member for your ward: A new challenge for all councillors*, London: Leadership Centre for Local Government (now part of the Local Government Association)

Keohane, NO, 2010, *Thinking about leadership*, Princeton, NJ; Princeton University Press

Kohn, M, 2004, *Brave new neighbourhoods: The privatisation of public space*, New York, NY: Routledge

Kriesi, H, Müller, L (eds), 2013, *Democracy: An Ongoing Challenge*, Zurich: Lars Müller Publishers

Krumholz, N, Forester, J, 1990, *Making equity planning work: Leadership in the public sector*, Philadelphia, PA: Temple University Press

Lacey, A, Miller, R, Reeves, D, Tankel, Y, 2013, From gender mainstreaming to intersectionality, in C Whitzman, C Legacy, C Andrew, F Klodawsky, M Shaw, K Viswanath (eds) *Building Inclusive Cities: Women's safety and the right to the city*, 143–61, Abingdon: Routledge

Laguerre, MS, 1999, *Minoritized space: An inquiry into the spatial order of things*, Berkeley, CA: University of California Press

Landis, D, Bennett, J, Bennett, M, 2004, *Handbook of intercultural training*, London: SAGE

Landry, C, 2006, *The art of city making*, London: Earthscan

Lansley, S, 2012, *The cost of inequality: Why equality is essential for recovery*, London: Gibson Square

Lapavitsas, C, 2013, *Profiting without producing. How finance exploits us all*, London: Verso

Larsen, JN, 2012, Voluntary community organisations in metropolitan development, Paper to the European Urban Research Association (EURA), Conference, Vienna, September

Layard, R, 2011, *Happiness: Lessons from a new science*, 2nd edn, London: Penguin

Le Grand, J, 2007, *The other invisible hand: Delivering public services through choice and competition*, Princeton, NJ: University of Princeton Press

Leach, S, 2006, *The changing role of local politics in Britain*, Bristol: Policy Press

Leadbeater, C, 2013, The systems innovator, Discussion paper in G Mulgan, C Leadbeater (eds) *Systems innovation*, January, 25–54, London: NESTA

Leadbeater, C, 2014, *The frugal innovator: Creating change on a shoestring budget*, Basingstoke: Palgrave

Leavy, J, Howard, J, 2013, *What matters most? Evidence from 84 participatory studies with those living with extreme poverty and marginalisation*, The Participate Initiative, Brighton: Institute of Development Studies

Ledwith, M, 2011, *Community development: A critical approach*, 2nd edn, Bristol: Policy Press

Lefebvre, H, 1996, The right to the city, in E Kofman, E Lebas (eds) *Writing on cities*, 63–181, Oxford: Blackwell, originally published as *Le Droit* à *la Ville*, 1968, Paris: Anthropos

Lefevre, C, 2010, The improbable metropolis: Decentralisation, local democracy and metropolitan areas in the Western world, *Analise Social* XLV, 197, 623–37

Leighton, D, Wood, C, 2010, *Measuring social value: The gap between policy and practice*, London: Demos

Levin, J, Rabrenovic, G, 2004, *Why we hate*, Amherst, NY: Prometheus Books

Levy, F, Meltsner, AJ, Wildavsky, A, 1974, *Urban outcomes*, Berkeley, CA: University of California Press

Lewis, M, Conaty, P, 2012, *The resilience imperative: Cooperative transitions to a steady-state economy*, Canada: New Society Publishers

Liddle, J, 2010, Twenty-first-century public leadership within complex governance systems: Some reflections, *Policy and Politics* 38, 4, 657–63

Livingstone, K, 2011, *You can't say that: Memoirs*, London: Faber and Faber

Lo, L, 2008, DiverCity Toronto: Canada's premier gateway city, in M Price, L Benton-Short (eds) *Migrants to the metropolis: The rise of immigrant gateway cities*, 97–127, Syracuse, NY: Syracuse University Press

Logan, JR, Molotch, HL, 1987, *Urban fortunes: The political economy of place*, Berkeley, CA: University of California Press

Low, S, 2003, *Behind the gates: Life, security, and the pursuit of happiness in fortress America*, New York: Routledge

Lukes, S, 2005, *Power: A radical view*, 2nd edn, Basingstoke: Palgrave

Lynch, K, 1960, *The image of the city*, Cambridge, MA: MIT Press

Lynch, K, 1981, *A theory of good city form*, Cambridge, MA: MIT Press

Lyons Inquiry into Local Government, 2007, *Place-shaping: A shared ambition for the future of local government*, March, London: The Stationery Office.

Maddock, S, 2009, *Change you can believe in: The leadership of innovation*, Whitehall Innovation Hub, London: National School of Government

Magnusson, W, 2010, Seeing like a city, in JS Davies, DL Imbroscio (eds) *Critical urban studies: New directions*, 41–53, Albany, NY: State University of New York Press

Maloney, T, Kirchberger, A, 2010, *Cities accommodating diversity: Findings from the peer review project 'Diversity and Equality in European Cities'*, Brussels: EUROCITIES

Maly, MT, 2005, *Beyond segregation: Multiracial and multiethnic neighbourhoods in the United States*, Philadelphia, PA: Temple University Press

Margerum, RD, 2011, *Beyond consensus: Improving collaborative planning and management*, Cambridge, MA: The MIT Press

Marris, P, 1987, *Meaning and action: Community planning and conceptions of change*, London: Routledge and Kegan Paul

Marris, P, Rein, M, 1972, *Dilemmas of social reform: Poverty and community action in the United States*, 2nd edn, Harmondsworth: Pelican

Marsh, PT, 1994, *Joseph Chamberlain: Entrepreneur in politics*, New Haven, CT: Yale University Press

Marshall, J, Coleman, G, Reason, P (eds), 2011, *Leadership for sustainability: An action research approach*, Sheffield: Greenleaf Publishing

Marshall, TH, 1950, *Citizenship and social class*, Cambridge: Cambridge University Press

Marshall, TH, Bottomore, T, 1992, *Citizenship and social class*, London: Pluto Press

Martinez-Fernandez, C, Audriac, I, Fol, S, Cunningham-Sabot, E, 2012, Shrinking cities: Urban challenges and globalisation, *International Journal of Urban and Regional Research* 36, 1, 213–25

Maslow, AH, 1943, A theory of human motivation, *Psychological Review* 50, 4, 370–96

Massey, D, 1994, *Space, place and gender*, Cambridge: Polity Press

Massey, D, 2005, *For space*, London: SAGE

Maude, B, 2011, *Managing cross-cultural communication: Principles and practice*, Basingstoke: Palgrave

Mayer-Schonberger, V, Cukier, K, 2013, *Big data: A revolution that will transform how we live, work and think*, London: John Murray

McCarney, PL, Stren, RE (eds), 2003, *Governance on the ground: Innovations and discontinuities in cities of the developing world*, Baltimore, MD: Johns Hopkins University Press

McGregor, D, 1960, *The human side of enterprise*, New York: McGraw-Hill

McInerney, CR, Day, RE, 2007, *Rethinking knowledge management*, New York: Springer

McKenzie, E, 1994, *Privatopia: Homeowner associations and the rise of residential private governments*, Newhaven, CT: Yale University

Meadows, DH, Meadows, DL, Randers, J, Behrens, WW, 1972, *The Limits to Growth*, New York: Universe Books

Meadows, DH, Randers, J, Meadows, D, 2005, *Limits to growth: The 30-year update*, London: Earthscan

Meijs, LCPM, 2012, Reinventing Dutch civil society, *ECSP Insight* 3, October, pp 16–18, Rotterdam: Rotterdam School of Management, Erasmus University

Meyer, WB, 2013, *The environmental advantages of cities: Countering commonsense antiurbanism*, Cambridge, MA: The MIT Press

Miliband, E, 2011, *Speech to the Labour Party Conference*, 27 September

Minton, A, 2009, *Ground control: Fear and happiness in the twenty-first-century city*, London: Penguin

Minton, A, Aked, J, 2012, 'Fortress Britain': High security, insecurity and the challenge of preventing harm, *Prevention Working Paper*, December, London: New Economics Foundation (nef)

Mitchell, D, 2003, *The right to the city: Social justice and the fight for public space*, New York: Guilford Press

Moloney, T, Kirchberger, A, 2010, *Cities accommodating diversity*, Report of the diversity and equality in European cities (DIVE) project, Brussels: EUROCITIES and Migration Policy Group, www.integratingcities.eu

Monaghan, P, 2012, *How local resilience creates sustainable societies: Hard to make, hard to break*, Abingdon: Routledge

Monbiot, G, 2013, Climate change? Try catastrophic climate breakdown, *Guardian*, 28 September, 1

Montgomery, J, 2007, *The new wealth of cities*, Aldershot: Ashgate

Montgomery, J, 2013, *Happy city: Transforming our lives through urban design*, London: Penguin

Moore, MH, 1995, *Creating public value*, Cambridge, MA: Harvard University Press

Moore, R, 2012, *Why we build*, Basingstoke: Picador

Morphet, J, 2010, *Effective practice in spatial planning*, Abingdon: Routledge

Mossberger, K, 2009, Urban regime analysis, in JS Davies, DL Imbroscio (eds) *Theories of urban politics*, 40–54, London: SAGE

Mossberger, K, Clarke, SE, John, P (eds), 2012, *The Oxford handbook of urban politics*, Oxford: Oxford University Press

Mossberger, K, Tolbert, CJ, McNeal, RS, 2008, *Digital citizenship: The internet, society and participation*, Cambridge MA: The MIT Press

Moynagh, M, Worsley, R, 2008, *Going global: Key questions for the 21st Century*, London: A and C Black

Mulgan, G, Leadbeater, C, 2013, *Systems innovation: Discussion paper*, London: National Endowment for Science Technology and the Arts (NESTA)

Neal, Z, 2013, *The connected city: How networks are shaping the modern metropolis*, Abingdon: Routledge

Nelson, AC, Allen, BL, Trauger, DL (eds), 2006, *Toward a resilient metropolis: The role of state and land grant universities in the 21st century*, Alexandria, VA: Metropolitan Institute at Virginia Tech

Neuwirth, R, 2005, *Shadow cities: A billion squatters, a new urban world*, London: Routledge

Newman, I, 2014, *Reclaiming local democracy: A progressive future for local government*, Bristol: Policy Press

Newman, P, Jennings, I, 2008, *Cities as sustainable ecosystems: Principles and practices*, Washington, DC: Island Press

Newman, P, Beatley, T, Boyer, H, 2009, *Resilient cities: Responding to peak oil and climate change*, Washington, DC: Island Press

Newton, PW, 2014, City transitions: Infrastructure innovation, green economy and the eco-city, in LJ Pearson, PW Newton, P Roberts (eds) *Resilient sustainable cities: A future*, 91–104, Abingdon: Routledge

Nicholson, N, 2013, *The 'I' of leadership: Strategies for seeing, being and doing*, Chichester: John Wiley

Nightingale, CH, 2012, *Segregation: A global history of divided cities*, Chicago, IL: University of Chicago Press

Norman, J, 2010, *The Big Society: The anatomy of the new politics*, Buckingham: University of Buckingham Press

Norquist, J, 1998, *The wealth of cities: Revitalizing the centers of American life*, Reading, MA: Addison-Wesley

Nye, JS, 2004, *Soft power: The means to success in world politics*, New York: Public Affairs

OECD (Organisation for Economic Cooperation and Development), 2008, *Growing unequal: Income distribution and poverty in OECD countries*, Paris: OECD

Oliver, B, Pitt, B, 2013, *Engaging communities and service users: Context, themes and methods*, Basingstoke: Palgrave

Osborne, D, Plastrik, P, 1997, *Banishing bureaucracy: The five strategies for reinventing government*, Reading, MA: Addison-Wesley

Osborne, H, 2014, Poor doors: the segregation of inner-city flat dwellers, *The Guardian*, 26 July, 1

Ouseley, H, 2005, *Community pride – not prejudice: Making diversity work in Bradford*, Bradford: Bradford Vision

Packard, V, 1957, *The hidden persuaders*, Harmondsworth: Penguin

Pallagst, K, Wiechmann, T, Marinez-Fernandez, C (eds), 2014, *Shrinking cities: International perspectives and policy implications*, Abingdon: Routledge

Parkin, S, 2010, *The positive deviant: Sustainability leadership in a perverse world*, London: Earthscan

Parnell, S, Pieterse, E (eds), 2014, *Africa's urban revolution*, London: Zed Books

Pateman, C, 1970, *Participation and democratic theory*, Cambridge: Cambridge University Press

Pearce, J (ed), 2010, *Participation and democracy in the twenty-first century city*, Basingstoke: Palgrave

Pearson, LJ, Newton, PW, Roberts, P (eds), 2014, *Resilient sustainable cities: A future*, Abingdon: Routledge

Peck, J, 2005, Struggling with the creative class, *International Journal of Urban and Regional Research* 29, 4, 740–70

Pelling, M, 2011, *Adaptation to climate change: From resilience to transformation*, Abingdon: Routledge

Pendleton, D, Furnham, A, 2012, *Leadership: All you need to know*, Basingstoke: Palgrave

Penninx, R, Martiniello, M, 2004, Integration processes and policies: State of the art and lessons, in R Penninx, K Kraal, M Martiniello, S Vertovic (eds) *Citizenship in European cities: Immigrants, local politics and integration policies*, Aldershot: Ashgate

Perry, DC, Wiewel, W (eds) 2005, *The university as urban developer: Case studies and analysis*, Armonk: ME Sharpe

Peters, TJ, Waterman, RH, 1982, *In search of excellence: Lessons from Americas best-run companies*, New York: Harper and Row

Peterson, PE, 1981, *City limits*, Chicago, IL: University of Chicago Press

Pew Partnership, 2004, *New directions in civic engagement: University avenue meets main street*, Charlottesville, VA: Pew Partnership for Civic Change

Pierre, J, 2011, *The politics of urban governance*, Basingstoke: Palgrave

Pierre, J, Peters, BG, 2000, *Governance, politics and the state*, Basingstoke: Palgrave

Pieterse, E, 2014, Filling the void: An agenda for tackling African urbanisation, in S Parnell, E Pieterse (eds) *Africa's urban revolution*, 200–20, London: Zed Books

Piketty, T, 2014, *Capital in the twenty-first century*, Cambridge, MA: Harvard University Press

Pollitt, C, 1990, *Managerialism and the public services*, Oxford: Blackwell

Porter, L, Shaw, K (eds), 2009, *Whose urban renaissance? An international comparison of urban regeneration strategies*, Routledge: Abingdon

Post, RC, 2010, *Urban mass transit: The life story of a technology*, Baltimore, MD: Johns Hopkins University Press

Price, M, Benton-Short, L, 2007, Immigrants and world cities: From hyper-diverse to the bypassed, *GeoJournal* 68, 2, 103–17

Price, M, Benton-Short, L (eds), 2008, *Migrants to the metropolis: The rise of immigrant gateway cities*, Syracuse, NY: Syracuse University Press

Provost, C, 2013, Bringing it all back home, *Guardian Weekly*, 8 March, 14

Putnam, RD, 1993, *Making democracy work: Civic traditions in modern Italy*, Princeton, NJ: Princeton University Press

Putnam, RD, 2007, *E Pluribus Unum*: Diversity and community in the 21st century, *Scandinavian Political Studies* 30, 2, 137–74

Quelch, JA, Jocz, KE, 2012, *All business is local: Why place matters more than ever in a global virtual world*, London: Porfolio Penguin

Quick, KS, Feldman, MS, 2011, Distinguishing participation and inclusion, *Journal of Planning Education and Research*, 31, 3, 271–90

Quirk, B, 2011, *Re-imagining government*, Basingstoke: Palgrave

Raja, S, Born, B, Kozlowski Russell, J, 2008, *A planner's guide to community and regional food planning: Transforming food environments, facilitating healthy eating*, Planning Advisory Service Report 554, Chicago, IL: American Planning Association

Ranney, D, 2003, *Global decisions, local collisions: Urban life in the new world order*, Philadelphia, PA: Temple University Press

Ravetz, J, 2013, Sustainable city regions and beyond: Towards urban synergy and social intelligences, *Journal of the Town and Country Planning Association* 82, 10, 402–6

Redekop, BW (ed), 2010, *Leadership for environmental sustainability*, Abingdon: Routledge

Reeves, D, 2005, *Planning for diversity: Policy and planning in a world of difference*, Abingdon: Routledge

Relph, E, 1976, *Place and placelessness*, London: Pion

Rhodes, R, Wanna, J, 2007, The limits of public value, or Rescuing responsible government from the platonic guardians, *Australian Journal of Public Administration* 66, 4, 406–21

Rich, RF, 1997, Measuring knowledge utilisation: Processes and outcomes, *Knowledge and Policy: The International Journal of Knowledge Transfer and Utilisation* 10, 3, 11–24

Richards, MG, 2006, *Congestion charging in London: The policy and the politics*, Basingstoke: Palgrave

Riley, K, 2013, *Leadership of place: Stories from schools in the US, UK and South Africa*, London: Bloomsbury Academic

Riots, Communities and Victims Panel, 2012, *After the riots: The final report*, March, London: Independent Report of the Panel

Rittel, H, Webber, M, 1973, Dilemmas in a general theory of planning, *Policy Sciences*, 4, 2, 155–69

Rivlin, G, 1992, *Fire on the prairie*, New York: Henry Holt

Rocke, A, 2014, *Framing citizen participation: Participatory budgeting in France, Germany and the United Kingdom*, Basingstoke: Palgrave

Rogers, R, Stirk, G, Harbours, I, 2012, *Cities of tomorrow: Cities and the language of architecture*, Lecture to the Royal Institute of British Architects (RIBA), London, 31 January

Rose, R, 1993, *Lesson-drawing in public policy: A guide to learning across time and space*, Chatham, NJ: Chatham House Publishers

Rose, R, 2005, *Learning from comparative public policy: A practical guide*, Abingdon: Routledge

Rosenzweig, P, 2007, *The halo effect*, New York: Simon and Schuster

Roulstone, A, Prideaux, S, 2012, *Understanding disability policy*, Bristol: Policy Press

Royal Commission on Auckland Governance, 2009, *Auckland governance report*, Auckland, New Zealand: Royal Commission on Auckland Governance, www.royalcommission.govt.nz

Royko, M, 1971, *Boss: Richard J Daley*, New York: Penguin

Ruble, BA, Stren, RE, Tulchin, JS, Varat, DH (eds), 2001, *Urban governance around the world*, Washington, DC: Woodrow Wilson Center

Rydin, Y, 2011, *The purpose of planning: Creating sustainable towns and cities*, Bristol: Policy Press

Rydin, Y, 2013, *The future of planning: Beyond growth dependence*, Bristol: Policy Press

Salgado, S, 2000, *Migrations: Humanity in transition*, New York: Aperture

Sanchez de Madariaga, I, Roberts, M (eds), 2013, *Fair shared cities: The impact of gender planning in Europe*, Abingdon: Ashgate

Sandel, M, 2012, *What money can't buy: The moral limits of markets*, London: Allen Lane

Sandercock, L, 1998, *Towards cosmopolis: Planning for multicultural cities*, Chichester: John Wiley

Sandercock, L, 2003, *Cosmopolis II: Mongrel cities of the 21st century*, London: Continuum

Sansom, G, 2012, *Australian mayors: What can and should they do?*, A discussion paper, Sydney: Centre for Local Government, University of Technology Sydney

Sashkin, M, Sashkin, MG, 2003, *Leadership that matters*, San Francisco, CA: Berrett-Koehler Publishers

Sassen, S, 1999, *Guests and aliens*, New York: New Press

Sassen, S, 2001, *The global city: New York, London, Tokyo*, 2nd edn, Princeton, NJ: Princeton University Press

Sassen, S, 2014, *Expulsions: Brutality and complexity in the global economy*, Cambridge, MA: Harvard University Press

Satterthwaite, D, Dodman, D, 2013, Towards resilience and transformation for cities within a finite planet, *Environment and Urbanization* 25, 2, 291–98

Satterthwaite, D, Mitlin, D, 2014, *Reducing urban poverty in the global south*, Abingdon: Routledge

Saunders, D, 2010, *Arrival city: How the largest migration in history is reshaping our world*, Heinemann: London

Saurugger, S, Radaelli, CM, 2008, The Europeanisation of public policies: introduction, *Journal of Comparative Policy Analysis* 10, 3, 213–19

Savitch, HV, Kantor, P, 2002, *Cities in the international marketplace: The political economy of urban development in North America and Western Europe*, Princeton, NJ: Princeton University Press

Scarman, LG, 1981, *The Scarman Report: The Brixton disorders, 10–12 April 1981*, Report of an inquiry by Lord Scarman, London: Her Majesty's Stationery Office

Scharmer, O, Kaufer, K, 2013, *Leading from the emerging future: From ego-system to eco-system economics*, San Francisco, CA: Berrett-Koehler

Schattschneider, EE, 1960, *The semi-sovereign people: A realist's view of the democracy in America*, New York: Holt, Rhinehart and Winston

Schon, DA, 1971, *Beyond the stable state*, London: Temple Smith

Schumpeter, JA, 1943, *Capitalism, socialism and democracy*, London: Allen and Unwin

Sclar, ED, Volavka-Close, N, Brown, P (eds), 2013, *The urban transformation: Health, shelter and climate change*, Abingdon: Routledge

Scott, J, 2001, *Power*, Cambridge: Polity Press

Scott, JC, 1998, *Seeing like a state: How certain schemes to improve the human condition have failed*, New Haven, CT: Yale University Press

Scullion, J, 2013, *Tweeting or retreating: The dilemma for modern councillors*, Paper to the Policy and Politics Conference, Bristol, 17–18 September

Sen, A, 1984, The living standard, *Oxford Economic Papers 36*, 74–90, Oxford: Oxford University Press

Sen, A, 2006, *Identity and violence: The illusion of destiny*, London: Penguin

Sepe, M, 2013, *Planning and place in the city: Mapping place identity*, Abingdon: Routledge

Shackle, S, 2013, Will the Delhi gang-rape case actually change women's lives in India?, *New Statesman*, 11 January, 12–17

Shaftoe, H, 2008, *Convivial urban spaces: Creating effective public places*, London: Earthscan

Sherriff, G, 2013, From burden to asset: The political ecology of sustainable transport, *Journal of the Town and Country Planning Association* 82, 10, 431–4

Shirky, C, 2008, *Here comes everybody: How change happens when people come together*, London: Penguin

Siegel, D, 2014, *Leaders in the shadows: The leadership qualities of municipal Chief Administrative Officers*, Toronto: University of Toronto Press

Skelcher, C, Sullivan, H, Jeffares, S, 2013, *Hybrid governance in European Cities: Neighbourhood, migration and democracy*, Basingstoke: Palgrave

Smith, C, 2006, *The plan of Chicago: Daniel Burnham and the remaking of the American city*, Chicago, IL: University of Chicago Press

Smith, G, 2009, *Democratic innovations: Designing institutions for citizen participation*, Cambridge: Cambridge University Press

Smith, I, Lepine, E, Taylor, M (eds), 2007, *Disadvantaged by where you live? Neighbourhood governance in contemporary urban policy*, Bristol: Policy Press

Snowden, DJ, Boone, ME, 2007, A leader's framework for decision making, *Harvard Business Review*, November, 1–8

Soja, EW, 2010, *Seeking spatial justice*, Minneapolis, MN: University of Minnesota Press

Sotarauta, M, Horlings, H, Liddle, J (eds), 2014, *Leadership and change in sustainable regional development*, Abingdon: Routledge

Spencer, S, 2011, *The migration debate*, Bristol: Policy Press

Spodek, H, 2011, *Ahmedabad: Shock city of 20th century India*, Bloomington, IN: Indiana University Press

Stacey, RD, 1993, *Strategic management and organisational dynamics*, London: Pitman Publishing

Stein, M, 2012, *Rethinking the gay and lesbian movement*, London: Routledge

Stern, N, 2010, *A blueprint for a safer planet: How we can save the world and create prosperity*, London: Vintage Books

Stewart, JD, 1971, *Management in local government: A viewpoint*, London: Charles Knight

Stewart, M, Collett, P, 1998, Accountability in contributions to sustainable development, in D Warburton (ed) *Community and sustainable development: Participation in the future*, 52–67, London: Earthscan

Stiglitz, J, 2006, *Making globalisation work*, London: Allen Lane

Stiglitz, J, 2012, *The price of inequality: How today's divided society endangers our future*, New York: WW Norton and Company

Stiglitz, JE, Sen, A, Fitoussi, JP, 2009, *Report by the Commission on the Measurement of Economic Performance and Social Progress*, September, Paris: Commission

Stone, CN, 1989, *Regime politics: Governing Atlanta, 1946–1988*, Lawrence, KS: University Press of Kansas

Stone, CN, 1995, Political leadership in urban politics, in D Judge, G Stoker, H Wollman (eds) *Theories of urban politics*, 96–116, London: SAGE

Stone, CN, 2005, Institutions count but resources decide: American mayors and the limits of formal structure, in R Berg, N Rao (eds) *Transforming local political leadership*, 180–94, Basingstoke: Palgrave

Strauss, A, 1978, *Negotiations: Varieties, contexts, processes and social order*, San Francisco, CA: Jossey-Bass

Sukopp, H, Werner, P, 1982, *Nature in cities*, Council of Europe: Strasbourg

Sun, PYT, Anderson, MH, 2012, Civic capacity: Building on transformational leadership to explain successful integrative public leadership, *The Leadership Quarterly* 23, 3, 309–23

Svara, JH, 1990, *Official leadership in the city: Patterns of conflict and cooperation*, Oxford: Oxford University Press

Svara, JH (ed), 1994, *Facilitative leadership in local government: Lessons from successful mayors and chairpersons*, San Francisco, CA: Jossey-Bass Publishers

Svara, JH, 2003, Effective mayoral leadership in council-manager cities: Reassessing the facilitative model, *National Civic Review* 92, 2, 157–72

Svara, JH (ed), 2009, *The facilitative leader in City Hall: Reexamining the scope and contributions*, Boca Raton, FL: Taylor and Francis

Svara, JH, Watson, DJ (eds) 2010, *More than a mayor or manager: Campaigns to change form of government in America's large cities*, Washington, DC: Georgetown University Press

Sweeting, D, 2002, Leadership in urban governance: the Mayor of London, *Local Government Studies* 31, 4, 465–78

Swianiewicz, P, 2007, Changing forms of urban government in central and eastern Europe, in R Hambleton, JS Gross (eds) *governing cities in a global era: Urban innovation, competition and democratic reform*, 93–112, Basingstoke and New York: Palgrave

Swinney, P, Smith, R, Blatchford, K, 2011, *Big shot or long shot? How elected mayors can help drive economic growth in England's cities?*, London: Institute for Government and Centre for Cities

Swyngedouw, E, 2010, Apocalypse forever? Post-political populism and the spectre of climate change, *Theory, Culture and Society* 27, 2/3, 213–32

Taket, A, Crisp, BR, Nevill, A, Lamaro G, Graham M, Barter-Godfrey, S (eds), 2009, *Theorising Social Exclusion*, Abingdon: Routledge

Taleb, NN, 2007, *The black swan: The impact of the highly improbable*, New York: Random House

Tallon, A, 2013, *Urban regeneration in the UK*, 2nd edn, Abingdon: Routledge

Tannerfeldt, G, Ljung, P, 2006, *More urban – less poor: An introduction to urban development and management*, London: Earthscan

Taylor, C, 2005, *Walking the talk: Building a culture of success*, London: Random House

Taylor, D, 2002, *The naked leader*, Chichester: Capstone Publishing

Taylor, FW, 1911, *Principles of scientific management*, New York: Harper and Brothers

Taylor, M, 2011, *Public policy in the community*, 2nd edn, Basingstoke: Palgrave

Taylor, N, 2003, More or less meaningful concepts in planning theory (and how to make them more meaningful): A plea for conceptual analysis and precision: An essay in memory of Eric Reade: 1931-2002, *Planning Theory*, 2, 91, 91–100

Tett, G, 2009, *Fool's gold: How unrestrained greed corrupted a dream, shattered global markets and unleashed a catastrophe*, London: Little Brown

Tewdwr-Jones, M, 2011, *Urban reflections: Narratives of place, meaning and change*, Bristol: Policy Press

Thaler, RH, Sunstein, CR, 2008, *Nudge: Improving decisions about health and happiness*, London: Penguin

Theodore, N, Peck, J, Brenner, N, 2011, Neoliberal urbanism: Cities and the rule of markets, in G Bridge, S Watson (eds) *The new Blackwell companion to the city*, 15–25, Chichester: Blackwell

Thompson Fullilove, M, 2004, *Root shock: How tearing up city neighbourhoods hurts America, and what we can do about it*, New York: One World Ballantine Books

Thörn, C, 2008, *Intervention, or The need for a new cultural critique*, Goteborg: Goteborgs Universitet, Faculty of Fine, Applied and Performing Arts, http://gup.ub.gu.se/publication/87287

Thorp, L, 2009, New migrants, citizenship and local governance: Poles apart?, in C Durose, S Greasley, L Richardson (eds) *Changing local governance, changing citizens*, 111–34, Bristol: Policy Press

Tidd, J, Bessant, J, Pavitt, K, 2005, *Managing innovation: Integrating technological, market and organisational change*, 3rd edn, Chichester: John Wiley

Tiebout, CM, 1956, A pure theory of local expenditures, *Journal of Political Economy* 64, 416–24

Townsend, AM, 2013, *Smart cities: Big data, civic hackers and the quest for a new utopia*, New York: WW Norton and Co Inc.

Travers, T, 2004, *The politics of London: Governing the ungovernable city*, Basingstoke: Palgrave

Tuan, YF, 1977, *Space and place: The perspective of experience*, Minneapolis, MN: The University of Minneapolis Press

Tuddenham, R (ed), 2010, *The Big Society: Next practice and public service futures*, London: SOLACE Foundation Imprint

Tulchin, JS, Varat, DH, Ruble, BA (eds), 2002, *Democratic governance and urban sustainability*, Washington, DC: Woodrow Wilson Center

UCLG (United Cities and Local Governments), 2008, *Decentralisation and local democracy in the World*, GOLD Report I, Barcelona: United Cities and Local Governments

UCLG (United Cities and Local Governments), 2010, Policy paper on urban strategic planning: Local leaders preparing for the future of our cities, *Paper on City Development Strategies*, Barcelona: United Cities and Local Governments

UCLG (United Cities and Local Governments), 2011, *Local government finance: The challenges of the 21st century*, GOLD Report II, Barcelona: United Cities and Local Governments

UCLG (United Cities and Local Governments), 2014, *Access to public services and world urbanisation*, GOLD Report III, Barcelona: United Cities and Local Governments

Uduku, O, 2010, Lagos: Urban gating as the default condition, in S Bagaeen, O Uduku (eds) *Gated communities: Social sustainability in contemporary and historical gated developments*, London: Earthscan

UN Expert Group, 2012, *The millennium development goals report 2012*, New York: United Nations

UN-DESA (Department of Economic and Social Affairs), 2012, *World urbanisation prospects: The 2011 revision*, New York: United Nations

UN-Habitat (Human Settlements Programme), 2010, *State of the world's cities 2010/2011. Cities for all: Bridging the urban divide*, London: Earthscan

UN-Habitat (Human Settlements Programme), 2011, *Cities and climate change: Global report on human settlements 2011*, London: Earthscan

UN-Habitat (Human Settlements Programme), 2012, *State of the world's cities 2012/13: Prosperity of cities*, World Urban Forum Edition, Nairobi: United Nations

UN-Habitat (Human Settlements Programme), 2014, *Urban equity in development: Cities for life*, Concept Paper for WUF 7, March, Nairobi: United Nations

UN-SDSN (Sustainable Development Solutions Network), 2013, *An action agenda for sustainable development: Report to the UN Secretary-General*, 23 October, New York: United Nations, www.unsdsn.org

Urban Task Force, 1999, *Towards an urban renaissance*, London: Department of the Environment, Transport and the Regions

Vertovec, S, 2007, Super-diversity and its implications, *Ethnic and Racial Studies* 29, 6, 1024–54

Vickers, G, 1965, *The art of judgment*, New York: Basic Books

Vickers, G, 1970, *Freedom in a rocking boat: Changing values in an unstable society*, Harmondsworth: Penguin

Viswanath, K, 2013, Gender inclusive cities programme, in C Whitzman, C Legacy, C Andrew, F Klodawsky, M Shaw, K Viswanath (eds) *Building inclusive cities: Women's safety and the right to the city*, 75–89, Abingdon: Routledge

Wainwright, H, 2003, *Reclaim the state: Experiments in popular democracy*, London: Verso

Walsh, K, 1995, *Public services and market mechanisms: Competition, contracting and the new public management*, Basingstoke: Palgrave

Walzer, M, 1992, The civil society argument, in C Mouffe (ed) *Dimensions of radical democracy: Pluralism, citizenship, community*, 89–107, London: Verso

Wang, BX, Chee, H, 2011, *Chinese leadership*, Basingstoke: Palgrave

Warburton, D (ed), 2009, *Community and sustainable development: Participation in the futures*, London: Earthscan

Watson, V, 2006, Deep difference: Diversity, planning and ethics, *Planning Theory* 5, 1, 31–50

Watson, V, 2009, Seeing from the South: Refocussing urban planning on the globe's central urban issues, *Urban Studies* 46, 11, 2259–75

WCED (World Commission on Environment and Development), 1987, *Our common future*, Oxford: Oxford University Press

Weaver, T, 2014, What does social justice in the city require?, Paper to the Urban Affairs Association Annual Conference, San Antonio, 20 March

Whitehead, M, 2012, The sustainable city: An obituary? On the future form and prospects of sustainable urbanism, in J Flint, M Raco (eds) *The future of sustainable cities: Critical reflections*, 29–46, Bristol: Policy Press

Whitfield, D, 1992, *The welfare state. Privatisation, deregulation, commercialisation of public services: Alternative strategies for the 1990s*, London: Pluto Press

Whitfield, D, 2012, *In place of austerity: Reconstructing the economy, state and public services*, Nottingham: Spokesman

Whitzman, C, Legacy, C, Andrew, C, Klodawsky, F, Shaw, M, Viswanath, K (eds) 2013, *Building inclusive cities: Women's safety and the right to the city*, Abingdon: Routledge

Wiechmann, T, Pallagst, KM, 2012, Urban shrinkage in Germany and the USA: A comparison of transformation patterns and local strategies, *International Journal of Urban and Regional Research* 36, 2, 261–80

Wiewel, W, Perry, DC (eds) 2008, *Global universities and urban development: Case studies and analysis*, Armonk: ME Sharpe

Wiggins, K, 2013, Fight of the navigator as the journey begins, *Local Government Chronicle*, 17 October, 10–11

Wilkinson, C, 2012, Social–ecological resilience: Insights and issues for planning theory, *Planning Theory* 11, 2, 148–69

Wilkinson, R, Pickett, K, 2010, *The spirit level: Why equality is better for everyone*, London: Penguin

Williams, K (ed), 2005, *Spatial planning, urban form and sustainable transport*, Aldershot: Ashgate

Williams, K, Burton, E, Jenks, M (eds), 2000, *Achieving sustainable urban form*, London: E & FN Spon

Williams, K, Gupta, R, Smith, I, Joynt, J, Hopkins, D, Bramley, G, Payne, C, Gregg, M, Hambleton, R, Bates-Brkljac, N, Dunse, N, Musselwhite, C, 2012, *Suburban neighbourhood adaptation for a changing climate (SNACC): Final report*, Bristol: University of the West of England

Williams, M, 2013, *Open data or closed doors? Supporting research in cities*, December, London: Centre for Cities

Williams, P, 2012, *Collaboration in public policy and practice: Perspectives on boundary spanners*, Bristol: Policy Press

Wilson, HF, 2013, Collective life: Parents, playground encounters and the multicultural city, *Social and Cultural Geography* 14, 6, 625–48

Winkler, T, 2013a, The future of our cities, *Quarterly Roundtable*, The Helen Suzman Foundation Series, July, Johannesburg: Helen Suzman Foundation

Winkler, T, 2013b, At the coalface: Community–University engagements and planning education, *Journal of Planning Education and Research* 33, 2, 215–27

Wolffe, R, 2009, *Renegade: The making of Barack Obama*, London: Virgin Books

Wollmann, H, 2014, The directly elected mayor in the German Lander – introduction, implementation and impact, *Public Money and Management*, 34, 5, 331–37

Wood, P, Landry, C, 2008, *The intercultural city*, London: Earthscan

Xu, J, Yeh, AGO, 2003, City profile, *Cities* 20, 5, 361–74

Xu, J, Yeh, AGO, 2005, City repositioning and competitiveness building in regional development: New development strategies in Guangzhou, China, *International Journal of Urban and Regional Research* 29, 2, 283–308

Yamanaka, K, 2008, Japan as a country of immigration: Two decades after an influx of immigrant workers, in S Yamashita, M Minami, DW Haines, JS Eades (eds) *Transnational migration in East Asia: Japan in a comparative focus*, 187–96, Senri ethnological reports 77, Osaka: National Museum of Ethnology

Yapp, C, 2005, Innovation, futures thinking and leadership, *Public Money and Management* 25, 1, 57–60

Yates, D, 1977, *The ungovernable city*, Cambridge, MA: Harvard University Press

Young, G, 2013, *Teardown: Memoir of a vanishing city*, Berkeley, CA: University of California Press

Young, IS, 2000, *Inclusion and democracy*, Oxford: Oxford University Press

Zachary, GP, 2000, *The global me: New cosmopolitans and the competitive edge*, New York: Perseus Books

Zavattaro, SM, 2013, *Cities for sale: Municipalities as public relations and marketing firms*, Albany, NY: State University of New York Press

Index

Note: page numbers in italic type refer to Figures; those followed by 'n' and another number refer to Notes; those in bold refer to a Table.

C

D

E

F

G

J

K

L

M

N

Q

R

S

T

U

V

W

X

Y

Z